2.00

BEYOND THE
PLEASURE DOME

BEYOND THE PLEASURE DOME

Writing and Addiction from the Romantics

Edited by
Sue Vice, Matthew Campbell & Tim Armstrong

Sheffield Academic Press

Copyright © 1994 Sheffield Academic Press

Sheffield Academic Press Ltd
343 Fulwood Road
Sheffield S10 3BP
England

Typeset by Sheffield Academic Press
and
Printed on acid-free paper in Great Britain
by Bookcraft
Midsomer Norton, Somerset

British Library Cataloguing in Publication Data

A catalogue record for this book is available
from the British Library

ISBN 1-85075-378-4

CONTENTS

Contents   7

ACKNOWLEDGMENTS

The editors would like to thank the following for various kinds of support, tangible and intangible, during the Literature and Addiction conference and in the preparation of this volume: Brian Britton; Valerie Cotter; Michael Ford; Roger Forseth; John Haffenden; Agnes McAuley; Neil Roberts; Erica Sheen; Elizabeth Vice; Pip Vice; Nick Warner; George Wedge; Sue Wiseman; Andrew Kirk and the staff at Sheffield Academic Press; the Department of English Literature, University of Sheffield; N.M. Rothschild and Sons; and Ian MacKillop, whose idea the conference was.

LIST OF CONTRIBUTORS

Tim Armstrong is a lecturer in the Department of English Literature, University of Sheffield.

Ros Ballaster is a university lecturer and college fellow in English at Mansfield College, University of Oxford.

Marcy Lassota Bauman is a professor of Composition and Rhetoric in the Writing Program at the University of Michigan-Dearborn.

Robin Burgess is Director of the Council on Addiction, Northampton.

Matthew Campbell is a lecturer in the Department of English Literature, University of Sheffield.

Caryn Chaden is a professor in the Department of English, De Paul University, Chicago

Mary Condé is a lecturer in the Department of English at Queen Mary and Westfield College, University of London.

Tom Dardis is a writer and author of *The Thirty Muse* living in New York City.

J. Gerard Dollar is a lecturer in the Department of English at Siena College, Loudonville, New York

Michael Ford was a lecturer in the Department of Law, University of Manchester, and now works in Chambers in London.

Roger Forseth is Emeritus Professor of English at the University of Wisconsin-Superior, and editor of *Dionysos: the Literature and Addiction Triquarterly.*

Renate Günther is a lecturer in the Department of French, University of Sheffield.

F.A. Jenner is Emeritus Professor of Psychiatry at the University of Sheffield.

Kevin McCarron is a lecturer in the Department of English at Roehampton Institute, London.

Catherine MacGregor is a high school English teacher in Nepean, Ontario, and is completing her doctorate at Ottawa University.

Brian McKenna is a postdoctoral fellow at Wolfson College, Oxford.

Barry Milligan is a professor in the Department of English, Cornell University.

Domhnall Mitchell is a lecturer in the English Institute, University of Trondheim.

Julian North is a lecturer in the Department of English, De Montfort University, Leicester

David Plumb is a teacher, writer and editor living in Fort Lauderdale, Florida.

Timothy Rivinus is Associate Clinical Professor of Psychiatry and Human Behaviour at Brown University School of Medicine, Providence, Rhode Island.

Neil Roberts is a lecturer in the Department of English, University of Sheffield.

Tom Roder has taken a break from working on his doctorate in the Department of English Literature, University of Sheffield to concentrate on journalism in London.

Danielle Schaub is a lecturer in English at the University of Haifa.

Erica Sheen is a lecturer in the Department of English Literature, University of Sheffield.

Sheila Smith has recently retired as lecturer in the Department of English, University of Nottingham.

Jean-Charles Sournia is the author of *A History of Alcoholism*.

Sue Vice is a lecturer in the Department of English Literature, University of Sheffield.

Nicholas O. Warner is a professor in the Department of Literature, Claremont McKenna College, California.

George Wedge has recently retired from the Department of English, University of Kansas.

Sue Wiseman is a lecturer in the Department of English Literature, University of Sheffield.

INTRODUCTION

Sue Vice

This collection of papers emerged from the Literature and Addiction Conference held at the University of Sheffield in April 1991. It was the first of its kind, but, with luck, will be not only not the last, but the initiator of a possible series of such conferences which might follow on from each other and perform a kind of 'work-in-progress' function, given the burgeoning of courses on addiction studies. Papers are included here by the co-editors (Roger Forseth, George Wedge and Nicholas Warner) of *Dionysos: The Literature and Addiction Triquarterly*, a fast-growing means of communication for those interested in the subject, whether as teachers, writers, students or even drinkers; and also one by Tom Roder, editor of the *Psycho-Active Journal*, for creative practitioners of the genre.[1]

One conceptual debate which is manifest in the essays in this collection is that surrounding accounts of the incidence of addiction, particularly alcoholism. Alec Jenner's paper raises questions about whether a disease-based or a societal model for addiction is more helpful. The relevance of the literary to medical, social and pharmacological approaches is a constantly recurring issue, and this joining together of two very different approaches to the area—that of treatment and that of textuality—is a reminder of what Mikhail Bakhtin says of the carnivalesque: only with its entry into the realm of the literary can it realize its full subversive potential.

The wide range, in both theme and methodology, of the essays in this collection points to what is both promising and problematic about the study of addiction in literary form. On the one hand, the rubric of addiction studies is exhilaratingly wide, and can encompass, as readers of this volume will realize, a weakening of boundaries between genres and periods of literature, which is a rare and refreshing experience. On the other hand, it is so wide that it is sometimes in danger of becoming a merely content-based issue (concerned simply with which writers feature addicts in their work, or were addicts themselves) rather than the subject of a more rigorous investigation.

While some categories seem clearly defined, as the Part sections of this volume suggest, others certainly involve the yoking together of heterogeneous material. Sometimes this works well. The deceptively simple section on 'The Novel' arose from a conference panel entitled 'Real Toads', and included Danielle Schaub on John Fowles, Kevin McCarron on William Golding and Brian McKenna on Patrick Hamilton. One of the speakers asked what the title of the panel suggested about their interconnections, noting that it is a quotation from Marianne Moore. It seemed clear that a complementary panel called 'Imaginary Gardens' might have been a good idea, to emphasize the point that different kinds of reality and realism are raised by any study of addictive writing. This was an issue the panel participants themselves discussed: Danielle Schaub's notion of addiction to writing itself is central to studying literature and addiction, and leads neatly into Brian McKenna's questioning of his own use of biographical detail about Hamilton—he also raises the issue of word-addiction by quoting the entry under 'drunk' from *Roget's Thesaurus*, a list of words which certainly ends up drowning the signified under the signifier.

Kevin McCarron's essay also effects a reversal of what might be expected in discussing alcohol and texts by pointing out that in Golding's *The Paper Men* alcohol is used as a metaphor, a situation unlike, say, that of Malcolm Lowry's *Under the Volcano*, where everything is a metaphor for alcohol. The metaphoric is implicit in Marcy Lassotta Bauman's paper on Faulkner and the processes by which his fiction turns the reader into an addict, and in Domhnall Mitchell's paper on Poe's *The Narrative of Arthur Gordon Pym*, where figurative language and words themselves are the elements of addictive writing, rather than any pre-existent experience of addiction which is being rendered as if confessionally. In her essay on Steven Spielberg and product placement, Erica Sheen points out that the series of films *Back to the Future* works along addictive lines, each one feeding the need to see the next, and incorporating into this form an imperative to consume Pepsi-Cola.

Two further significant non-literary and non-generic categories featured prominently in the conference and therefore also in this collection: politics and gender. The political dimension of addiction often involves the same issues of metaphor and the ways in which addiction can become a potent image for itself and for other things (for Lowry, for instance, it figured, among other things, the 'drunkenness' of a world at war). The conference panel 'Welcome to the Pleasure Dome' which included papers on Goldsmith and gambling (Caryn Chaden), opium and the corrosion of empire (Barry Milligan) and R.S. Hawker (Sheila Smith) was followed by a lively discussion. The discussion united the metaphoric qualities of opium as a transforming and fear-inducing substance, which Barry Milligan likened to contemporary paranoia about viral infection and AIDS, and literary representations of such experiences: the case of

Charlotte Brontë's *Villette* was raised, and the thorny biographical problem discussed in relation to Lucy Snowe's hallucinatory experiences—was Brontë writing about her own life, or only an imaginative experience? Does her description of Lucy's drugged wanderings share formal features with other opiate writings? Does it matter, and if so, how? In another panel, J. Gerard Dollar, speaking on 'Addiction and the Other Self in Three Late-Victorian Novels', interestingly cited the Gulf War as an instance of addictive behaviour: the West is addicted to oil, and the war could be seen as an instance of pernicious withdrawal symptoms.

The area of codependency, a subject not yet very familiar to British addiction-theorists, is also raised in this collection in Caryn Chaden's paper and in Cathy MacGregor's on Dostoevsky's *Crime and Punishment*, and these provide a particularly useful introduction, to the topic.

Matthew Campbell's paper on the Joyces and conversion unites politics, religion and alcohol, while Michael Ford shades into philosophy and jurisprudence in his critical discussion of liberal notions of the subject and what this means for our conception of addiction. Ros Ballaster's essay 'Addicted to Love?' provides the interface between politics and gender; she analyses the use and usefulness of models of addiction in assessing women's role as both consumers and the means of disseminating products through advertising. Other papers on the subject include Mary Condé's on women, food, eating disorders and the improper body and Renate Günther's on Marguerite Duras and *écriture féminine*.

Another feature of this volume is the expansion of the remit of addictive writing to include new and previously little discussed writers: Tim Armstrong writes on Theodore Dreiser, electricity and desire, and Sue Wiseman deals with Alexander Trocchi and the avant-garde. These essays are a complement to those on the kinds of writer readers would expect to read about: Tennessee Williams (David Plumb), Sinclair Lewis (Roger Forseth), William Faulkner (Tom Dardis), Jack Kerouac (George Wedge), Theodore Roethke (Timothy Rivinus) and the Beats (Robin Burgess).

Sue Vice's essay is on the construction of Yvonne in Lowry's *Under the Volcano* as an alcoholic by virtue of her femininity, using Luce Irigaray's rereading of Freud's 'Mourning and Melancholia', an article often used in psychiatric treatment of alcoholics. Masculinity is not entirely neglected here: Neil Roberts's paper is on 'Drink as Menses Envy' and Peter Redgrove's reversal of the usual priorities, arguing that rather than seeing femininity as lack, Redgrove sees the masculine as constructed in this way.

NOTES

1. *Dionysos: The Literature and Addiction Triquarterly* (University of Wisconsin); *The Psycho-active Journal* (University of Sheffield).

PART I

Medical and Legal Paradigms

MEDICINE AND ADDICTION

F.A. Jenner

A medical man addressing the literati is wise, as is the cobbler, to stick to his last. Or, as one would not wish to reduce the good physician to a plumber and druggist, he can most usefully offer those aspects of his education which are, he suspects, least available to students of general literature. So, despite awareness of the relevance of the social and psychological factors influencing the addicted, here discussion will be of brain function.

This should not stimulate a howl of 'reductionist' because of the apparent irrelevance of brain function to, inter alia, explanations of gambling and other non-pharmacological addictions. A lack of awareness of the seductive chemical explanations of addiction to substances which affect the brain can hardly be a sign of an all-round education. Further, those who are thoroughgoing materialists can find theories to cover other addictions analogously. They can use concepts of pleasure centres electrically stimulated in the brain by behaviour.

It is clearly of significance, however, to note how the pharmaceutical industry's dream of effective drugs to make others, and indeed ourselves, compliantly and contentedly or happily normal without unwanted side effects, is faced by mounting evidence that all its products produce withdrawal phenomena. That is, despite any benefits there are, there is a price to pay if you no longer wish to indulge, and especially if you are in a hurry to desist. This fact about anxiolytics, antidepressants, hypnotics, analgesics and major tranquillisers is shared with illicit drugs. It must play a role in maintaining addictions. It must be further noted that the classification into licit and illicit is legal and not medical. Alcohol is medically more dangerous than heroin. Diazepam (Valium) may be nearly as addicting.

Of course, it is a central feature of all of biology, as adumbrated by Claude Bernard, that life is itself the result of much that is maintained constant despite the environment. This the brain exemplifies par excellence. To some extent it is protected by the blood–brain barrier: few substances get in. Those it makes itself it controls by a plethora of negative feedback circuits, like central heating thermostats. Our individuation, and partially our identity, depends on this. In this idiom a complex entity is created by a separately definable set of homeostatic systems.

The degree to which our moods are reflections of, or are reflected in, the homeostatic activity of the limbic system of the brain, approximately— on the analogy of an onion—the layers that are neither the core nor the rind, presents philosophical questions. However, in the language of an identity theory (of brain and mind) which psychopharmacology tends to use, one can talk much sense by assuming they are two sides of one coin. Further, homeostatic mechanisms must be presumed to explain our fairly frequent states of equanimity. Gross defects of mood control are, in this language, manic-depressive psychoses, which can frequently be regulated by taking lithium salts. They stop those particular swings from dejection to elation in some people.

Whatever the aims of being human are, if there are any, not wishing to be depressed, apathetic or anxious seems fairly ubiquitous. Of course, it is usually others who do not let you enjoy the elation of mania, a most delectable disease for some. Similarly, many of the delusions of schizo- phrenia are as troublesome to those who must suffer the sufferer, and drug addiction is significantly a problem for others. One should not so spend one's days dazed and bemused and not working. But I am erring towards a sociological paradigm that must see heroin addiction as less dangerous than motor car racing, certainly medically less so than excessive alcohol intake, but made a disease by social forces whatever the amount involved.

The strictly biological paradigm values eschewing values and seeking mechanisms. The nature of the creature is a product of random variations of genetic material and natural selection of phenotypes. Other talk is scientifically meaningless. The outline of the individual is written on the double helixes of the deoxyribonucleic acid molecules inherited. Their complex interaction with the environment produces the physico-chemical brain and especially determines its protein content, much of which is enzymes catalysing its chemical processes.

The quasi-values are, or the telemony is, survival and reproduction. That which fails to further those ends is by definition ephemeral trivia, a side effect of the tautological reality that not to survive and reproduce is to die. So much then for our art, philosophy, religion and literature. In fact logical positivism, though mortally wounded, is not quite dead. Its fatal, logical flaws have not been universally biologically noted.

The details of how the brain works have only been lightly sketched so far by the neurosciences, yet it may be of value to take the example of how heroin addiction might be caused biochemically. I confess gross simplification.

Figure 1 represents the brain schematically as four sub-units. The first is in the front and inhibits social indiscretion and initiates motor activity. Damage or tumours or trauma to it lead to altered personality. The second system at the back receives information from the outside world to some extent as it is. The first and second systems are essentially cortical, the third is subcortical and has more to do with pain, pleasure and evaluation of experiences in personal terms. Below the third system is the fourth, which controls functions like being awake and asleep, and levels of awareness. From our point of view, and taking our cue from Freud, the pleasure principle resides at level three and determines our needs, recalling what fulfilled or thwarted them. System two takes external reality into account in the interest of system three, and system one makes executive decisions in their light and those of the social mores. System four turns the set on and off and controls the volume.

Psychopharmacology can be moderately specific because the brain is not, like most computers, simply dependent on the wiring diagram. The brain uses chemical transmitters produced by one nerve cell to stimulate others. This allows specific one-to-one contacts and more diffuse modulations, but to the delight of pharmacologists there are not only several chemical neurotransmitters, there are for most, if not for all, several different sensitive receptors, usually numbered for example D_1, D_2 ... D_7 and so on (in that example dopamine 1, 2, 3 and so on receptors). The stimulating nerve not only secretes its transmitter but economically takes it back, and so has another mechanism which can be pharmacologically influenced. This delicate system has evolved successfully because in the 'natural' world it has maintained its integrity. Millions of substances producible by modern synthetic chemistry challenge the 'defences'. Often those which are like naturally-occurring products 'fool' the system.

The various chemicals and areas of the brain subserve different functions. The brain contains, for example, its own opiates, several so-called endorphins and encephalins. These are relevant in controlling pain and pleasure. There have been attempts to identify pleasure centres, by, for example, wiring up animals to stimulate particular parts of the brain by pressing levers, and looking at those parts chosen for repeated stimulation. While exogenous opiates, for instance heroin, interfere with this system and 'improve' the individual's state of being, the homeostatic mechanisms are also brought into play so that there is a reduction in the brain's own pleasure and analgesic compounds in the interest of the sacred homeostasis. These responses take time but produce tachyphylaxis, that is, decreasing efficacy of the drug after continued use, and also a rebound effect if use of the drug stops. There are many other factors by the nature of things. For example, there is a conditioning effect; if you take your tipple at the same time each day, you will be aware of needing it then. The familiar environment is also demonstrably relevant to awareness of need; much in it is a conditional stimulus in the Pavlovian sense. Many of these aspects of addicts' behaviour and responses can be reproduced in animal experiments and much of so-called human biology is based on extrapolations from such experiments. As would be expected for biological experiments apparently innate differences in individual responses are striking and possibly due to inherited factors. I am not aware of studies showing what aspects of the DNA molecules are important for this variability but I would anticipate some such studies in due course. That is not to deny the relevance of infection, experienced trauma, the season of birth and so on, but just to assert that we have increasing ways of expressing and measuring innate susceptibility chemically.

Even if our lives are merely the brown paper which literature describes, and which encloses the precious DNA molecules we exist to deliver, our society has in particular shown how important the difficult-to-remove wrappings are. To some extent then we do not and indeed cannot live in the world in which we think, especially if we are thinking biologically. Sometimes both worlds are so painful that we seek solace, probably mistakenly, in drugs. What I have tried to do is to illustrate how far what some might call medicalizing could go. In further defence, however, of my own trade union, let me suggest that those critics should speak about biologizing and leave the physician as a learned, and hopefully humble, compassionate person, intent on helping by all available means. To see the other as ill can be more compassionate, but it is disenfranchizing. Although many medics have also produced contributions to the world's literary works, most, like myself, lack the ability and time to be adequately involved.

Yet it is not a matter of the truths of neurophysiology; they are fairly undeniable in the Popperian sense. The question is how far one explores this rather than humanistic studies, and why. There is no doubt that medicine can be seen as aiming to control, or to help others to control. We can produce, and to some extent have produced, drugs which inhibit the effects of extraneous opiates, so we can treat opiate addiction with drugs. We nevertheless require literature or other guides to help us answer for what purpose, and what directions are to be valued. That requires some grasp of the phenomenology of being human, and it will not do to explain to someone that her amygdala is playing up when you mean she is anxious.

Yet, despite the delight of operas and the complexities of family life, the biological underpinning and purpose of sexual love seems on reflection, but not performance, obvious. By and large the organisms' search for pleasure 'should' serve with some efficiency survival and procreation. The degree to which the system is defective or not foolproof is a measure of its likelihood to be ephemeral. As Leibniz might have written, even God could not change that. Drug addiction as a pleasant partial alternative to sex, though for some very real, is still only a questionable threat in this regard in an over-populated world. Nevertheless it can be viewed as something breaking through to mechanisms usually giving individuals pleasure in order to further the mechanism's own perpetuation.

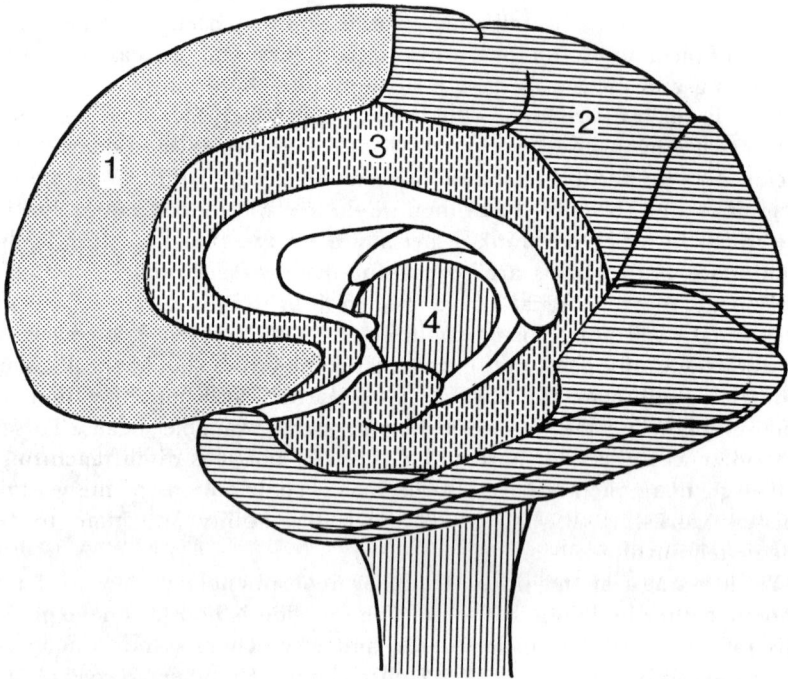

FIGURE 1

This figure is a representation of the brain simplistically presenting it as four functional units: (1) the frontal and executive lobes controlling expressed speech and movement; (2) the occipital and superficial parietal and temporal areas recording information about the world as it is; (3) the limbic system recording in terms of past experience the hedonistic or threatening aspects of things; (4) the brain stem and reticular formation controlling degrees of awareness and sleep.

CODEPENDENCY AND *CRIME AND PUNISHMENT*

Catherine MacGregor

It is well known that *Crime and Punishment*[1] is an extraordinary fusion of what Dostoevsky originally conceived of as two different novels: the Raskolnikov murder/repentance story and a rather Dickensian exposé of Russian alcoholism in the portrait of the Marmeladov family. No serious attention, however, has yet been paid to the textual implications of Dostoevsky's own experience of codependency; that is, to the impact on *Crime and Punishment* of Dostoevsky's reactions to his father's alcoholism.[2] Understanding the issues which have emerged during the last decade in the Adult Children of Alcoholics movement provides a fresh approach to addiction-related texts in general and helps to illuminate a remarkable consistency in this complex and crowded novel in particular. That 'rescuing' others from the consequences of their own behavior is pathetic and futile at best and contemptible and dangerous at worst is not only a recent insight of clinicians and self-help groups; it is also a recurring theme which unifies both segments of *Crime and Punishment*. More than a century before the interpersonal dynamics of addiction and the concomitant failure of 'rescuing' were described by addiction professionals, Dostoevsky explored those issues in his fiction with an insight—perhaps not entirely conscious—derived from his experience of his father's alcoholism.

For our purposes, there are five relevant areas of discussion. The first is an abbreviated overview of what are now understood to be the predictable consequences of parental alcoholism on the family unit. The second and third are biographical, and provide a useful point of departure for a consideration of the text: Dostoevsky's dreadful relationship with his alcoholic father, and the evidence of his own 'Family Hero' role in later life, particularly significant in the circumstances surrounding the publication of *Crime and Punishment*. The fourth and fifth concern the text: Dostoevsky's original intention for the novel, a narrative with a sociological interest in Russian alcoholism, and most important, of course, the final version of the book, with its subtle but powerful struggle with codependency. Sensitivity to addiction issues will help to clarify two puzzles in the text. First is the problem of the relationship between suffering and redemption. The idea that embracing suffering is the key to one's personal renewal and freedom is so important in *Crime and Punishment*, Dostoevsky's other novels, letters, and in the commentaries of his myriad biographers and critics, that yet another treatment of this theme might seem as superfluous as a refutation would be impossible. What I suggest, however is that the suffering/redemption theme in *Crime and Punishment* needs a more nuanced treatment than is usually given in conventional readings, which maintain their consistency only at the price of misconstruing or ignoring outright the many instances in the text of suffering which is clearly non-redemptive. If we speculate that one of Dostoevsky's purposes (among others) in creating the world of this novel was to dramatize the moral and pragmatic implications of two different ways codependents can respond to misery, then some of the apparent contradictions can be resolved rather than evaded. The second textual puzzle, regarding Raskolnikov's renewal, is related to this: closure is deferred beyond the final chapter into an epilogue, and then again beyond the epilogue to another, unwritten, story. The urge to escape narrative closure, I believe, is related to Dostoevsky's intuitive sense that recovering codependents must move beyond the psychological closure of the addiction-related roles generated by their experience of alcoholism.

1. *Current Thinking about Codependency*

In North America, counselling professionals and self-help recovery groups in the last decade have increasingly turned their attention to 'System Enabling'; that is, to the dynamics which perpetuate rather than initiate addiction.[3] This shift in focus is partly due to the serious controversies among researchers about the origins of alcoholism.[4] There are two reasons for interest in codependency roles; that is, in the predictable behaviours and attitudes assumed inadvertently by the alcoholic's family members and sometimes by friends and colleagues (who may or may not have their own drinking problems). An early and still valid reason for making alcoholics and codependents aware of these roles was to enhance the alcoholic's recovery, but a more recent and equally compelling justification is to promote the recovery of the codependents themselves, whose emotional problems are now understood to be just as serious, predictable and treatable as the alcoholic's disorder. 'Denial' is an important characteristic of both substance addiction and codependency. After years of maladaptive reactions to the drinker, by the time the family of an alcoholic seeks professional counselling or support from a self-help group, the addict's troubles and their own problems have become very serious. Since codependents almost always seek help because they see counselling as an escalation in their attempt to control the alcoholic's problem drinking, three basic assumptions about addiction which emerge very quickly in an initial discussion will often disturb them and challenge their self-image.

First, they are told that they cannot control the alcoholic's drinking; they can change only their own behaviour and hope that the alcoholic may respond. Secondly, they are invited to re-evaluate their own behaviour, particularly the likelihood that in a well-meaning attempt to protect the alcoholic and the family from the natural consequences of the drinking, they have tended to 'rescue' or inappropriately assume responsibility for the alcoholic, enabling the drinker to persist in the illusion that the problem drinking is acceptable. A distinction is made between 'helping', actions which often involve loving but firm confrontations with the drinker, and 'rescuing', which is ultimately and ironically self-defeating. Thirdly, the family is made aware of the typical roles family members slowly and unconsciously assume in their attempts to distract the hostile or pitying gaze of outsiders and to maintain, at all costs, the equilibrium of the family unit. These roles not only enable the alcoholic to progress in the spiral of his or her self-destructive drinking but also become rigid, constricting personae for the spouse and the offspring who become 'Adult Children of Alcoholics' or ACOAs. These inauthentic, rigid roles are eventually carried over into other relationships and situations outside the family where they generate other personal disasters. In smaller families, roles can overlap, and in all families they can be exchanged from time to time. Without help, however, they can rarely be outgrown.

Typically, the spouse assumes the role of Prime (or Chief) Enabler, who buys time for the alcoholic by trying to convince employers, friends and, worst of all, their children that nothing is wrong. This ploy 'teaches' the children that honest discussion of issues is forbidden and that they should distrust the evidence of their own senses. The Family Hero role is usually assumed by the eldest and most successful child, not often recognized by outsiders as having any problems; Family Heroes become addicted to successes or to quixotic failures and wear themselves out taking on responsibilities which belong to others. Family Heroes often marry alcoholics and become Chief Enablers. The second child takes on the role of Scapegoat, the rebel in conflict with authorities, often a substance abuser in his or her own right. The third child plays the role of Mascot, the witty clown who defuses tension with his or her antics. The last child's role is that of the Lost Child, dreamy, withdrawn, often artistic, prone to eating disorders, overlooked by everyone. The astonishing speed with which codependents can usually identify their own roles in a preliminary counselling session is an indicator of the degree of closure the experience of alcoholism has imposed on their lives. The challenge then for the recovering codependent individual is to detach himself or herself from the inappropriate centrality of the alcoholic and the addiction, reclaiming his or her own life as central, and to replace the inauthentic self-image to which he or she has become addicted with a sense of self which is capable of growth.

2. *Dostoevsky's Relationship with his Father*

Why is codependency relevant to *Crime and Punishment*? During my first reading of this novel, the Gibian translation, which happened to coincide with my first exposure to alcoholism studies, I was struck by the clarity with which the dynamics of an alcoholic family are rendered in the predicament of the Marmeladov family. In particular, Dostoevsky's portrait of Marmeladov's daughter Sonia, the innocent prostitute who sells herself to care for her destitute step-mother and step-siblings, provides us with an Adult Child Family Hero par excellence. As this family is so obviously alcoholic, however, I was not surprised by this; what disturbed me was the nagging impression that several other characters who had no apparent connection with problem drinking, particularly Raskolnikov himself, acted as if they also were ACOAs. I dismissed this notion, initially deciding that my interest in addictions was interfering with my reading of the text. Picking up the Garnett translation, however, I was startled into a reconsideration of my original reaction. The second sentence of its lurid introduction sent me back to Dostoevsky's biographies, which confirmed the history of alcohol problems in his life, and kindled a lingering preoccupation with codependency issues in fiction: 'He was born in Moscow in 1821, the son of a former army surgeon whose drunken brutality led his own serfs to murder him by pouring vodka down his throat until he strangled'. Although this melodramatic titbit turned out to be problematic, for reasons I will discuss shortly, it was a useful beginning.

Roger Forseth has argued that biographers of alcoholic writers become at least temporarily codependent themselves, ignoring, excusing or misunderstanding the implications of so much in the alcoholic's life which can only be understood in terms of addiction,[5] and I suggest that a similar case must be made for biographers of writers who were adult children of alcoholics. The failure to recognize the centrality of codependency in an adult child's life will obscure patterns easily recognized by an addiction-sensitive reader.

Many standard biographies of Dostoevsky[6] indicate that he had an alcoholic father and that alcoholism was a family problem. Fyodor's uncle and two brothers died of their 'dipsomania'.[7] No biographer, however, has sought to link this experience with textual issues beyond the observation that there are a lot of compulsive drunkards in his fiction. I therefore offer this view of the novel: although we cannot determine the extent to which Dostoevsky was able to come to terms with his own experience of addiction-related problems in his personal life (the biographies all discuss his own gambling compulsion but are too sketchy to permit much beyond speculation), the design of *Crime and Punishment* makes clear that at some level he recognized the futility of the 'Hero' role and its constitutive element of 'rescuing', repudiating both.

What do we know about Dr Dostoevsky from the standard biographies? Fyodor refused even to discuss his father for most of his life; he emerges from most accounts as an ill-tempered, demanding, miserly drunk given to utterly unjustified accusations about his wife's fidelity, physical brutality to his serfs, irrational, impossible expectations of those around him and, after his wife's death, sexual indiscretions with servant girls in their early teens, one of whom bore him a child.[8] He also carried on loud conversations with what he believed to be his wife's ghost, answering his own questions in a voice mimicking hers.[9] All the biographers agree that Dr Dostoevsky was drinking very heavily in the last few years of his life. There are conflicting accounts of his death, but the most widespread belief is the one mentioned earlier, that he was murdered by his own serfs who strangled him by pouring vodka forcibly down his throat. The conspirators' motive, according to some, was revenge for the sexual abuse of their daughters.[10] The family, revolted by his behaviour in life and embarrassed by the circumstances of his death, bribed officials to cover up the murder and record it as a death by 'natural causes'.[11] Another suggested murder motive was revenge for his 'drunken rages and habit of ordering floggings in his fiefdom'.[12] Biographers who are skeptical of this melodramatic account (for instance, Frank and Kjetsaa) argue plausibly that impoverished peasants could not have managed to bribe so many doctors and investigators. The skeptics suggest that Dr Dostoevsky's death was of 'natural causes', occurring during an 'apoplectic fit' (a stroke or heart attack) brought on by the heat, his drunkenness, and by his anger that his peasants were spreading manure on the fields incorrectly. Magarshack suggests that the apoplexy may have been delirium tremens.[13] The murder story was concocted, it is argued, by a rival landowner who had his own reasons for wishing to cause scandal. As interesting as this dispute is, it is a red herring, as far as I am concerned, since what the biographers are ignoring is that one way or another it was Dr Dostoevsky's drinking which precipitated his death. The reason this oversight is so important is that children of alcoholics always blame themselves for their parents' drinking problems; that is simply the way they think. If drink caused Dr Dostoevsky's death, then his children would feel responsible for his death as well as for the misfortunes of his life.[14] Fyodor, because he had sent his father a confrontational letter about his stinginess around the time of his death, did feel guilty for his father's demise for the rest of his life. Some biographers suggest that he felt guilty about not loving his father and about feeling relieved at his death. These contradictory reactions are as understandable as they are irrational, and it is not necessary to subscribe to Freudian dogma to account for his ambivalence.[15] In addition to the unhappiness it caused during his lifetime, Dr Dostoevsky's mismanagement of the estate created debts and hardships afterwards, one example being the necessity of a rather unpleasant marriage between Fyodor's sister Varvara and a much older businessman. Anyone feeling responsible for Dr Dostoevky's drinking problem and its consequences would thus have a huge burden on his or her conscience.

What I want to concentrate on is the struggle in *Crime and Punishment* to repudiate distorted notions of responsibility for other people's problems, but in passing I should mention briefly how Dr Dostoevsky is represented in the text. Dostoevsky may have dealt with his ambivalence about his alcoholic father by differentiating aspects of that complex relationship across four different characters whom he inspired: Dr Zossimov, Marmeladov, Alyona and Svidrigailov. Dr Zossimov, the impecunious physician who is that rare thing in this novel, an abstainer, may be on one level a 'wishful-thinking' version of Dr Dostoevsky. So, perhaps, is Marmeladov. Raskolnikov ministers to the dying drunk 'as earnestly as if it had been his father' (p. 154).[16] In this scene, one could argue, he gets to have his cake and eat it too: the drunken father who has been a source of misery to his family is killed off, but with a filial figure standing by to exude compassion. If one chooses to see the hapless Marmeladov as a fictional version of Dr Dostoevsky, however, one must deal with the obvious difference between the bumbling and rather affectionate Marmeladov and the harsh, miserly father. It may be that Svidrigailov and Alyona are projections of those elements of his character, Svidrigailov's sexual deviance and Alyona's life-denying miserliness being ways in which Dostoevsky could exorcise the memories he was unwilling to discuss. This possibility is particularly interesting in the case of Alyona, whom Raskolnikov hates with an extraordinary force. As if he has been Alyona's victim, rather than she his, he makes an odd remark: 'I shall never, never forgive the old woman!' (p. 239). In any case, if at least on one level Dostoevsky is Raskolnikov, he gets to explore his contradictory feelings several ways: first, through Alyona, he murders his miserly father figure and moves slowly towards repentance; secondly, through Marmeladov, he attends compassionately the dying father; thirdly, through Svidrigailov's suicide, he learns that the sexually deviant father in a sense administers his own punishment. Interestingly, Marmeladov's death is a possible suicide as well; in some communities, coroners identify deaths attributed to alcoholism as suicides.

3. *Portrait of the Writer as a Family Hero*

In addition to his unnecessary appropriation of guilt for his father's death, the younger Dostoevsky seems to have exemplified the Family Hero role in other ways. All the biographies offer a wealth of anecdotes about Fyodor's life-long involvement with alcoholics other than his father and with other troubled people, many of whose problems stemmed from their own relationships with alcoholics, which Fyodor took on as his own. I can cite only a few here. His first marriage, a very unhappy one, was to the consumptive widow of an alcoholic who had attracted his pity and ardor long before the death of her husband. Dostoevsky committed himself to taking care of her, her difficult son and a rival lover, for whom he secured a teaching position. In fact, getting the rival a job seems to have been a condition for the marriage. Among the relationships he had with women between his two marriages, one was with Martha Brown who lived with and cared for an alcoholic lover.[17] Despite life-long financial problems of his own, he was burdened by the debts of his two alcoholic brothers, Mikhail and Nikolai.[18] One motive for the writing of *Crime and Punishment* was financial necessity: in addition to his own debts, which were pressing, he had voluntarily assumed responsibility for the debts of his brother Mikhail, who had died of cirrhosis of the liver shortly after being released from debtors' prison[19] and for the maintenance of the widow and four children. Keeping Mikhail's journal *Epoch* functioning was made even more difficult by the death of Apollon Grigoriev, 'the journal's foremost contributing editor', another alcoholic.[20] To stay out of debtor's prison himself, Dostoevsky made desperate overtures to publishers for cash advances, finally committing himself in the summer of 1865 to an unscrupulous publisher to whom he promised an entire new novel by 1 November 1866. The agreement was that all his existing and future works would become the property of the bookseller if the deadline were not met. This was a gamble, and his ambivalent reaction to the crisis, recorded in a letter to his friend Baron Wrangel, is utterly typical of a tired Family Hero, artificially invigorated by the challenge:

> And now I've been suddenly been left alone and things have become simply terrible for me. My whole life is broken in two... Oh my friend, I'd readily go back to penal servitude for as many years, just to pay off my debts and feel free again. Now I'll start writing a novel with a stick over my head, i.e. from need, in haste. And meanwhile, it always appears to me that I'm really just beginning to live. Funny, isn't it? A cat's vitality.[21]

This addiction to crises was related in Fyodor's case to his problem with gambling, itself a compulsive behavior. He fled from his creditors to Wiesbaden, gambled all his money away in five days, and then worked feverishly, in his own words, to beat the almost impossible deadline. In fact, he churned out not only *Crime and Punishment*, but *The Gambler* as well.

As the deadline loomed, friends suggested that he hire a stenographer and dictate the text of *The Gambler*; when the stenographer, Anna Snitkina (who was to become Dostoevsky's second wife) left after their first session, Dostoevsky said, 'I am glad that you are a woman and not a man'. Anna asked 'Why?' and he responded, 'Because a man would be quite sure to get drunk, but you, I hope, won't'.[22] Clearly, Dostoevsky's overwhelming sense of responsibility for his family's misfortunes was one of the motivations for his journalism and his fiction.

4. *The Original Intention: The Drunks*

Not only was the context in which *Crime and Punishment* written suggestive of Dostoevsky's experience of addictions, the original intention for the novel was explicitly concerned with the miseries of alcoholism. In his letter to the publisher Krayevsky, he made his purpose clear: 'My Novel is called *The Drunks* and will deal with the current problem of drunkenness. Not only is the question analyzed, but I am also exposing all its ramifications, especially pictures of families, the upbringing of children in this atmosphere and so forth...'.[23] This is obviously the Marmeladov story. Dostoevsky's interest in the ramifications for families is especially intriguing and remains clear even in the final version of the novel with its murder and repentance plot.

5. *Crime and Punishment*

My principal concern is with the inner dynamics of the text of *Crime and Punishment*. I have drawn attention, nevertheless, to extra-literary considerations—to Dostoevsky's personal experience of addiction and to current thinking in addiction counselling—because they account for a striking feature of the text which has not been paid much critical attention by those who think that he was promoting suffering of an undifferentiated kind. The saintly prostitute Sonia and the murderer Raskolnikov learn, as most of the others do not, to be reconciled to authentic, undistorted notions of personal responsibility which open the possibilities of genuine, inter-subjective bonds. They grow beyond the manipulative, power-oriented relationships which characterize those around them.

The necessity of briefly summarizing this great baggy monster of a novel almost equals the impossibility of doing so. Raskolnikov, an impoverished student whose widowed mother and sister have made many sacrifices for his education, murders a loathsome old woman, a pawnbroker who has victimized him and many others. His motives are tangled. Another suspect is apprehended and then released although he has confessed to the crime; Raskolnikov fears that the wise detective Porfiry, so interested in psychology, knows that he is the killer. Having met the drunkard Marmeladov shortly before both the murder and Marmeladov's own death under a horsedrawn coach, which he witnesses, Raskolnikov becomes emotionally involved with the wretched family whom he aids: the half-mad consumptive widow, Katerina, who also dies shortly after her husband's scandalous funeral, her starving children and, especially, Marmeladov's daughter Sonia—the timid and religious prostitute who is their only means of support and to whom Raskolnikov eventually confesses the great secret which has been torturing him. She encourages him to confess publicly and to repent to God; he similarly challenges her to realize that she cannot go on as a prostitute. Raskolnikov's mother Pulcheria and sister Dounia, who is engaged briefly to Luzhin, a domineering and unscrupulous business-man, arrive in St Petersburg, as does Dounia's former employer Svidrigailov, a sexual deviant who may be responsible for the deaths of his wife Marfa Petrovna, a deaf-mute adolescent girl whom he has sexually abused and a male servant. Svidrigailov, having eavesdropped and learned that Raskolnikov is the killer, promises Dounia to get him out of the country in exchange for sexual favours from her. She refuses. After having made arrangements to care for Sonia and Katerina's children, Svidrigailov commits suicide. Sonia, Dounia and Raskolnikov's friend Razumihin, whom Dounia will marry, stand by Raskolnikov at his trial; Sonia follows him to Siberia, where he is sentenced, and where he eventually moves beyond his formal confession of his transgression toward authentic repentance.

This skeletal outline fails to disclose the text's fascination with alco-holism and codependency, but the explicit references to problem drinking in the novel itself are overwhelming. The Marmeladov family's predicament is treated with compassion, but no sentiment: the narrator gazes unflinchingly at every detail of their suffering. Their cycle of misery is so obvious that any detailed analysis here would be superfluous: the exposure of the degradation, material poverty, fear, anger, pathos and tissue of illusions on the part of the three adult Marmeladovs has few literary parallels. Katerina's delusions about the grandeur of her past and future, and Sonia's naive faith that her prostitution is helpful, are extreme and pathetic examples of system enabling. But the Marmeladovs are not alone; their sort of misery is everywhere in St Petersburg. A casual enumeration of incidental references to drunkards and drunkenness yields approximately thirty examples. Obviously, Dostoevsky's horrified fascination with intoxication is far broader than the particular miseries of the Marmeladovs. It is hard to imagine another novel in which alcohol abuse is so prominent.

The magnitude of the social problem is staggering. What is at stake, however, is not just a question of the sociological novel suggested to Krayevsky. The fusion of the experience of addictions with the

Raskolnikov murder plot creates a metaphysical level. This is no patch-work job: the fundamental unity of the novel derives from the informing principle of the language of addictions which provides a symbol for human evil, and of recovery from addiction as spiritual reconciliation of God and humanity. That this is so is evident from the astonishing fact that although none of the principal characters—with the exception of poor Sonia—comes from an alcoholic household, *to some degree, all of them behave as if they did.* And not only do they respond to situations the way that adult children of alcoholics do; they respond as 'Family Heroes' specifically would. They waste much energy attempting to 'rescue' one another from situations which are not their responsibility and, in doing so, they raise the level of tension in their relationships. That Dostoevsky was repudiating 'rescuing' is exposed by the fact that all the rescue attempts fail, whereas the only characters to grow beyond their roles— Raskolnikov and Sonia—help each other to see and deal with reality, which is always open to growth and genuine recovery. Raskolnikov and Sonia are defined over and against the other characters—some of them likeable and some not—all of whom overestimate the extent of their own power.

Let us see how Dostoevsky undermines the concept of rescuing through dramatizing its futility; he does so sometimes with poignancy and some-times through caricature. First, there are some extraordinary dreams or fantasies of rescue. It is striking that none of these succeeds, even as fantasy. Raskolnikov's heartbreaking and horrifying dream of the death of the mare is a case in point. In it, a small mare, given the impossible task of pulling a wagonload of drunken peasants, is beaten to death for her failure by the driver, who is cheered on by the tavern crowd. In the dream, Raskolnikov is a helpless child, impotent to protect the mare. But he is also the mare and the killer.[24] Without repeating the critical argu-ments for this position, I will point out that it is consistent with the emotional experience of a child of an addicted household: he tries to stop the suffering, his own and his parent's (or parents'); he fails, and at some level he concludes that the perpetuation of the suffering is his fault because he did not try hard enough.

In the fantasies and behaviour of the contemptible Luzhin we see a caricature of a rescuer; Dostoevsky here exposes an unpleasant truth about rescuing, that its primary purpose is not genuinely altruistic but is self-serving instead. Luzhin indulges himself in absurd reveries about Dounia's total dependence on him. He wanted Dounia to perceive him as her benefactor, rescuing her from her poverty; in turn, he imagines that Dounia would be 'one who would all her life look on him as her saviour, worship him, admire him, and only him' (p. 266). The incongruously religious language here is a clue to how inappropriate his desire is. That we are meant to repudiate his role of rescuer is emphasized by the fact that in his unsuccessful scheme to win back Dounia's affection, he poses as Sonia's benefactor in order to humiliate her. After Marmeladov's death, Luzhin offers Sonia a small sum, ten roubles, for her impoverished family, and furtively places a hundred roubles in her pocket without her knowledge. At the funeral dinner, he accuses her of theft (Part V, Chs. 1 and 2). The point is that his ludicrous fantasies undermine any inclination a reader might have to romanticize heroic fantasies of rescue.

Svidrigailov's rescue fantasies are more complex, as he is a far more complex character, but the theme is nonetheless similar. He dreams of rescuing a pathetic waif (the abused child of a drunken cook), but the child metamorphoses into a harlot figure, thus tempting him with his own desires, which is all a rescue can do since it is not genuinely concerned with the welfare of the other. The problem here is very complicated and beyond the scope of this discussion; one might argue that there is something unselfish in Svidrigailov's choice of death rather than submission to his deviant fantasies. Even so, the point is that associating a failed rescue fantasy with the character of Svidrigailov certainly undermines it as an appropriate response to suffering.

Similarly, in Raskolnikov's painful struggle to understand his own motives for the murder, he recognizes (and then repudiates) his self-deceptive philanthropic urge (p. 360).[25] He acknowledges that he did not really kill Alyona to save others from suffering but to be a Napoleon, to dare.

In addition to these fantasies, there are many actual rescue attempts, all of which also fail. Here is a brief sketch of some of these attempts:

1. Marmeladov's attempt to rescue the unhappy Katerina from her misery by marrying her was obviously an absolute failure. The unemployed drunkard cannot provide even the most basic necessities for her and her children. Dounia's willingness to marry Luzhin for the sake of her mother and brother is inappropriate, as she learns. Although ostensibly more respectable, it invites comparison with Sonia's prostitution. And although it is certainly not as revolting as Luzhin's scheme to pose as her and Sonia's benefactor, Dounia has a similarly exaggerated notion of her responsibility for her mother and brother; she actually asks Raskolnikov what right he has to refuse her sacrifice (p. 172).

2. Svidrigailov's wife, the late Marfa Petrovna—a rescuer par excellence—not only paid Svidrigailov's card debts, thus freeing him from debtors' prison (p. 407), but also bribed officials so that he would escape a murder charge (p. 258). These rescues neither won her Svidrigailov's love, nor made Svidrigailov feel loved. Her well-meaning attempts to protect him from the consequence of his actions are obviously futile. His suicide is the closest he

can come to assuming moral responsibility for himself, and it is a hollow parody of Raskolnikov's struggle.

3. Another failed rescue is Pulcheria's attempt to protect Raskolnikov from the painful knowledge of Dounia's troubles. As governess in Svidrigailov's household, Dounia had been slandered, dismissed and disgraced. Pulcheria's presumption enrages Raskolnikov; moreover, the intolerable manipulation one reads between the lines of her letters is symptomatic of an unhealthy relationship in which one partner wishes to have control.

4. Raskolnikov's attraction to his first fiancée and his feeling that he would have preferred her had she been a lame hunchback (p. 201) are disturbingly reminiscent of Luzhin's sick imagination.

5. The absurd willingness of the painter Nikolay (arrested for the murder committed by Raskolnikov) to bear the guilt for the crime should not be seen as a Christ-like sacrifice; his confession is an inauthentic martyrdom rooted in false, neurotic piety. Interestingly, the name of Nikolay's religious sect in Russian is Raskolniki. Raskolnikov's inner fragmentation is indicated by his surname, derived from the same word, meaning 'schism'. Nikolay is a pathetic character, not an admirable one, and his action is not in Raskolnikov's interest.

6. Dounia, as Svidrigailov correctly sees (p. 404), was a rescuer, though one who grew somewhat beyond her role. She had tried to save his servant girl Parasha from him (p. 410), and had attempted to reform him. Counting on that element of her nature, Svidrigailov attempts to win her affections by offering to rescue Raskolnikov, getting him out of the country. He appeals to her exaggerated sense of responsibility by saying that both Raskolnikov's and Pulcheria's future depends on whether she chooses to be seduced by him (pp. 424-26). His history of seductions had followed this pattern; he was able to 'protect' women from the reality of their own moral responsibilities by claiming that they were innocent of all lusts and that he was guilty for both parties (p. 410), but this skill certainly brought him no lasting satisfaction. All in all, the association of Svidrigailov's unsavory seductions with rescuing once again undermines its validity as a mode of response to suffering.

7. Raskolnikov's and Lebeziatnikov's rescue of Sonia from Luzhin's malicious charges is also interesting. Lebeziatnikov had witnessed Luzhin's surreptitious placing of the hundred rouble note in Sonia's pocket and confronted him with the disgraceful truth in the presence of the funeral dinner guests before whom

8. Sonia had been humiliated. While motivated by worthy intentions, this rescue too is futile, since the outraged landlady evicts them all anyway, despite Sonia's vindication.

8.   Dounia has not really learned her lesson: after Raskolnikov's trial, she and Razumihin ineffectually try to protect Pulcheria from the knowledge of Raskolnikov's imprisonment (p. 461); Pulcheria, in turn, conceals her intuitive awareness of the truth from them (p. 464). The strain undoubtedly contributes to her mental and physical decline, which is reminiscent of poor mad Katerina's hysterical delusions. Similarly, Dounia and Razumihin fail in their attempt to protect Raskolnikov from the knowledge of Pulcheria's death (p. 464). This familial dishonesty, the urge to protect one another from reality, is clearly pointless.

All in all, the failure of both the rescue fantasies and of the actual rescue attempts dramatizes the inappropriateness of trying to save others from responsibility and reality. Although I have argued that this pattern among the novel's characters who have no apparent connection with problem drinking is a subtle but strong displacement in the text of Dostoevsky's own anxieties about codependent rescuing, we should return, of course, to the explicitly codependent Sonia. Her pathetic attempt to save her family from destitution fits this pattern too. It is astonishing that critics uniformly praise her salvific influence on Raskolnikov without attending to the parallel influence he has on her. Her encouragement of his reconciliation to life is so much a matter of consensus that it needs no discussion here, except to stress that she makes him see the reality that he can be loved, despite his great sin. What I want to stress is the generally ignored passage in which he makes her see reality too, that she has also made a great mistake:

> But you are a great sinner...and your worst sin is that you have destroyed and betrayed yourself for nothing. Isn't that fearful? Isn't it fearful that you are living in this filth which you loathe so, and at the same time you know yourself (you've only to open your eyes) that you are not helping anyone by it, not saving anyone from anything? (pp. 279-80).

He makes her see that she too has destroyed a life, her own (p. 286). Interestingly, the problem of Svidrigailov is pointedly relevant here. Raskolnikov has argued that her prostitution cannot save her family and that her little step-sister, Polya, will probably follow the same route, a likelihood which Sonia has resisted up to this point. Without Svidrigailov's gift of money, which for once has no strings attached, Raskolnikov's prediction would have become the reality which Sonia had denied. If one adopts a particular theological perspective, it is possible to see Svidrigailov's gesture as a channel of grace: it is free, surprising, unconnected to the recipients' efforts, and is not manipulative. Moreover, Svidrigailov reinforces Raskolnikov's repudiation of Sonia's rescuing by warning her that she cannot get through life paying other people's debts (p. 431). I am conscious of a contradiction here; it would seem that Sonia's liberation from self-destructive rescuing is dependent on Svidrigailov's rescue of her, which coincides with (though is not causally related to) his suicide. If this paradox can be resolved, perhaps it will be only by underlining the tragic deficiency in Svidrigailov's imagination: he cannot envisage a life free of exploitative relationships and hence chooses death. If it cannot be resolved, it nevertheless points to Dostoevsky's obsession with rescuing.

Although Raskolnikov (prompted by Sonia) confesses to the police in the last line of the novel proper, his spiritual renewal or conversion is deferred until the Epilogue and deferred again beyond it. It is clearly an ongoing process, not merely a one-time leap into a stasis of belief. That Sonia and Raskolnikov can *help* one another is the psychological fulcrum of the novel. They challenge one another to turn from familiar and wretched paths, paths which are nonetheless enthralling for being so wretched, paths whose misery is addictive because it sustains strong but inappropriate images of their respective selves. Their gift is reciprocal, and both their 'pale, sick faces were bright with the dawn of a new future, of a full resurrection into a new life' (p. 471). The language of healing is unmistakable. In their Siberian exile, they are recovering not just from their Siberian physical maladies but from the infected relationships of St Petersburg. This apparently sudden recovery is not at all discontinuous with the rest of the novel, as is sometimes argued by critics who think that the Epilogue is flawed by a clumsy *deus ex machina* quality. This continuity is borne out by the Lazarus allusion in the Epilogue: Raskolnikov is surprised that Sonia had not pressed her Bible or her faith on him; she waited for him to ask. Similarly, he had asked her to read the Gospel to him on the night of his confession.

I want to comment very briefly on this controversial Epilogue; sophisticated theories of narration have been used to attack and defend it, and while I do not wish to dispense with these responses, even though I cannot discuss them here, I cannot resist passing on a much simpler reaction. While preparing an earlier draft of this paper, I noticed that a very bright friend of mine, a recovering alcoholic untainted by any academic exposure to literary criticism or even much formal education, was reading *Crime and Punishment* just for fun. Curious, I asked her what she thought precipitated Raskolnikov's change of heart in the Epilogue. There was no hesitation: Sonia 'got off his case', as she put it; Raskolnikov 'bottomed out' when Sonia involuntarily withdrew because of her minor illness. Much more is involved, of course, I would argue. The Epilogue is all of a piece with the novel for various and complex reasons.

Nevertheless, her answer is closer to the truth than the arguments of those who think that it is an aesthetic blunder.

The room Sonia leaves Raskolnikov for his own healing is consistent with the design of the plot and both are consistent with what we know about codependency and recovery. Dr Zossimov, much earlier, had told Raskolnikov that 'your recovery depends solely on yourself' (p. 194). Raskolnikov, who has trouble accepting affection from anyone, is mystified at the attention he has been getting and says, frowning, 'I simply don't know what I have done to deserve such special attention from you. I simply don't' (p. 195).

The answer is, of course, 'nothing'. The free gift of regeneration in the Epilogue is perfectly consistent with the design of the whole, with its powerful identification of distorted notions of human responsibility with the illness and limitations associated with addiction experience. In this regeneration, we come to understand something of Dostoevsky's own spiritual illumination, his sense of grace. But that is the beginning of a new story.

I hope that I have not implied that any of the characters, no matter how ineffectual or contemptible, is beyond redemption. Even Svidrigailov, one could argue, has fed the hungry and clothed the naked. It is clear, however, that the novel promotes not the vain delusions of rescue, but the painfully acquired wisdom of Sonia and Raskolnikov who assist one another in honestly acknowledging the reality of their limitations. In doing so, they implicitly leave room for grace. Seen in this light, the Epilogue which brings them closer together and brings Raskolnikov closer to repentance is part of the trajectory of the whole novel. The well-known 'Serenity Prayer' of Alcoholics Anonymous asks for three gifts: 'the serenity to accept the things I cannot change, courage to change the things I can, and the wisdom to know the difference'. The fatalists of the world, like Marmeladov (and possibly Svidrigailov) settle too easily for pseudo-tragic and illusory acceptance of misery rather than the first gift, serenity. The rescuers, trapped in the accelerating cycle of their own pride, mistakenly think that they possess the second. Only Raskolnikov and Sonia, who learn to be open to the third gift, acquire this most difficult of all powers of discernment.

That Dostoevsky's own experience of codependency helped to shape this novel is beyond doubt; the degree to which he was conscious of the impact of this experience remains, however, well beyond the reach of this paper. Even the best of his biographical critics have failed to come to grips with the centrality of addiction in his life for all the same reasons that ordinary people involved with alcoholics have usually failed in the same task—lack of awareness and denial. Now that the enigmas of alcoholism in general and codependency in particular have become better under-stood, critics and readers have a new responsibility to be sensitive to this

dimension of texts such as *Crime and Punishment,* which invite and repay
rereading.

NOTES

1.   The text to which the page references in this paper correspond is
F. Dostoevsky, *Crime and Punishment* (trans. C. Garnett; Toronto: Bantam, 1982). How-
ever, to avoid being sent astray by nuances of translation, I also read the translation by
J. Coulson (ed. G. Gibian; New York: Norton, 1975), and the translation by S. Monas
(New York: New American, 1980).

2.   I am grateful to Roger Forseth, who drew my attention to G.C. Noelke's
'Alcoholism in *The Brothers Karamozov*', *The Counsellor* (Nov–Dec. 1986), after the
completion of this paper. Noelke's reading of *The Brothers Karamazov* also uses alcoholic
family roles in its analysis and is therefore similar to my reading of *Crime and
Punishment.* As far as I know, Noelke's paper is the only study of alcoholism in
Dostoevsky's texts.

3.   The important texts about codependency from which my summary is drawn
are these: S. Wegscheider, *Another Chance: Hope and Health for the Alcoholic Family* (Palo
Alto, CA: Science and Behavior, 1981); C. Black, *It Will Never Happen to Me: Children of
Alcoholics as Youngsters, Adolescents, Adults* (Denver: M.A.C., 1982); J.G. Woititz, *Adult
Children of Alcoholics* (Hollywood, CA: Health, 1983); H.L. Gravitz and J.D. Bowden,
Recovery: A Guide for Adult Children of Alcoholics (New York: Simon, 1985); A.W. Schaef,
Co-Dependence (San Francisco: Harper, 1986); and Rachel V., *Family Secrets: Life Stories of
Adult Children of Alcoholics* (San Francisco: Harper, 1987).

4.   A special issue of *The Journal of Drug Issues* (issue 17 1987), guest edited by
psychosocial theorist Stanton Peele, was devoted to a scholarly overview of the relevant
debates; for a briefer account for general readers, see Peele's 'Second Thoughts About a
Gene for Alcoholism', *The Atlantic* 266.2 (August 1990), pp. 52-69.

5.   R. Forseth, 'Alcohol and the Writer: Some Biographical and Critical Issues
(Hemingway)', *Contemporary Drug Problems* 13 (1986), pp. 361-86.

6.   H. Troyat, *Firebrand: The Life of Dostoevsky* (trans. N. Guterman; New York: Roy,
1946); K. Mochulsky, *Dostoevsky: His Life and Work* (trans. M. Minehan; Princeton, NJ:
Princeton University Press, 1967); L.P. Grossman, *Dostoevsky* (trans. M. Mackler;
London: Penguin, 1974); D. Magarshack, *Dostoevsky* (New York: 1963); Ronald
Hingley, *Dostoevsky: His Life and Works* (London: Hamilton, 1978); and G. Kjetsaa,
Fyodor Dostoevsky: A Writer's Life (trans. S. Hustvedt and D. McDuff; New York: Fawcett,
1987).

7.   Magarshack, *Dostoevsky*, p. 11.

8.   Grossman, *Dostoevsky*, p. 39.

9.   Troyat, *Firebrand*, p. 49.

10.   Magarshack, *Dostoevsky*, pp. 10-11; Grossman, *Dostoevsky*, p. 40.

11.   Grossman, *Dostoevsky*, p. 40.

12.   Hingley, *Dostoevsky*, p. 35.

13.   Magarshack, *Dostoevsky*, p. 11.

14.   Troyat, *Firebrand*, p. 52; Mochulsky, *Dostoevsky*, pp. 4-6

15.   Nonetheless, Freud's own assessment of Dostoevsky as a parricide, based on his
reading of *The Brothers Karamazov*, is fascinating reading. See Freud's 'Dostoevsky and
Parricide', in R. Wellek (ed.), *Dostoevsky: A Collection of Critical Essays* (Englewood
Cliffs, NJ: Prentice Hall, 1962), pp. 98-111, and J. Frank's assessment of both the
murder and Freud's insights into Dostoevsky in *Dostoevsky: The Seeds of Revolt*

(Princeton, NJ: Princeton University Press, 1976), pp. 81-91, 379-91.

16. Monas's and Coulson's translations here have 'own father'.

17. Grossman, *Dostoevsky*, pp. 329-33.

18. Magarshack, *Dostoevsky*, pp. 39, 174, 271, 331.

19. Grossman, *Dostoevsky*, p. 322.

20. Kjetsaa, *Fyodor Dostoevsky*, p. 173.

21. Kjetsaa, *Fyodor Dostoevsky*, p. 177; Mochulsky, *Dostoevsky*, pp. 268-69.

22. Magarshack, *Dostoevsky*, p. 248.

23. Mochulsky, *Dostoevsky*, p. 271.

24. W.D. Snodgrass's 'Crime and Punishment: The Mare Beating Episode', in E. Wasiolek (ed.), *Crime and Punishment and the Critics* (Belmont, CA: Wadsworth, 1961) has an excellent account of the triple role of Raskolnikov in his own dream.

25. For the confusion of his motives and his gradual recognition of them, see M. Beebe, 'The Three Motives of Raskolnikov' in Gibian's edition of the novel.

WALTZING WITH PAPA, DANCING WITH THE BEARS: ILLNESS, ALCOHOLISM AND CREATIVE REBIRTH IN THEODORE ROETHKE'S POETRY

Timothy Rivinus

I

Poetry: essential action outward.[1]

For one answer to the question, 'how do creative effort, great poetry, mental illness and alcoholism coexist?' we may examine Theodore Roethke's life and work. Roethke (1908–63) was one of the finest of twentieth-century North American poets. But according to available documents Roethke was probably dependent on alcohol, as were many prominent literary members of his generation. Alcohol use caused him distress in his work and personal life, particularly early in his career. It both heightened and relieved the angst of a painful childhood; it unleashed and heightened manic-depressive illness with which he struggled through most of his adult life.

In his early poetry, Roethke mined the experience of childhood trauma, alcoholic excess and mental illness using rigorous poetic discipline. In the craft of his later poetry he came to seek and, in part, achieve an intoxication with life and the cosmos. The practice of poetry may have developed in him a kind of resiliency in the face of a traumatic past and the threat of progressive alcoholic and mental breakdown. Roethke's poetry also offers the reader the wonder of joining an artist who gives poetic voice to his own creative rebirth and who is uplifted by his own ability to create.

II

All I ask is a way out of slop
Loose me into grace, papa,
I'm up to here and I can't stop.[2]

Theodore Roethke was born in 1908 to German American parents who had settled in Saginaw, Michigan. His father, Otto Roethke, was a driven man: a gardener, a grower of roses, laboring with old-world skills to achieve the American dream in a culture that was already beginning to view gardeners as manual laborers and servants, not artists. As a father, he provided Theodore with an existential Oedipal opponent. Theodore yearned for his father's friendship, but Otto was a stern and punitive workaholic who died when Theodore was barely an adolescent. Otto wanted Theodore to become a lawyer; Theodore chose to become a teacher and a poet. Otto demanded toughness and endurance; Theodore was sensitive and introspective. However, as a grower and a friend to 'little things' Otto Roethke also gave his son an important metaphor of vocation: to explore the subterranean, to nurture, to view nature as organic, growing, flowering, living, dying and resurrecting.

The available evidence suggests that Otto Roethke was a heavy drinker. He usually drank after work. Otto probably also abused his son Theodore, psychologically, if not physically, when he drank. Theodore's experience of this early abuse became a lifelong wound.[3] Regarding the anger and woundedness dating from childhood Roethke made early poetic resolutions. In the title poem in his first published collection, 'Open House' (1941), he concluded,

> The anger will endure
> The deed will speak the truth
> In language strict and pure.
> I stop the lying mouth:
> Rage warps my clearest cry
> To witless agony.[4]

Roethke's frequently anthologized early poem 'My Papa's Waltz'[5] is, among other things, a poem by the child of an alcoholic parent, of wounding and abuse:[6]

> The whiskey on your breath
> Could make a small boy dizzy;
> But I hung on like death:
> Such waltzing was not easy.

With delicate ambivalence this first verse implies that waltzing with a drinking father may cause his son to identify himself with death. Writing this poem in retrospect, Roethke had already experienced his father's early death (Theodore was fourteen at the time) and the poem implies, perhaps, the death wishes of a hurt and angry son.

> We romped until the pans
> Slid from the kitchen shelf;
> My mother's countenance
> Could not unfrown itself.

A mother's disapproval heightens the Oedipal conflict for a small boy.

> The hand that held my wrist
> Was battered on one knuckle,
> At every step you missed
> My right ear scraped a buckle.

The understated violence of this moment, the excitement, the implication of parental disregard for the child's safety are memorable for Roethke— and for all readers, especially those who have known a parent out of control.

> You beat time on my head
> With a palm caked hard by dirt,
> Then waltzed me off to bed
> Still clinging to your shirt.

What do we have from this early autobiographical poem? A household poem, it shows us the helplessness of the small boy still clinging to his father's shirt—feeling anger, mortal power and fear of death. A poem of seduction and family conflict; a boy clings to his intoxicated father, disapproval 'frowning' from his mother's countenance. A memorial poem; Roethke captures, in a short space, filial anger and the image of a powerful, even wonderful, overworked, rough, preoccupied, and drunken father soon to die. A poem about creativity; Roethke gives a stunning lyric to the waltz (a Germanic dance form) and recreates the moment, its rhythm and its poetry as drummed into memory by a 'palm caked hard by dirt'. Roethke achieves in this early poem the wildness, the ecstasy, the intoxication and healing that animate most of his mature work.[7]

III

> To gain a contemplative mind
> All these extremes I have endured.[8]

Theodore, like his father, drank too much. There is ample evidence for this. His friend and biographer Allan Seager notes that Roethke's engagements at three of the first four colleges at which he taught (Lafayette, Michigan State and Bennington) were marred by drunken revels and overinvolvement with students. At least two of his six hospitalizations for manic-depressive illness were precipitated by heavy alcohol use. Seager, though generally an apologist for Roethke's drinking, leaves us other important observations on the subject: Roethke drew inspiration, release and relief from intoxication; he was an inspired entertainer and intrepid Bacchus; he had friends smuggle him beer into hospital against medical advice.[9] Seager quotes two observers of Roethke's behavior at parties who were indignant at his drunkenness and sexual innuendo. Seager also makes the following important observation of Roethke's use of alcohol as self-medication, describing Roethke on his days not teaching at Bennington (Vermont) College (c. 1944): 'On days when he was not teaching he moped around Shingle Cottage alone, scribbling lines in his notebooks, sometimes, he told me, drinking as a deliberate stimulus (later he came to see alcohol as a depressant and used [it] to curb his manic states)...'.[10] In later years Roethke often drank in the morning, a pattern suggestive of efforts to reverse withdrawal symptoms and a mark of problem drinking.[11] Roethke, in fact, fulfilled at least four (three being necessary for the diagnosis) of nine currently accepted criteria for alcohol dependence:[12] (1) he continued to drink despite knowledge of its adverse consequences; (2) he developed tolerance to alcohol (and other sedative drugs); (3) he suffered physical consequences of drinking and triggered psychiatric illness and hospitalization; (4) his drinking caused him recurrent vocational and interpersonal difficulties. Whether Roethke died as a consequence of alcoholism is, presently, unclear. The circumstances of his early death, in a swimming pool, having just made mint juleps for daytime consumption, and attributed by a coroner's report to cardiovascular causes, raises unanswered questions (for alcohol-related deaths are commonly attributed to other causes).

But to demonstrate the diagnosis of alcoholism alone is too reductionistic for an informed and sympathetic view of a rich and productive life. In Roethke's case (as in most cases), alcoholism was a double-edged sword. He enjoyed and reveled in the use of alcohol, but it caused him painful consequences. It temporarily numbed the wounds of a painful childhood and blunted the experience of mania and depression, but it perpetuated painful memories and unresolved conflicts with his father, triggered manic attacks and complicated his depressions.[13]

Although Roethke drank heavily until his death, he began, after his first bout of manic illness, to view his alcohol use as problematic. In an early poem, 'Long Live the Weeds' (a phrase from Gerard Manley Hopkins's poem 'Inversnaid'), he sings of the ambiguity of his relationship to illness and a substance that may have mortal consequences:

> Long live the weeds that overwhelm
> My narrow vegetable realm!...
> The rough, the wicked, and the wild
> That keep my spirit undefiled.
> With these I match my little wit
> And earn the right to stand or sit,
> Hope, love, create, or drink and die.
> These shape the creature that is I.[14]

In the poem 'The Longing' he probably comments on his frequent abuse of prescribed sedative pills:[15]

> On things asleep, no balm:
> A kingdom of stinks and sighs...

and on the agony of drunkenness:

> Saliva dripping from warm microphones,
> Agony of crucifixion on barstools...
> How to transcend this sensual emptiness?[16]

In one of his last poems, 'The Marrow', he again acknowledges that inspirational sources in alcohol have turned to agony and a will to die:

> The wind from off the sea says nothing new.
> The mist above me sings with its small flies.
> From a burnt pine the sharp speech of a crow
> Tells me my drinking breeds a will to die...

He concludes 'The Marrow' by acknowledging that he has lost control:

> Yea, I have slain my will, and still I live;
> I would be near; but I shut my eyes to see;
> I bleed my bones, their marrow to bestow
> Upon that God who knows what I would know.[17]

Roethke confesses the harmful power of alcohol in his life and admits that his own will is 'slain'. His confession is akin to the strivings of those who struggle to embrace the first steps of Alcoholics Anonymous, which call upon alcoholics to acknowledge their powerlessness over alcohol, to accept the inability of solitary will to halt drinking and its consequences, and to surrender themselves to a 'higher power'.[18]

IV

Dissociation often precedes a new state of clarity.[19]

As clinical knowledge and awareness of psychiatric disorders increase, the list of authors and artists who have had affective disorder combined with alcohol or other drug dependence is growing and will probably continue to grow. Table I presents a selected list of twentieth-century American poets who received psychiatric treatment for affective disorder, many of whom were alcoholic and/or commited suicide.[20] Epidemiologists who have studied artists (writers, painters and composers especially) have suggested a genetic or constitutional association between manic-depressive (or bipolar) illness, alcoholism and creative excellence.[21] The gifts of these artists may also reside in their unique ability to draw from what psychoanalysts call 'primary process' for their creative sources.[22] Artists are able to make associations that are new, startling, and speak to certain as yet unspoken, universal and hitherto secret elements within each of us. As such, they are able to break through the organized defenses that make us hold to old structures, reason and logic. As they offer us new, unalloyed 'discoveries', these artists may also be struggling, through creative efforts, to heal themselves.[23]

Manic-depressive illness, unlike schizophrenia, is a cyclic disorder in which there are periods of generally normal functioning interspersed with periods of abnormally elevated or depressed mood, thinking and activity. The morbidity of these disorders can be measured in three ways. They can lead to accidental, suicidal or other catastrophic events that may impair or terminate the afflicted person's life; they can, over time, erode the cognitive, coping and creative abilities of the people who have them; they can lead the afflicted person to seek dangerous and self-imposed relief. An example of the latter is when the afflicted person 'self-medicates' with an addicting intoxicant.[24]

The co-occurrence of mental illness and self-medication with a psycho-active chemical, this co-occurrence is currently called 'dual or multiple diagnosis'. Dual diagnosis may work in various ways. Substance use (and abuse) may lead to depression or trigger episodes of mania or depression in those predisposed toward mental illness but not previously ill. Or substance abuse may follow mental illness. Often it is not clear which came first, only that both may coexist, the one fueling the other.[25]

Theodore Roethke had 'dual diagnosis'. He had manic-depressive episodes and he triggered and treated them with alcoholic binges and abuse of sedative drugs prescribed to him. His notebooks at the time of his first breakdown quote Rimbaud's philosophy of *deréglement de tous les sens* by use of chemicals. He confided, 'My first breakdown was in a very real sense deliberate. I not only asked for, I prayed that it would happen'.[26] Soon, however, Roethke came to suffer the pain of illness, its recurrence, *and* its possibilities.[27]

Once confined to hospital Roethke usually benefited from the pro-longed rest and curtailment of alcohol use during hospitalization. While in institutions Roethke wrote prodigiously in his notebooks and began poems. For the most part, he 'finished' the work begun in hospitals after he was discharged. Sometimes, however, he also underwent in hospitals painful, primitive and perhaps harmful organic treatments including electroconvulsive therapy (ECT) and temporarily paralyzing neuroleptic drug treatments.[28]

V

The pit and the peak are the same.[29]

The first of Roethke's six breakdowns came in 1936 when he was 27. His hospitalizations regularly preceded his publications and paralleled his flowering and twenty-five year harvest as a writer (see Table II). How was it possible that a man who endured such turmoil became such a fine poet? I believe that Roethke did it by an extraordinary transformation of inchoate grief, rage and mental disintegration into reconstructive healing by writing poetry, teaching, and cultivating supportive friendships and associations. His notebooks are remarkable documents of self-exploration, self-healing and source material. His poetry probably appeals to us because it ultimately triumphs over regression, suffering and travail. About the father with whose memory he struggled in his early work, Roethke wrote while in hospital, and in the midst of a manic episode:

> By grubbing among the stones, in the cluster I found out
> Where my father left his heart...
> Where my lost father is: There I would be.[30]

But grubbing among the stones of painful memory is exhausting work:

> The point is, dear father, if I don't stop soon,
> I am going to become a suntanned idiot boy...
> All I ask is a way out of slop;
> Loose me into grace, Papa,
> I'm up to here and I can't stop...
> I can't scratch anymore. My lips need more than a snifter.[31]

Alcohol may provide temporary release from memory and mental anguish but 'the snifter' does no more than 'lip' service to a mythic struggle. Grace, perhaps in the clarity of poetry, is the real object of the search.

Of manic and depressive breakdown Roethke quips in his notebooks,

> Sure I'm crazy
> But it ain't easy.[32]

He also observes: 'My own agonies which I once thought comic have become more terrible with the passing of time...'.[33] Of manic (or alcoholic) excitement he says,

> It is very hard work trying to be naughty for a whole community.[34]

Of its isolation he drily rhymes,

> When I go mad I call all my friends by phone;
> I'm afraid they might think they're alone.[35]

Writing born of psychotic dissolution may not be easy or the finished product, but it can be a source of fearful inspiration:

> In euphoria, the terrible fear that I would not live long enough
> to achieve the full essence of experience
> In euphoria, little work. But perhaps the source?[36]

In an analytic, diagnostic vein Roethke searches the detritus of breakdown for a 'creative source':

> Manic: a limitless expanding of the ego with no controlling princi
> [sic]
> (1) an intense communion with nature in which subject
> and object seem identical
> (2) abdication of the ego to another centre the 'self' of[37]

Roethke came to view his illness as a transcendent calling to poetry:

> I can't go on flying apart just for those who want the
> benefit of a few verbal kicks. My God, do you know that
> poems like that *cost*? They're not written vicariously:
> they come out of actual suffering, *real* madness.
> > I've got to go beyond. That's all there is to it.
> > Beyond what?
> > The human, you fool. Don't you see what I've done. I've
> > come this far, and now can't stop. It's too late, baby, it's
> > too late.[38]

During his breakdowns, Roethke imagined and found himself in the company of other mad mentors in the poetic tradition. In his late poem 'Heard in a Violent Ward' he declares,

> In heaven, too,
> you'd be institutionalized
> But that's all right,—
> If they let you eat and swear
> With the likes of Blake,
> And Christopher Smart,
> and that sweet man, John Clare.[39]

Of healing and creative rebirth in the craft of poetry he observes,

> Slowly the speech of the dead is beaten into praise. An eye
> walked there, wily as an adder, making a new place pure.
> Even I can be a mother, giving birth to my father.[40]

His art consists of the psychic pain it takes to create *and* the joy of its product:

> I am proud to suffer; to know
> I can and can make it something else.[41]

Regarding the courage it takes to write: 'To write poetry: you have to be prepared to die', he told his students.[42]

VI

> And I acknowledge my foolishness with God
> My desire for the peaks, the black ravines, the rolling mists
> Changing with every twist of wind,
> The unsinging fields where no lungs breathe,
> Where light is stone.[43]

Theodore Roethke was, is, a poet's poet. His knowledge of poetry was prodigious and he used the phrases and rhythms of other poets like a jazz musician uses the melodies, inflections and rhythms of a musical past. He saw the poets of the past as friends: Henry Vaughan, Thomas Traherne, Christopher Smart, John Clare, William Shakespeare, Sir John

Davies, William Blake, Gerard Manley Hopkins, Emily Dickinson, Walt
Whitman, T.S. Eliot, Wallace Stevens, William Butler Yeats. He turned to
and drew from contemporary poets who were his friends and mentors:
Louise Bogan, Stanley Kuntiz, Rolfe Humphries and Dylan Thomas.
Writers of fiction, particularly William Faulkner and James Joyce, served
as models of revolutionary artistic expression of the unconscious and the
child within. He also drew inspiration from the mystical writings of St
John of the Cross and the spiritual and philosophical works of Evelyn
Underhill, William James, Paul Tillich and his contemporary critic,
philosopher and friend, Kenneth Burke.[44]

Theodore Roethke was also a great teacher. He taught literature and
writing to university students for thirty years. Despite recurrent illness he
held his last teaching post (at the University of Washington) for fifteen
years. He was also a great reader of poetry, his own and others; his
readings were command performances. His voice booms forth with
drama, pathos and play in the taped readings that survive him. He drew
on theatrical gifts in his personal, poetic and teaching life. Roethke's
biographer and critics have noted that poetry, for Roethke, *was* his life. His
collected poems and notebooks are a poetic, psychological and spiritual
odyssey and autobiography; the references in his work are objective
correlatives of his own life, its struggles, its defeats and victories.[45]

As autobiography, Roethke's early poetry is a poetry of survival. It
appeals to us because it speaks to the survivor in us. He survived many
things including childhood trauma, the early loss of a parent, a long
struggle with alcoholism, five manic-depressive episodes and hospitalizations, the struggle to be a teacher, academic and poet in the United
States during the 1930s, 1940s and 1950s ('dark times' for many North
American academics), and the engulfing appetites of a passionate man.

Freud's dyad, 'love [i.e. a significant relationship] and work', emerges,
in research from the many variables studied, as identifying the two basic
ingredients of healthy adaptation in adult life. They appear to confer
relative protection against crippling developmental illness during
adulthood.[46] As the work of his poetry developed further, Roethke realized
the other of these two elements of psychological health. In midlife,
having come to relative terms with childhood trauma, his father, himself
and his vocation, Roethke met Beatrice O'Connell, who agreed to be his
wife and partner. (Beatrice was probably also an unwilling 'enabler' to
Roethke's drinking and neglect of his health.) He explored his *anima* by
writing memorable poetry from a woman's point of view ('Meditations of
an Old Woman'[47]). To Beatrice he wrote some of the great love poems of
the language.

Much of the poetry of Roethke's midcareer is the poetry of love, of play
and of growth. Theodore and Beatrice never had children, but Theodore
wrote many fine children's poems, brilliantly capturing the voice,

whimsy and imagination of the child. His interest in youth, nurture and the cycles of life also became his vocation as he developed his career as a teacher. His preoccupation with birth, death and rebirth is reflected in his memorable nature poems.[48]

Ultimately Roethke developed himself as a mystic, transcendental, inspirational, confessional poet who staked out high ground above cool order and reason, above frenzy, disillusion and dissolution, achieving a position firmly beside Ezra Pound, T.S. Eliot, Robert Frost, Wallace Stevens, Robert Lowell and Elizabeth Bishop in mid-twentieth century American poetry. In progressing from the painful, self-absorbed, exposition of his childhood and his 'dark time' to become an existential poet of light, Roethke followed a developmental path commonly seen in the successful outcome of involvement in psychotherapy, psychoanalysis, mysticism (of which Roethke had extensive knowledge) or other spiritual practices.[49] From this point of departure the stages of Roethke's poetic development may be outlined as follows:

I. *The Beginning*
  1. Statement of purpose
  2. Dealing with pain and the self (e.g. 'The Open House')
  3. Dealing with suffering and its limitations
  4. The development of his vocation and craft

II. *The Middle*
  1. Finding and hearing voices outside the self, his models and mentors
  2. Loving another (e.g. 'I Knew a Woman')
  3. Loving and writing for children
  4. Writing of (and joining) nature (e.g. 'North American Sequence') and the cosmos (e.g. 'Sequence, Sometimes Metaphysical')

III. *The End*
  1. Recapitulation
  2. Dark night of the soul (e.g. 'The Abyss', 'In a Dark Time', 'The Marrow')
  3. Transcendence (e.g. 'The Right Thing')
  4. Union
  5. Facing the eternal (e.g. 'In Evening Air')

Roethke's first two volumes, *Open House* and *The Lost Son and Other Poems*, begin his odyssey. Their purpose is to master trauma and mental illness and bring them into creative poetic perspective. In the volumes *Praise to the End*, *The Waking* and *Words for the Wind*, his love poems and poetry for children, Roethke emerges from himself in work to join others, nature and the universe. Poems from his last (posthumous) volume, *The Far Field* (as well as a number of earlier poems) prefigure death, recapitulate themes of agony and acceptance, and roughly correspond to the third and final stage of his work. Roethke's last poems recapitulate earlier themes but also transcend them to affirm the roundedness and completeness of an artist who has come to terms with his past *and* his coming death.

VII

> Now I adore my life...
> And everything comes to One.
> As we dance on, dance on, dance on.[50]

The study of Roethke's poetry rewards the reader with inspirational material drawn from the 'fetor of weeks', 'rubbish', 'the riddled foliage, by the muddy pond edge/by bog holes', 'from the crucifixion on barstools', the padded cell, or the hard stone of the sarcophagus. From these unenviable places Roethke emerges, the universal lover, as in his late sensual love poem 'The Wraith':

> Did each become the other in that play?
> She laughed me out and then she laughed me in;
> In the deep middle of ourselves we lay;
> When glory failed, he danced upon a pin.
> The valley rocked beneath the granite hill;
> Our souls looked forth, and the great day stood still.[51]

Roethke was a wild man who sang, danced, lost it in alcoholic excess and madness, and got it back again. He allows us as readers to revel and vicariously fulfill our own Dionysian necessities when he takes us in his exuberant, bearlike arms and waltzes us, intoxicated by poetry itself into madness and back again:

> Is that dance slowing in the mind of man
> That made him think the universe could hum?
> The great wheel turns its axle when it can;
> I need a place to sing, and dancing-room,
> And I have made a promise to my ears
> I'll sing and whistle romping with the bears.
>
> For they are all my friends: I saw one slide
> Down a steep hillside on a cake of ice,—
> Or was that in a book? I think with pride:
> A caged bear rarely does the same thing twice
> In the same way: O watch his body sway!—
> This animal remembering to be gay.
>
> I tried to fling my shadow at the moon,
> The while my blood leaped with a wordless song.
> Though dancing needs a master, I had none

To teach my toes to listen to my tongue.
But what I learned there, dancing all alone,
Was not the joyless motion of a stone.

I take this cadence from a man named Yeats;
I take it, and I give it back again:
For other tunes and other wanton beats
Have tossed my heart and fiddled through my brain.
Yes, I was dancing-mad, and how
That came to be the bears and Yeats would know.[52]

Modern psychiatry still knows far less than 'Yeats would know' of the causes of manic-depressive disorder or addiction to alcohol and other mind-altering chemicals. In Roethke's case, however, we know something of the origins of his kind of suffering, of his experiences with psychiatric illness and with alcohol. He has told us much in his poetry, notebooks, essays and letters. He also has told us how, in an effort to transcend suffering, illness and addiction, he taught himself to compose, dance and sing, for himself and others, to the music of something surpassing. We may, as Roethke did, survive by becoming intoxicated by poetry, even addicted to it. It may be for us, as it was for him, in part, a healing and a rebirth.

Table I *Some Major Twentieth-Century American Poets Born between 1890–1935 with Histories of Manic-Depressive Illness and Alcoholism*[53]

Poet	Pulitzer Prize in Poetry	Treated for Major Depressive Illness	Treated for Mania	Committed Suicide	Alcohol Abuse/Dependence
Edna St. Vincent Millay (1892–1950)	X	X			X
Hart Crane (1899–1932)		X	X	X	X
Theodore Roethke (1908–63)	X	X	X		X
Delmore Schwartz (1913–66)		X	X		X
John Berryman (1914–72)	X	X	X	X	X
Randall Jarrell (1914–65)		X	X	X	X
Robert Lowell (1917–77)	X	X	X		X
Anne Sexton (1928–74)	X	X	X	X	X
Sylvia Plath (1932–63)	X	X	X	X	X

Table II

Theodore Roethke: Relation of Illness to Creative Output

Illnesses and Hospitalizations	Publications
1. 1935–36	First published poems (1935)
	Open House (1941)
2. 1945–46	*The Lost Son and Other Poems* (1948)
	Praise to the End (1951)
3. 1953–54	*The Waking* (1953)
4. 1957–58	*Words for the Wind* (1958)
	Party at the Zoo (1958)
5. 1960–61	*I am! Says the Lamb* (1961)
Death 1963	*The Far Field* (1964)

NOTES

1.   This quote originates from unpublished papers and notebooks by Theodore Roethke in archives at the library of the University of Washington. Quotations used in this paper drawn from the archives are taken from two secondary sources: A.T. Foster, *Theodore Roethke's Meditative Sequences: Contemplation and the Creative Process* (Lewiston, NY: Edwin Mellen, 1985), and N. Bowers, *Theodore Roethke's The Journey from I to Otherwise* (Columbia, MO: University of Missouri Press, 1982). The numbers in parentheses indicate the archive box and folder in which a piece is located. This citation is from Foster, *Roethke's Meditative Sequences*, p. 1 (Roethke Notebook 8.115).

2.   *Straw for the Fire: From the Notebook of Theodore Roethke 1943–63* (ed. D. Wagoner; Seattle: University of Washington Press, 1980), pp. 28-29. This volume is an edited selection from the unpublished archival material cited in note 1.

3.   See Wagoner (ed.), *Straw for the Fire*, pp. 23-27. Evidence of Roethke's childhood paternally inflicted wound can also be seen clearly in the poems 'The Open House', 'Feud', 'Prognosis', 'Sister', 'Premonition', 'Orders for the Day', 'Silence', 'On the Road to Woodlawn', 'The Lost Son', 'Where Knock Is Open Wide', 'Unfold! Unfold!' and 'Fourth Meditation'. All of these poems can be found in *The Collected Poems of Theodore Roethke* (New York: Anchor Press/Doubleday, 1975). Current works that examine the creative impact of childhood trauma and loss on writers can be found in L. Terr, 'Childhood Trauma and the Creative Product', *Psychoanalytic Study of the Child* 42 (1987), pp. 545-72; *idem*, 'Terror Writing by the Formerly Terrified', *Psychoanalytic Study of the Child* 44 (1989), pp. 369-90;' *idem*, 'Who's Afraid of Virginia Woolf?', *Psychoanalytic Study of the Child* 45 (1990), pp. 531-44; D. Aberbach, *Surviving Trauma: Loss, Literature and Psychoanalysis* (New Haven: Yale University Press, 1989); A. Miller, *The Untouched Key: Tracing Childhood Trauma in Creativity and Destructiveness* (trans. H. & H. Hanumm; New York: Doubleday, 1990 [originally published in German in 1988]); and L. Shengold, *Soul Murder: The Effects of Childhood Abuse and Deprivation* (New Haven: Yale University Press, 1989).

4.   In *Collected Poems*, p. 3.

5.   In *Collected Poems*, p. 43.

6.   Brian Ford and I introduce the moving literature written of and by children of alcoholic parents in 'Children of Alcoholics in Literature: Portraits of the Struggle', *Dionysos: The Literature and Intoxication Triquarterly* 1.3 (Winter 1990), pp. 13-23, and 2.1 (Spring 1990), pp. 10-26. Issues of the self-healing aspects of writing and art are treated in O. Rank, *Art and Artist: Creative Urge and Personality Development* (New York: Norton, 1989), pp. 305-31. Freud's contributions to the self-healing aspects of art are discussed in L. Feder, *Madness in Literature* (Princeton, NJ: Princeton University Press, 1980), pp. 23-26 and A. Rothenberg, *Creativity and Madness: New Findings and Old Stereotypes* (Baltimore, MD: Johns Hopkins University Press,1991), pp. 149-64. For a discussion of the failure of writing poetry alone to promote self-healing see M.A. Silverman and N.P. Will, 'Sylvia Plath and the Failure of Emotional Self-Repair through Poetry', *Psychoanalytic Quarterly* 60 (1986), pp. 99-129.

7.   A seminal discussion of the growth-promoting aspects of the search for truth and meaning in the face of a traumatic past appears in V. Frankl, 'Psychiatry and Man's Quest for Meaning', *Journal of Religion and Health* 1 (1962), pp. 93-103.

8.   N. Bowers, *Roethke's The Journey*, p. 76 (Roethke Notebooks 32a.1).

9.   Roethke's biographer A. Seager (*The Glass House: The Life of Theodore Roethke* [New York: McGraw-Hill, 1968]) makes it clear that Theodore was a heavy drinker during his college years (p. 56). Roethke's reputation in an early teaching post at Lafayette College was that he often drank heavily with students (*The Glass House*, pp. 72, 98). Roethke's failure to get tenure at Michigan State appears to have been related, in part, to his reputation for excessive drinking (*The Glass House*, pp. 98-100). Seager notes that Roethke drank heavily at Bennington College (*The Glass House*, p. 144) and that he was not invited to return despite being cited as the college's most popular teacher in 1946 (*The Glass House*, pp. 153-54). The description of Roethke's self-induction of his first illness episode occurs in *The Glass House* (p. 205) and appears also in a letter to James Wright (cited in R.J. Mills, Jr (ed.), *Selected Letters of Theodore Roethke* [Seattle: University of Washington Press, 1968], p. 220). Comments on Roethke's behavior at parties can be found in the accounts by Seager, by his department chair at the University of Washington, Robert Heilman, and in a letter to Seager by Veronica Henriques (*The Glass House*, pp. 238-41).

10.   Seager, *The Glass House*, p. 144.

11.   Seager, *The Glass House*, p. 242. Another reference to Roethke's use of alcohol to 'control' mania occurs in *The Glass House*, p. 251. References to early morning drinking are also on p. 252. Early morning drinking is often seen in problem drinkers and is one of four indicators of problem drinking in the CAGE Questionnaire, a widely used clinical screening device for problem drinking. See J.A. Ewing, 'Detecting Alcoholism: The CAGE Questionnaire', *Journal of the American Medical Association* 252.14 (1984), pp. 1905-1907.

12.   See American Psychiatric Association, *Diagnostic and Statistical Manual III, Revised* (Washington, DC: Author, 1987), pp. 123-62.

13.   Seager, *The Glass House*, p. 285.

14.   In *Collected Poems*, p. 17.

15.   Seager documents two occasions when Theodore dosed himself with large amounts (suggesting tolerance, that is, the progression to larger and larger doses to achieve the desired effect—an indicator of chemical dependence) of sedatives, phenobarbital (*The Glass House*, pp. 147-48) and unknown pills (p. 277) without medical advice. 'Seager: "What are the pills for" [Roethke]: "Ah, I'm nervous"...[Roethke] growled contemptuously as if nervousness were China, a place I'd never been...' (p. 227). Why, with so many examples of problems with alcohol and pills in his subject, would a biographer such as Seager minimize the issue in his subject? This is

an issue beyond the scope of this paper except to note that in 1968 when *The Glass House* was published there was a very different understanding of the consequences of alcohol and drug use by clinicians and the general public than there is today. Furthermore, as Tom Dardis has put it in his examination of the biographies of alcoholic writers, 'If great authors are called alcoholics or said to have alcoholism [or by implication, other chemical addictions] then how can they be called great any more? After all, what does a drunk know?' (see his paper in this volume). The examination of Roethke's and other alcoholic writers' lives reveals how much addicted writers may indeed know despite and because of their suffering and dependence on a drug.

16. In *Collected Poems*, p. 181.

17. In *Collected Poems*, p. 238.

18. The issue of acceptance of powerlessness over the addictive process and surrender to it are discussed in *The Big Book* (New York: Alcoholics Anonymous World Services, 1976), pp. 58-60, and G. Bateson, 'The Cybernetics of "Self": A Theory of Alcoholism', *Psychiatry* 33 (1971), pp. 1-18. See also E. Kurtz, *Not God: A History of Alcoholics Anonymous* (Center City, MN: Hazelden, 1980), and G.A. Vaillant, *The Natural History of Alcoholism* (Cambridge, MA: Harvard University Press 1983), p, 193.

19. R.J. Mills, Jr (ed.), *On the Poet and His Craft: Selected Prose of Theodore Roethke* (Seattle: University of Washington Press, 1965), p. 41.

20. Affective disorders are characterized by prolonged instability of mood, with depression, mania or both, usually associated with disturbances of thinking and behavior. D. Goodwin (*Alcohol and the Writer* [Kansas City: Andrews & McMeel, 1988], p. 4) presents a long list of American writers who were alcoholics, many of whom also received psychiatric treatment for various (mostly affective) disorder diagnoses. See also Table 1.

21. The genetic hypothesis linking creativity and manic-depressive illness is presented in K.R. Jameson, 'Manic-Depressive Illness, Creativity and Leadership', in F.K. Goodwin and K.R. Jameson (eds.), *Manic Depressive Illness* (New York: Oxford University Press, 1990), pp. 349-56. See also N.J.C. Andreasen and A. Canter, 'The Creative Writer: Psychiatric Symptoms and Family History', *Comprehensive Psychiatry* 5.2 (1974), pp. 123-31; N.J.C. Andreason, 'Creativity and Mental Illness: Prevalence Rates in Writers and Their First-Degree Relatives', *American Journal of Psychiatry* 144.10 (1987), pp. 1288-1292.

22. Rothenberg (*Creativity and Madness*, pp. 149-57) challenges the genetic hypothesis of a connection between creativity and manic-depressive illness on the basis of biased sampling and inadequate diagnosis cited in the studies in n. 21.

23. A classic debate arose in American literary circles as a result of Edmund Wilson's (implied) thesis that psychic 'wound' was integral to the creative effort, 'the bow' in his essay 'Philoctetes: The Wound and The Bow', in *The Wound and the Bow* (Boston: Houghton Mifflin, 1941), pp. 272-95. Lionel Trilling, with whom I would agree, pointed out that a wound may not be necessary but can be sufficient to provide a source of creative drive. He notes that the artist 'is what he is by virtue of his successful objectification of his neurosis, by his shaping it and making it available to others in a way which has its effect upon their egos in struggle...It is, as we say, a gift' (L. Trilling, 'Art and Neurosis', in *The Liberal Imagination* [New York: Charles Scribner's Sons, 1976], p. 179). Although the 'wound' or 'gift' may be painful, crippling and even ultimately lethal, this self-healing and restorative action of art for artist and audience is the essence of much great art. See for further elaboration of this theme R. Coles, *The Call of Stories* (Boston: Houghton Mifflin, 1989).

24. E.J. Khantzian, 'The Self-Medication Hypothesis of Addictive Disorders', *American Journal of Psychiatry* 142 (1985), pp. 1259-1264.

25. A useful discussion of 'dual diagnosis' appears in E.C. Penick *et al.*, 'The Emerging Concept of Dual Diagnosis: An Overview and Implications', in D.F. O'Connell (ed.), *Managing the Dually Diagnosed Patient: Current Issues and Clinical Approaches* (New York: The Haworth Press, 1990), pp. 1-42.

26. Bowers, *Roethke's The Journey*, p. 12 (Roethke Notebooks 42.194).

27. See n. 15 above for references to Roethke's self-medication with sedatives. The reference to Rimbaud is discussed in Seager, *The Glass House*, p. 101. It is probably no coincidence that a number of the modern writers from whom Roethke drew inspiration were also alcoholic: Dylan Thomas, Louise Bogan, James Joyce and William Faulkner.

28. Seager, *The Glass House*, pp. 220, 287.

29. Bowers, *Roethke's The Journey*, p. 93 (Roethke Notebooks 43.200).

30. Wagoner (ed.), *Straw for the Fire*, p. 131.

31. Wagoner (ed.), *Straw for the Fire*, pp. 28-29.

32. Wagoner (ed.), *Straw for the Fire*, p. 20.

33. Wagoner (ed.), *Straw for the Fire*, p. 34.

34. Wagoner (ed.), *Straw for the Fire*, p. 87.

35. Wagoner (ed.), *Straw for the Fire*, p. 87.

36. Wagoner (ed.), *Straw for the Fire*, pp. 86-87.

37. Bowers, *Roethke's The Journey*, p. 19 (Roethke Notebooks 43.206).

38. Wagoner (ed.), *Straw for the Fire*, p. 87.

39. *Collected Poems*, p. 220.

40. Seager, *The Glass House*, p. 167.

41. Seager, *The Glass House*, p. 168.

42. Wagoner (ed.), *Straw for the Fire*, p. 262.

43. From 'The Long Waters', *Collected Poems*, p. 190.

44. For a more complete discussion of Roethke's sources of mysticism, see Bowers, *Roethke's The Journey*, pp. 2-19, and Foster, *Roethke's Meditative Sequences*, pp. 1-28.

45. Roethke's booming (melo)dramatic voice can be heard on a posthumous compilation, entitled *Theodore Roethke Reads His Poetry*, by Caedmon Records LDL 51351 (New York, 1972) also available as a tape (Tape C-1616) from Poet's Audio Center, 6925 Willow St. NW, #201, Washington, DC, 20012, USA. In these readings Roethke can frequently be heard to slur words, suggesting that he may be reading under the influence of sedatives as he reads ('Saliva dripping from warm microphones...', see n. 16). For commentary on Roethke's life and influence as a poet see for example a letter in Roethke's support to Frederick Thieme, Vice President of the University of Washington by his department chair Richard Heilman (Seager, *The Glass House*, p. 254) and the statement by his former student and later editor of his notebooks, David Wagoner (*Straw for the Fire*, p. 14). Roethke's recorded readings can be found on *Theodore Roethke Reads his Poetry* (New York: Caedmon, 1972), LDL 51351.

46. Freud's discussion of the principles of love and work appears in 'Three Essays on the Theory of Sexuality' (1950), in J. Strachey (ed.), with A. Freud, *The Standard Edition of the Complete Psychological Works of Sigmund Freud*, XVII (London: Hogarth Press, 1961), pp. 135-243. See also G.E. Vaillant and E.S. Milofsky, 'Natural History of Male Psychological Health, IX: Empirical Evidence for Erikson's Model of the Life Cycle', *American Journal of Psychiatry* 137 (1980), pp. 1348-1359; and G.E. Vaillant and C.O. Vaillant, 'Natural History of Male Psychological Health X: Work as a Predictor of Positive Mental Health', *American Journal of Psychiatry* 138, pp. 1433-1440.

47. *Collected Poems*, pp. 151-72.

48. An 'enabler' can be defined as a partner-in-living who, for compassionate reasons, makes it easier for an addicted person to deny and cope with the process and

consequences of addiction. Roethke's children's volumes are *I am! Says the Lamb* (Garden City, NY: Doubleday, 1961), *Party at the Zoo* (New York: Crowell-Collier, 1963), and *Dirty Dinkey and Other Creatures: Poems for Children* (Garden City, NY: Doubleday, 1973). Roethke's great popularity and success as a teacher is documented by Seager (*The Glass House*, pp. 137-38), and by the fact that many of his former students went on to become poets themselves (Seager, *The Glass House*, pp. 253-56). Roethke's great nature poems appear in *Words for the Wind* (1958) and in *The Far Field* (1964).

49. For discussions of Roethke's study, knowledge and acceptance of mysticism see Bowers and Foster who provide evidence that Roethke had studied two texts on mysticism by E. Underhill: *The Mystic Way: A Psychological Study in Christian Origins* (London: J.M. Dent, 1913) and *Mysticism: A Study in the Nature and Development of Man's Spiritual Consciousness* (New York: Meridian Books, 1955). Hierarchical discussions of the progress of successful psychotherapy and the transformation of consciousness that parallel the transformations undertaken by the mystic and by Roethke in his poetic development can be found in A.D. Weisman, *The Existential Core of Psychoanalysis* (Boston: Little, Brown, 1965), and in a collection of essays, K. Wilbur, J. Engler and D.P. Brown (eds.), *Transformations of Consciousness: Conventional and Contemplative Perspectives on Development* (Boston: New Science Library, 1986).

50. *Collected Poems*, p. 243.

51. *Collected Poems*, p. 102.

52. *Collected Poems*, p. 101 ('The Dance' [Part I from 'Four for Sir John Davies']).

53. Table adapted and expanded from K. Jameson, 'Manic-Depressive Illness, Creativity, and Leadership', in F.K. Goodwin and K.R. Jameson (eds.), *Manic Depressive Illness* (New York: Oxford University Press, 1990), p. 347, reprinted and adapted with permission of the publisher.

ALCOHOLISM, GAMBLING AND CREATIVITY

Jean-Charles Sournia

Medical interest in patterns of behaviour considered abnormal, for instance addictive behaviour, can lead us to study in more detail those forms of behaviour considered normal. We can view any act of creation, indeed perhaps any act at all, as a kind of challenge: we are aware of potential obstacles or means of failure and it is this awareness that challenges us to act, to create, to assert ourselves in the face of our audience or the world as a whole. So actors coming on stage, although confident of success, will at the same time be stimulated by the risk of failure; the same risk stimulates novelists, political candidates, military officers planning battle tactics or artists. We create for ourselves but also for the public; our achievement will exist by itself, but it will be judged by others, who will glorify us or ignore us.

1. *Alcoholism and Creativity*

Sociologists and psychiatrists are familiar with the notion of roles, particular patterns of behaviour, as central in human society. In relation to this, the common experience described above of stimulation by risks and hazards can lead to extreme behaviour patterns among people suffering some kind of addiction. Classically, alcoholics for example may be warned that they are 'gambling with their health' but will continue their alcohol consumption regardless.

Such extreme behaviour patterns will tend to give a particular character to the artistic creations of addicts. We have many examples of literature produced by alcoholics, whose addiction certainly did not prevent them from writing. William Faulkner, when living in Paris, drank large quantities of brandy while managing to work on his novels, send short stories to his agent and film scripts to Hollywood—and he was not in any financial difficulties, since his writing was becoming more and more successful. Faulkner knew that he was endangering his life by his excessive drinking, but he persisted in provoking the fates, both physically and literarily. Jack London, on the other hand, wrote most pathetically about his addiction and related that he was quite unable to write when intoxicated with whisky.

It is interesting to note the different patterns of behaviour typically exhibited by male and female alcoholics—which are often depicted in films or theatre productions. The male alcoholic drinks openly, in public houses and on the streets while the female alcoholic drinks alone, sadly, in the house. This difference may be the result of society's differing attitudes: in Western societies male drunkenness is regarded with indulgence, but female drunkenness with contempt and disgust.

In recent years more than fifteen accounts have been published in France by former alcoholics, describing how the authors escaped their hells of addiction. Such publications both serve to encourage other addicts to conquer their addictions and reflect the will of the writers to narrate their experiences even after recovering (although some of these authors relapsed into addiction and even ended their lives by suicide, as did Jack London, who related his illusory victory over alcohol in *John Barleycorn*).

We have established, then, that excessive use of alcohol does not prevent people from writing. If drinking were to make writing *easier*, we might expect France to produce the highest number of authors of any country, since it is here that alcohol consumption is highest in the world. In fact it is noticeable that alcoholic writers have proliferated in America and Ireland, an issue which will perhaps be addressed by some of the other contributors to this volume.

We can see in the careers of many alcoholic artists a pattern of alternating phases of unproductiveness and unbridled creativity. Beethoven, the son of wine merchants, frequented public houses where he took part in wine-drinking contests. Mussorgsky, who suffered from manic-depression, went through several phases of excessive alcohol consumption, although, contrary to the warnings of his contemporaries, he did not suffer attacks of delirium tremens.

Alcohol appears to have had a positive effect on the career of Utrillo, who began drinking when he first went to college and whose painting demonstrated great originality and met with increasing success. After his marriage at the age of 53, at the peak of his career, he stopped drinking and was satisfied, until his death at the age of 72, with copying postcards. Modigliani, on the other hand, seems to have suffered from his alcoholism. He began his career as a sculptor (perhaps surprisingly, as far as I am aware, there have been no alcoholic sculptors), then took up painting and drinking and died aged 36 from toxicosis and tuberculous lesions. In the last years of his life his artistic ability decreased, his portraits becoming stiffer and less vivid. After his death his partner committed suicide, as did his mistress, the English journalist Beatrice Hastings, who was also an alcoholic. It is perhaps misleading to describe Van Gogh as an alcoholic, since he described in his letters his negative physical reactions to only small amounts of alcohol, but he did experience phases of acute alcoholism, which he linked to his consumption of low-quality wine.

2. *Drinking and Gambling*

In his novel *The Gambler* Dostoyevsky depicts the problems of another sort of addiction: gambling. I suggested earlier that alcoholism itself is often considered as a type of gambling (the drinker 'gambling' with his or her health, career or life). The main difference is that, unlike alcoholism or drug addiction, compulsive gambling is not related to the consumption of some substance but to the effects of the excitement on the body itself—that is, the gambler may become addicted to the adrenaline rush produced by gambling.

As in the case of alcoholics, for compulsive gamblers their actual social position, their futures or the futures of their families are of little interest. Rather, each throw of the dice is a new departure, a rebellion against the established order, a chance to master life and fate, a Faustian pact which will confer on the gambler godlike status, universal titles of glory. Like the drunkard in the public house, the gambler performs his drama before an audience, narrating his feats and successes, the victorious hero until disaster strikes. Behind the gaming table and at the bar gambler and drinker find friendships and complicities: they are no longer alone.

But this is only temporary. Alone again, even after a big win or a successful novel, the gambler and alcoholic feel powerless, permanently defeated in the face of addiction. Although they may maintain a façade or happiness, lying to everyone, they cannot ignore the sad truth of the situation. Sometimes, aware of their senseless slavery, they promise themselves that today they will drink or gamble for the last time. They are obsessed by the fear of relapsing, and when they do they are consumed by guilt.

Both alcoholism and addiction to gambling may be caused by depression or anxiety, and both may induce such states. Dostoyevsky describes this toxicosis very well. He was not himself an alcoholic but he knew many alcoholics, probably including his father, and there is at least one alcoholic character in each of his novels (for example the father Karamazov is a heavy drinker and he raves at the intemperance of his son Mitia). Dostoyevsky was, however, a gambler; he spent money he did not have in the casinos of Wiesbaden and Baden-Baden, squandering advance payments from his publishers for pages he had not written and which his compulsive gambling prevented him from writing.

Alcoholics and gambling addicts may also experience similar withdrawal symptoms, including insomnia, gastro-intestinal disorders, headaches, violent mood swings and changes in temperament.

3. *Addiction and Creation*

Every act of creation involves a risk to ordinary, everyday life, because each new painting, novel or throw of the dice cancels out or supersedes the previous ones, and aims to alter, to affect in some way the social situation and even the personality of the creator. Creation involves a constant fear of failure; at the end of his life Cézanne, who had persisted in his paintings of the Montagne Sainte Victoire, trying to capture it in all the different lights of the different times of day, regretted that he could never succeed in his task. Addiction raises to an extreme and even a tragic level the common elements of creativity, effort (towards the desired goal) and the enjoyment of risks.

We may all have felt at some time the desire to alter our personalities in some way, and there is no society in the world in which certain activities and substances are not used for these ends. We may engage in particular activities or take particular drugs even though we know that there is a risk of addiction, perhaps leading to ruin and even death. However, not every person who tries gambling, alcohol or other drugs will become an addict. The processes by which addiction develops are not fully understood; sometimes the enjoyment of risks and dangers which is developed to an abnormal degree in some people indicates an underlying inclination towards self-destruction, a 'death-wish'.

The widespread human fascination with risk renders any act of creation a challenge against the forces of chance, against fate. Fortunately creation is possible without the extreme expression of this behaviour: addiction.

ADDICTION IN ACTION:
DRUGS, ADDICTION, LIBERALISM AND LAW

Michael Ford

One view of our political institutions sees them as largely drawing their justification, their legitimacy, from liberalism.[1] On this account, ours is a society which purports officially to respect the equal personal autonomy of each rational agent and, correspondingly, to treat individuals as responsible for their freely chosen actions. In this paper I want to discuss in greater detail the kind of liberal human subject and the model of action that these institutions can be seen to appeal to, and specifically to draw out the problems that drugs and addiction pose for this subject and the institutions premised on it. Naturally, I am fully aware that any attempt to establish the broad, often unarticulated, principles underpinning a wide variety of institutions that in some cases have a lengthy history is bound to be contentious; the difficulties of finding any consistency in a single text, by now well known, are multiplied many times over. For instance, one obvious empirical objection is that there is no one set of principles to which our diverse institutions appeal because we live in a social world without any consensus, even among official institutions.[2] Another, more theoretical, objection is to show the deep tensions between competing sets of principles to which *individual* institutions implicitly or explicitly appeal, and the impossibility of resolving by any neutral method which one provides the 'best' account of institutional practices.[3] For, it seems, no such neutral metatheory transcending the competing accounts is available, since any such theory will already prejudge the issue in virtue of its own conceptual presuppositions—the current suspicion of foundationalist arguments is here once more to the fore.

Although I appreciate the force of these arguments, I continue to think that there can be better or worse principled explanations of the model of subjectivity presupposed by our social practices without the necessity of appealing to standards of transcendental rationality, in just the manner that Habermas grounds his theorizing in the (contingent) consensus underlying communication;[4] whether these practices as a matter of fact exhibit a generally shared model of subjectivity is, of course, a separate empirical question. But in any case we can put the wider philosophical issue to one side while continuing to see some sense in examining what a particular justificatory model, here taken to be liberalism, might look like. For, first, there plainly are those, as I have mentioned, who do claim that liberalism and its accompanying conception of the human subject do supply the deep-level foundations of our social practices. If we accept the theoretical possibility of such a principled account, we can see whether these arguments work on their own terms in respect of particular institutions. Secondly, it is clear that some of the institutions themselves at times more or less explicitly appeal to liberal arguments for their legitimacy: I am thinking here especially of our legal institutions. By analysing how the institutions do actually justify their treatment of what they categorize as drug users, I then hope both to show that essentially liberal standards are those to which they do in fact appeal and to bring to light the internal tensions in the legitimating arguments which they put forward, and the tensions between the arguments and institutional practice—tensions which are to some extent present in liberalism itself. Hence even without addressing the more difficult problem of whether liberalism can be seen as supplying the most coherent set of legitimating principles for our institutions in general, principles which often may not be articulated at all within the institutions themselves, there remain significant issues to confront.

First, however, what in broadest terms is liberalism? Put most simply, liberalism is a political doctrine that claims to adopt a stance of a certain neutrality towards different conceptions of the good. Whilst I want to leave the exact nature of this neutrality vague for the moment, it is clear that it does not mean neutral in the sense that any good is permissible, for that would hardly give it the character of a *political* theory—that is, a theory governing social relations—at all. But it is neutral in the sense that each person is left free to decide for herself what the good life is to be for her, subject only to the condition that those goods will be disallowed which undercut the ability of others freely to pursue their own conception of the good life. The idea at root is that the Right is logically prior to the Good; it is why Rawls characterizes liberalism as a deontological, and not a teleological, theory.[5] Such a theory is egalitarian, in that each rational agent is deemed to be equally well-placed to decide what her good life is to be, and is therefore accorded a private sphere within which she can pursue it. No other agent, or institution, may interfere with this exercise of choice, other than by means such as discussion and persuasion which respect the autonomy of the agent concerned. The point is most famously expressed in John Stuart Mill's harm principle, by which only acts that harm others can be prohibited: 'His own good either physical or moral is not a sufficient warrant'[6] (I ignore here the inherent uncertainty as to what is to count as 'harm').

What concrete political arrangements such a theory requires is, of course, not self-evident. It is significant, for instance, that Rawls admits that his theory could in practice be consistent with either capitalist or socialist institutions. More specifically, there is always room for argument as to how far the redistribution of economic resources from one group of agents to others (to enable the others genuinely to pursue their goods) amounts to an illegitimate interference in the private autonomy of the first group.[7] But it is clear that on any version of liberalism certain important rights are to be accorded equally to all agents; Rawls characterizes these as the rights an agent must have if she is meaningfully to pursue *any* good, which would include rights to freedom of conscience, freedom of association, freedom from arbitrary arrest and freedom of speech.[8] The emphasis upon citizens freely choosing their own good life—because it seems there are no rational criteria for judging one good as superior to another, except for rational prohibition of goods that infringe rights—is matched by a stress on responsibility. If an agent breaches the liberal principles of justice (which are assumed to be publicly known) then she will be punished—and not just in order to deter others, but because she freely decided, *qua* rational agent, with knowledge of the consequences, to do so. Choice thus cuts both ways: the enhanced status given to my capacity for choice as the necessary condition of neutrality among goods, and which leads to the protection of my private sphere of autonomy, also means that a liberal cannot consistently claim that I did not choose in the majority of instances when a rational agent would have realized that the consequence of her action would be to infringe the principles of justice. To assert otherwise would be either to undercut the fundamental value given to choice or radically to question the extent to which empirical agents do resemble the subjects of liberal theory.

There are other unifying strands that can be picked out in liberalism. For instance, it tends to be anti-conservative, in that the fact that institutions of a particular sort have been respected in the past is not seen as a reason to respect them now. It is irrelevant that the members of a society have hitherto shared a form of the good life—perhaps they have clustered around a religious world-view—because the impossibility of rationally demonstrating the superiority of one such form above other kinds of goods would disallow politically entrenching that way of life. Instead, the important issue is whether societal arrangements that allow differing individual goods are capable of rational justification in the public sphere: the search is one for the concrete articulated principles of liberal justice. It follows, too, that liberalism is also anti-utopian, in that there seems little hope of a future society where there is common agreement as to the good life; a certain amount of conflict is endemic—by contrast, for example, to

Marxist accounts of communism in which individuals all act together in pursuit of their shared good of self-realization through creative and social labour. At best, it seems, there can only be agreement that the (liberal) principles of justice are the fairest ones that we can arrive at, and to which it is hoped rational citizens will therefore give their assent; they are the principles which 'can require and secure allegiance in and to a form of social order in which individuals who are pursuing diverse and often incompatible ways of life can live together without the disruption of rebellion and internal war'.[9] Society would then still be conflictual but in a weak sense; as Gutmann and Thompson argue,[10] it would amount to a dialogue about the good life, to continue indefinitely, in a context of an underlying consensus.

Before concluding this crude summary of liberalism, I want to say a little about the concept of human action which underlies it. Once each agent accepts that her choice of goods should be constrained by the right— and there is no inconsistency in liberal institutions forcing her so to do— then she acts rationally to the extent that she pursues rational means to attain her personal conception of the good. Rational action is thus largely reduced to purposive-rational action: rationality enables him or her to determine whether certain factual circumstances do, or probably will, obtain and to select the most efficient means to his or her good. This is broadly in line with Hume's account of reason, by which reason cannot motivate us to act in the first place but can only supply us with the means of best achieving whatever our contingent goals happen to be.[11] In practice, of course, it is very difficult to claim in any actual circumstances that another subject is using irrational means to pursue her ends, given the often interwoven nature of ends and means and the likelihood that her ends are not explicitly stated but rather reveal themselves in action. Hence the danger of a slip into a tautological theory of human action, perhaps illustrated by much economic writing, in which agents are simply assumed rationally to maximize their welfare or whatever. For my purposes, however, the significant point is that it will be rare on this conception of liberalism that a person can be said to be acting irrationally. If she interferes with others' pursuits of their goods then she may be punished for this, but it is not clear (yet) whether a liberal is entitled to assert that she is being irrational. That she chooses the means to reach her ends, something which to a degree is almost presumed of adult human agents, is in general a sufficient condition for deeming her action rational.

It is possible to view a variety of our official institutions as being normatively grounded upon just such a conception of the subject, that is, one who is ostensibly left free to choose her own good without outside interference and whose choosing of itself confers value upon those goods without the need for further justification. Consider, for example, the

doctrine of freedom of contract and the accompanying arguments legitimating the market which flows from it. Each rational, autonomous agent
decides which goods she wishes to exchange for which other goods;
because there is no objectively ascertainable hierarchy of needs, the value
of a particular commodity is simply what an individual is willing to
exchange for it; since the agent is rational, she would not have made the
exchange at all unless it benefitted her; therefore, the exchange should be
upheld, since the state is then doing no more than protecting the
autonomous, private choices of its subjects. By contrast, any distribution by
a centralized authority of specific goods—say food—would infringe the
principle that it is for each agent to decide what are her true wants and
needs. It is for this reason, incidentally, that classical economics can with
difficulty accommodate the notion of a subject whose wants are distorted
by the operation of power, and for whom the market can be seen to
exercise an ideological function.

It does not follow, however, that liberals must accept that all contracts are
morally justifiable. They can point to features of a market which lead to
some exchanges diverging more or less from the ideal of free exchange.
Certain categories of persons, especially the young, may be treated as not
yet having attained a sufficient level of rationality to know what their
wants really are; alternatively, the presence of monopolistic power may
mean that some exchanges are forced upon the economically weaker
party, who does not then genuinely choose the relevant exchange. In this
way, some paternalistic intervention and some market regulation may be
justifiable. But essentially these are only devices to ensure that the ideal
market continues on the whole to be present, and they leave in place the
fundamental assumption that the state should not prevent adult agents
with a choice of suppliers from making whatever bargains they wish. It is
interesting to note that *laissez-faire* arguments of just this kind were put
forward by the British in the nineteenth century when the Chinese
sought to prohibit the sale of opium in their territories;[12] and, of course,
'freedom of choice' continues to figure as one of the reasons put forward
for ending the illegality of drugs in modern political rhetoric.[13] To what
extent the illegality of drugs can be reconciled with a liberal justification
of the market is something considered implicitly later in this essay. If
they cannot, it may lead us to conclude that our existing 'market' is not as
neutral to human wants and needs as its supporters claim or, indeed, that
no empirical market can ever by neutral in this manner.[14]

A second area in which legal institutions have been brought into
contact with drugs is the criminal law. Here the courts have been forced
most clearly to face the reasons why someone may take drugs and what
effects her doing so may have on the ascription of responsibility to her.
And it is perhaps also here that the courts appeal most explicitly to a liberal
model of the subject: legal subjects are taken to be free and rational,

knowing both what the law is and the consequences of their actions. Now while it is true that some crimes require the prosecution to establish a subjective intent on the part of the defendant—that she intended to cause the harm that followed from her action—it seems plausible to assume that in most cases the fact that another (reasonable?) person would have foreseen that a particular consequence would ensue from a given act is enough, in practice, to lead to a presumption that the defendant too knew this would be so; the legal wording of the burden of proof can easily be misleading, because the need to understand the action usually entails mapping onto the agent internal reasons which would be acceptable to other agents if they were to perform the relevant act. Moreover, many crimes—those which can be committed negligently or recklessly—judge an individual by objective standards of intention, so that if an abstract 'reasonable person' would have foreseen the consequences of a particular act, the defendant is deemed to have done so too. In addition, the lack of defences involving recognition of a constrained voluntariness of action similarly emphasizes the treatment of the accused person as a fully free subject: it is no defence to theft, for example, to argue it was brought about by acute economic need.

Drugs present a particular problem here. First, consider the case of the person, otherwise taken to be fully rational, who commits a crime while intoxicated. Temporarily she has left the realm of the autonomous and rational subject; she may not even know in any real sense what she is doing. Should she be held responsible as if she were fully aware? The law is in something of a mess here. For some crimes, those involving 'specific intent', intoxication is a defence if it prevents the actor having the required state of mind; for other offences, comprising the majority of crimes, the jury is supposed to ignore the effects of the drugs which led to the altered mental state. For instance, in *R. v. Newell*[15] the defendant, an alcoholic whose girlfriend had just left him, was drunk on whisky (having earlier consumed a bottle of surgical spirits, three bottles of shaving lotion and half a bottle of vodka). When his friend insulted the departed lover and invited the defendant to sleep with him instead, Newell battered him to death with an ashtray. On the question of provocation, a defence to murder, the trial judge directed the jury that they should consider whether a reasonable man, sober, because a reasonable man is assumed to be sober, who had this observation made about his girlfriend, would have behaved as the accused did?[16] A clearer statement of the contrast between the hypothetical reasonable subject and the actual empirical subject would be hard to find.

The general attitude of the law, then, is that occasional lapses from the realm of rational autonomy are ignored. This could be seen as either a straightforward refusal to admit that individuals do not meet the necessary standards of voluntariness and rationality—after all, it is plain that elsewhere in the law the distance between the located subject and her reasonable counterpart is overlooked, albeit perhaps less blatantly—or as being grounded in the notion that because individuals are rational, knowledge that intoxication will not avail them as a defence will deter them from becoming drugged in the first place (why they should want to become intoxicated is not very relevant on this version of liberalism: intoxication can be a good if a person chooses it, like any other). It is only the first approach which seems to undermine liberal ideas of subjectivity: the less liberalism can claim to articulate what we are as subjects, the greater difficulty it has in claiming legitimacy. But it is unclear that such an approach presents any fundamental challenge, since to admit that on occasions an agent may not be fully responsible, whether through drugs or other causes, hardly attacks the assumption that she acts voluntarily and rationally in the normal course of affairs. The portrayal of intoxication as a sporadic, intermittent intervention in an individual's life can thus serve paradoxically to reinforce the notion that otherwise she is rational and free. The more significant question of whether she would have acted rationally were she not intoxicated, which would begin fundamentally to undermine liberal theories of responsibility, is not addressed at all.

But whilst the temporarily intoxicated subject can be retained without too much difficulty in the community of rational subjects in her 'normal' condition, like the permitted lapses of all (autonomous) subjects into frequent periods of sleep, a different set of issues concerns those subjects who did not choose to become intoxicated. First, there are those rare cases where someone is tricked into intoxication—her drinks are spiked or whatever—and this will afford a defence. Such an attitude is consistent with liberal views: if a person did not choose to enter into a state where she briefly lost her rational autonomy, then she should not be held accountable for what she did during that period. Addicts, however, are in a separate category. They, it seems, cannot choose whether or not to take drugs and therefore should not be held responsible for the consequences which afterwards ensue. There remains the possibility that an addict might be held blameworthy on a long-term notion of responsibility, in that she 'chose' to become an addict in the first place. An examination of this sort would involve complex questions of what aspects of an agent's character she can be held responsible for, and would doubtless begin to collapse together current legal concepts of responsibility; for this reason, perhaps, it is not a matter to which the courts have accorded much attention, and so I shall ignore it for the moment.

How then do the courts deal with defendants who are addicts? The usual stance is for them to ignore addiction. It would be no defence to theft, for example, for an addict to claim that she stole in order to service her habit and had no choice whether or not so to do. She is just treated in accordance with standards appropriate to the abstract liberal subject; the tension between her presumed voluntariness and her actual compulsion is simply ignored. But in some areas of law the courts have been forced to address more directly the nature of addiction. If a defendant claims that she was provoked into murder, her addiction may be a relevant consideration. In *Newell*, the court made it clear that the jury could take into account characteristics of the accused which affect the gravity of the provocative statement made to him, and that being a chronic alcoholic *might* be a matter of sufficient permanence and significance to amount to a 'characteristic' for these purposes (unlike being drunk, which would be too transitory). Thus, if Newell's friend had called him 'a drunken bastard' instead of insulting his girlfriend, the jury would here consider whether such a remark would prompt the reasonable and sober alcoholic to attempt murder. In this manner, personal characteristics are referred to in determining the strength of the provocation, since it is unclear how an abstract subject could ever be provoked, lacking any personal attributes save rationality. (The only plausible insult would appear to be that she was 'irrational'.) But the reaction to that provocation continues to be judged by the standards of the fully rational person, now without those very personal features which caused her to be initially provoked. A more bizarre oscillation between empirical and abstract subject, and a more tortuous thought-experiment for the jury to carry out, is difficult to imagine.

Another area of the law in which the courts have expressly considered addiction relates to the doctrine of diminished responsibility. If a person accused of murder can establish this 'defence', she will be convicted of the lesser crime of manslaughter. The defendant must show 'such abnormality of mind (whether arising from ... any inherent causes or induced by disease) as substantially impaired [the defendant's] mental responsibility for his act'.[17] Because it has been held that a depressive illness can amount to an inherent cause, the way seems open for addiction to be similarly treated, an issue which arose in *R. v. Tandy*.[18] In this case, Tandy, an alcoholic accustomed to drinking Cinzano (I assume these two facts are not mutually exclusive), drank a bottle of vodka and then strangled her eleven-year-old daughter; she had no recollection of the act of killing. Although two out of three medical experts called at the trial felt that alcoholism was a disease, the judge decided that this was not the crucial consideration. Instead, he directed the jury that the question was whether the defendant had no immediate control over her behaviour. She would not have this control if either her alcoholism meant that her judgment was grossly impaired *in the absence of any drink*—once more, it is her 'normal', sober state that matters and the fact that she was drunk at the time of committing the crime is irrelevant—or if it meant that she had no control over her decision to drink, and hence the consequences that flowed from that drinking. In both cases a permanent loss of rational judgment is therefore required. As regards the second issue, the judge directed that if the defendant had any choice at all whether to drink or not, her drinking was not involuntary: 'The choice [of the appellant whether to drink or not] may not have been easy but...if it was there at all it is fatal to this defence, because the law simply will not allow a drug user...to shelter behind the toxic effects of a drug which he or she need not have used'.[19] The jury convicted her.

On appeal, the direction was upheld. Only if the appellant's drinking was involuntary—'that is to say she was no longer able to resist the impulse to drink'[20]—would the defence apply. Because here she had decided to drink vodka instead of her usual Cinzano, and because there was evidence that she did not drink every single night, the Court of Appeal concluded that she had chosen to drink on the night of the killing; and 'if the taking of the first drink was not involuntary, then the whole of the drinking on [that occasion] was not involuntary'.[21] In the court's view, this conclusion was reinforced by evidence that she did not finish the entire bottle of vodka that night: she could even choose to stop drinking once she had begun (perhaps, therefore, someone who tries to commit suicide by drinking her way through a wine cellar chooses to stop if any bottles are left when she becomes unconscious...). Alcoholism is thus treated by the court in a clearly divided fashion. Either the addict's drug-taking is entirely involuntary, the product of a diseased state, which following *Tandy* is clearly going to be almost impossible to establish, or it is the result of an autonomous choice for which the defendant is fully responsible, like any other rational subject. There is, it seems, no intermediate position, no recognition of differing degrees of autonomy.[22]

I want to concentrate upon two features that emerge from these judgments. One is a reluctance of the court to allow that an act, here to take a particular drug, can be involuntary or at least not entirely voluntary. Caught in a framework which sees individual choice as alone determinative of whether someone is to be held responsible, the court views any voluntariness of action at all as a sufficient condition of rationality. Like the liberalism I characterized earlier, the courts hold what Richardson has termed a 'present aim' theory of the good, by which 'something is good just in case it satisfies a current desire'.[23] Because the ends of action cannot be critically addressed within this liberal framework, the addict in choosing to pursue her current desire for a drug is acting in a purposive-rational manner like any other rational agent. True, the court in *Newell* did grudgingly admit that chronic alcoholism might (it expressly declined to go further than that) amount to a 'characteristic', hence pointing to a model of personality in which different goods are evaluated differently by the agent, which would explain more complex motivational patterns since some goods may be constitutive of what she is, and so less obviously chosen in any straightforward sense. But while the judgment admits of this interpretation, it is hardly one that the court makes explicit, and still does not indicate how an agent acquires the constitutive goods she does nor provide any substantive grounds for judging between the goods, whether constitutive of identity or not, that *different* agents pursue. It seems, then, that the court lacks the legal resources to criticize the ends of the addict's action.

On the other hand, the court in *Tandy* did at least recognize the theoretical possibility that in some, exceptional, circumstances an addict will not have any choice over her habit. In that case, she is no longer acting as a rational subject and hence can be afforded a defence. What is perhaps curious, however, is the apparent lack of any middle ground here: either the agent is acting freely in choosing whether or not to have the first drink of the day, or she is in the grip of a disease over which she has no control whatsoever. Either, that is, the defendant is placed squarely in the realm of the free reflective mind or she is dumped in the world of the body and its imperatives that are beyond the reach of conscious control. The straightforward dichotomy seems to indicate a weakness in the descriptive power of liberalism: the drawing of clear boundaries where there are surely only gradual shifts appears empirically untenable. But how forceful a challenge is this? The use of a plain division between voluntary and involuntary action does at least make the law certain—after all, a person is either to be convicted or not—and so may be a fiction that is morally necessary; and, it might be contended, the courts are open to change their conceptualizations of action in the light of improved scientific understanding, an attitude demonstrated by the court consulting doctors in *Tandy* as to whether alcoholism should be viewed as a disease.

What is possibly more disconcerting for liberals is that in fact the line is not as clearly drawn as concentrating on the judgment alone might imply; the same individual tends to oscillate uncomfortably between the two categories of voluntariness and involuntariness within institutions which form part of the same official power complex, and without any of the open disagreement that typifies the decision of the court whether to convict or not. Indeed, at times the courts display an ambivalence of this nature when, having decided a person is responsible for her actions, they then proceed to sentence her on the assumption that she was not. We may suppose, for example, that once convicted on the basis of her status of responsible agency, Tandy would be treated in prison for her addiction, now being conceived of as an actor lacking full autonomy; the woman convicted in Florida for 'voluntarily' administering cocaine to her foetus was dealt with in this way.[24] Foucault has shown how a dichotomy of this sort has historically pervaded official institutional attitudes towards criminals in general, and not only addicts, as part of his account of the aliberal foundations of liberal democracies.[25] Again, however, it is not clear how serious a challenge this divergence in institutional attitudes is to liberalism. It would be open to a liberal to argue that the present confusion serves to demonstrate that we do not live in a society whose official institutions are liberal: some are, but others are not, and the discordance exhibited would enable a powerful immanent critique of the institutions that fail to meet liberal standards of legitimacy. Thus a liberal could contend that many of our current prison practices, premised upon an individual's being determined to act as she did, are simply inconsistent with liberal assumptions, supported by empirical evidence, that agents on the whole choose what to do. What is needed is a more thoroughly liberal society which would punish criminals because they chose their criminal actions, and not for any other reason; someone like Tandy should therefore be punished as any other offender. To do otherwise would be to attempt to force an individual to reject her particular good, which liberals lack the normative resources to do.

But there remains, I think, a certain discomfort among liberals with this conclusion. One reason for this is that an addict may satisfy the requirements for voluntariness yet may herself wish she did not have the set of wants that she does actually have; in that sense she differs radically from the other kinds of criminal that Foucault alludes to, since few of them would wish for a restructuring of their goods—and this would explain in part the remarkable lack of success prisons have had in their efforts to persuade inmates to accept different sets of values. The idea of a subject who can desire on a higher level not to have the desires which she has on another level, but be unable to fulfil that desire, draws upon a more complex model of subjectivity than that advanced so far, one which presents difficulties to the version of liberalism outlined earlier: how, for instance, is a political authority to determine whether it should help or force a subject to alter her wants in accordance with the higher-level desires which she sometimes claims to have? More generally, liberals are unhappy with a subject who through her own choices comes progressively to lose her capacity genuinely to exercise choice and yet for whom the only point at which intervention seems permissible is precisely at the stage when that capacity has been lost, by which time it may be too late. There is no coherent account of how some people—and Tandy was not yet taken to be one of them—can slip from the realm of the free subject into that of the diseased body. The 'present-aim' structure of the court's analysis eliminates a historical explanation of how a desire can become a disease, of how (rationally) pursuing a good can remove the capacity for rational action altogether. Covertly, that is, liberals want to say that there is *more* to acting rationally than choosing the best means to achieve my current wants, but their ostensible neutrality towards different goods precludes them from expressly articulating what this additional requirement of rationality is, and of why they feel uncomfortable with drug-taking subjects who have failed to meet it.

This discomfort is exhibited, I feel, in a variety of rather unsatisfactory explanations given to account for drug-taking, which either treat the individual as never having been autonomous at all or as inexorably losing her autonomy almost immediately the first drop, grain or puff of the addictive substance is taken. For example, the subject who takes drugs can be portrayed as pathological, as genetically determined to resort to them, and thus already in the grip of the body—although liberalism cannot admit that too many individuals are so afflicted or it would cease to be grounded in a conception of what we (mostly) are like. Along the same lines, the subject can be viewed as immature and hence not yet fully autonomous, as not representative of our adult condition; a strategy that may then be adopted is to aim at an early development of rational autonomy, as in Nancy Reagan's 'just say no' campaign. The other set of arguments, stressing the power of the substance, can invoke the notion of evil 'pushers' who force drugs on innocent victims, who through deceit may not even know that they are being given a drug and who then find themselves dominated by the power it wields over their bodies.[26] Now all these explanations are no doubt inadequate as explanations of why people come to take drugs in the first place or come to be addicted to them; they also conflict markedly with the type of individual choice portrayed in *Tandy*. That they are resorted to, however, is hardly surprising, for the drug addict threatens liberals' idea of a society that is strongly neutral among goods in a manner which points to flaws at the heart of such a version of liberalism.

First, there is the nightmare of a drug-taker who is so bent on pursuing her own private ends that she is not susceptible to arguments of liberal justice at all. While the law may punish her for her acts if she is caught, there is no prospect of her internally accepting the principles of liberal justice. Only on condition that the risk of detection and punishment outweighs, in purely self-interested terms, the utility she derives from the drugs will she cease to use a given means of servicing her habit; and the enormous pleasure that her drugs are assumed to give her makes this an unrealistic possibility (to what extent this truly represents the state of the addict is not a matter I want to consider; clearly much media rhetoric does present them in this way, for instance linking rising crime to addicts desperate to finance their habits). Liberals are presented with an egoistical subject, acting rationally to further her own ends like any other human subject, but whose absorption by those ends threatens the maintenance of the order that protects others' private spheres. The difficulty is similar to that faced by utilitarians when they are unable to explain why, if we are essentially self-interested as their theory claims, we should accept utilitarian principles at all; deprived of explaining *that*, the ideal of individual pursuit of self-interest of itself producing the best collective outcome depends upon the assumption that no one has ends that radically attack others' interests, only resolvable by describing our wants as harmonious or as placing a priority on the happiness of others, both of which are surely untenable. The greater the number of persons who do behave in this damaging egoistical manner, the less the prospect of any cooperation, and the greater the need for rigorous centralized control, with its accompanying dangers, as the only means to preserve the private spheres of each agent.

This in turn leads to another central problem, ignored by liberal arguments that concentrate on fairness among agents, relating to motivating agents to abide by liberal principles of justice. The drug addict, because of the massive utility she is presumed to derive from her habit, forces liberals to confront more squarely a fundamental tension that underlies much of their theorizing, and specifically their claim to neutrality among goods: how are liberal principles to appeal to a subject with a strong sense of the good which opposes those principles? Drugs are not, of course, the sole threat here—it is evident, for example, that religion could similarly undermine the acceptability of liberalism to a group of agents—but they present special difficulties in that they remain more readily compatible with advances in the sphere of technological knowledge. To attempt to answer this question is implicitly to address another, more fundamental, question of what is supposed to motivate rational agents in general to abide by the just liberal principles on those occasions, which may be numerous, when they oppose their self-interest; drugs only present the dilemma in a concrete, visible form. How long can liberal institutions survive if more and more members of society do not internalize the liberal principles but simply happen to be in a society which still has, as a historical accident, some such institutions?

To see these difficulties is not, however, necessarily to reject liberalism, although they do cast some doubt upon the acceptability of the crude version of good-neutral, utilitarian liberalism I have characterized up to now. Instead, in considering why it is that individual subjects should be motivated to accept liberal principles, the debate switches to issues of citizenship, of what conditions are needed in order that persons do in fact abide by liberal principles, of how liberal institutions can survive in a feasible social world, rather than questions of what is fair between different abstract subjects whose motivations are ignored. Such an explanation demands a somewhat different conception of the human subject than that of the means-rational pursuer of private, given ends. On the one hand, as regards her attitude towards herself, she is a subject whose rationality is not confined to the purposive-rational pursuit of her desires but is elevated to the status of constraining those desires themselves. Her rationality tells her that goods vary both across subjects and within the narrative history of individual subjects—individuals may learn that what once appeared a good no longer is one for them—and hence any commitment to a single good, and in particular a good that may lead to her losing her capacity rationally to reject it in the future, may turn out to be an error. She thus stands at a certain rational distance from her goods, whatever they may contingently happen to be.[27] Hence her actions are not merely forced on her by her desires but instead are the result of a process of reasoning in which she considers her own goals from a radically impersonal perspective; all her wants can then ideally be viewed as dispensable features of her personality, to be rejected if rationality so dictates.[28] The subject now proposed, then, is autonomous in a stronger sense than the agent who merely opts for the means to meet her chosen ends. Her stance to some extent is exemplified by the attitude of the ancient Greeks to their bodily wants that Foucault has described;[29] on this model, obsessive goods of all kinds, and not just drugs, stand condemned.

On the other hand, there is also supposed to be involved here a transformation of this subject's relationships with other subjects. The level of strong autonomy that she should reach—for it would be mistaken to argue that there is not a model of the good life put forward here—is not something that is achieved alone: others, and outside institutions, are crucial in fostering this stance. Others are then much more than means or obstacles to the satisfaction of her private ends. Rather, her identity is itself constituted and her impersonal attitude to her goods, itself her central good, arrived at through dialogue and interaction with others; she is thus closer to Charles Taylor's portrayal of the located subject and Michael Sandel's depiction of communitarian conceptions of the good[30] than our earlier version of the abstract liberal subject would allow, although the end-state of strong autonomy is more fixed than some communitarian arguments appear to permit. There is a further similarity to models of located subjectivity, too, in that an agent's goals can be seen as formed in dialogue with others (whether that debate is subject to standards of immanent rationality is not something I want to discuss here). To some extent, the good life is just a free, public debate among agents open to argument as to what their ends are. This enhanced degree of reciprocity among agents, the sense that they are engaged in a common venture, means that the motivations to accept liberal principles of justice are to the same degree rendered more understandable.

But this different account of a liberal subject is less clearly grounded in straightforward appeals to fairness, and hence it meets fresh problems of justification. There is, first, the problem that a liberalism resting upon strongly autonomous subjects implicitly claims that some forms of existence are better, because nearer the truth, than others, in that this kind of subject is viewed as in some sense more rational than other kinds; the subject who cannot stand at a reflective distance from her current desires has failed in some important sense to grasp the truth of her condition, to see that her possibilities are more open and her ends less sure than she currently considers them. Connected to this, it follows that an evaluation of this sort is not securely grounded in a theory of what we (ahistorically) are. The liberalism that draws its support from a depiction of human agents as rationally pursuing their goods does at least offer an account of action that purports to be universal—that is, to explain the action of all human agents at all times, including Tandy and her drinking—however misplaced and tautological it turns out to be. But the strongly autonomous rational subject invoked in the second version of liberalism is more obviously not an account of universal features of human action; rather, it is an aspiration of a stage to be reached, and a stage that individuals, and societies as a whole, can fail to attain.

On the one hand, such a theory demands a more complex theory of human action, involving different degrees of voluntariness. For instance, Tandy would plainly not be seen as acting autonomously in the strong sense, despite her retaining the capacity for choice at another level. This differing extent of voluntariness and responsibility is matched by greater uncertainty as to what form of punishment, or treatment, could justifiably be imposed on her: for even if we accept that strong autonomy is a better condition for an agent to be in, it does not follow that any other agency is entitled to force her to attain that state.[31] Moreover, a recognition that individuals in differing societies differ in the extent to which they stand at a rational distance from their goods entails acknowledging the importance of institutions which support the emergence of, and sustain, such subjective attitudes. Not only do liberal democracies then appear rather fragile, dependent upon all forms of institutions for fostering citizenship which do not seem necessary to the election process itself, but also notions of blame and responsibility are less clearly individualized: communities can thus be responsible for the subjects within them. Tandy's drinking was, at the risk of sounding trite, not entirely her fault. This does not mean, of course, that the response is to prohibit drugs of any form, since the important issue is rather what institutional responses will engender the type of citizens who are sufficiently autonomous not to become captured by any of their desires, not only drugs, and for whom straightforward prohibitions are generally unnecessary? Prohibition may be a particularly inefficacious means of achieving this end.

On the other hand, there are further difficulties in explaining at a deeper level what justifies a liberalism that draws upon a model of human subjectivity as something to be achieved. There is the possibility of appealing to metaphysical notions of what our true nature is, in an Aristotelian fashion or in the way that Kant argued that his rationalist morality bound the transcendental subject; the problems with arguments of this nature are well known.[32] In particular, they seem irreconcilable with scientific world-views which deny any underlying goal of life forms, with our knowledge of the vast differences between societies, and with the understanding that any language in which such goals are articulated will already have built into it, as it were, socially relative assumptions as to the ends of action. Alternatively, then, an attempt can be made to ground liberal politics in what our current self-understandings are. This approach avoids the appeal to a transcendental subject and a universal teleology of human existence. Instead, it is grounded within the social life in which we find ourselves, and the dialogue about our self-understandings which is partially constitutive of that life; hence it does not claim universal, ahistorical application. If made out, it would show that we see ourselves as changing in our commitment to the goods and hence should realize that it is irrational ever to make a binding commitment to any one good—or if we do not, we can be persuaded in uncoercive conditions to accept the superiority of this position; unlike a transcendental argument, a general requirement here would be that agents who do not share this point of view do in fact come to do so, in just the way that psychoanalysis if it is to effect a successful emancipation demands that the patient agrees with the explanation of her action that is presented to her. In the end, our rationality will be triumphant.

There are, of course, many objections that can be levelled at such an argument; one is simply to deny that there are any shared self-understandings within our societies. Attempts to explain what are the shared features of modern, Western subjectivity generally draw upon a very narrow range of sources, it seems to me, usually close to the author's own social position.[33] The issue, however, is too large to address here; instead, I want to offer some tentative concluding remarks on the relevance of drugs to our modern self-understandings, specifically relating to their cognitive functions. For parallel to the history of drugs as an escape from reality and a denial of true autonomy is another of drugs as a means of access to the truth, to ways of seeing the world as it really is—even if this involves the existence of different worlds or the drift into a subjectivist notion of reality. On this account, they may show us that our world-view is only one among many and that our view of ourselves as separate, reflective, self-controlling subjects is merely one possible, perhaps mistaken, self-understanding. I think that there is a similarity here with Nietzsche's treatment of art in *The Birth of Tragedy*,[34] that is as either an escape from reality (the Apollonian) or as a surrender to the privileged unity beyond all phenomena (the Dionysian). The latter is an experience, through intoxication, of a reality beyond the individual and beyond all conscious articulation which throws doubt upon our articulated, conscious world-views.

To some extent the truth-revealing function of drugs has even received official recognition: in the treatment of madness, for instance, drugs have often been used both as a means of understanding the mad and as a means of enabling the mentally ill to see the reality which their madness hides from them, and so to reassert control over their condition.[35] But this use of drugs in the service of institutionalized medicine, and the knowledge claims associated with it retains at its heart the purposive-rational subject; through drug therapy, that rational subject, representing the truth or highest stage of human existence, comes to dominate the individual psyche and so to reunify it. But another understanding of drugs, closer to Nietzsche's Dionysian art, opposes the notion of a privileged rational world-view, including the idea that we are rational, unified subjects, or that we should seek to attain this state. The relevance for liberalism of drugs is then ambiguous. On the one hand, it may be supposed that the access to different experiences of consciousness to which drugs give rise serves to reinforce the liberal ideal of standing at a distance from one's current goods: how can I retain certainty about those goods when the truth of any single account of affairs, even relating to the existence of external objects, seems questionable? But, on the other hand, these experiences may be taken in some sense to be privileged, like Dionysian intoxication was for Nietzsche, and not merely another aspect of the same reality. In this case, they can reveal depths within us, or a lack of any real separation between ourselves and the rest of the world (something not to be equated with simply revealing an unconscious in a Freudian fashion, for here there is no prospect of emancipation, of any reunification of conscious and unconscious subject through under-standing subconscious motivations: this 'unconscious' is beyond all articulation). Instead of our highest state then being a controlled distance from commitment to goods, a permanent rational vigilance, it appears as a surrendering process in which we abandon control and let ourselves be carried by the (irrational) forces that underlie conscious reality; indeed, on this Nietzschean account, any attempt to acquire rational control over our lives can only, like Christian morality, suppress conflict, stifle the life forces within us and deprive us of a true celebration of all reality. The parallel with religious accounts of contact with transcendental reality, Nirvana and the like, is clear. Drugs may thus undermine the very motivation to achieve the rational distance liberalism appears to require.

One last point: I am not trying to say that our present institutions are in fact being undermined by the use of drugs. We are a long way from 'legalize marijuana or revolution'. On the contrary, drugs can serve the function of explaining inequalities, by individualizing what are more probably social deprivations—hence the sort of argument that if only individuals could refuse drugs, they would be able to do as well as anyone else in the mythical meritocracy. Nor should the hermeneutic doubt which drugs may throw upon the rational subject of liberalism be understood as fundamentally undermining liberal politics, for it is unclear that this entails anything concrete as a political system to replace it, other than as an unspecified Utopian dream in which everyone may express herself or himself through an individual aesthetics of consciousness. That we are not rational subjects tells us little as to how we should mediate real conflicts over resources or adjust our conflicting desires.

NOTES

1.   For example, Ronald Dworkin has tried to argue that liberalism provides the deep principles that best justify our existing legal practices in *Taking Rights Seriously* (London: Duckworth, 1978) and *Law's Empire* (London: Fontana, 1986); and John Rawls has recently claimed that the liberal politics of *A Theory of Justice* (Oxford: Oxford University Press, 1972) should be primarily understood as an articulation of the underlying consensus of Western democracies, and less as an attempt to ground liberalism in a metaphysical conception of the self (see his 'Justice as Fairness: Political not Metaphysical', *Philosophy and Public Affairs* 14 [1985], pp. 308-22, and 'The Idea of an Overlapping Consensus', *Oxford Journal of Legal Studies* 7 [1987], pp. 1-25).

2.   A view advanced by Alisdair Macintyre in *After Virtue* (London: Duckworth, 1985), ch. 17: 'Modern politics is civil war carried on by other means' (p. 253).

3.   Roberto Unger, for example, has devoted much attention to the lack of principled foundations in our legal system, which he argues is locked in an irresolvable conflict between principles and counter-principles, neither of which provides a better account of the courts' decisions; see his *The Critical Legal Studies Movement* (Cambridge, MA: Harvard University Press, 1983). His argument operates in the context of institutions, namely the courts, that are expressly aiming at consistency and so may apply with yet greater force to other institutions more plainly guided by policy than principle.

4.   See J. Habermas, *The Theory of Communicative Action*, I (London: Heinemann, 1984) and II (Cambridge: Polity Press, 1987).

5.   Rawls, *Theory of Justice*, ch. 1.

6.   J.S. Mill, *On Liberty* (London, 1859), ch. 1.

7.   For an argument opposing redistribution along these lines see R. Nozick, *Anarchy, State and Utopia* (Oxford: Basil Blackwell, 1980).

8.   See Rawls, *Theory of Justice*, pp. 60-65.

9.   A. Macintyre, *Whose Justice, Which Rationality* (London: Duckworth, 1988), p. 210.

10.   A. Gutmann and D. Thompson, 'Moral Conflict and Political Consensus', in R. Douglass, G. Mara and H. Richardson (eds.), *Liberalism and the Good* (London: Routledge, 1990).

11.   See D. Hume, *A Treatise of Human Nature*, II (Oxford: Oxford University Press, 1958). I say 'broadly' Humean because what Hume's concept of action amounted to is a matter of debate. Macintyre argues that for Hume the passions are pre-linguistic and do not figure as a premise in practical reasoning; rather, the action is internally related to the passion in the sense that it is expressive of it. He contrasts this with modern liberal accounts of action in which the 'I want X' does figure as an articulated premise, and hence appears as an impersonal reason for the agent concerned (see *Whose Justice, Which Rationality*). This distinction begins to reveal, I think, a tension in liberal accounts of action between its utilitarian and Kantian sides, rather than the contrast between two competing accounts of rational action which Macintyre describes, a tension which I deal with later in the essay. For a detailed exposition of Hume's theory of action see B. Stroud, *Hume* (London: Routledge & Kegan Paul, 1977), and for

a recent defence of a Humean explanation of action see B. Williams, 'Internal and External Reason', in P. Moser (ed.), *Rationality in Action* (Cambridge: Cambridge University Press, 1990).

12. See C. Bachmann and A. Coppel, *La drogue dans le monde* (Paris: Albin Michel, 1989), ch. 4.

13. It would be mistaken, however, to see all arguments advocating decriminalization of drugs as deriving their force from a morality of choice, for drugs might be viewed as an unqualified evil, which criminalization is an ineffective means of preventing; but clearly whether liberals can consistently claim that drug-taking should be illegal is a different matter.

14. For a discussion of this nature see R. Unger, *Social Theory: Its Situation and Task* (Cambridge: Cambridge University Press, 1987), pp. 120-29.

15. (1980) 71 Cr. App. Rep. 331.

16. Quoted in the judgment of Lord Lane at p. 335.

17. Homicide Act 1957, section 2.

18. (1989) 1 WLR 350.

19. At p. 354.

20. Lord Justice Watkins at p. 356.

21. Lord Justice Watkins at p. 357.

22. It is interesting to note that the courts in the US have adopted a similar approach. In a recent case an addict was convicted for delivering cocaine to her newborn baby through its umbilical cord; the judge said that 'she voluntarily took cocaine into her body, knowing it would pass to her foetus' (reported in the *New York Times*, 20 April 1991).

23. H. Richardson, 'The Problem of Liberalism and the Good', in Douglass, Mara and Richardson (eds.), *Liberalism and the Good*.

24. See the article in the *New York Times* (n. 22 above).

25. M. Foucault, *Discipline and Punish* (London: Peregrine Books, 1979), especially Part 4.

26. For an interesting account of how just such an explanation of drug-taking is to some extent self-reinforcing in the courts, see J. Young, 'The Role of the Police as Amplifiers of Deviance etc.', in S. Cohen (ed.), *Images of Deviance* (London: Penguin, 1971).

27. For a powerful critique of this model of the rational, liberal subject, see M. Sandel, *Liberalism and the Limits of Justice* (Cambridge: Cambridge University Press, 1982).

28. For a more detailed discussion of the liberal first-person perspective to action, see MacIntyre, *Whose Justice, Which Rationality*, pp. 338-43.

29. See M. Foucault, *Historie de la sexualite*. II. *L'usage des plaisirs* (Paris: Gallimard, 1984).

30. C. Taylor, *Sources of the Self* (Cambridge: Cambridge University Press, 1989), and M. Sandel, *Liberalism and the Limits of Justice* (Cambridge: Cambridge University Press, 1982). See too the article by W. Kymlicka, 'Liberalism and Communitarianism', defending liberalism against communitarian challenges, in *Canadian Journal of Philosophy* 18.2 (June 1988), pp. 181-204.

31. See B. Williams, *Ethics and the Limits of Philosophy* (London: Fontana, 1985), ch. 10.

32. For example, see Williams, *Ethics and the Limits of Philosophy*, chs. 3–4.

33. For example, Charles Taylor's lengthy description of modern self-understanding (in *Sources of the Self*) draws almost exclusively on traditional philosophical and literary texts, whose attitudes there is no reason to suppose are generally shared.

34. F. Nietzsche, *The Birth of Tragedy* (New York: Vintage, 1967).
35. See e.g. Bachmann and Coppel, *La drogue dans le monde*, ch. 6.

PART II

Romantic Beginnings

THE PROMISE OF MODERATION:
ADDICTION, CODEPENDENCE, DECEPTION AND DISGUISE IN GOLDSMITH'S SATIRES

Caryn Chaden

Oliver Goldsmith's problems with money are legendary. Commenting on a gift of fifty pounds he received from his parents as he headed off to London, Stephen Gwynn rues that, 'they might as well have put water in a sieve'.[1] Indeed, his friend and first biographer the Reverend Thomas Percy reports that from the time he went to study chemistry at Leyden at the age of 25 (in 1755) he was 'unhappily addicted' to gambling, and he remained addicted until his untimely death at the age of 44.[2]

Goldsmith also carried the notion of benevolence to what he himself describes as 'excess'.[3] If anyone asked him for money, or anything else for that matter, he felt compelled to satisfy them, even when, as was usually the case, he was in debt himself. Once, he was found asleep in the ticking of his bed; he had passed a beggar woman with children on the street, gone to his rooms and taken the blankets off his own bed to give her.[4] Some years later when he was seriously in debt and looking for a job, he borrowed a suit from his publisher to wear to an interview, only to pawn the suit and give the money to his neighbor who was also unemployed.[5] Episodes like these abound in his biographies.[6] While his actions might initially appear endearing, Goldsmith himself recognized his own pathology and its inevitable consequences. 'In proportion as he became contemptible to others', Goldsmith writes of the similarly afflicted Sir William Thornhill in *The Vicar of Wakefield*, 'he became despicable to himself'.[7]

In the works I will consider, Goldsmith does not discuss gambling—or 'gaming' as he refers to it in essays that offer predictably negative views of the activity.[8] However, as critics have long been aware, each of his major prose works includes a character—the man in black from the *Citizen of the World*, Sir William Thornhill in *The Vicar of Wakefield*, Mr Honeywood in *The Good Natur'd Man* and Charles Marlow in *She Stoops to Conquer*—who exhibits some kind of addictive or compulsive behavior; most often, but not exclusively, the kind of obsessive generosity Goldsmith saw in himself.[9] What has not been noticed, to my knowledge, is that he also often includes a character (sometimes the addict himself) who engages in what we would now call codependent behavior. Sir William Honeywood in *The Good Natur'd Man* and Kate Hardcastle in *She Stoops*, for example, each offer so-called assistance which, from the vantage point of recent research on compulsive behavior, has all the makings of codependence.

In every case, the method that some character introduces to resolve whatever specific dilemma Goldsmith has created involves deception, and that deception often involves disguise. In fact, deception is presented as a necessary component of moral instruction in a world Goldsmith sees as corrupt. In *An Enquiry into the Present State of Polite Learning in Europe*, Goldsmith writes that, 'Dry reasoning, and dull morality, have no force with the wild fantastic libertine. He must be met with smiles, and courted with the allurements of gaiety. He must be taught to believe, that he is in pursuit of pleasure, and be surprized into reformation.'[10] For Goldsmith, straightforward, rational discourse has lost its power to persuade; hence, to his mind, instructive deception is the order of the day.

Anne Wilson Schaef, author of the 1987 study *When Society Becomes an Addict*, might well agree with Goldsmith's view of society, but would likely find his response equally unhealthy. For the result of this approach is that basic questions Goldsmith continually raises about the relationship between social convention and moral behavior are never resolved; either the addict simply moves on to a new situation, as the man in black does in *Citizen of the World*, or else some codependent saves the day, and works like *The Vicar of Wakefield*, *The Good Natur'd Man*, and *She Stoops to Conquer* conclude before their duly repentant addictive characters are forced to confront a new situation. Several critics have found these happily-ever-after conclusions unsatisfying.[11] What makes them unsatisfying, I will argue, is that the characters remain locked into their addictive/codependent systems. The same affliction that limited Goldsmith's life—he apparently died a lonely, dissipated man—thus limits his art as well; both remain bound by his inability to step outside the addictive systems he portrays.

My definitions of terms like 'addict', 'codependent' and 'addictive behavior' come from recent literature on these subjects which suggest that the object of addiction need not be limited to drugs. In *The Addictive Organization* (1988), Schaef and Diane Fassel define addiction as 'any substance *or process* that has taken over our lives and over which we are powerless'.[12] Stanton Peele, in *Love and Addiction* (1975), helps us understand what 'powerless' means in this context:

> An addiction exists when a person's attachment to a sensation, an object, or another person is such as to lessen his appreciation of and ability to deal with other things in his environment, or in himself, so that he has

become increasingly dependent on that experience as his sole source of gratification.[13]

These two definitions go a long way to informing the behavior of Goldsmith's addicts. Goldsmith and the characters he portrays as 'good natur'd men' are all addicted to the sensation they feel when they relieve others in distress. While generosity is a virtue, it has been distorted here into what Peele describes as 'a malignant outgrowth, an extreme, unhealthy manifestation, of normal human inclinations'.[14] The man in black describes himself as a 'mere machine of pity...incapable of withstanding the slightest impulse made either by real or fictitious distress',[15] while Sir William Thornhill describes the condition in terms of disease:

> Physicians tell us of a disorder in which the whole body is so exquisitely sensible, that the slightest touch gives pain: what some have thus suffered in their persons, this gentleman felt in his mind. The slightest distress, whether real or fictitious, touched him to the quick, and his soul laboured under a sickly sensibility of the miseries of others.[16]

These passages reveal Goldsmith's acute understanding of the danger posed by such compulsive behavior. What is so insidious about this particular addiction, however, is that it is so close to the virtue of generosity, a trait Goldsmith sees all too lacking in mid-eighteenth-century England, where, in his opinion, a rapidly expanding economy has led people to become obsessed with greed and ambition.[17] Whether it be the prostitute who steals Altangi's money, the myriad nameless characters in *The Citizen of the World* who collect 'useless' imported goods only for display, fortune-hunting Mr Lofty, fashion-conscious Mrs Primrose, materialistic Mrs Hardcastle, or the ruthless Squire Thornhill, characters whose actions are controlled by greed dominate the world of Goldsmith's satires. Thus the man in black, Sir William Thornhill, and Mr Honeywood in *The Good Natur'd Man* are depicted to be among Goldsmith's most honorable, if also, to use Primrose's description of Sir William, most 'whimsical', characters. Indeed they bear out Peele's contention that 'addiction is a complex and wide-ranging reaction in society to the constriction and subjugation of the individual psyche'.[18] While Goldsmith depicts most of society as retreating into self-enclosed worlds of conspicuous consumption, he sees seeds of real virtue in these characters' 'natures', if not their actions. As Sir William Honeywood says of his nephew, 'There are some faults so nearly allied to excellence, that we can scarce weed out the vice without eradicating the virtue'.[19] The assumption here is that, if only these men would moderate their behavior, they would be happy and the world would be a better place. That promise, of course, leaves the addictive system intact, and it is no wonder that the complement to the addicts in these works is a whole troop of codependents ready to offer their assistance.

In *Codependent No More* (1987), Melody Beattie defines the co-dependent person as 'one who has let another person's behavior affect him or her, and who is obsessed with controlling that person's behavior'.[20] Goldsmith's works are dotted with characters who fit this description, and who, moreover, are lauded for their efforts. In the *Vicar of Wakefield*, Sir William Thornhill might be described as a recovering-addict-turned-codependent. Although he has stopped doling out money to anyone who asks, he has done so not by learning to resist their pleas, but by disguising himself as the hapless 'Burchell' so that no one will ask; hence he can enjoy 'respect uncontaminated by flattery'[21] from good people like the Primroses. While wearing that disguise, however, he busily goes about taking care of that family, not only rescuing Sophia after she falls from her horse, but later writing a letter to his own nephew to caution him against 'ruining' the Primrose daughters, and then pursuing Sophia's kidnappers to save her from the kind of ruin her sister endured. At the end of the novel Sir William, now unmasked, uses his fortune and influence to mete out punishments and rewards to deserving parties, and asks for the hand of his beloved Sophia, 'a woman, who, a stranger to my fortune, could think that I had merit as a man'.[22]

Goldsmith never *presents* Sir William in any kind of negative or ironic light. On the contrary, his depiction of Sir William in all his 'native dignity'[23] invites the kind of interpretation Martin Battestin offers when he describes the character's actions echoing those of Jesus.[24] But the conclusion of *The Vicar of Wakefield* invites debate over artistic integrity because the resolution it offers is superficial at best. Throughout the novel, Goldsmith has illustrated again and again that the nation's obsession with wealth and social advancement has led to greed, corruption and deception on every level. Indeed, Brissenden argues that the society Goldsmith portrays here is 'so irrational, so cruel, and so economically inefficient and inequitable' that it *requires* the kind of 'magical assistance' Sir William provides.[25]

But by having the novel's wealthiest character disguise himself as poor and then use his money and influence to save the day, Goldsmith inadvertently reifies the values that created the corruption in the first place. Moreover, the character who resolves the thorniest private dilemma Goldsmith sets up—restoring Olivia's 'honor' after young Squire Thornhill lures her into a fake marriage—is not Sir William at all, but repentant con-artist Mr Jenkinson, who confesses that when the Squire

> commissioned me to procure him a false licence and a false priest, in order to deceive this young lady...what did I do but went and got a true licence and a true priest...my only design was to keep the licence and let the Squire know that I could prove it upon him whenever I thought proper, and so make him come down whenever I wanted money.[26]

While Curtis Dahl observes that 'the deceit of Jenkinson plus the deceit of

Thornhill results in truth and good',[27] and prompts Battestin to argue that 'the vicar's world is in part redeemed' by Jenkinson's actions,[28] I would argue the opposite; the juxtaposition of Jenkinson's and Sir William's actions suggests to me that Goldsmith has created a system in which its participants on both sides of the law are similarly compelled to exert control over one another. Hence the novel's so-called resolution only distracts us from the author's—and his characters'—inability to address the social ills he has exposed.

While the codependent's rescue of an addictive situation is fairly subtle in *The Vicar of Wakefield*, it is pronounced in *The Good Natur'd Man*. In order to stop his nephew's misapplied benevolence, Sir William Honeywood plans a pretence of sending him to debtor's prison and thus 'involving him in fictitious distress before he has plunged himself into real calamity'.[29] Mr Honeywood feels the pinch only for a moment, however, because his beloved Miss Richland immediately pays off the debt. At the end of the play, when Mr Honeywood has his fortune restored and wins Miss Richland's hand, we may well ask with him, 'Heavens! how can I have deserved all this?'.[30] He may resolve that 'it shall be my study to reserve my pity for real distress; my friendship for true merit, and my love for her, who first taught me what it is to be happy',[31] but there is nothing in the play to suggest how he will go about this task, or that his friends will not simply bail him out again in the future. Like a true addict, the most Goldsmith can envision for the characters whose problems he knows best is the promise to do better.

Goldsmith's last and most sophisticated work also portrays the most subtly codependent system. The troubled character in this instance is Charles Marlow, and though he does not share the 'good natur'd men's' compulsive benevolence, he, too, behaves by extremes. Tongue-tied almost to the point of autism with women of his own class and both arrogant and presuming with women he considers social inferiors, he shares with the 'good natured men' a profound sense of isolation: 'I'm doom'd to adore the sex, and yet to converse with the only part of it I despise'.[32] Marlow is compelled to exert his influence, especially over women; if he cannot achieve a feeling of superiority, then all others are out of reach. Like his creator, Marlow is well aware of his own pathology, and he expects never to marry, 'unless as among kings and princes, my bride were to be courted by a proxy. If, indeed, like an Eastern bridegroom, one were to be introduced to a wife he never saw before, it might be endured' (V. 130).[33] In this passage, Marlow all but asks to be tricked, and the rest of the play can be seen as an answer to his request.

The codependent here is Kate Hardcastle, daughter of a longtime friend to Charles Marlow's father, and so a good candidate to be Marlow's bride. Indeed, Marlow has come to the Hardcastle home to meet Kate. In a compromise with her self-proclaimed 'old-fashioned' father, Kate has agreed to wear a plain 'housewife's dress' for half the day in exchange for permission to wear whatever fashionable attire she desires the rest of the time. Kate's different costumes allow her and the audience to witness the extremes in Marlow's behavior. When Marlow is formally introduced to Kate in her fashionable clothes, he is so nervous that he stares at his toes and never sees her face,[34] but when he meets her in her plain clothes and mistakes her for a barmaid, he immediately makes advances.[35]

While Goldsmith explores Marlow's problems in some detail, he presents Kate's response—one that some might consider equally disturbing—as a model of virtuous behavior. Having experienced Marlow's impudence as well as his anxiety first-hand, she does not reject this clearly troubled man as a potential spouse. On the contrary, Goldsmith portrays her as penetrating and sympathetic, willing and able to see behind Marlow's behavior to what he suggests is the man's true character. When Marlow is shy, she observes 'good sense...buried in his fears',[36] and when he is not, she dismisses his impudence as 'faults that will pass off with time', while continuing to praise 'the virtues that will improve with age'.[37] Her object then, is to trick him into moderating his behavior, and she, of course, has everything to gain. 'If I could teach him a little confidence,' she predicts, 'it would be doing somebody that I know of [namely, herself] a piece of service'.[38]

Not surprisingly, the scheme works as planned. In the course of a few hours' intermittent conversation, Marlow comes to love this woman who has gently refused his advances and whom he continues to believe is his social inferior. 'What at first seem'd rustic plainness, now appears refin'd simplicity. What seem'd forward assurance, now strikes me as the result of courageous innocence, and conscious virtue.'[39] For her part, Kate comes to realize that Marlow shares her traditional values and is similarly looking for a spouse who will be acceptable to himself and his father alike. When he puts aside his own feelings and steels himself to leave, explaining, 'I owe too much to the opinion of the world, too much to the authority of a father', Kate's heart is won: 'I never knew half his merit till now. He shall not go, if I have power or art to detain him.'[40]

Through this relationship, Goldsmith demonstrates the way that courtship rituals, particularly among the upper classes, had degenerated into what Kate, early in the play, describes as 'so like a thing of business'[41] that it was impossible for two people to get to know each other before it was too late. Kate's disguise thus enables both characters to circumvent conventions surrounding arranged marriages—for instance meeting in the presence of their fathers, getting acquainted with the prospect of marriage always looming—and meet in a psychological space they create behind their respective social masks where they can presumably discover each other's true beliefs. Thus their private union, shown to be based on shared beliefs and mutual growth, at once precedes and reaffirms the social appropriate 'match' their fathers desire.

Notwithstanding Bernard Harris's view that Goldsmith has created in *She Stoops* 'a prose comedy of ideal, romantic love',[42] the problem with this depiction of Kate and Marlow is that their relationship never moves beyond deception. Marlow's most heartfelt words are addressed to a person he thinks is someone she is not, and the tears he evokes in her by saying he must leave—tears that truly touch him and which he describes as 'the first mark of tenderness I ever had from a modest woman'—turn out to be fake; the stage directions tell us Kate was only 'pretending to cry'.[43] When Marlow does discover Kate's true identity, his impulse is to flee. 'Zounds,' he cries, 'there's no bearing this; it's worse than death...O, curse on my noisy head. I never attempted to be impudent yet, that I was not taken down, I must be gone.'[44] He stays only because Mr Hardcastle stops him, saying, 'Take courage, man'. Once again, we never *see* this supposedly reformed man engage in moderate behavior or see him and Kate engage in anything like a frank discussion. At the conclusion of the play Goldsmith leaves us, as always, with only the promise of improvement, one that his art never fulfills.

Goldsmith's feelings of alienation from a society he understandably viewed as corrupt give him a good vantage point from which to portray the problems that he sees new wealth creating in his country. But Goldsmith never successfully finds his way out of the mazes he creates—even to the kind of religious or ethical sanctuary that Samuel Johnson can at least imagine—because his own unresolved feelings of inadequacy and profound impotence stand in the way. In 1758, when his writing career was just beginning, he wrote to his former schoolmate Robert Bryanton, 'God's curse, Sir! who am I? Eh! what am I?'[45] The question was posed half in jest, but Goldsmith never seems to have found a satisfying answer. Samuel Johnson reports that, on his deathbed, when his doctor asked, 'is your mind at ease?' Goldsmith answered, 'It is not'.[46]

In *A Room of One's Own*, Virginia Woolf writes of Shakespeare:

> The reason perhaps why we know so little of Shakespeare['s life]...is that his grudges and spites and antipathies are hidden from us. We are not held up by some 'revelation' which reminds us of the writer. All desire to protest, to preach, to proclaim an injury, to pay off a score, was fired out of him and consumed. Therefore his poetry flows from him free and unimpeded. If ever a human being got his work expressed completely, it was Shakespeare. If ever a mind was incandescent, unimpeded...it was Shakespeare's mind.[47]

It seems to me that the opposite can be said of Goldsmith. No matter what else he was dong in these works, he was continually searching for an elusive sense of moderation while playing hide and seek with his own demons. Sadly, in both his life and art, the demons won.

NOTES

1. S. Gwynn, *Oliver Goldsmith* (New York: Henry Holt, 1935), p. 53.

2. R.M. Wardle, *Oliver Goldsmith* (Laurence: University of Kansas Press, 1957), p. 304 n. 26.

3. O. Goldsmith, *Collected Works* (ed. A. Friedman; 5 vols.; Oxford: Clarendon Press, 1966), IV, p. 29.

4. J. Forster, *The Life and Times of Oliver Goldsmith* (London: Ward, Lock, 1871), I, p. 27.

5. Forster, *Life and Times*, I, pp. 157-60.

6. See for example Forster, *Life and Times*, I, p. 56; Wardle, *Oliver Goldsmith*, pp. 12, 34, 41-42, 100, 115, 245-46; J. Ginger, *The Notable Man: The Life and Times of Oliver Goldsmith* (London: Hamish Hamilton, 1977), pp. 57, 123, 277-82; L. Wibberley, *The Good-Natured Man: A Portrait of Oliver Goldsmith* (New York: William Morrow, 1979), pp. 24-25, 61, 66, 82, 85-87, 96-97, 173-74, 229; A.L. Sells, *Oliver Goldsmith: His Life and Works* (London: George Allen & Unwin, 1974), pp. 81-82.

7. Goldsmith, *Collected Works*, IV, p. 30.

8. See Goldsmith, *Collected Works*, II, pp. 401-403; III, pp. 108, 298, 299, 379-87.

9. See for example O. Ferguson, 'Oliver Goldsmith: The Personality of the Essayist', *PQ* 61 (1982), pp. 183-87; C. Knight, 'Ironic Loneliness: The Case of Goldsmith's Chinaman', in H. Bloom (ed.), *Modern Critical Views: Oliver Goldsmith* (New York: Chelsea House, 1987), pp. 93-96; R. Helgerson, 'The Two Worlds of Oliver Goldsmith', *SEL* 13 (1973), pp. 523-29; M. Golden, 'The Family-Wanderer Theme in Goldsmith', *ELH* 25 (1958), pp. 183-87; R.H. Hopkins, *The True Genius of Oliver Goldsmith* (Baltimore: Johns Hopkins University Press, 1969), pp. 125-37; Ginger, *The Notable Man*, pp. 144-45, 232-41.

10. Goldsmith, *Collected Works*, I, p. 319.

11. See Golden, 'Family-Wanderer Theme', p. 187; Ferguson, 'Oliver Goldsmith', p. 189; R.F. Brissenden, 'The Sentimentality of *The Vicar of Wakefield*', in Bloom (ed.), *Modern Critical Views*, p. 19. All of these critics are primarily interested in Goldsmith's social commentary. Hopkins (*True Genius*, pp. 207-30), also primarily interested in his social commentary, does find the conclusion to *The Vicar* satisfying, but only because he finds the entire novel ironic. Critics who see *The Vicar* as a kind of religious allegory (M.C. Battestin, 'Goldsmith: The Comedy of Job', in *The Providence of Wit* [Oxford: Clarendon Press, 1974]; C. Dahl, 'Patterns of Disguise in *The Vicar of Wakefield*', *ELH* 25 [1958], pp. 90-104; Lehman, Ferguson, 'Dr Primrose and Goldsmith's Clerical Ideal', *PQ* 54 [1975], pp. 323ff.) are more likely to be satisfied with the conclusion.

12. A.W. Schaef and D. Fassel, *The Addictive Organization* (San Francisco: Harper & Row, 1988), p. 5 (my italics).

13. S. Peele with A. Brodsky, *Love and Addiction* (New York: Signet, 1975), p. 56.

14. Peele with Brodsky, *Love and Addiction*, p. 4.

15. Goldsmith, *Collected Works*, II, p. 114.

16. Goldsmith, *Collected Works*, III, p. 29.

17. For discussions of Goldsmith's politics see H.J. Bell, Jr, 'The Deserted Village and Goldsmith's Social Doctrines', *PMLA* 59 (1944), pp. 747-72; D. Davie, 'Notes on Goldsmith's Politics', in A. Swarbrick (ed.), *The Art of Oliver Goldsmith* (New Jersey: Vision/Barnes & Nobel, 1984), pp. 79-89.

18. Peele with Brodsky, *Love and Addiction*, p. 37.

19. Goldsmith, *Collected Works*, V, p. 20.

20. M. Beattie, *Codependent No More: How to Stop Controlling Others and Start Caring for*

Yourself (New York: Harper & Row [by arrangement with the Hazelden Foundation], 1987), p. 31.

21.   Goldsmith, *Collected Works*, IV, p. 168.

22.   Goldsmith, *Collected Works*, IV, p. 181.

23.   Goldsmith, *Collected Works*, IV, p. 167.

24.   Battestin, 'The Comedy of Job', pp. 209-10.

25.   Brissenden, 'Sentimentality', p. 19.

26.   Goldsmith, *Collected Works*, IV, p. 178.

27.   Dahl, 'Patterns of Disguise', p. 101.

28.   Battestin, 'The Comedy of Job', p. 207.

29.   Goldsmith, *Collected Works*, V, p. 20.

30.   Goldsmith, *Collected Works*, V, p. 81.

31.   Goldsmith, *Collected Works*, V, p. 81.

32.   Goldsmith, *Collected Works*, V, p. 131.

33.   Goldsmith, *Collected Works*, V, p. 130.

34.   Goldsmith, *Collected Works*, V, pp. 142-48.

35.   Goldsmith, *Collected Works*, V, pp. 170-73.

36.   Goldsmith, *Collected Works*, V, p. 148.

37.   Goldsmith, *Collected Works*, V, p. 174.

38.   Goldsmith, *Collected Works*, V, p. 148.

39.   Goldsmith, *Collected Works*, V, p. 211.

40.   Goldsmith, *Collected Works*, V, p. 186.

41.   Goldsmith, *Collected Works*, V, p. 111.

42.   B. Harris, '*She Stoops to Conquer*', in Bloom (ed.), *Modern Critical Views*, p. 141.

43.   Goldsmith, *Collected Works*, V, p. 185.

44.   Goldsmith, *Collected Works*, V, p. 213.

45.   K.C. Balderston (ed.), *The Collected Letters of Oliver Goldsmith* (repr.; New York: Kraw Reprint Company, 1969 [1928]), p. 38.

46.   Forster, *Life and Times*, II, p. 518.

47.   V. Woolf, *A Room of One's Own* (New York: Harcourt, Brace & World, 1929), pp. 58-59.

OPIUM SMOKING AND THE ORIENTAL INFECTION OF BRITISH IDENTITY*

Barry Milligan

Elsewhere in the work from which this paper is taken,[1] I argue that the opium visions of Coleridge and De Quincey offer a scenario in which ingestion of the Oriental substance opium allows the Orient to enter, occupy and oppressively rule the author's consciousness. This literary paradigm, I argue, is metaphorically comparable to a contemporary historical phenomenon: the growing British colonial commerce with the Orient, by means of which the metaphorical body of Britain similarly ingests Oriental substances which these authors fear are diluting British culture and identity, perhaps ultimately paving the way for an Oriental takeover. The authors' fears apparently were not shared by many of their contemporaries, among whom so-called 'Orientalism' was becoming hugely popular, with the rage for 'Chinoiserie' in fashionable decor, Chinese gardens on the best estates, and Byron and Southey's Oriental Tales on the bookshelves of those in the know. But Coleridge and De Quincey found the ascendance of these versions of Oriental culture particularly frightening because England had 'grievously offended and been most tyrannous' in the Orient, as Coleridge unpopularly put it in 'Fears in Solitude', and the internalization of the supposed culture of these grudge-bearing Orientals represented a silent but significant threat. De Quincey especially associated these supposedly vindictive Orientals with what Edward Said calls 'the nineteenth-century academic and imaginative demonology of "the mysterious Orient"',[2] and the result was a mythologized enemy, the pernicious, demonic Oriental, who could be expected to use subtle and evil means to gain the field and to bide his time and endure privations in doing so.

Although Coleridge and De Quincey's fears were somewhat anomalous early in the century, they gained a broader base by the middle of the century, when many Britons were critical of the policies behind the so-called opium wars with China and began to fear retribution for what they saw as immorally forcing a detrimental product onto an unwilling customer. With the appearance of more and more Oriental immigrants on British shores, some believed they saw that retribution taking shape in a practice these Orientals brought with them: opium smoking, which one British critic of the Indo–Chinese opium trade tellingly called 'the plague spreading and attacking our vitals...the reflex action and retributive consequence of...the opium traffic at the hands of our government'.[3]

This impression of opium smoking as at once infectious epidemic and hostile invasion informs a number of examples of a new literary genre that grew and thrived late in the century: narratives about mysterious and evil opium dens in the East End of London, a region which itself is repeatedly figured as an Orient in miniature within the capital of the empire. In these narratives, Orientalism is repeatedly portrayed as a sort of transmittable disease, with opium smoke as the means of transmission. So when the aforementioned critic of the opium trade speaks of 'the plague spreading and attacking our vitals', he does not necessarily mean only, or even primarily, an increased incidence of addiction to opium smoking; he also seems to fear a more comprehensive infectious 'Chineseness' eating away at the very identity of the British people.

The majority of this article deals with Dickens and Conan Doyle; but first I would like briefly to sketch some outlines of the body of other portrayals of opium dens surrounding and leading up to these authors' works.

The typical opium den is represented as being run and mostly frequented by vaguely threatening Orientals who are silent and patient but seem ready to well up with violence. The typical Oriental smoker 'don't care for no drink and seem[s] to live without eating', according to one early account, and he 'looks a little dangerous as he brandishes his opium pipe'.[4] The stamina and implicit violence of these aliens is made more frightening by their subtle ability to assimilate British persons who come in contact with their opium smoke—especially poor dockside women, who in the early examples of the genre are the only English people found in the dens. One opium-smoking woman says of her Oriental neighbors who operate an opium den, 'I've lived here these dozen year, and naturally have got into many of their ways'. Indeed she herself is known by no other name than the pseudo-Oriental one of 'Mother Abdallah' ('Lazarus Lotus-Eating', pp. 423-44). The Englishwoman is being absorbed by the Oriental culture as mediated by the opium den, and this alien absorption is taking place right in the heart of the capital of the British Empire. Several reporters dwell on the fact that some Chinese proprietors of opium dens have British wives, who are even more obviously and menacingly being Orientalized by the insidious influence of opium smoke. One typical account shows the English wife of a Chinese opium master undergoing a macabre metamorphosis that is expected to leave her as a sort of mystical Oriental living-dead: 'Poor English Mrs Chi Ki looks as though she is being gradually smoke-dried, and by and by will present the appearance of an Egyptian mummy'.[5]

This almost invisible but dangerous incursion of the Orient onto English soil is more developed in Dickens's *The Mystery of Edwin Drood* (1870). Again we see a female casualty of contagious Orientalism who 'has opium-smoked herself into a strange likeness of the Chinaman. His form of cheek, eye, and temple, and his color are repeated in her.'[6] But we also see, for the first time, an English *man* in the den. This man is also being infected as a result of his close contact with the Orientalized woman: 'As he watches the spasmodic shoots and darts that break out of her face and limbs...some contagion in them seizes upon him: insomuch that he has to withdraw himself...until he has got the better of this unclean spirit of imitation' (p. 39).

This infected Englishman, John Jasper, represents a significant departure from previous opium den writings. All of the previous smokers were either Oriental men or English women from the dock districts, suggesting that, if the practice of opium smoking was spreading to English people, it was reaching only the most marginal groups. But this smoker is neither Oriental nor female nor one of the poor of the London docks; he is instead white, English, male, and—of all things—a choirmaster in an English cathedral town. The reader is presented with an outwardly upright, middle-class citizen who unexpectedly leads a second, hidden life centered around and enabled by the Oriental influence of opium. Thus we see an important new twist on the opium den narrative in *Edwin Drood*: the portrayal of the Orient's infection of a more mainstream English scene *outside* the opium den.

We see an illustration of this merging of a threatening Orient with the English domestic scene in the novel's first paragraph. The reader views the den through Jasper's dazed opium visions as a corroded and corrosive agent which pierces the boundary between the English cathedral town and the teeming, violent Orient. In his hallucination, Jasper sees 'the well-known massive grey square tower of [his town's] old cathedral', but it appears behind an unfamiliar 'spike of rusty iron' which is not visible 'from any point of the real prospect'. He drowsily decides that the mysterious spike is a tool of Oriental violence, 'set up by the Sultan's orders for the impaling of a horde of Turkish robbers, one by one'. This exotic and threatening Oriental imagery then dominates his vision: 'cymbals clash, and the Sultan goes by to his palace in long procession' as 'ten thousand scimitars flash in the sunlight' (p. 37). The rusty Oriental spike actually turns out to be a much more mundane object which comes to be the distinguishing mark of the opium den in *Edwin Drood*: the top of a broken down bedpost in the East End den. This earmark of the opium den is the only actual physical presence to be incorporated into Jasper's vision, where the corroding rusty spike punctures the boundary between the

English domestic scene and the violent Orient, allowing one to enter the open wound in the other. The opium den acts much like a dirty, rusty nail: you had best avoid it unless you want to get a nasty infection.

Jasper carries this strange contagion from his secret life to his daylight one. Back in the cathedral town, Jasper's secret opium life is gradually taking over his outwardly respectable existence to the extent that he even smokes opium in his English village home, polluting it too with 'the evil spectres it invokes at midnight' (p. 77), evil spectres which were described in the novel's first paragraph as a violent Oriental horde. *Edwin Drood* draws a scenario in which a malignant foreign influence has already infected the seemingly upright citizen next door, and may thus be working its way outward from the landing site into the fundamental fabric of the invaded culture.

The idea of Oriental infection continues to be developed in many of the popular opium den narratives of the 1870s and 1880s, and the character of the middle-class Englishman who leads a second, secret life to which he passes through an East End opium den is picked up and elaborated in Wilde's *The Picture of Dorian Gray* (1891). But after Dickens, the next extensive development of the opium den as the medium of Oriental contagion infesting the English domestic environment is Conan Doyle's 'The Man With the Twisted Lip'.[7] In this Sherlock Holmes adventure the double identity of the middle-class man explodes into a surprising double identity of all the trappings of middle-class existence, including home, occupation and income. The slippery, too permeable boundary between these pairs of identities is again the opium den, whose contagious Oriental influence is shown to have so fully permeated the English domestic scene that it is discoverable beneath a number of conventions previously taken for granted as middle class and English.

The adventure itself is initiated by a series of disruptions of the proper domestic order, disruptions ultimately originating in what Holmes calls 'the vilest murder-trap on the whole riverside', an East End opium den run by what he calls a 'rascally Lascar' and a 'sallow Malay'. First Watson is shaken from his easy chair, where he sits sleepily as his wife does needlework, to answer another young wife's request that he return her husband from the opium den to his empty hearthside. In the den, Watson finds Holmes investigating the disappearance of yet another young husband who was last seen peering from a window upstairs. Thus we see the den draw three young middle-class husbands from their homes, leaving fretting wives next to empty easy chairs.

And once these men are drawn from their homes into the East End dens, they assume second identities appropriate to their haunts. The man for whom Watson searches becomes quasi-Oriental, 'with yellow, pasty face, drooping lids and pin-point pupils' (p. 623); Holmes is at first unrecognizable in his disguise as a hardened opium smoker, 'very thin, very wrinkled...an opium pipe dangling down from between his knees' (p. 625); and, as Holmes discovers in the end, the man for whom he has been searching has also been leading two lives with the opium den as gateway between them. The missing man, Neville St Clair, turns out to have been spending his weekdays earning a fortune as a beggar in the City, and his evenings and weekends as a husband and father in the suburbs. He has been going to a rented room in the opium den in the mornings and evenings to change from suburban family man to beggar and back again.

The opium den serves as the catalyst for St Clair's identity change, the gateway between the two poles of his double life. It seems at first as if the den acts as a closable valve between the two existences, opening twice a day to allow only the beggar into the City and only the suburban family man out of it. But it becomes increasingly evident that assorted detritus accompanies the man in each of his passages until the two existences are in many ways indistinguishable from one another. Most obviously, the St Clair family's suburban existence is, ironically, financed by St Clair's begging. But the two realms also mesh in other, more subtle, ways. When St Clair, disguised as the beggar, wants to hide his dual identity from the police, his secret is nearly revealed by the presence of a middle-class man's clothes and some children's building bricks in the room at the opium den. The two existences mix with one another until it is impossible to say whether St Clair is a family man impersonating a beggar or a beggar impersonating a family man.

One may well question my insistence on the *Oriental* nature of this contagion in the Holmes adventure. At first glance, it appears as if the Orient is more or less safely contained in the 'vile murder-trap' on the river-side. But a closer look reveals that the Orient is initially unapparent elsewhere only because it has so fully integrated with what at first seems to be inconspicuously English.

The story opens with Dr Watson's description of Isa Whitney, who appears to be the quintessential respectable member of the middle class. He is first presented as the 'brother of the late Elias Whitney, DD, Principal of the Theological College of St George's' (p. 623); but we are then immediately told that he is 'much addicted to opium', and now even physically resembles the Oriental smokers as described in previous opium den accounts, 'with yellow, pasty face, drooping lids and pin-point pupils' (p. 623). One might attempt to argue that this habit which has reduced the promising Whitney to 'the wreck and ruin of a noble man' (p. 623) has an English rather than an Oriental source since it originates in De Quincey; Watson claims that 'the habit grew upon him...from some foolish freak when he was at college, for having read De Quincey's description of his dreams and sensations, he had drenched his tobacco with laudanum' (p. 623). But even this tenuous Englishness drops away.

Apart from the fact that De Quincey himself associated his own habit with Oriental contagion, he also never *smoked* opium, but only drank it in the form of laudanum. Smoking opium was an exotic Oriental practice essentially unheard of in England in De Quincey's time, and—as I have indicated—was thought of as a peculiarly Oriental vice even in Dickens's day. The fact that Whitney's habit was acquired not from a bamboo pipe in an East End den but from a regular English tobacco pipe smoked in rooms at Oxford or Cambridge suggests that the Englishness and Orientalness of the habit have become inseparable—that what was peculiarly Oriental is now unexceptionably English, and vice versa.

If Whitney's laudanum-laced tobacco smoking *suggests* that English and Oriental are not differentiable, Holmes' peculiar tobacco-smoking practices *insist* that they are merged. Watson describes Holmes' ritual as he prepares to spend the night in a guest bedroom in the St Clairs' house:

> He...wandered about the room collecting pillows from his bed, and cushions from the sofa and armchairs. With these he constructed a sort of Eastern divan, upon which he perched himself cross-legged, with an ounce of shag tobacco and a box of matches laid out in front of him. In the dim light of the lamp I saw him sitting there, an old brier pipe between his lips, his eyes fixed vacantly upon the corner of the ceiling, the blue smoke curling up from him, silent, motionless, with the light shining upon his strong set aquiline features (p. 633).

Holmes' tobacco-smoking posture of course echoes that of the opium smoker, but with a strange amalgam of incongruous English elements. Holmes sits on an 'Eastern divan', but it is composed of arm-chair and sofa cushions. With 'pipe between his lips, his eyes fixed vacantly upon the corner of the ceiling, the blue smoke curling up from him, silent, motionless' (p. 633), he resembles the Oriental smokers in the den, but he is nonetheless clearly Occidental, 'with the light shining upon his strong set aquiline features' (p. 633). The room, 'full of a dense tobacco haze', looks much like the 'room, thick and heavy with the brown opium smoke' Watson described in the East End den (p. 624), but this room is a bedroom in a suburban villa, and the smoke is from shag tobacco rather than opium.

This last incongruity is particularly significant: previously, those who warned against Oriental contagion attributed it to the spread of opium dens. But 'The Man With the Twisted Lip' gradually takes that assumption apart. At the beginning, we found Isa Whitney smoking opium from a regular tobacco pipe at an English college; in the midst of the adventure, we see St Clair's passage through the opium den blending the East End with the suburban domestic scene, even though he never smokes opium; and by the end of the story, the influence of the opium den is discernible in English domestic elements that are disconnected, in any physical sense, from opium, the Orient, or the East End. Objects and practices are simultaneously characteristic of both the opium den and the English domestic scene: the sofa cushions are also an Eastern divan, the shag tobacco is also opium and the suburban bedroom is also an opium den.

I would like to sum up some of the more salient characteristics of these opium den narratives by borrowing a metaphor from modern medical research, as this nineteenth-century 'Oriental contagion' interestingly has much in common with late-twentieth-century theories about viral diseases. Unlike bacterial infections, which besiege the body for a time and either kill it or are killed themselves, viruses are currently believed to enter the cells of the organism, sometimes even becoming a part of its very genetic structure. The viruses thus invisibly reproduce themselves with each reproduction of the host cell, of which they are now a permanent part. These viruses may go on replicating and integrating with the host cells for years without manifesting noticeable symptoms, only to cause unpredictable complications in the later life of the organism.[8]

A similar process seems to be at work in Conan Doyle's non-differentiable Anglo–Oriental domestic scene, in which Oriental elements enter British culture by way of the opium den and become permanent but almost invisible components of the culture, integrating and reproducing along with the host culture, and perhaps causing unexpected complications later on. Just as the opium smoke enters the smoker's body, permanently altering the cells and restructuring the smoker's identity, so do foreign elements similarly introduced into a culture become part of that culture, restructuring the national identity until what were previously perceived as rigidly divided cultures are now inseparable, as in Conan Doyle's subtly Orientalized suburban bedroom. This cultural blending is both enticing and frightening; enticing perhaps because it brings the often romanticized, adventurous frontiers of colonialism to one's doorstep, but frightening because those frontiers themselves are often frightening; bringing them home gives a seemingly hostile culture a foothold, and replaces a national identity which at least *seemed* predictable with an unpredictable changeling. The late-nineteenth-century wariness of the opium den, then, is probably inseparable from simultaneous anxieties about the imperial process. The end of the century saw a growing awareness that the British Empire could no longer be viewed as an entity in which the home culture of England overwrites the Oriental culture of the colonies, but must instead be viewed as an unpredictable multinational identity—at every level from nation to individual, and from the outposts in the colonies to the hearthsides in London.

NOTES

*   I use the terms 'Orient' and 'Oriental' in the sense in which they were used in England and Europe throughout much of the nineteenth century, when the alien 'Orient' included roughly everything east of Greece (all the way to Japan) and south of the territory of the former USSR (but north of Australia). See, for instance, E. Said, *Orientalism* (New York: Random House, 1979), and R. Kabbani, *Europe's Myths of Orient* (Bloomington: Indiana University Press, 1986).

1.   The work in question is my *Pleasures and Pains: Opium and the Orient in Nineteenth-Century English Culture* (University Press of Virginia, forthcoming).

2.   Said, *Orientalism*, p. 26.

3.   G. Piercy, 'Opium Smoking in London', *Friend of China* 6 (1883), pp. 239-40.

4.   'Lazarus Lotus-Eating', *All the Year Round* 15 (1866), pp. 421-25.

5.   'East London Opium Smokers', *London Society* 14 (1868), pp. 68-72.

6.   C. Dickens, *The Mystery of Edwin Drood* (New York and London: Penguin, 1974), p. 38. Subsequent references are by page number to this edition.

7.   A. Conan Doyle, 'The Man with the Twisted Lip', *Strand Magazine* (1891), pp. 624-26. Subsequent references in the text are by page number to this edition.

8.   For an accessible and informative overview of contemporary theory and research on viruses, see F. Hapgood, 'Viruses Emerge as a New Key for Unlocking Life's Mysteries', *Smithsonian* (November 1988), pp. 117-27.

DRINK AND DISORDER IN *THE NARRATIVE OF ARTHUR GORDON PYM*

Domhnall Mitchell

According to David Ketterer, in his survey of *Pym* criticism from 1980–90,[1] recent approaches to the text have included psychoanalytical, mythic, psychological, existential, social, formal, hoax-based, satiric and ironic, deconstructive and visionary studies. As far as I am aware, drink is treated as a serious preoccupation in only a few of those readings. Given Poe's reputation, this is rather surprising. The singer Dean Martin once defined sobriety as the ability to lie on a floor without having to hold on, and somehow the image we have of Poe is of a man struggling to maintain his grip, not only on sobriety, but on sanity as well. Rufus Griswold's portrait of the artist as a drug addict and alcoholic, permanently in search of some gutter to stagger into, is, like all depictions of excess, excessive in itself. Poe was certainly never addicted to opium, however much he used it, and he was easily, rather than always, drunk: although the part played by alcohol in his early death cannot be underestimated, the truth is that for much of his life he drank scarcely, but could never hold it. As I hope to demonstrate in the course of this paper, his problems were at once more banal, and more deeply disturbing.

In *Poetry and the Age* Randall Jarrell wrote that, 'after a few decades or centuries almost everybody will be able to see through [Emily] Dickinson to her poems'.[2] The same point might be made with equal justice about Poe, for, like Dickinson, his reputation can often get in the way of his writing. The drunken episode at the beginning of *Pym* is a case in point. Pym is fooled into believing his friend Augustus to be sober when he suggests that they go out sailing at night and in rough weather, only to discover after a while that Augustus, who is at the helm and is therefore supposed to be steering, is in fact 'so drunk—beastly drunk—he could no longer either stand, speak, or see'.[3] The temptation is to feel that the writer somehow approves of their actions: such a combination of Romantic recklessness and vision seems close to our own views on Poe himself. But the incident is significant for other reasons. It is the first example of deception in a book where deception inevitably leads to disaster or to destruction. Pym's trust in Augustus is, of course, totally misplaced, since what initially appears to be a 'most delightful and most reasonable' proposition (p. 48) turns out to be the very opposite of anything rational, a 'mad idea' (p. 48) brought on by intoxication. Augustus, in fact, never lives up to a name which is meant to suggest a degree of reason and intellectual control: he is able only to '*imitate* the outward demeanor of one in perfect possession of his senses' (p. 50, my italics).

The issue of failing to control the senses is a significant and stimulating one, for there is a recurring failure to maintain order of one sort or another throughout the book. Images of inebriation, or delirium, are one way of recognizing this preoccupation, for drinking leads to a lack of control, a disorientation which has social as well as psychological consequences. Drinking overcomes reason in the same way that a largely drunken crew overcome the captain of the *Grampus*, and with exactly the same result—shipwreck, or the loss of the ability to navigate, and therefore to control. In fact, Augustus is not only the son of a ship's captain but, at the rudder of the *Ariel*, he is effectively a ship's captain himself, and is therefore the first of many who come out of the book rather badly. Despite occupying positions of command, Block, Barnard, and Guy all make crucial and often disastrous errors of judgment. All three are like Augustus in the sense that they are trusted, and fail to live up to that trust. But the three are also like Pym, in the sense that they are too trusting, and often confuse appearance with reality. Block, captain of the *Penguin*, trusts his instinct as a sailor and makes the near-fatal mistake of believing that no one could have survived the wreck of the *Ariel*. It is only the persistence of his crew which results in Augustus and Pym being saved from certain death by drowning. Barnard, captain of the *Grampus*, makes the mistake of entrusting his safety, and that of others, to a suspect crew and boat—described as 'an old hulk, and scarcely seaworthy' (p. 58) at one stage—and if he cannot be blamed directly for the mutiny, he can be blamed for not supervising the proper loading of the ship's cargo. Finally, Guy, captain of the *Jane Guy*, makes the mistake of trusting Too-Wit and his island savages. This is something that not even the chief himself does, for, seeing his own reflection in a mirror on board the ship, he reacts with considerable fear and alarm: the reaction is so excessive, in fact, that Pym tells us that the 'thought the savage would go mad' (p. 191), a word which crucially links him with other deceivers in the book. The truth is that, for Poe especially, the Chief *is* mad; the mirror is a trick device to show us Too-wit as he really is, and not as he appears to be: confronted with himself, he reacts with a clearly appropriate terror. But all three captains are easily misled, in the sense that they are too credulous, too ready to believe what they think they see. And Poe appears at one stage to suggest that this is a failing shared by all humankind; it is said that in 'no affairs of mere prejudice, pro or con, do we deduce inferences with entire certainty even from the most simple data' (p. 53), and even though this is Pym speaking, it seems to reiterate the narrative preoccupation with the human inability to interpret facts properly.

Throughout the narrative, drink is associated not only with various forms of deception but with mania. According to Pym, the adventure with Augustus is 'the result of a highly concentrated state of intoxication—a state which [is] like madness' (p. 50). At a later stage, when they are left without provisions on what remains of the *Grampus*, Augustus, Peters and Parker all suffer from 'a species of delirium' (p. 136) induced by wine, and all three persuade Pym to explore the submerged cabin of the ship so that they can drink while he dives. Of course, this takes place not long after the crew have overthrown the captain and been overthrown in their turn, and indeed madness and mutiny, drink and deception are all closely related in *The Narrative of Arthur Gordon Pym*. It is interesting that Poe chooses to bring Pym, suffering from a combination of hunger, hangover and sensory deprivation in the hold of the *Grampus*, close to an insane despair at the same time as an intoxicated crew indulge in a desperately bloody, and barbaric, form of insanity on the upper decks. Pym, of course, has already indulged in a parallel rebellion against parental authority by stowing away on the ship in the first place, and it is especially significant that he only just manages to evade a representative of that authority, in the shape of his grandfather, Mr Peterson, by impersonating a drunken sailor. The rule of order is disrupted in all three cases, with nightmarish consequences.

It is particularly intriguing, then, that much of this revolt against authority is accompanied by references to letter-writing, story-telling and fictional masquerading of one sort or another, and connected to the theme of deception in the book. Pym admits to boarding the *Grampus* by using a 'scheme of deception' (p. 58), and again places his trust in Augustus, who conceals his disappearance by forging a letter from Mr Ross, a distant relative, to his family. But from the very beginning of the book, Augustus is associated with tall tales of one sort or another. Pym observes at the start of the first chapter that he 'was always talking to me of his adventures in the South Pacific Ocean' and 'telling me stories' (p. 47), then complains at the beginning of the second chapter that, at dinner especially, Augustus 'had a manner of relating his stories of the ocean (more than half of which I now suspect to have been fabrications)' (p. 57). But since he is so closely connected with Augustus, he suffers from a sort of guilt by association. Besides, Pym deceives his grandfather, and his minor role-playing leads him into a theatre of the absurd where roles are unrehearsed, the script is illegible, the director has been murdered and total breakdown ensues. Stuck in the hold, Pym is no longer able to comprehend, or to communicate with, the world outside him. The fact that he is unable to read the message sent to him by Augustus is crucial at this point, for it indicates not only that Pym is on the verge of collapse, but that there is a more widespread slide into anarchy taking place above deck. The ship is a universe without an authority figure, and because of that signs no longer make sense, and both the rules of language and the rule of law break down.

Poe seems to be pointing out that, in such a world, all human perception is suspect. The imagination in particular is potentially destructive: to overreach is to run the risk of toppling over into chaos. At a very basic level, there is an obvious critique of the more excessive claims for the imagination made by the Romantics—indeed, Pym's middle name, Gordon, is one that he shares with Lord Byron, and at times he seems to be acting out the part of a Byronic hero. In addition, Pym and Augustus have their first, and nearly their last, adventure at sea in the *Ariel*, which is, of course, the name of the boat Shelley drowned in. Still attracted by fictional visions of 'shipwreck and famine: of death or captivity among barbarian hordes' (p. 57), their next journey on the *Grampus* ends in a horrible death for one and a mysterious disappearance for the other. Nonetheless, Poe's criticism is not simply a literary one, but extends to the social, and even to the racial, sphere. It is therefore useful to note that the mutineers themselves finally fall foul of their own drunken imaginations. Soon after taking over the *Grampus* they are divided into opposing camps, the stronger side having come together less out of loyalty than out of a liking for the picture Dirk Peters paints, in words, of life in the South Pacific. We are told that Peters 'dwelt on the world of novelty and amusement to be found among the innumerable islands of the Pacific', until finally 'the pictures of the hybrid line manager [took] strong hold upon the ardent imaginations of the seamen' (p. 93). Faced with a choice between competing narratives, the seamen vote for the one which is most skilfully presented. In the process they subtly change from being a group of actors, in control of their own destinies, to a passive audience in a drama not of their own making. In the end, this is their undoing. Their ability to reason considerably weakened by alcohol, again, and the combination of superstition and more stories from Dirk Peters, the mutineers are momentarily deceived by the appearance of Pym, disguised as Rogers' ghost. All of them are either killed right away, or die later, and the fact that their deaths seem implausible suggests, I think, that Poe's political will took precedence over his creative imagination in the writing of these scenes: the justice is not poetic, but socially conservative and reactionary. Pym plays dead because he represents the angel of death, messenger from a dark and vengeful deity.

If the living can impersonate the dead, the dead prove just as capable of impersonating the living. One of the most grotesque contributions to the preoccupation with deception in the book is the appearance of the Dutch trading ship, which seems to represent salvation for the shipwrecked survivors of the *Grampus*, but is eventually shown to be peopled only by a crew and passengers who are dead. This is a confidence trick, again, though one with several implications for the narrative as a whole. At one level, the ship is a parody of different kinds of hope. The survivors ask for 'deliverance'—an important word in the text, with obvious religious connotations—and are sent a different kind of message. The vessel does not ferry passengers from one location to another, and nor will it carry Pym and his comrades from the world of death and disorder to the land of the living and of the known, the familiar. In that sense, it seems to defeat the desire for solid ground, for certainty, while also deflating the traditional images of death as a journey from this life to the next. Ultimately, therefore, the boat is an image not of Christian promise and reward but of a more Calvinistic system of punishment and retribution. In particular, the image of 'a huge seagull, busily gorging itself with the horrible flesh' from one corpse is meant to remind us of the Promethean myth: Pym records with horror the 'portion of clotted and liverlike substance in its beak' (p. 133). It is worth pointing out that, as Harold Beaver has argued, 'this myth of rebellion against fathers'[4] has obvious implications for both Augustus and Pym, and puts their punishment into a new and interesting context. The book does not simply concern itself with filial disobedience, but with the consequences of Adam's disobedience, and the subsequent expulsion from Eden. The father is first rejected, then sought after and returned to, and the book charts that movement. But the suggestion that the Deity can at times be a terrible, vengeful figure not only echoes the views of Puritan preachers like Jonathan Edwards but goes some way to explaining the preponderance of suspect signs, hoaxes and deception in the book. For this is a fallen universe, and it is to that fact that Poe draws our attention, by using fiction to point out that all facts are appearances only.

In *The Narrative of Arthur Gordon Pym*, things are never quite what they seem. The book itself is an adventure story which pretends to be a factual account of a journey so incredible that it must masquerade as a fiction if it is to be given any credence at all. This is only 'pretended fiction', Pym informs us in the preface; it is 'a narrative,' he goes on to claim, 'publish(ed)...under the garb of fiction' (p. 44). The immediate, and intriguing, effect of this authorial decoy is, of course, to make the relationship between reader and writer much more ambiguous and problematic. The suspicion that the entire book may be a gigantic hoax, an absurd joke at the reader's expense, is hardly a way to inspire confidence in the facts of the narration. On several occasions in what is a highly self-conscious text we are told that particular events are nearly too fantastic to be believed. Pym himself admits that the 'incidents to be narrated' could only seem like 'an impudent and ingenious fiction' (p. 43). He and Augustus are

saved from the remnants of the wrecked *Ariel* because of 'almost incon-
ceivable pieces of good fortune' (p. 53). And Pym puts his own extended
survival down to a 'vast chain of apparent miracles' (p. 194). Lines such as
these are playful but unsettling: it is as if one can hear behind them a
ghostly laugh emanating from Poe, the would-be ghost-writer.

Part of the unspoken narrative contract of any book is that, as readers,
we choose to believe what we are being told, but of course this can only
happen if the person who is doing the narrating, and the narrative itself, is
credible. But from an early stage Augustus in particular is identified as
being unreliable. 'Schoolboys,' it is pointed out towards the end of the
opening chapter, 'can accomplish wonders in the way of deception'
(p. 56). The point being made here is not so much that Pym and Augustus
are dishonest, but that it is extremely difficult to maintain trust in
characters whose reading of events and other people is so consistently
open to question. In fact, Poe takes every opportunity to remind us that the
vessel of narration is just as suspect as the vessels of navigation it purports
to describe. The *Grampus* is packed 'full of books, chiefly books of voyages
and tales' (p. 61). Pym sets off on his adventure in the hold of the ship by
selecting an account of 'the expedition of Lewis and Clark to the mouth of
the Columbia' (p. 63). The narrative itself ends by literally dissolving in
front of us, as Poe removes the curtain of writing to reveal the white page
underneath. As readers, our confidence in the facts of the narration is
constantly undermined, and it is as if Poe is deliberately trying to encode
a kind of permanent sense of unease and wariness within his text. We are
told in the Preface, for instance, that Pym 'kept no journal during a greater
portion of the time in which [he] was absent' (p. 43), but a journal form is
adopted at several stages in the narrative. Pym even goes so far as to
produce 'a pocketbook and pencil' (p. 223) from nowhere in order to record
the mysterious hieroglyphics on Too-Wit's island. Poe borrows
extensively from other narratives and inserts them into his own. Clearly
then, this undermining of our trust as readers is as systematic as it is
deliberate. The writer is not only drawing attention to the suspect status of
his text, but to the fallibility of his audience. We ourselves are constantly
capable of being deceived, and part of the logic of Poe's method is to
remind us of this at every opportunity. We are as implicated in the facts of
the Fall as the protaganists of his book.

If the mind is fallen, it is because the world itself is fallen also. Evidence
of this is partly argued by the appearance of Nature in the text, for even it is
capable of deceit. Desolation Island, for instance, appears lush with
vegetation, but is in fact covered in saxifrage. Yet another island turns out
to be 'a low rocky islet' containing nothing more than a species of prickly
pear, a desert in all but name (p. 185). The Auroras, a group of islands
discovered by the Spanish in 1762, and seen again in 1790, are in fact
non-existent, and therefore revealed as a hoax. Observing a breed of

penguins, Pym remarks that 'the resemblance to a human figure is very striking, and would be apt to deceive the spectator at a casual glance or in the gloom of the evening' (p. 166). But Nature's crudest deception is the co-habitation on Kerguelen Island of the white albatross, king of the sea-birds, with the black penguins who pretend to be human. These two species seem to live together in great friendship and apparent harmony, and we are told that 'nothing can be more astonishing than the spirit of reflection evinced by these feathered beings, and nothing surely can be better calculated to elicit reflection in every well-regulated human intellect' (p. 169). In fact this invitation to consider the possible human significance of two breeds sharing the one living space is a trap, and one which prefigures the brief co-habitation of white sailors and black islanders on Tsalal. Speaking just before the ambush which ends this idyll, Pym claims that during 'the whole of this adventure we saw nothing in the demeanor of the natives calculated to create suspicion, with the single exception of the systematic manner in which their party was strengthened during our route from the schooner to the village' (p. 200). This of course is the most spectacular deception in the book, and one which results in the deaths of most of the crew of the *Jane Guy* and the horrific destruction of nearly a thousand natives when the boat is eventually blown up.

In fact this breach of trust on the part of the natives is at once the most bloody and the most significant one in the narrative, and it is possible to argue that the device of alerting the reader to one deception after another indicates a conscious and cumulative agenda at work in the book. Poe is warning his gullible public not about the dangers of fiction but about the perceived threat posed by the slave community in antebellum America. As the ship is navigated southwards to the whiteness and purity of Antarctica the narrative becomes increasingly concerned with historical Southern fears of black insurrection and massacre. The signposts are obvious. Towards the close of the novel, Pym is able to see from the *Jane Guy* 'a singular ledge of rock...projecting into the sea, and bearing a strange resemblance to corded bales of cotton' (p. 185). And the inhabitants of Tsalal are clearly projections, caricatures rather than characters. The males are associated with the biche-de-mer, the sea cucumber, and therefore with white prejudices about black sexual prowess. Speaking of the native women, Pym remarks on their nakedness but goes on to note that 'their lips, however, like those of the men, were thick and clumsy, so that even when laughing, the teeth were never disclosed'. In reality, of course, the teeth are not disclosed because Poe cannot bring himself to admit a possible connection, however small, between the natives and the whites.

The book ends as a kind of racist allegory, a sort of Pogrom's Progress. And its message is sanctioned by Scripture. Entering the native village for the first time, Pym refers to 'as many as forty (of them) sitting on their hams' (p. 198), and Harold Beaver has again demonstrated how Poe him-self believed that the practice of slavery was literally justified by the Bible, since it was a direct result of the curse of Ham, whose dark sons were 'fated to occupy the southernmost zones of the earth'.[5] Shortly after this, when he comes across the hieroglyphics, Pym believes that he is being deceived, but these figures turn out to be partly in Hebrew, the language of the Old Testament. The final lines of the book, 'I have graven it within the hills, and my vengeance upon the dust within the rock', are taken from the book of Job, and again demonstrate a continuing belief on Poe's part in the reality of the biblical curse, which has yet to be satisfactorily completed in his eyes. The point seems to be that only the signs of the Bible endure and are real, and only they can be relied upon. As I have argued, Poe develops the idea of men falling about drunk to argue that all humanity is in fact fallen. From this proceeds not a literary classic but a relentlessly literal reading of Scripture as it applies to the world of pre-Civil War America. Poe's delusions were not fostered by any alcoholic addic-tion, but by the Southern dream of white supremacy and the nightmare of racial hatred.

NOTES

1.   D. Ketterer, 'Tracing Shadows: *Pym* Criticism, 1980–90', in R. Kopley (ed.), *Poe's Pym: Critical Explorations* (Durham, NC: Duke University Press, 1992), pp. 233-74.

2.   R. Jarrell, *Poetry and the Age* (London: Faber & Faber, 1973), p. 106.

3.   E.A. Poe, *The Narrative of Arthur Gordon Pym* (ed. H. Beaver; Harmondsworth: Penguin, 1975), p. 50. All subsequent references in my text to the book are by page number to this edition.

4.   Beaver, *Commentary*, p. 257.

5.   Beaver, *Introduction*, p. 24.

OPIUM AND THE ROMANTIC IMAGINATION: THE CREATION OF A MYTH

Julian North

Two years after the *Confessions of an English Opium-Eater* was published in 1821, a reviewer commented that De Quincey had presented the public with 'a striking and almost a new subject'.[1] The *Confessions* celebrated opium not merely as a medicinal cure-all but as a source of hedonistic pleasure. The drug was described in terms of a religious cult: opium was God; the opium-eater a worshipper. De Quincey also made a significant and seductive link between opium and the creative imagination:

> thou buildest upon the bosom of darkness, out of the fantastic imagery of the brain, cities and temples, beyond the art of Phidias and Praxiteles... oh, just, subtle, and mighty opium![2]

The association between opium and the Romantic imagination has proved a potent one for a number of twentieth-century commentators who have tried to attribute certain effects in the work of De Quincey and other opium-addicted writers specifically to the action of the drug. The central question posed by Alethea Hayter, for instance, in her book *Opium and the Romantic Imagination*, was: '[d]oes opium affect the creative processes of writers who use it?'[3] In asking this she was following in the wake of M.H. Abrams and Elizabeth Schneider, both of whom produced studies trying to find out what it was about the work of an opium addict, if anything, that was traceable to the opium itself.[4]

Schneider concluded that there was, in fact, nothing in the work of Coleridge that was a product of opium alone. But both Abrams and Hayter singled out groups of images commonly found in opium addicts' writing, thereby suggesting a shared source of imaginative stimulus in the drug itself. Hayter further suggested that opium addicts could gain a special awareness of their own creative processes through the use of the drug, since, as she argued, opium at once retrieves thoughts and memories from the depths of the mind and allows the addict to observe the mechanisms of that retrieval.[5]

Clearly there are problems with this effort to trace the imagery and structures of a text to the action of opium—problems recognized to some extent by all the critics mentioned above. To begin with, the images favoured by opium addicts are, of course, used by non-addict writers too. Although De Quincey's idea of the 'involute', for example, may have derived, as Hayter suggested, from his observation of the action of opium on his own memory, it might equally well have been influenced by his reading of *The Prelude*, and particularly by Wordsworth's 'spots of time'.[6] As De Quincey argues at the beginning of the *Confessions*, even under the influence of opium, the man ' "whose talk is of oxen"...will dream about oxen' (p. 5), and Hayter has to acknowledge that '[o]pium works on what is already there in a man's mind and memory'.[7] In trying to trace the effects specifically attributable to opium in addict writing, Abrams and Hayter are inevitably engaged on a circular quest.

Few would now argue with the dubiousness of using the *Confessions*, or any other such text, as a source for speculations upon opium's effects on the imagination of the writer. Coleridge's attribution of 'Kubla Khan' to a certain 'anodyne' has long been regarded as a fiction, and De Quincey's representation of opium's power over his mental faculties must also be looked at sceptically as a self-serving mythic construction.[8] The trouble is that both Abrams and Hayter are seduced by the opium myth as they are by the discourse of Romantic imagination—Hayter's book even ends with an account of a dream she had while writing it. Perhaps as a consequence, neither critic recognizes the important senses in which the opium vision, as represented by nineteenth-century writers, is at odds with dominant Romantic conceptions of the imagination.

Instead of asking whether opium produced certain common effects in work by writers addicted to the substance, what I want to do in the following discussion is to look more closely at the nature of the literary myth of opium's power over the imagination, as it first evolved in Britain in the last century. In so doing I am particularly interested in the ways in which that myth altered the Romantic models of the imagination it inherited. Although I will touch on a fairly wide range of material, the focus of this discussion will be on De Quincey's *Confessions of an English Opium-Eater* as the most important English text dealing with the subject of opium.

In the years leading up to the publication of the *Confessions* it is noticeable how rarely and tentatively any association was made between opium and imaginative stimulation. Indeed, opium was almost always written about in the early Romantic period as a sedative rather than a stimulant, reflecting the widespread use of the drug at the period as a household painkiller.[9] For instance, in an anonymous poem of 1796, entitled 'A Sonnet to Opium; Celebrating its Virtues. Written at the Side of Julia, when the Author was Inspired with a Dose of Laudanum, more than Sufficient for two Moderate Turks', although the author is 'inspired' by the drug, far from being a stimulant, it is shown to be the only way he can suppress his passions: 'Guardian you are of Julia's innocence, / When madd'ning rapture, goads to vice my throbbing sense'.[10] In Charles Lloyd's novel *Edmund Oliver* (1798), the hero, modelled on Coleridge, samples laudanum as a means of escaping his sorrows. '[D]elerious daydreams' are mentioned, but there is no development of this.[11] Lloyd condemns opium as a passive indulgence, both for the hero and for Gertrude, the fallen heroine, who commits suicide by swallowing a bottle of laudanum.[12]

Coleridge, too, represents opium as a sedative, dangerously destructive of the will. The crux of his anxieties about his own use of the drug was whether it was for the attainment of pleasure or the release from pain. Sensual gratification as an end in itself he considered a manifestation of 'the will not to be in God'.[13] Even in his prefatory note to 'Kubla Khan' Coleridge does not directly associate the drug with mental stimulation. He has been prescribed the 'anodyne' to cure an illness (dysentery as we learn from the unpublished MS), and the drug induces a deep sleep during which the poem is composed, significantly, 'without any sensation or consciousness of effort'.[14] Certainly, this does not conform to Coleridge's conception of the secondary imagination, voiced in the *Biographia Literaria*, as an 'essentially vital' faculty.[15] Rather than suggesting that opium can stimulate the imagination, Coleridge uses the note to 'Kubla Khan' as a way of suggesting his mental passivity, thereby devolving responsibility from himself both for what he has written and for what has supposedly been lost.

Against this background, the provocations of De Quincey's association between opium and imaginative stimulation in the *Confessions* are all the more in evidence. The suggestion that opium is a sedative eroding the will is still present in De Quincey's account, of course; he writes for instance of the 'Circean spells of opium' which prevented him from finishing his *Prolegomena to all Future Systems of Political Economy* (p. 66). However, this image of the drug is countered throughout by irony (the *Prolegomena* was 'itself...sufficient opiate') and by a competing image of the drug as a stimulant, whether physical, as on his Saturday night wanderings, or, more often, mental, in his night-long meditations and his frantic dreams.[16]

This association between opium and the imagination does not fit comfortably into the context of a Romantic interest in drugs and dreams, as Hayter's book suggests, but undercuts and even parodies dominant contemporary models of the imagination. In many senses, for instance, the *Confessions* sets itself up in rivalry to Coleridge's *Biographia Literaria*.[17] As De Quincey writes in his 'Preliminary Confessions' this will be the autobiography of a man who 'boasteth himself to be a philosopher', and the only other Englishman who can truly lay claim to this title is Coleridge (p. 5). However, where the theory of the imagination forms the centrepiece of Coleridge's philosophical autobiography, De Quincey's work hinges on his apostrophe to the powers of opium, 'Oh! just, subtle, and mighty opium!' (p. 49). Where Coleridge, famously, reneges on his promise of a full exposition of the theory of imagination in chapter thirteen of the *Biographia*, De Quincey withdraws the promised self-justification for his opium habit. Like Coleridge, he reserves explanation for publication at a later date and merely '*postulate[s]*' as much as is necessary for his purpose.[18] Such parallels seem parodic. In place of imagination De Quincey holds up the much more equivocal agency of opium, characterized as at once a divine power ('thou hast the keys of Paradise' [p. 49]) and an artificial commodity ('happiness might now be bought for a penny, and carried in the waistcoat pocket: portable ecstasies might be had corked up in a pint bottle' [p. 39]).

The impression of parody is enhanced by the fact that the *Confessions* contains a thinly-veiled attack on Coleridge for his moral censure of De Quincey's opium habit.[19] This attack was continued in later years when De Quincey carried on a long public dispute with Coleridge about whether he used the drug as a stimulant or a sedative. At first each writer accused the other of using opium as a sensual indulgence, but in his essay 'Coleridge and Opium-Eating' (1845) De Quincey shifted his ground and openly defended the drug as a 'voluptuous stimulant', and a cure for '*ennui*'.[20] The 1856 revised version of the *Confessions* includes a prolonged and open dispute with Coleridge over the use of the drug as a stimulant. It is perfectly justifiable, De Quincey argues, to take the drug as a source of '*extra* power and enjoyment', not merely to ward off '*extra* torment'.[21] The quarrel with Coleridge gave De Quincey a public platform from which to define his defence of the drug, in opposition to what was essentially an objection to ungodly mental passivity. In so doing De Quincey moved from a combative anti-earnestness to a progressively more serious defence of opium as a pleasurable mental stimulant.

De Quincey's dispute with Coleridge was a significant factor in shaping his representation of opium as an agent of imaginative power. However, the response to Wordsworth in the *Confessions* may be even more important here. De Quincey recorded the gradual souring of his personal relationship with the poet in essays published in 1839 and 1840.[22] Although he maintained that he had never lost his admiration for Wordsworth's poetry, he seems to have become alienated from Wordsworth's belief in his own special relationship with the natural world. He describes, for instance, Wordsworth's belief that no one but himself and his close family circle were fit to comment on the natural beauties around them. After seeing Wordsworth cold-shouldering all who stood outside the 'sacred and privileged pale' of nature-worshippers, De Quincey '[s]ystematically...avoided saying anything, however suddenly tempted into any expression of my feelings, upon the natural appearances whether in the sky or on the earth'.[23]

The quarrel with Wordsworth, and particularly this aspect of it, had important ramifications for the *Confessions*, De Quincey's first book, written immediately after leaving the Lakes in 1821. Not only had Wordsworth and his family expressed open dismay at De Quincey's opium habit; they had made it clear he was an outsider to their natural paradise.[24] De Quincey's decision to make his mark as a writer on the London literary scene with a book about the paradise of opium might be seen as a riposte in itself, and there is much in the *Confessions* to confirm that suspicion.

Although the book is, in many respects, a homage to Wordsworth—a kind of prose *Prelude*—it is also a gesture against Wordsworth's nature-dominated aesthetic. By making his landscape the city and his source of mental stimulation opium, De Quincey replaces the natural with the artificial and offers an image of himself as opium-eater which parodies the Wordsworthian poet. Thus, as in the case of his quarrel with Coleridge, the terms in which De Quincey shapes his representation of opium are, to some extent at least, dictated by the grounds of his dispute with Wordsworth. This becomes particularly clear in relation to the network of parodic allusion to Wordsworth's poetry that can be found in the *Confessions*.

For instance, as I have argued elsewhere, the opening of 'The Pleasures of Opium' contains an important allusion to Wordsworth's poem 'Resolution and Independence'.[25] The poet in this latter piece is cured of his despondency by the intervention of a leech-gatherer, 'like a Man from some far region sent, / To give me human strength, and strong admonishment'.[26] As an emanation of nature and a seemingly divine emissary the leech-gatherer provides the crucial therapeutic stimulus to the poet's imagination.[27] However, in the *Confessions*, instead of a leech-gatherer on a moor De Quincey meets, on Oxford Street, '[t]he druggist—unconscious minister of celestial pleasures!', who 'has ever since existed in my mind as the beatific vision of an immortal druggist, sent down to earth on a special mission to myself' (p. 38). Wordsworth's natural setting is thus replaced by the artificial and urban; his divine agency of imagination, working through nature, is, in De Quincey's account, an artificial stimulant available for sale.

Even the famous apostrophe, 'O! just, subtle, and mighty opium!' (p. 49), the rhetorical centrepiece of the *Confessions* and De Quincey's most unequivocal hymn of praise to the drug, contains in the space of a single sentence three quotations from Wordsworth. The very fact that De Quincey thus appropriated the words of a poet who so vigorously opposed artificial stimulants suggests at least some kind of oedipal struggle. Added to this, the quotations, which come from *The White Doe of Rylstone* and *The Excursion*, have again been recontextualized in such a way as to replace Wordsworth's praise of the restorative powers of poetry, God, nature, duty and reason with opium.[28]

These allusions, both general and specific, to Coleridge and Wordsworth suggest the degree to which De Quincey's construction of a myth of opium's power over the imagination depended on current models of the poetic imagination, but also subverted them. However, perhaps because this image of opium challenged notions, sacred to many, of artistic free will and the communion of the poet with a divine spirit in nature, De Quincey's representation of opium as a mental stimulant was slow to catch on in British writing.

Despite the immediate and continuing popularity of the *Confessions* in this country, it was not until the mid-nineteenth century that evidence of an increased interest in opium's stimulant possibilities and in its effects upon the imagination began to emerge. Signs of this can be seen in Charlotte Brontë's *Villette* (1853), when Lucy Snowe, under the influence of laudanum, gets up from her bed ('Imagination was roused from her rest') and wanders the streets experiencing the town as a multi-coloured hallucination (chapter 38). In *The Mystery of Edwin Drood* (1870), Dickens attempted to recreate the waking dream of an opium addict, if rather artificially with visions of Turkish dancing girls, and suggested that Jasper had dreamt in the past of 'great landscapes and glittering processions' (chapter 1). In *Middlemarch* (1871–72) Ladislaw's sensation-seeking past has included not only experiments with wine and lobster but also with 'doses of opium' (chapter 10).

All these writers refer implicitly or explicitly to De Quincey, suggesting the extent of his influence upon what references there are to opium and the imagination. However, it is more remarkable that he was so comparatively little followed in nineteenth-century British writing in this respect. This is especially puzzling when we consider how enthusiastically he was taken up in France from the 1830s onwards by Gautier, Baudelaire, Huysmans, de Goncourt and others.[29] It was the French influence that produced, in British writing of the 1890s, the nearest equivalents to De Quincey's assertions of opium's power over the imagination, rather than any native tradition.

Late nineteenth-century British writers such as Symons and Wilde followed Baudelaire, Gautier and Huysmans, in particular, in representing opium as an agent of dream and an adjunct of the artistic life; this can be seen for instance in Symons's poem 'The Opium-Smoker', or Wilde's *The Picture of Dorian Gray* (1890–91).[30] Like their French forebears, and like De Quincey, Symons and Wilde at once employ a Romantic image of the artist and challenge it by introducing an artificial stimulant. Symons's opium smoker, in an urban garret, has pawned his soul to his pipe. Wilde's hero, Dorian Gray, uses hashish and opium as part of his self-conscious quest to live a life against nature. The artificiality of the drug experience is emphasized by the enshrinement of his hashish as itself an art object, placed within a cabinet 'made out of ebony, and inlaid with ivory and blue lapis' and a 'Chinese box of black and gold-dust lacquer, elaborately wrought'.[31]

The social and cultural differences which may have produced this divergence of reactions to the *Confessions* in Britain and France are far-reaching, and there is no space to do justice to the subject here. However, one reason would seem to be the existence in France of a tradition of literary Decadence which challenged the Romantic hegemony of nature over art to an extent that was not paralleled in Britain. Interest in the links between opium, hashish and the imagination was, for Baudelaire and his followers, part of a wider questioning of the Romantic religion of nature.[32] Although always highly equivocal on the subject of the artist's recourse to artificial stimulants, these writers used opium and hashish polemically, to show imagination pitched against nature in what Baudelaire referred to in the title of his seminal work on drugs as 'artificial paradises'.

It is, perhaps, a measure of the challenge offered by the myth of opium's creative potential to existing models of artistic genius that, on the whole, nineteenth-century British writing makes such tentative links between opium and the imagination. Although De Quincey, Baudelaire and those writers who followed them use a familiar Romantic vocabulary of solitary vision and aspiration to the infinite and the ideal, they also emphasize the artificiality of opium. The 'paradise' of opium was a complex and provocative construction which can neither be read simplistically as a record of the addict-writer's actual experience, nor merely be assimilated to the more familiar models of Romantic imagination.

NOTES

1.   Anon., *New Edinburgh Review* 4 (January 1823), p. 273. T. De Quincey, *Confessions of an English Opium-Eater* (first published in *London Magazine* 4.21 [September 1821], pp. 293-312; 4.22 [October 1821], pp. 353-79).

2.   T. De Quincey, *Confessions of an English Opium-Eater and Other Writings* (ed. G. Lindop; World's Classics; Oxford: Oxford University Press, 1985), p. 49. All subsequent references to the *Confessions* will be to this edition.

3.   A. Hayter, *Opium and the Romantic Imagination* (London: Faber & Faber, 1968), p. 12.

4.   M.H. Abrams, *The Milk of Paradise: The Effect of Opium Visions on the Works of De Quincey, Crabbe, Francis Thompson, and Coleridge* (Cambridge, MA: Harvard University Press, 1934); E. Schneider, *Coleridge, Opium and 'Kubla Khan'* (Chicago: University of Chicago Press; London: Cambridge University Press, 1953).

5.   Hayter, *Opium*, p. 334.

6.   Hayter, *Opium*, p. 335. See W. Wordsworth, *The Prelude* (1805), book ix, l. 257.

7.   Hayter, *Opium*, p. 331.

8.   See Coleridge's prefatory note to 'Kubla Khan: Or, a Vision in a Dream. A Fragment' (1816), in E.H. Coleridge (ed.), *The Complete Poetical Works of Samuel Taylor Coleridge* (2 vols.; Oxford: Clarendon Press, 1975 [1912]), I, p. 296.

9.   See V. Berridge and G. Edwards, *Opium and the People: Opiate Use in Nineteenth-Century England* (London: Allen Lane; New York: St Martin's Press, 1981).

10.   R. Lonsdale (ed.), *The New Oxford Book of Eighteenth-Century Verse* (Oxford: Oxford University Press, 1987), p. 818.

11.   C. Lloyd, *Edmund Oliver* (2 vols.; Bristol: Bulgin & Rosser, for Joseph Cottle, 1798), II, p. 213.

12. Lloyd, *Edmund Oliver*, II, p. 172.

13. See J. Gillman, *The Life of Samuel Taylor Coleridge* (London: Pickering, 1838), pp. 249-50.

14. E.H. Coleridge (ed.), *The Complete Poetical Works of Samuel Taylor Coleridge*, I, p. 296. See also J. Shelton, 'The Autograph Manuscript of "Kubla Khan" and an Interpretation', *A Review of English Literature* 7.1 (January, 1966), pp. 32-42.

15. *Biographia Literaria* (1817), in K. Coburn (ed.), *The Collected Works of Samuel Taylor Coleridge* (Bollingen Series, 75; Princeton: Princeton University Press; London: Routledge & Kegan Paul, 1971–), VII.ii, p. 304.

16. See *Confessions*, pp. 66, 46-49, 67-77.

17. For a discussion of the *Confessions* as 'a materialist "assassination" of Coleridge's *Biographia Literaria*' see N. Leask, *British Romantic Writers and the East: Anxieties of Empire* (Cambridge: Cambridge University Press, 1992), pp. 170-228.

18. *Confessions*, p. 52. Coleridge applies the term 'postulates' from mathematics to philosophy in chapter xii of the *Biographia*. This is listed by the *OED* as the first English usage of the word in the sense of 'to assume the possibility of (some construction or operation)'. The fact that De Quincey italicizes the word on introducing it and uses it four times in the space of a few lines may suggest a parody of this.

19. See *Confessions*, p. 2, where Coleridge is alluded to in a note, though not by name, as the only man to have exceeded De Quincey in his opium doses. For Coleridge's disapproval of De Quincey's opium habit, see Gillman, *Life of Coleridge*, pp. 248, 251.

20. D. Masson (ed.), *The Collected Writings of Thomas De Quincey* (14 vols.; London: A. & C. Black, 1896–97), V, p. 210.

21. *Confessions of an English Opium-Eater* (1856), Masson (ed.), *Collected Writings*, III, p. 224.

22. 'William Wordsworth' (1839); 'The Lake Poets: William Wordsworth and Robert Southey' (1839); 'Gradual Estrangement from Wordsworth' (extracted from 'Walking Stewart'; 1840), in Masson (ed.), *Collected Writings*, II, pp. 229-332; III, pp. 197-206.

23. 'Gradual Estrangement from Wordsworth', Masson (ed.), *Collected Writings*, III, pp. 198-99.

24. See for example the letter from Mary Wordsworth to Dorothy Wordsworth, 29 October 1814, in M.E. Burton (ed.), *The Letters of Mary Wordsworth, 1800–1855* (Oxford: Clarendon Press, 1958), pp. 24-25.

25. See my 'Leeches and Opium: De Quincey Replies to "Resolution and Independence" in *Confessions of an English Opium-Eater*', forthcoming in *Modern Language Review*.

26. 'Resolution and Independence' (1807), ll. 118-19, in J. Curtis (ed.), *Poems in Two Volumes, and other Poems by William Wordsworth, 1800–1807* (Ithaca, NY: Cornell University Press, 1983), p. 128.

27. See 'Resolution and Independence', ll. 134-47, p. 129.

28. *The White Doe of Rylstone* (1815) and *The Excursion* (1814). For a full discussion of these parodies see my 'Thomas De Quincey and the Early History of Aestheticism and Decadence' (D.Phil dissertation; Oxford University, 1990), pp. 283-85.

29. For the general and specific influence of De Quincey on these writers see T. Gautier, 'La Pipe d'opium', *La Presse* (27 September 1838), 'Le Hachisch', *La Presse* (10 July 1843) and 'Le Club des hachischins', *Revue des deux mondes* (1 February 1846); C. Baudelaire, *Les Paradis artificiels: opium et hachisch* (Paris: Poulet-Malassis & De Broise, 1860), which included a free translation of the *Confessions*; J.-K. Huysmans, *A Rebours* (1884), reprinted in *Oeuvres complètes de J.-K. Huysmans* (Paris: Editions G. Crès, 1928–54), VII, pp. 155-56; E. de Goncourt, *La Faustin*, *Le Voltaire* (November 1881).

30. Arthur Symons's 'The Opium-Smoker' is closely modelled on Baudelaire's prose poem 'La Chambre Double'. The fact that Dorian Gray takes hashish as well as opium suggests Wilde's French allegiances.

31. R. Ross (ed.), *The Works of Oscar Wilde* (15 vols.; London: Methuen, 1908–22 [facsimile reprint; London: Dawsons of Pall Mall, 1969]), II, pp. 295-96.

32. For Baudelaire's discussion of the term 'decadence' and his anti-naturalism see for example his 'Notes nouvelles sur Edgar Poe' (1857), in C. Pichois (ed.), *Baudelaire; Oeuvres complètes* (Pléiade; 2 vols.; Paris: Gallimard, 1975–76), II, pp. 319-25.

'HO! FOR THE SANGRAAL!'
OPIUM AND R.S. HAWKER'S ARTHURIAN LEGEND

Sheila Smith

In June 1875, after months of ill-health, Robert Stephen Hawker (1803–75), his second wife Pauline and their three young daughters vacated their vicarage at Morwenstow on the North Cornish coast for the new curate and his large family, to enable them to settle more easily into their own new abode, and went to stay with Hawker's brother Claud in nearby Boscastle. But Claud was also ill so, as they could not immediately return home, Hawker and his family went on to Plymouth, his birthplace, where he died in private lodgings on 15 August. On 24 September Claud wrote to the Reverend Frederick George Lee, an early biographer of Hawker's:

> My brother was an opium eater for 40 years of his life. Under the influence of opium he was all the time he was here (i.e. in Boscastle). His wife gave him the doses and he was in a state of oblivion all the time he was here and at Plymouth.[1]

(In 1875 opium addiction was something to be ashamed of.[2] Alethea Hayter in *Opium and the Romantic Imagination*[3] points out that many earlier opium eaters, such as Coleridge, felt distressed by the effects of the addiction and longed for release from it, but were not ashamed that they were addicts. Opium was used as a readily available medicine.)

Hawker had certainly read De Quincey, and refers to him in his notebooks, but it seems that he first took opium, like so many Victorians, as a medicine. His son-in-law C.E. Byles, writing of his picturesque belief in demons and angels, says:

> He took opium, at first as a medicine, afterwards from habit, and there can be little doubt that this explained a great deal in his character and mental attitude. [Hayter might have argued that his character and mental attitude were such as to require opium for stimulus or as a tranquillizer.] Under its influence, perhaps, much of his finest work in poetry was written; but it had its inevitable reaction, in irritability, and moods of profound depression. He broke himself of the habit after his second marriage [i.e. wedding], but renewed it some years before his death.[4]

Perhaps. As Hayter says, the connection between opium and the writing of poetry is always conjecture; we cannot know what the poet would have written without the drug.[5] In Hawker's case it is arguable that the taking of opium helped him write his finest and most ambitious poetic fragment, *The Quest of the Sangraal* (1864). Despite its unpromising first line, 'Ho! for the Sangraal! vanish'd Vase of Heaven!', typical of Hawker's stubborn antiquarianism in the use of 'vase' despite its inappropriate modern connotations, it is one of the most interesting Victorian evocations of the Arthurian legend. Its power lies in the success with which Hawker makes the supernatural immanent in the Cornish landscape and seascape. It can be argued that opium helped focus a previously fragmented imagination on King Arthur as an emblem of Hawker's own predicament and on Cornwall, as Hawker knew it in his daily life, as Arthur's kingdom.[6] For, although he wrote the poem in 1863 after the death of his first wife Charlotte when he was almost certainly using opium to combat his grief and depression, there is evidence that the subject had long been in his thoughts. Nicholas Ross, writing to Cecil Woolf on 26 June 1963, says 'at least parts of it, and certainly notes for it which I possess in Hawker's hand, were in his desk as early as 1839'.[7]

Morwenstow—which is not a village, but a scatter of hamlets—was extremely isolated in Hawker's day. He felt this isolation, particularly the lack of intellectual stimulus; yet he loved the moors and the cliffs, and particularly the sea, despite the distress it caused him when it destroyed the ships which passed so close to his church. He saw them all as emblems of God; and from his study window at the top of the vicarage he could see the Atlantic cupped as in a grail between two cliffs. His imagination responded to his remote Cornish parish not least because, when he arrived there in 1834, it was still, as Margaret Burrows points out, medieval.[8] His jottings in his many notebooks, as well as his poems and tales, reveal his love for the Celtic Church, his belief in its continuing presence and his affinity with its mixture of mysticism and superstition. He also had the power to locate ancient legend, especially Celtic legend, in the places and events of his own life. He delighted that his beautiful church stood on the site of a Saxon shrine and insisted that 'Morwenstow' meant 'the place of St Morwena', the Christian missionary daughter of the Celtic Welsh King Breachan. There are no records to support this. But, for Hawker,

> How all things glow with life and thought,
>   Where'er our faithful fathers trod!
> The very ground with speech is fraught
>   The air is eloquent of God.[9]

Apart from his Newdigate Prize Poem, *Sangraal* is his only poem of a sustained length. Its power was recognised by both Longfellow and Tennyson (who said 'Hawker has beaten me on my own ground').[10] Like

Emily Brontë in *Wuthering Heights* echoing the late medieval ballads, Hawker in *Sangraal* accepts the supernatural as part of ordinary human experience and, like the medieval dramatist of the Wakefield Second Shepherds' Play who locates the angels' appearance to the shepherds before Christ's Nativity outside Wakefield, he describes King Arthur, the Knights of the Round Table and Merlin inhabiting the Tintagel, not of contemporary literary fashion, but the place he could see from his own cliffs; although, typically, he gives it its old name, Dundagel. The Knights, prepared to set forth on the quest for the Holy Grail, are

> Of the siege perilous, and the granite ring—
> They gathered at the rock, yon ruddy tor.
>> [Routor, the 'red hill', covered in heather]

When Merlin shows the king the vision of the battle for the Grail

> ...Dundagel shuddered into storm—
> The deep foundations shook beneath the sea;
> Yet there they stood, beneath the murky moon,
> Above the bastion, Merlin and the King.
> Thrice waved the sage his staff, and thrice they saw
> A peopled vision throng the rocky moor.

When they see Galahad holding the Grail light falls from it

> As though the pavement of the sky brake up,
> And stars were shed to sojourn on the hills,
> From Grey Morwenna's stone to Michael's tor
>> [St Michael's Mount],
> Until the rocky land was like a heaven.

'The rocky land' was Hawker's phrase for Cornwall.

Near the end of the poem comes Merlin's vision of contemporary Victorian England, materialistic, intent on war, bereft of the Grail. The horrific intensity of the vision might owe something to opium dreams:

> Troops of the demon-north, in yellow garb,
> The sickly hue of vile Iscariot's hair,
> Mingle with men, in unseen multitudes!...
> The shrines were darkened and the chalice void:
> That which held God was gone: Maran-atha!
> The awful shadows of the Sangraal, fled!
> Yet giant-men arose, that seemed as gods,
> Such might they gathered from the swarthy kind:
> The myths were rendered up: and one by one,
> The Fire—the Light—the Air—were tamed and bound
> Like votive vassals at their chariot-wheel.
> Then learnt they War...

Merlin responds:

> 'Ah! native England! wake thine ancient cry;
> Ho! for the Sangraal! vanish'd Vase of Heaven,

That held, like Christ's own heart, an hin of blood!'
['hin' was a Hebrew measure used for the wine
of the sacrifice]

The poem ends on the Cornish coast:

He ceased; and all around was dreamy night:
There stood Dundagel, throned: and the great sea
Lay, a strong vassal at his master's gate,
And, like a drunken giant, sobb'd in sleep!

The whole poem, as we have it, needs to be read to get its cumulative effect, and the appeal of the blank verse which Hawker made a vehicle for his own sonorous voice; in extracts his sometimes florid figures of speech are obtrusive. Only four lines of the three other planned 'Chants' of *Sangraal* were ever written, seemingly supporting Byles's argument that opium eventually had a destructive effect on Hawker's life. It could be argued that, with his marriage in December 1864 to the young governess in a clergyman friend's family and the birth of his three daughters, day-to-day concerns of life overwhelmed him so that sustained literary creation became impossible. His last letters, despite love for his wife and delight in his babies, are a catalogue of ill-health and depression. He had always been given to self-dramatization and to self-pity, but his increasing sense of his isolation as he wrestled alone in his study with the terror of not being able to provide for his young family during his life or of leaving them penniless on his approaching death might have an element of the addict's growing feeling of isolation described so vividly by Alethea Hayter.

NOTES

1.   Bodleian Ms. Eng. Misc. d. 16 f105.
2.   Mr W. Waddon Martyn, owner of Tonacombe near Hawker's vicarage, who was kind enough to show me some of Hawker's books in his possession and to discuss some of Hawker's letters written to the Reverend William Waddon Martyn who owned Tonacombe in Hawker's day, said that there was suppressed scandal after Hawker's death about his taking opium. The other scandal, which provoked controversy in the national press, was Hawker's death-bed conversion to Roman Catholicism.
3.   A. Hayter, *Opium and the Romantic Imagination* (London: Faber & Faber, 1968), pp. 29, 34.
4.   C.E. Byles, *The Life and Letters of R.S. Hawker* (New York: John Lane; London: Bodley Head, 1906), p. 102.
5.   Hayter, *Opium*, p. 334.
6.   Piers Brendon in his *Hawker of Morwenstow* (London: Jonathan Cape, 1975) has a useful chapter, 'Opium', in which he argues that the drug possibly helped Hawker to focus previously fragmented images in *Sangraal*, but does not remark on the unifying power of Hawker's vision of Cornwall in the poem.
7.   Bodleian Ms. Eng. Misc. d. 650/3 f46.

8.   M. Burrows, *Robert Stephen Hawker: A Study of his Thought and Poetry* (Oxford: Oxford University Press, 1926), p. 100.

9.   'Morwennae Statio', from *Ecclesia* (1840).

10.   Byles, *Life and Letters of R.S. Hawker*, p. 41.

PART III

Theories of Consumption

FAT WOMEN AND FOOD

Mary Condé

Audrey Eyton, author of *The F-Plan Diet*, points out pitilessly that, 'unfortunately, if your bosom is drooping over your stomach, people tend to think you're a dreary old bat'.[1] How is it then that fat women allow themselves to get so fat? What is the cause of fatness? The London Fat Women's Group, which held its first national conference in March 1989 and had to turn away four hundred women (for lack of space),[2] denies that the simple cause of fatness is overeating.[3] But the popular view remains that of Joan, the once-fat narrator of Margaret Atwood's *Lady Oracle*: fatness is 'a disgusting failure of will'.[4] Mrs Hawkins, another once-fat narrator, of Muriel Spark's *A Far Cry from Kensington*, offers this implacable wisdom:

> I can tell you that if there's nothing wrong with you except fat it is easy to get thin. You eat and drink the same as always, only half. If you are handed a plate of food, leave half; if you have to help yourself, take half. After a while, if you are a perfectionist, you can consume half of that again... I offer this advice without fee; it is included in the price of this book.[5]

Few people seem to dispute that for Western women the gaining of weight has come to mean the loss of power. Shelley Bovey in her polemic *Being Fat is not a Sin* claims that 'it is only on the telephone that a fat woman can claim equality'.[6] Many feminist writers, like Kim Chernin, the author of *Womansize: The Tyranny of Slenderness*, who looks back nostalgically to the days when Marilyn Monroe (a size 16)[7] was admired by all of us,[8] see this as a growing male conspiracy. Susie Orbach argues in *Fat is a Feminist Issue* that fat women may become fat precisely because they fear the power of being thin.[9] The 'disgusting failure of will' is really a disgusting failure of nerve, so that Mrs Hawkins is addressing very few fat women with her caveat 'if there's nothing wrong with you except fat'.

Addiction to food, then, has an underlying purpose. Joan in *Lady Oracle* is at times frightened by her new, thin, state, and rushes to 'eat all the dry doughnuts and pieces of fishglue pie' she can afford because she 'longed to be fat again. It would be an insulation, a cocoon. Also it would be a disguise. I could be merely an onlooker again, with nothing too much expected of me.'[10] Similarly, Mrs Hawkins in *A Far Cry From Kensington* realizes that the advantage of her fatness was that the aggrieved authors at the publishers where she worked perceived her as too vulnerable to be attacked.[11]

Paradoxically, the weakness conferred by fatness can become a source of strength. Mrs Manson Mingott in Edith Wharton's *The Age of Innocence*, immobilized by the 'immense accretion of flesh' which had descended on her 'like a flood of lava on a doomed city',[12] uses it to compel the society of old New York to come to her. Faith, the narrator of Grace Paley's short story 'The Long-Distance Runner', negotiates her way into the apartment building where she used to live through her disarmingly stout appearance. ('When you seen a fatter ass?'[13] the neighbours ask each other companionably.) The grieving war mother Mamaw, 'so fat she has to sleep in a special brassiere',[14] becomes the epitome of survival at the climax of Bobbie Ann Mason's *In Country* as she clambers up the Vietnam Veterans Memorial, 'her flab hanging loose and sad'.[15] The Fat Lady, the audience for J.D. Salinger's prodigies the Glass children, pictured by them as 'sitting on this porch all day, swatting flies, with her radio going full-blast from morning till night',[16] is revealed, in an epiphany of narcissism, as Christ himself. In all these instances fatness, with its pathos of the dispossessed, is used to smuggle through an unsuspected power. But in all these instances, too, fatness carries a strong sense of the absurd.

A sense of the absurd is not far removed from the censorious when it comes to fat women. Henry James's real-life model for Miss Birdseye in *The Bostonians* was Elizabeth Peabody, by then a venerable old reformer nicknamed 'the Grandmother of Boston'. Unlike Miss Birdseye, Elizabeth Peabody was fat, and her nephew Julian Hawthorne, Nathaniel Hawthorne's son, tells this anecdote about her:

> We had a cat, and the cat had had kittens a day or two before. Aunt Lizzie came into the nursery, where Una and I were building houses of blocks, and sat down in the big easy-chair. The cat was in the room, and she immediately came up to my aunt and began to mew and to pluck at her dress with her claws. Such attentions were rare on pussy's part, and my aunt noticed them with pleasure, and caressed the animal, which still continued to devote its entire attention to her. But there was something odd in the sound of her mewing and in the intent regard of her yellow eyes. 'Can anything be the matter with pussy?' speculated my aunt. At that moment my father entered the room, and my aunt rose to greet him. Then the massacre was revealed, for she had been sitting upon the kittens. Their poor mother pounced upon them with a yowl, but it was too late. My dear aunt was rather a heavy woman, and she had been sitting there fifteen minutes. We all stood appalled in the presence of the great mystery.[17]

Henry James himself denied that he had used Elizabeth Peabody as a model for Miss Birdseye (although circumstantial evidence is against him), claiming in a letter to his brother William that 'Miss Birdseye was evolved entirely from my moral consciousness, like every other person I have ever drawn'. He goes on to say that Miss Birdseye originated in his desire to embody humanity and transcendental tendencies 'in a sympathetic, pathetic, picturesque, and at the same time grotesque way'.[18] Bruce A. Ronda, the editor of Peabody's letters, gives as his verdict: 'Henry James had portrayed Elizabeth Palmer Peabody in his novel. He had reversed only the physical size of the real and fictional reformers, and had kept true to the weight of her impact.'[19]

But the weight of her impact is not in the least altered by the weight of Peabody's fictional counterpart. Miss Birdseye would have been equally grotesque had James left her fat, and indeed he could easily have used the real-life episode of the kittens in his novel to illustrate Miss Birdseye's hopelessly well-meaning incompetence. The difference a fat Miss Birdseye would have made is the intrusion of that question, 'How is it that fat women allow themselves to get so fat?' There is something troubling about a fat reformer. Reactions to fatness are usually tinged with something of the spitefulness of John Steinbeck's description in *Tortilla Flat* of 'fat ladies in whose eyes lay the weariness and the wisdom one sees so often in the eyes of pigs'.[20]

John Waters, the director of *Hairspray*, has explained that, 'to me, Fat stands for every minority',[21] and fatness is often linked to the examination of race in fiction. In Flannery O'Connor's story 'The Artificial Nigger' the ten-year-old white boy Nelson is sexually mesmerised by an enormous black woman and 'her tremendous bosom'.[22] There is a similarly farcical scene in Ann Petry's *The Narrows* (a work similarly bleak about racial stereotyping), in which the white patriarch Old Copper insists on 'a big fat colored woman' as his grandson's nurse, a woman who turns out to have a soporific effect even on adults.[23]

In two later African-American novels two hugely fat black women move from the comic to the terrifying. Ruby in Gloria Naylor's *Mama Day*, described as not so much a woman as an event,[24] becomes murderous through sexual jealousy. Another Ruby, in Mary Monroe's *The Upper Room*, tears a man's arm off his body.[25] Jokes are made at these women's expense, but their size signals their power to transgress social boundaries. In Dorothy West's novel *The Living is Easy*, where black fatness becomes explicitly tragic, it does so because it is presented not as a basic premise but as the result of an involuntary crippling addiction. The black heroine Cleo, trying to find her niche in the Boston of the 1940s, deprives all her sisters of their husbands in a disastrous bid for upward social mobility. One sister, Charity, turns to food as a substitute for sexual pleasure, and rapidly becomes disablingly obese. When the family fortunes collapse, it is ironically Charity who helps to restore them by being hired out as a cook—because she fits the stereotype of a fat black woman. Her painful joke to her white employer at her own expense, 'You can see by just looking at me I'll be well at home in a kitchen',[26] expresses her conscious loss of social power, but at the same time her relief at finding a working identity through the food which has almost destroyed her.

In Alice Walker's short story 'Nineteen Fifty-Five' an immensely fat black blues singer, Gracie Mae, is set against an immensely fat white Elvis Presley figure. Only almost at the very end of the story does Gracie Mae tell us that 'I finally faced up to the fact that my fat is the hurt I don't admit, not even to myself, and that I been trying to bury it from the day I was born'.[27] The impact of this sudden disclosure depends on the extent to which we have unthinkingly accepted the stereotype of the big fat happy black woman, who is serenely in control of her appearance.

Wittman Ah Sing, the Chinese-American hero of Maxine Hong Kingston's *Tripmaster Monkey*, wants 'the fattest lady on earth' to dance in his Chinese extravaganza because, he claims, 'she busts through stereo-types. That we're puritanical. That Han people don't dance. That a fatty can't hold center stage.'[28] Here it is noticeable that none of the women to whom he pontificates wants to challenge a stereotype at the cost of playing a fatty herself.

Fat women seem often to be recollected nostalgically by others as part of a vanished past. For example, the heroine of Tsitsi Dangarembga's *Nervous Conditions* remembers with affectionate amusement her huge black aunt Gladys disembarking from 'a gallant if rickety old Austin': 'because she was so large, it was not altogether clear how she had managed to insert herself into her car in the first place. But her mass was not frivolous. It had a ponderous presence which rendered any situation, even her attempts to remove herself from her car, weighty and serious. We did not giggle, did not think of it.'[29] This impressive, obsolete figure is set against the obsessive dieting which leads to disaster in the next generation: the title of *Nervous Conditions*, a novel set in the colonial Rhodesia of the sixties, puns on the 'nervous condition' of 'native',[30] and anorexia nervosa and bulimia. These eating disorders are directly connected with the pressures of an alien education, like the compulsive gorging of Zoë Wicomb's black South African heroine Frieda, who says, 'at night a hole crept into my stomach, gnawing like a hungry mouse, and I fed it with Latin declensions and Eetsumor biscuits'.[31]

Another alienated heroine, 'fat to the point of parody',[32] who stuffs learning and food into herself together, is the American student Ramona in Jean Stafford's short story 'The Echo and the Nemesis'. Ramona crams her mind and her pigskin satchel with philology, and her mouth and stomach with assorted goodies including 'little pots of caviar, as black as ink'.[33] The setting of the story is Heidelberg on the brink of the Second

World War, a barely contained Tower of Babel. Ramona prides herself on her 'gift of tongues', but she has become so driven by her addiction to food that she nightmarishly perceives her whole self as 'an enormous mouth and a tongue, trembling lasciviously'.[34] Ramona is tormented by the memory of her slender, beautiful twin sister Martha, who wasted away and died five years before. We finally discover that Martha '*was* dead, dead and buried under layers and layers of fat'[35]—since Martha is Ramona's younger, slimmer self. Fatness interferes violently with its victims' views of the past. The narrator of *Lady Oracle* denies that a youthful, fat photograph is of herself,[36] and the narrator of a Canadian short story, 'April First' by Irena Friedman Karafilly, still cannot believe that she has escaped from being overweight.[37] A difficult mother may also translate herself, deceptively, into a fat mother. The mother in Anne Tyler's *Earthly Possessions*, remembered eating chocolate caramels and playing hostess in a pink tulle evening gown, 'looking like a giant hollyhock',[38] is buried in a coffin 'oddly narrow', making her daughter wonder whether after all she had 'made up her fatness'.[39]

Fatness, however, as anyone who has ever been fat knows, interferes far more with the future than with the past. It can be seen as one of the ultimate catastrophes: 'I want to get fat. Or be addicted to heroin. I want to be a disaster'[40] says a college girl in Mary Gaitskill's story 'Connection'. High-school girls 'fear for the future' when they see the cellulite on the thighs of Carol Shields' splendid heroine in 'Mrs Turner Cutting the Grass'.[41] Bill Bryson's travel article 'Fat Girls in Des Moines' muses on the metamorphosis of beautiful women as fruit into ugly women as meat, and the shock in store for the male consumer:

> Iowa women are almost always sensationally overweight—you see them at Merle Hay Mall in Des Moines on Saturdays, clammy and meaty in their shorts and halter-tops, looking a little like elephants dressed in children's clothes, yelling at their kids, calling names like Dwayne and Shauna...I will say this, however—and it's a strange, strange thing—the teenaged daughters of these fat women are always utterly delectable, as soft and gloriously rounded and naturally fresh-smelling as a basket of fruit, I don't know what it is that happens to them, but it must be awful to marry one of these nubile cuties knowing that there is a time bomb ticking away in her that will at some unknown date make her bloat out into something huge and grotesque, presumably all of a sudden and without much notice, like a self-inflating raft from which the stopper has been abruptly jerked.[42]

More often, though, fatness invades the future with the promise of its absence. 'Everything would be all right,' Stacey tells herself in Margaret Laurence's *The Fire-Dwellers*, 'if only I was better educated. I mean, if I were. Or if I were beautiful. Okay, that's asking too much. Let's say if I took off ten or so pounds.'[43] Jane, in Muriel Spark's *The Girls of Slender Means*, 'was miserable about her fatness and spent much of her time in eager dread of the next meal, and in making resolutions what to eat of it and what to leave'.[44] Sophie in Kate Pullinger's short story 'The Self-Loathing Diet or How to Hate Yourself Into Thin Air' has some thin days, but far more frequent fat days, on which she drags herself along by her spare tyre

> to the big sign on the side of the hill that reads, YOU ARE FAT. When she reached this point she would get down on her knees and blubber incoherently, 'I shouldn't have eaten it, I should do more leg-lifts, I should swim five times a week, I should cut out breakfast completely, I should get a night-job as well so I don't have time to eat, I should get my jaw wired shut, I should take a big pair of shearing scissors and cut all this extra bulk away, I should sell my refrigerator, I should fast for a week, I should take diet pills and laxatives and speed, I should buy all my clothes two sizes too small and not give in until I can wear them'.[45]

The story ends with a newly cellulite-free Sophie savagely slapping a man who has told her she is sweet enough to eat: 'As he howled she realised that perhaps cellulite wasn't her only enemy after all'.[46]

The enemy is firmly identified in a novel by Lesléa Newman called *Good Enough to Eat*. The heroine Liza dislikes fellatio because 'she'd read somewhere that each ejaculation had about 500 calories in it. That was enough to blow her diet for an entire day.'[47] By the end of the novel she has recognized that she dislikes men too, and looks forward to a lesbian future free from eating disorders. Liza's conviction that women's debilitating anxiety about weight is an aspect of male control is echoed by Susan in Fay Weldon's *The Fat Woman's Joke*. Susan tells Brenda, who has fat legs, 'You're supposed to bother. You've got to bother if you're a woman. Otherwise you might as well be a man.'[48]

Susie Orbach has been criticized in *Feminist Review* in an article by Nicky Diamond called 'Thin is the Feminist Issue' for proposing that food should be reduced to the satisfaction of physical needs. Diamond argues that this is like proposing that sex should be linked only to reproduction.[49] Food, it seems, should be an indulgence.

However, it is an indulgence which costs the fat woman dear in social esteem. To speak of 'fat women' or 'fat ladies' at all, phrases reverberating with the suggestion of the circus freak, is to embark on a series of judgments—like the word 'fat' itself. If fat women's habitual and excessive indulgence in food may be defined as addiction, how may 'excessive' be defined, except in terms of exceeding social expectations? Fat women in fiction derive their literary, if not their social, power from the ways in which they illuminate and challenge society's expectations about gender, race and identity.

NOTES

1.   Cited in *The Independent on Sunday*, 31 March 1991.

2.   S. Bovey, *Being Fat is not a Sin* (London: Pandora, 1989), p. 94.

3.   *The Guardian*, 20 March 1989.

4.   M. Atwood, *Lady Oracle* (London: Virago, 1990), p. 90. See D. Jones, 'Decolonizing Women's Romance', in A. Rutherford (ed.), *From Commonwealth to Post-Colonial* (Sydney: Dangaroo Press, 1992), pp. 390-98 for her valuable insights into the connections between fatness, the transgressing of male boundaries and the writing of women's romance.

5.   M. Spark, *A Far Cry From Kensington* (Harmondsworth: Penguin, 1989), p. 11.

6.   Bovey, *Being Fat is not a Sin*, p. 1.

7.   Bovey, *Being Fat is not a Sin*, pp. 156-57.

8.   K. Chernin, *Womansize: The Tyranny of Slenderness* (London: Women's Press, 1983), pp. 88-89 (first published in 1981 as *The Obsession: Reflections on the Tyranny of Slenderness*, 1981).

9.   S. Orbach, *Fat is a Feminist Issue* (London: Arrow Books, 1983).

10.   Atwood, *Lady Oracle*, p. 141.

11.   Spark, *A Far Cry From Kensington*, p. 86.

12.   E. Wharton, *The Age of Innocence* (Harmondsworth: Penguin, 1974), p. 27.

13.   G. Paley, 'The Long-Distance Runner', in *Enormous Changes at the Last Minute* (London: Virago, 1979), p. 181.

14.   B.A. Mason, *In Country* (London: Flamingo, 1987), p. 4.

15.   Mason, *In Country*, p. 243.

16.   J.D. Salinger, *Zooey* (New York: Penguin, 1964), p. 156.

17.   J. Hawthorne, *Hawthorne and his Circle* (New York: Harper & Brothers, 1903), pp. 17-18, quoted in B.A. Ronda (ed.), *Letters of Elizabeth Palmer Peabody* (Middletown, CT: Wesleyan University Press, 1984), p. 41.

18.   P. Lubbock (ed.) *The Letters of Henry James* (New York: Charles Scribner's Sons, 1920), I, pp. 115-17, quoted in Ronda (ed.) *Letters of Elizabeth Palmer Peabody*, p. 41.

19.   Ronda (ed.), *Letters of Elizabeth Palmer Peabody*, p. 41.

20.   J. Steinbeck, *Tortilla Flat* (London: Pan, 1981), p. 43.

21.   *The Guardian*, 10 July 1990.

22.   F. O'Connor, 'The Artificial Nigger', in *A Good Man is Hard to Find and Other Stories* (London: The Women's Press, 1980), p. 119.

23.   A. Petry, *The Narrows* (Boston: Beacon Press, 1988), pp. 183-84.

24.   G. Naylor, *Mama Day* (London: Hutchinson, 1988), p. 134.

25.   M. Monroe, *The Upper Room* (London: Allison & Busby, 1986), p. 49.

26.   D. West, *The Living is Easy* (New York: Feminist Press, 1982), p. 311.

27.   A. Walker, 'Nineteen Fifty-Five', in *You Can't Keep a Good Woman Down* (London: The Women's Press, 1982), p. 19.

28.   M. Hong Kingston, *Tripmaster Monkey* (London: Vintage, 1990), pp. 146-47.

29.   T. Dangarembga, *Nervous Conditions* (London: The Women's Press, 1988), pp. 35, 36.

30.   The epigraph is, 'The condition of native is a nervous condition. From an introduction to Fanon's *The Wretched of the Earth.*'

31.   Z. Wicomb, 'When the Train Comes', in *You Can't Get Lost in Cape Town*, (London: Virago, 1987), p. 33.

32.   J. Stafford, 'The Echo and The Nemesis', in *The Collected Stories* (London: Hogarth Press, 1986), p. 36.

33. Stafford, 'The Echo and the Nemesis', p. 51.

34. Stafford, 'The Echo and the Nemesis', pp. 42, 43.

35. Stafford, 'The Echo and the Nemesis', p. 51.

36. Atwood, *Lady Oracle*, p. 91.

37. I. Friedman Karafilly, 'April First', in *Montreal Mon Amour: Short Stories from Montreal* (Toronto: Deneau, 1989), p. 263.

38. A. Tyler, *Earthly Possessions* (London: Arena, 1987), pp. 10, 11.

39. Tyler, *Earthly Possessions*, p. 182.

40. M. Gaitskill, 'Connection', in *Bad Behavior: Stories* (New York: Sceptre, 1989), p. 102.

41. C. Shields, 'Mrs Turner Cutting the Grass', in *Various Miracles* (Toronto: General Paperbacks, 1989), p. 19.

42. B. Bryson, 'Fat Girls in Des Moines', *Granta* 23 (Spring 1988), pp. 28-32.

43. M. Laurence, *The Fire-Dwellers* (London: Virago, 1988), p. 2.

44. M. Spark, *The Girls of Slender Means* (Harmondsworth: Penguin, 1966), p. 32.

45. K. Pullinger, 'The Self-Loathing Diet or How To Hate Yourself Into Thin Air', in *Tiny Lies* (London: Cape, 1988), p. 53.

46. Pullinger, 'The Self-Loathing Diet', p. 57.

47. L. Newman, *Good Enough to Eat* (New York: Firebrand Books, 1986), p. 60. My thanks to my student, Natasha Roe, who temporarily shared my preoccupation with fatness, for drawing this novel to my attention.

48. F. Weldon, *The Fat Woman's Joke* (London: Coronet, 1990), p. 14.

49. N. Diamond, 'Thin is the Feminist Issue', *Feminist Review* 19 (Spring 1985), p. 59.

ADDICTION, ELECTRICITY AND DESIRE*

Tim Armstrong

> The study of thinking machines teaches us more about the brain than we
> can learn by introspective methods. Western man is externalizing
> himself in the form of gadgets. Ever pop coke in the mainline? It hits you
> right in the brain, activating connections of pure pleasure. The pleasure of
> morphine is in the viscera. You listen down into yourself after a shot. But
> C is electricity through the brain...The C-charged brain is a berserk
> pinball machine, flashing blue and pink lights in electric orgasm.
> C pleasure could be felt by a thinking machine... Of course the effect of
> C could be produced by an electric current activating the C channels...
>
> William Burroughs, *Naked Lunch*[1]

Thus Burroughs's Dr Benway, defining that integration of body and
machine which has become so much a part of modern experience,
whether in 'cybernetic' fiction and film or in biofeedback therapy and lie-
detector tests. In this essay I want to look at one aspect of bodily
mechanization at the point early this century where emergent technologies begin to crystallize its impact, namely the play of electrical
energies, electrical pleasures and electrical addictions, and what could be
called the technology of addiction, in relation to Theodore Dreiser's novel
Sister Carrie (1900) and (briefly) George Cukor's film *A Star is Born* (1954).
Both involve plots in which a woman rises to stardom on an upwards
trajectory, while a man sinks downwards to ruin; both nevertheless pose
the question of who is really the addict, since the same interactive system
that de-energizes one individual enables the other to become a centre of
energy, a 'star'. I will explore two postulates: that this flux of energies is
linked with new ways of figuring the body; and that it tells us something
about the body's relation to consumption itself.

Sister Carrie and the City

To suggest that *Sister Carrie* is a novel about addiction may seem odd, since
there is no alcoholic or drug-taker in the book. Nevertheless addiction is
central to its depiction of desire and the city, in a number of ways—firstly,

in Hurstwood, the character who declines over the course of the novel and whose death ends it. Hurstwood, it seems to me, is consistently depicted in terms of a displaced alcoholism, even though we are told 'he had no vices'.[2] We see it in his closeness to the drink trade: he manages an expensive establishment in Chicago when we first meet him, and later works at a series of less salubrious bars in New York, where there is constant reference to the possibility of a job from the brewery. The general pattern of his decline, with his increasing inability to energize himself, his shabbiness, poverty and hopeless anger shading into apathy and death, seems alcoholic—perhaps unspeakably so and 'invisible', as the disease so often is. In fact a material explanation of his decline is offered, which Dreiser derived in part from the theories of the physiological chemist Elmer Gates:[3]

> Constant comparison between his old state and his new showed a balance for the worse, which produced a constant state of gloom, or at least depression. Now it has been shown experimentally that a constantly sub-dued frame of mind produces certain poisons in the blood, called katas-tates, just as virtuous feelings of pleasure and delight produce helpful chemicals, called anastates. The poisons, generated by remorse, inveigh against the system and eventually produce marked physical deterioration. To this Hurstwood was subject (p. 339).

What he is addicted to is, in part, his old life, to an established pattern of behavior and self-perception, to comfort and ease. Thus at the midpoint of his decline he escapes from a fight with Carrie and goes off to an expensive hotel for a dinner he can ill afford: 'Like the morphine fiend, he was becoming addicted to his ease. Anything to relieve his mental distress, to satisfy his craving for comfort. He must do it. No thoughts for the morrow' (p. 373).

But there is a second, related, strand of addictive thinking in *Sister Carrie*, linked to the excitements of the city rather than to its depletive effects, and in particular to the new technology of electricity which so interested Dreiser in the 1890s.[4] We might use Burroughs's distinction between the downward pull of morphine and the electric flash of cocaine to describe it. Within this second addictive pattern it is the upwardly mobile character Carrie who is truly addicted, in her constant trophism with respect to light, lustre and shining surfaces. Throughout *Sister Carrie* there is a circuit of lights which are switched on, off, on again; which attract and enlighten some, leaving others in the darkness. The differentiation of light and lustre on the one hand and darkness and poverty on the other is closely related, via a flux of desire and exchange, to the ever-present metaphor of the 'light in the eyes'—a commonplace of the romantic novel which in *Sister Carrie* acquires a signalling function, and eventually merges with the novel's structural patterning. In particular, it is in the eye that the novel's concern with the specular—with commodities and stars, theatres and department stores—meets with its analysis of the commerce of the heart, the switching of personal allegiances, and ultimately the transfer of energy within society. The light in the eye moves, in the course of the novel, from the private and domestic sphere to the public stage, the theatrical marketplace within which the power to radiate desire can be exploited.

The intercourse of eyes begins when Carrie meets her first lover Drouet on the train: she looks at him 'out of the side of her eye' and flirts with him. On arrival in Chicago 'she smiled into his eyes' (p. 11) before parting, and then gazes down the platform at him while talking to her sister. This eye-play parallels the developing contrast between the 'burden of toil' and a vision of a lighted world of material possessions: 'Says the soul of the toiler to itself, "I shall soon be free. I shall be in the ways and the hosts of the merry. The streets, the lamps, the lighted chamber set for dining are for me"' (p. 10). Carrie's sister is, literally, lack-lustre, representing 'cold reality...no world of light and merriment', in contrast to Drouet's well-lit world (p. 11). The tragic structure of the novel is figured within this exchange of light and darkness. The play which marks Carrie's beginnings as an actress is an effect of lights, supported by businessmen who are 'the lights of a certain circle' (p. 178), orchestrated by Hurstwood who was 'a light among them' (p. 180). It is through learning to manage light-effects that Carrie plots her upward path. After the play, the balance of power in her relationship with Drouet changes: he 'was feeling the shadow of something which was coming' (p. 198) and his question about the source of her dramatic power releases 'a flood of light on the matter of superiority. She began to see the things which he did not understand' (pp. 198-99). Drouet departs into 'shadow' as the more powerful Hurstwood, with his radiating power, moves into the light of Carrie's affection. This pattern continues throughout the novel. As the declining Hurstwood sinks into darkness, Carrie moves on to 'that gilded state which she had so much craved' (p. 377): the light of the salons which she sees early in the novel, but more importantly the light of public acclaim, of her representation as spectacle and commodity. The two merge when Carrie is offered effectively free residence at a new hotel which wishes to use her as a an in-house advertisement, her domestic arrangements becoming public.

Deploying this recurrent pattern of figuration, Dreiser is thinking in terms of a specific technology. Throughout *Sister Carrie* the pulse of the city is linked to the new world of electric lights, conspicuous consumption, American energy—and, as Rachel Bowlby has shown, of the emergent institution of the department store.[5] The newly speeded-up world of instant gratification is suggested by the first large electric sign on Broadway, which Dreiser reported seeing in the mid-1890s, 1500 lights flashing the message:

SWEPT BY OCEAN BREEZES
THE GREAT HOTELS
PAIN'S FIREWORKS
SOUSA'S BAND
SEIDEL'S GREAT ORCHESTRA
THE RACES
NOW—MANHATTAN BEACH—NOW[6]

An example of similar effects in the novel, one of many, is the first time Carrie ventures out into fashionable New York (and meets Ames), entering a world of lights, branded commodities and, incipiently, the instant gratifications of consumer society (which I will come back to)— notice the waiter's 'yes', parallelling the sign's 'now':

> On the ceilings were colored traceries with more gilt, leading to a centre where spread a broad circle of light—incandescent globes mingling with glittering prisms and stucco tendrils of gilt...
>   The tables were not so remarkable in themselves, and yet the imprint of 'Sherry' upon the napery, the name of 'Tiffany' upon the silverware, the name of 'Haviland' upon the china, and over all the glow of the small red-shaded candelabra, and the reflective tints of the walls on garments and faces, made them seem remarkable. Each waiter added an air of exclusiveness and elegance by the manner in which he bowed, scraped, touched and trifled with things. The exclusively personal attention which he devoted to each one, standing half-bent, ear to one side, elbows akimbo, saying 'soup—green turtle, yes—one portion, yes. Oysters—certainly—half-dozen—yes. Asparagus! Olives—yes' (pp. 332-33).

Light effects are thus linked to individual aspirations, and electricity and lighting modify 'human nature' in the book. Carrie and Ames, the man set up by the novel as her ideal partner, are electric people. Carrie is constantly 'turned on' by lighting effects, while her ability to 'electrify' her audience (as one critic puts it) is central to her aspirant role.[7] Ames is partly modelled on Edison: he is called 'a very bright mind, which was finding its chief development in electrical knowledge' (p. 335). Neither Ames nor Carrie drinks, seeing it as a needless 'burning off' of energy (p. 333). Hurstwood is, on the other hand, associated not only with alcohol but with gas-light, the out-moded technology of desire—and kills himself, at the novel's end, with the single gas-jet which represents his poverty.

Both the addictive paradigm offered by Hurstwood and that demonstrated by Carrie involve a diagnosis of the city as the site of addiction: for Hurstwood the comforts of home, position; for Carrie the light-effects which pull her towards the public gaze. An analysis of both cravings is offered in the great description of the city in Chapter 33. The author is explaining why Hurstwood will be destroyed by New York, to which the couple have fled from Chicago after he has left his wife and stolen money from his employer. The paradigm is chemical, but addiction is nevertheless associated with what we have come to call the 'buzz' of the city:

> The great create an atmosphere which reacts badly upon the small. This atmosphere is easily and quickly felt. Walk among the magnificent residences, the splendid equipages, the gilded shops, restaurants, resorts of all kind. Scent the flowers, the silks, the wines; drink of the laughter springing from the soul of luxurious content, of the glances which dream like light from defiant spears; feel the quality of smiles which cut like glistening swords and of strides born of place and power, and you shall know of what is the atmosphere of the high and mighty...It is like a chemical reagent. One day of it, like one drop of the other, will so affect and discolour the views, the aims, the desires of the mind, that it will thereafter remain forever dyed. A day of it to the untried mind is like opium to the untried body. A craving is set up which, if gratified, shall eternally result in dreams and death. Aye, dreams unfilled—gnawing, luring, idle phantoms which beckon and lead, until death and dissolution dissolve their power and restore us blind to nature's heart (p. 305).

Here, the city itself becomes an addiction: the craving for light, luxury, commodities is a poison to those who are not able to master it; the individual is 'plugged in' to its energies, desires and rewards.

There are thus two types of addiction in *Sister Carrie*, and two contexts in which they are situated: that of alcohol and degeneration; and an addiction to the light and lustre of the modern city. What is involved, it seems, is a shift in the paradigm of addiction: from the romantic portrayal of degeneration to a modernist analysis of commodification and desire. In the former, the focus is not so much the addictive substance's price, distribution, and so on as the 'weakness' of the individual (with a resulting fascination with the squalid areas of the city where the 'fallen' congregate). The result of opium addiction in literary terms is the dream-visions which represent (as Barry Milligan argues elsewhere in this volume) an Oriental decadence.[8] In the second addictive paradigm which emerges in *Sister Carrie*, the 'content' of the addiction, its flow into the body, is identical to its mode of presentation; the addict simply plugs in and becomes part of what she desires.

Addiction, Electricity and the Commodity

How do we theorize the flux of energies and attractions which we see in *Sister Carrie*, involving both the personal and the social? One possible framework is offered by Teresa Brennan's recent work on the relation between objects and desires, working within a Freudian paradigm which attempts (at least to some extent) to locate itself historically. Brennan proposes that 'the desires encapsulated in commodities reflect an underlying trans-historical fantasy'.[9] Her argument begins with the visual representation of commodities; the primal hallucination which Freud suggests covers up for the instant gratification of the breast—a hallucinated breast which both covers up the need and in fact acts as an index of the delay in fulfilling it. Fantasy, in this reading, acts as a hallucinatory gratification which Brennan (to summarize her argument rather crudely), maps directly onto the commodity as image, whose origins in labour (the labour of the maker/mother) are effaced by the fantasy. She links this in turn to Melanie Klein's theories about the aggression of the child against the mother, motivated by envy, producing a desire to control and dominate as well as to receive instant gratification; to dismember or pollute.

In *Sister Carrie* the fantasy of instant gratification is certainly present—visible in the waiter's 'yes', as in the flashing 'NOW' of the Broadway sign, a spectacular visual effect which emphasizes its own temporal immediacy. Indeed, it is worth reflecting on David Nye's report, in his *Electrifying America*, that early displays of public electrical lighting (beginning with the lighting of the Wabash Court House in 1880) struck watchers dumb, as if they were seeing a hallucination. Nye also reports some of the more inflated hopes associated with such lighting—that wheat crops would reach huge sizes, growing night and day, and so on.[10] The electric image seems to help open a space for unreal returns. *Sister Carrie* is also interesting for its aggression against or indifference to actual mothers (Carrie's is absent; Hurstwood's wife is heartless). But more importantly, we can use Brennan's Kleinian theories in order to interpret its division of addiction into two paradigms: Hurstwood's attraction to comfort and fall away from family life and nurturance via his crime and the 'bad chemicals' of depression, and Carrie's attraction to the flux of energies at the city's core, the instant gratification offered by the consensual fantasy of the theatre. What is suggested here is, in part, the 'poisoning' of the old-fashioned purveyor of addictive substances, and the entry of a new producer, who deals in the production of fantasies—a division which might in some ways reflect Klein's distinction between the 'good' (internal) and 'bad' (external) breasts of psychic genesis. Indeed Hurstwood, as Carrie's patron, stands in the place of a mother to some extent, enabling her entry into the dramatic world before he is sloughed off. The aggression of the passage on the city quoted above, with its 'smiles which cut like glistening swords', reflects the ambivalence of the relation between aspirants and achievers.

Yet the worrying aspect of Brennan's analysis of the commodity (as with much work which attempts to link Freudian theory to a historical perspective) is its lack of specificity and its inattention to the placement of 'theory' within the same historical continuum to which it is applied. In some ways it seems equally productive to approach this whole question from the point of view of the discursive framework which informs Dreiser's novel—as to some extent does Avital Ronel in *The Telephone Book: Technology, Schizophrenia, Electric Speech*, which begins with the technology and shows the way in which it has shaped the thought of its users.[11] Thus both Freud and Dreiser share the inheritance of nineteenth-century biophysics with its understanding of the body as a mass of impulses and circuits, in a way which directly parallels Edison's own speculations about the relationship between his apparatus and the nervous system. Of particular interest in this respect is the work of George Beard, who was at the centre of a group of American psychologists and physiologists interested in electrical effects. Beard was known especially for his theory of neurasthenia or 'nervous exhaustion', a diagnosis which was widely influential in Europe, on Freud among others. He saw neurasthenia in electrical terms, as a depletion of the body's neuro-electrical energies, to be treated by stimulants of various kinds, including drugs and techniques of bodily electrification like 'central galvanization'. Beard, with A.D. Rockwell, was also the author of the standard text on electricity and medicine in the period, in which he pictures the body as an electrical system with a set level of energy, like the voltage of a battery. Even more importantly, he sees the body as plugged into other energy systems: the major causes of neurasthenia are the demands of the modern world— transport, technology, the telegraph, speed and the inventions, in particular, of his friend Edison.[12] The self is thus not isolated, but implicated within a technological structure which determines its equilibria, energy levels, and perhaps even its desires.

Like Freud, Beard was interested in stimulants (his book on addictive substances includes an account of the violent effects of taking hashish). He also wrote on alcoholism; according to Henri Ellenberger in *The Discovery of the Unconscious*, 'Beard was one of the first if not the first physician to seek a dynamic psychological explanation of alcoholism'.[13] He postulated that drinking was linked to levels of nervous energies, and to the discrepancy between the amount of nervous force which they felt within themselves and the effort which they had to furnish in their lives. It is thus a way of artificially restoring those energies drained off by modern life, a product of the energy-grid which is the modern city. These ideas are close to those in Dreiser's novel: Hurstwood cannot match the energy levels of the city from his own resources, and is described as dosing himself on the 'morphine' of comfort, while Carrie plugs herself into the cycle of energization, mastering the production and consumption of images. If for Beard the self is electric, both Carrie and Ames epitomize the opportunities generated for those who can manipulate electric effects. Indeed the book as a whole explores the idea that the self (in particular the body) may itself be a commodity in the sense defined by Baudrillard when he talks about a political economy of the sign rather than an economy of use–value: the projection of a surface—but within a context where the social space itself creates the possibility of these fantasies and these particular addictions.[14] It is an electric image we are dealing with, not because the self is *a priori* electric, but because the technology exists for it to be so, in the electric lights, pulses, flashes, signals and exchanges which dot the pages of the novel. Indeed, that twentieth-century analysis of social interaction in terms of 'networks' of power, 'grids' and the like—metaphors dominating the work of Foucault and others–finds its founding moment in late-nineteenth-century technological developments. What a reading of Beard adds to Brennan's speculations on the relationship between the body, fantasy, and the commodity is a sense of the body's own status not as engram but as itself a commodity and image, produced and reproduced.

In Carrie herself this sense of the self's position is reflected in the extraordinary fluidity of the way she is depicted, both as replica or mimic, and as 'heart' or subjectivity. She is one moment malleable and open, subject to the desires of others, and the next moment an agent of her own desires and destiny. This is true from the beginning, when she seems open to penetration by the first voice which whispers in her ear, but where she nevertheless is already a self-propelling agent, casting her past off behind her. She is, in a parallel way, both addictive substance and addict. At the end of the novel she appears almost wholly sublimated into the apparatus of publicity and desire, her name in lights, besieged with marriage offers, and furnished free accommodation. She barely needs to carry money any more, so ready are people to put things her way, to offer her instant gratification; in her last encounter with Hurstwood she has only seven dollars in her purse to give him, having transcended banknotes well in advance of the credit card. That, in part, explains why Carrie is such a 'blank' character in the novel, less a person than a series of interchanges.

A Star is Born

An important question which I have not yet asked of the cyclic rise and fall patterns of *Sister Carrie* is what they have to do with gender. Is it incidental, or is it that only a woman (or a woman's body) which is the subject of a commercially exploited gaze, and thus can achieve 'star' status? One answer is that in the novel's scheme (as in most Western cultural stereotypes) the male body is 'productive', it works for what it gets in an obvious, physical way, whereas the female body is defined as the subject of male gazes, an image. But in the novel images are not simply a matter of subject-positions; they involve their own 'work', as we have seen, within a technology of display—the conscious deployment which Carrie learns and eventually discusses with Ames. This represents a part reversal of the Freudian/Kleinian paradigm which Brennan develops, where it is the maternal body which produces in the primary sense. It seems at first that in *Sister Carrie* the poisoning of the *male* body represents the liberation of the commodity from the 'base' of work, that process of alienation which Marx calls 'fetishism', but which Brennan describes in terms of the destructive attack on the maternal body, in the interests of fantasy. But this liberation and its control has in turn become a kind of work—the work of the 'star'.

One area of cultural production in which we can see these problems being played out is that of film. Rachel Bowlby's remarks in *Just Looking* help us here:

> The transformation of merchandise into a spectacle in fact suggests an analogy with an industry that developed fifty years after the first department stores: the cinema. In this case, the pleasure of looking, *just* looking, is itself the commodity for which money is paid. The image is all, and the spectator's interest, focused from the darkened auditorium onto the screen and its story, is not engaged by the productive organization which goes to construct the illusion before his/her eyes, or with any practical use for the viewing experience. In the way it appears, the Hollywood 'dream factory' necessarily suppresses its mechanical laboured parts, and works against any notion of stable need by providing something characterized by its very separation from the relative ordinariness of everyday life.[15]

The cinema, as many theorists have suggested, involves the consumption of fantasy, with the accompanying suppression of 'laboured parts'. *Sister Carrie* points forward to the era of the commoditized image, of the star, the name in lights and the body on the screen. Moreover, the film industry also enables us to link addiction and popular culture. The post-war period was characterized by anxiety about mass culture, consumption and its influence: in the field of alcohol, Prohibition (which ended in 1933); in the field of entertainment, concern from the Catholic hierarchy and government over the influence of film images, culminating in establishment of the Hays office by the MPPDA in 1926, and eventually the Hollywood Production Code enforced by the Legion of Decency. It is from within this context—questions about morality and the star as 'commodity'—that *A Star is Born* was originally produced (in Wellman's 1937 screenplay; here I will deal with George Cukor's better-known 1954 version). The plot of *A Star is Born* parallels that of *Sister Carrie*: the rise of a star, the fall of the older man attached to her. It is, both in the context of its production and in its contents, a profoundly 'addict-ridden' film: its star Judy Garland, a famous pill-taker, one of its scriptwriters the alcoholic Dorothy Parker, and in the film James Mason giving a famous performance as a drunken actor.[16] *A Star is Born* is, obviously enough, a film about the apparatus of stardom, and as such it constantly reproduces itself: from the initial two-mirrors image to the still sequences, to the figuring of the newly re-christened Vicky's rise to stardom as pure 'story' (and pure immediacy) in the musical which actually makes her a star—a fantasy story-within-the-story which comes complete with a stage birth, a role as child-actor, and time in the chorus. The technique of reproduction is thus constantly foregrounded—as it is in detail in the film, most obviously in the 'playback' sequence at the rehearsal, in which Mason's proposal to Garland is recorded surreptitiously by the sound engineers and broadcast publicly. The film also contrasts the 'acting' of Garland (she never stops acting, from her initial rescue of Mason on stage to her role as his widow) with the 'real' and thus disruptive, anti-diegetic performance of Mason. This contrast climaxes in the scene in which he staggers on stage during the Oscars and cries 'I need a job'; she, in contrast, and like Carrie after her stardom, does not need to work in the sense that 'work' involves delay and frustration; she is simply 'plugged in' to the studio apparatus.

But if self-commodification is the aim of the modern performer, then *A Star is Born* surely suggests a return of the repressed: the star who rises is portrayed by an actor who is herself a victim and addict, whose story of decline and occasional revival it becomes part of. 'Judy Garland' stands, in movie mythology, for Hollywood's tendency to 'waste' its products by isolation and the denial of 'real' human needs—a loss which Dreiser seems to be suggesting in *Sister Carrie* (though the critique is never realized). That is the final, negative, by-product of the addictive energies which I have discussed, the self-commodification of the individual 'star' and its dissemination (via the electric image) as fantasy producing a bodily disruption, a loss of energies which George Beard would have seen as inevitable. A final question is, perhaps, whether there is any 'solution' to this complex, given that all notions of 'organic' existence seem equally like nostalgic fantasies—or perhaps a drive towards death and the dissipation of energies, as in Mason's final swim towards the sunset in the film. What, for any of us, is the alternative to the addictive desires of modernity?

NOTES

*   A portion of the material on Dreiser in this essay has appeared in a different form in 'The Electrification of the Body at the Turn of the Century', *Textual Practice* 5.3 (1990), pp. 303-25.

1.   W. Burroughs, *Naked Lunch* (London: John Calder, 1964), pp. 33-34.

2.   T. Dreiser, *Sister Carrie*, unexpurgated edition (Harmondsworth: Penguin, 1981), p. 396. Subsequent references in text.

3.   See E. Moers, *Two Dreisers* (New York: Viking, 1969), pp. 161-62.

4.   Dreiser visited the Electricity Hall at the Chicago World's Fair in 1893, and in his capacity of journalist he published articles on electrical technology in *Demorest's* and *Success* in 1899; see Y. Hakutani (ed.), *Selected Magazine Articles of Theodore Dreiser* (London: Associated Universities Press, 1987).

5.   R. Bowlby, *Just Looking: Consumer Culture in Dreiser, Gissing, and Zola* (London: Methuen, 1985).

6.   T. Dreiser, *The Color of a Great City* (New York: Boni & Liveright, 1923), p. 119. This and other comments on electricity by Dreiser are discussed in David Nye's fascinating *Electrifying America: Social Meanings of New Technology, 1880–1940* (Cambridge, MA: MIT Press, 1990), p. 50 *et passim*.

7.   H. Witemeyer, 'Gaslight and Magic Lamp in *Sister Carrie*', *PMLA* 86 (1971), pp. 236-40.

8.   See also A. Hayter, *Opium and the Romantic Imagination* (London: Faber & Faber, 1968).

9.   T. Brennan, 'The Age of Paranoia', *Paragraph* 14 (1991), pp. 20-45.

10. Nye, *Electrifying America*, p. 111.

11. A. Ronel, *The Telephone Book: Technology, Schizophrenia, Electric Speech* (Lincoln: University of Nebraska Press, 1989). On Edison, see Nye, *Electrifying America*, p. 242.

12. G. Beard, *American Nervousness* (New York: George Putnam, 1881), p. 98. On Beard in general, see C.E. Rosenberg, 'The Place of George M. Beard in Nineteenth-Century Psychiatry', *Bulletin of the History of Medicine* 36 (1962), and J. Oppenheim, *'Shattered Nerves': Doctors, Patients and Depression in Victorian England* (New York: Oxford University Press, 1991).

13. H. Ellenberger, *The Discovery of the Unconscious* (New York: Basic Books, 1970), p. 243.

14. J. Baudrillard, *Selected Writings* (ed. M. Poster; Cambridge: Polity Press, 1988), pp. 57-97.

15. Bowlby, *Just Looking*, pp. 6-8.

16. See the discussions in J. Cook and M. Lewington (eds.), *Images of Alcoholism* (London: British Film Institute, 1979).

ADDICTED TO LOVE? WOMAN AND/AS MASS CULTURE

Ros Ballaster

A group is extraordinarily credulous and open to influence, it has no critical faculty, and the improbable does not exist for it. It thinks in images, which call one another up by association...and whose agreement with reality is never checked by any reasonable agency (Sigmund Freud, 'Group Psychology and the Analysis of the Ego').[1]

It is impossible to dissociate the questions of art, style and truth from the question of the woman. Nevertheless the question 'what is woman?' is itself suspended by the simple formulation of their common problematic. One can no longer seek her, no more than one could search for women's femininity or female sexuality. Yet it is impossible to resist looking for her (Jacques Derrida, *Spurs: Nietzsche's Styles*).[2]

In this book we will take a hard look at the reasons why so many women, looking for someone to love them, seem inevitably to find unhealthy, unloving partners instead. We will see that loving turns into loving too much when our partner is inappropriate, uncaring, or unavailable and yet we cannot given him up—in fact we want him, we need him even more. We will come to understand how our wanting to love, our yearning for love, our loving itself becomes an addiction (Robin Norwood, *Women Who Love Too Much*).[3]

This paper seeks to address the place of women in contemporary theories of mass culture. The three quotations above illustrate a certain peculiar symmetry: women, it seems, have something to do with 'group psychology' (Freud's comments on the psychology of the group sound suspiciously like his understanding of women's lack of 'ethics'), with 'art, style and truth' and with 'addiction'. All three are linked, centrally, by the understanding that women have a particular, if different in each case, relation to love. Above all, and perhaps most interestingly, this relation to love is 'fictional'. The love that for Freud is the motor for commitment to a group ('love relationships...constitute the essence of the group mind'[4]) is a wilful commitment to illusion, to the image. So too for Robin Norwood who tells her reader that she can recognize herself as 'emotionally addictive' if 'in a relationship, you are much more in touch with your dream of how it could be than with the reality of your situation'.[5] And finally, of course, for Derrida, where woman is not so much the victim of this fiction of 'love' than the figure of it, the 'unrepresentable', the 'simulacrum' (copy without original)—woman *is* fiction. My interest here is in two parallel narratives or 'fictions' that concern themselves with the relation of women to a fictional 'love'. The first is a narrative of women's 'addiction' to a fiction of romance, a narrative of women *and* mass culture. The second is a narrative of 'woman' as the figure of addictive romance, of femininity as seduction whether threatening for (for a certain brand of 'high modernism') or to be embraced by (for a certain inflection of postmodern or post-structuralist theory) the male creative imagination, that is, a narrative of woman *as* mass culture. These two narratives, of woman as consumer and woman as object to be consumed, I will argue are the dominant models of contemporary theories of mass culture that both obscure and explain the problem of imagining/imaging the woman as *producer* or *agent* of culture.

The trope of women's unhappy alliance with the fictional is a long established and tediously familiar one, of course. As early as 1712, the *Spectator* of April 29 made explicit links between a number of 'addictive' substances and their dangerous effects on the adolescent female mind, warning its 'fair Readers to be in a particular manner careful how they meddle with Romances, Chocolate, Novels and the like Inflamers; which I look upon as very dangerous to be made use of during this Carnival of Nature'.[6] The addiction to fiction has something to do with women's vulnerability to love. Most frequently in the eighteenth century the complaint is that fiction teaches women to overinvest in the power of love. Charlotte Lennox's 'female Quixote' of 1752, Arabella, 'supposing Romances were real Pictures of Life, from them she drew all her Notions and Expectations. By them she was taught to believe, that Love was the ruling Principle of the World, that every other Passion was subordinate to this; and that it caused all the Happiness and Miseries of Life'.[7] 'Romance' is dangerous because it persuades women wrongly that love is the 'ruling principle of the World' and that they as arbiters and objects of amorous desire have power over the world. In the twentieth century, theorists of a very different kind of romance, the mass-market 'pulp' fiction of Mills and Boon or, in the States, Harlequin, identify the same kind of fictional 'compensation' for women readers in romance. The authors of *Rewriting English* point out that romantic fiction entails 'a reversal of the common view of history, allowing the usually marginalized female sphere to dominate'.[8] Romantic fiction not only reverses public history, it constantly renarrates the same moment in the heterosexual woman's 'personal' history when she perceives herself to be powerful, the period of courtship, women's 'one socially acceptable moment of transcendence', according to Ann Barr Snitow.[9] Snitow's comments on the genre in her

essay 'Mass Market Romance: Pornography for Women is Different' echo
Robin Norwood's understanding of women's 'addiction to love'. Snitow
identifies all pornography as driven by 'the universal infant desire for
complete, immediate gratification, to rule the world out of the very core of
passive helplessness';[10] Norwood identifies 'emotionally addictive'
behaviour as the desire for control and power over men veiled in terms of
support, help and passivity on the part of the woman who 'forgives' everything. Tania Modleski in her ground-breaking book on mass market texts
for women, despite the claim to challenge the orthodoxy of presenting the
romantic fiction reader as victim of the text's 'illusions', uncomfortably
restores this rhetoric of addiction in the closing considerations of her
chapter on romance. Modleski argues that romance ultimately induces
dependence rather than liberation. The heroine is 'cleared' of blame, her
innocence and total passivity are rewarded by 'winning' the desirable
man, but the reader in the process acquires precisely that guilty
knowledge of sexual motivation that makes it impossible for her to 'be' the
heroine herself. Her only recourse is to read another romance text. This,
Modleski argues,

> renders credence to the other commonly accepted theory of popular art as
> narcotic. As medical researchers are now discovering, certain tranquilliz-
> ers taken to relieve anxiety are, though temporarily helpful, ultimately
> anxiety-producing. The user must constantly increase the dosage of the
> drug in order to alleviate problems aggravated by the drug itself.[11]

The long history of invective and analysis of women's addiction to
romance fiction is evidence, it seems to me, of a deeper structure whereby
the concept of the 'addictive personality' is engendered through identifying it as feminine—passive, helpless, dependent, paradoxically self-
loathing and power-seeking. The 'addictive' personality is 'unselfconscious' and therefore 'unproductive', marked by the compulsion to
repeat rather than to transform. The 'addict' is, above all else, a consumer
not a producer, a reader not a writer. We should not forget, however, that to
'consume' also means 'to use up; to destroy'; if women are the archetypal
'consumers', then, they figure not only as victims of addiction, but also as
sources of addiction. It is in this association that the figure of woman
functions *as* mass culture in an equally long and time-honoured tradition
of critical thinking.

Andreas Huyssen in the essay that prompted this paper, 'Mass Culture
as Woman', turns to the late nineteenth and early twentieth century to
point out a 'striking' phenomenon whereby 'political, psychological and
aesthetic discourse…consistently and obsessively genders mass culture
and the masses as feminine, while high culture, whether traditional or
modern, clearly remains the privileged realm of male activities'.[12]
Whether this takes the shape of Lukacs' privileging 'social realism' or
Adorno's privileging 'modernism', the aesthetic form that 'wards off' the

evils of industrial, modern consumerism is identified as 'masculine'. Huyssen points to the consistency with which the 'great' modern theories (Freud's ego over the id, Marx's production over consumption, modernist artistic autonomy over a slavish servitude to the desires of the masses) develop an image of a 'paranoid' self, endlessly engaged in warding off an unspecified force that threatens to consume and engulf it. Protection from this threat is secured by a form of 'inoculation' rather than outright rejection. The modern artist adopts a posture of 'imaginary male femininity', mastering the threat through putting it to use in his own project without falling victim to its seductive power. This is, of course, only a step away from the 'postmodern' aesthetics of Jean Baudrillard or Jacques Derrida, advocating a 'feminization' of culture where the seductive alterity of a figure of the feminine is put to use by the male artist or critic in order to *challenge* the transcendental signifiers of masculinity. As Teresa de Lauretis puts it, with reference to Derrida's *Spurs*, 'If Nietzsche and Derrida can occupy and speak from the position of woman, it is because that position is vacant and, what is more, cannot be claimed by women'.[13] Feminists have not been slow to point out that the 'models' of 'l'écriture féminine', that disruptive capacity with language that interferes with our belief in its referential and mediatory power, are almost exclusively male—Joyce, Artaud, Lautréamont. Woman is in this equation a 'position' to be adopted, a masquerade, a simulacrum and, it seems, only men are in the position to adopt the role without being consumed by it. Thus, Jean Baudrillard self-righteously informs his female readers to beware of feminism, a dangerous addiction to 'truth', which undermines woman's only 'real' power, the seductive power of appearance:

> Now, woman is but appearance. And it is the feminine as appearance that thwarts masculine depth. Instead of rising up against such 'insulting' counsel, women would do well to let themselves be seduced by its truth, for here lies the secret of their strength which they are in the process of losing by erecting a contrary, feminine depth.[14]

Baudrillard here crystallizes the polarity of women's relation to love that modern theory itself compulsively repeats: woman 'embodies' seduction, the illusion of love; women are particularly vulnerable to love and should allow themselves to be seduced by it. In doing so, however, they necessarily absent themselves from the sphere of production. Women do not 'produce'; at best they 'repeat', reflect back to a masculine productive force its own instability, which serves ultimately to confirm, rather than dismantle, its aesthetic superiority. If 'love is a drug', women take the role of both drug and addict in the drama of seduction.

I would like to suggest, in conclusion, that we need ourselves to think 'outside' of the frame of reference that these different narratives have constructed for our understanding of women's relation to mass culture. The 'other' or spectre that haunts what I would identify as contemporary 'masculinist' theories of mass culture is that women as consumers and producers of mass cultural forms may be involved in a 'different' project from their own, that the 'undoing' of masculinity is a preoccupation *of* the masculine that has little to do with women's desire, history and aesthetics. The mass cultural form of romantic fiction, for example, may provide an opportunity for the exploration of different kinds of female subjectivity for its female readers, rather than an imaginary resolution of gender division through the 'feminization' of masculine power. Let us postulate that the romance reader does not necessarily identify solely with the central female character, the heroine, as Cora Kaplan suggests in her essay on *The Thorn Birds*, but rather with multiple subject positions and the pleasure in fantasy of abandoning a fixed and directive consciousness for the blurring of boundaries between self and other, person and object, character and environment.[15] The pleasure of romance fiction might then lie in the possibility of exploring multiple positions for a 'female subjectivity' which may equally encompass that of seducing 'hero', dangerous 'other woman', or that of innocent heroine. Women as producers and consumers of mass culture might then be indulging in, to reverse Andreas Huyssen's phrase, an imaginary female masculinity which has as little to do with the historical, social and cultural 'reality' of being a man as masculine appropriations of the 'feminine' from the eighteenth century to the present day have to do with the historical, social and cultural 'reality' of being a woman. Women's addiction to romance might then be less a compensation, a revenge fantasy, a source of anxiety, than a discursive field in which we find a space to talk to each other, rather than respond to men. The 'engulfing' nightmare of woman, whether figured as mass culture, seduction, or style, for masculinist theory might be that women's dismantling of subjectivity, our 'giving away' of ourselves to fiction, our 'addiction', has, ultimately, nothing to do with men.

NOTES

1.   S. Freud, 'Group Psychology and the Analysis of the Ego' (1921), in *Civilization, Society and Religion* (The Pelican Freud Library, 12; Harmondsworth: Pelican, 1985), p. 104.

2.   J. Derrida, *Spurs: Nietzsche's Styles* (trans. B. Harlow; Chicago: University of Chicago Press, 1979), p. 71.

3.   R. Norwood, *Women who Love Too Much* (London: Arrow Books, 1986), p. 1.

4.   Freud, 'Group Psychology', p. 120.

5.   Norwood, *Women who Love Too Much*, p. 11.

6.   J. Addison and R. Steele, *The Spectator 1711–1712* (ed. D.F. Bond; Oxford: Clarendon Press,1982), III, p. 374.

7.   C. Lennox, *The Female Quixote* (1752; London: Oxford University Press, 1970), p. 7.

8.   J. Batsleer, R. O'Rourke, C. Weedon and T. Davies, *Rewriting English: Cultural Politics of Gender and Class* (London: Methuen, 1985), p. 92.

9.   A.B. Snitow, 'Mass Market Romance: Pornography for Women is Different', in A.B. Snitow, C. Stansell and S. Thompson (eds.), *Desire: The Politics of Sexuality* (London: Virago, 1984), p. 265.

10.   Snitow, 'Mass Market Romance', p. 269.

11.   T. Modleski, *Loving with a Vengeance: Mass-Produced Fantasies for Women* (1982; London: Methuen, 1984), p. 57.

12.   A. Huyssen, 'Mass Culture as Woman: Modernism's Other', in T. Modleski (ed.), *Studies in Entertainment: Critical Approaches to Mass Culture* (Bloomington: Indiana University Press, 1986), p. 191.

13.   T. de Lauretis, 'The Violence of Rhetoric: Considerations on Representation and Gender', in *Technologies of Gender: Essays on Theory, Film and Fiction* (Bloomington: Indiana University Press, 1987), p. 32.

14.   J. Baudrillard, *Seduction* (trans. B. Singer; London: Macmillan, 1990), p. 10.

15.   See C. Kaplan, '*The Thorn Birds*: Fiction, Fantasy, Femininity', in *Sea Changes: Culture and Feminism* (London: Verso, 1986), pp. 117-46.

PETER REDGROVE: DRINKING AS MENSES-ENVY

Neil Roberts

> I have wondered about the reason why men drink. I think it's because
> they're creating sensation in their bodies. The alcohol stills thought and
> allows them to attend to sensation in the same manner as meditation will
> but also, of course, they're pissing, which is feeling the world pass through
> their bodies.[1]

This is Peter Redgrove in an interview for the *Manhattan Review* in 1983,
incorporating alcohol into the discourse about gender that pervades his
work. A moment before he has said of women,

> Whether or not it's because they're a 'slave class', or whether they are
> connected with their senses by the menstrual cycle, women may be more
> in the world than men are by culture.

Here, in his references to 'slave class' and 'culture', he is stepping more
cautiously than he and Penelope Shuttle do in their influential study of
menstruation, *The Wise Wound*, where they write,

> Every month, all through the month, the woman goes through a series of
> bodily changes of ineffable sensitivity that are a total response of her
> being, arguably more deeply actual and rooted in this physical world than
> any man can attain. Man is like the waterfly of existence, for the weight of
> his body-fruits do not pull him below the surface of existence.[2]

The function of alcohol, then, is to drag waterfly-man below the surface.
As Redgrove writes in one of his drinking poems,

> I find I
> Have prepared myself by weeks of abstinence
> For a descent into alcoholic flux.[3]

The role of alcohol in Redgrove's writing focuses a fascinating and
important aspect of his view of gender. His drinker, known in some of the
poems as Grand Buveur, is like the aboriginal men who according to
some anthropologists practise subincision out of envy at the women's
menstrual bleeding. The menstrual flow is mimicked by the metaphorical 'alcoholic flux' and by the literal flow of the drinker's urine. This

is one of the ways in which Redgrove inverts the Freudian view, which has recently enjoyed a resurgence with a revised ideological colouring under the influence of Lacan, according to which the feminine is the sign of lack. His earlier poetry is peopled by a series of masculine personae who suffer from a sense of lack culminating in the speaker of 'The Haunted Armchair', who is so alienated from his body that he thinks it out of existence:

> The body is gone. I sit here alone. A nothing, a virgin memory.
> A grease-spot. A dirty chair-back.[4]

The masculine consciousness in Redgrove is always threatened by this fear that it is 'a nothing'. His most elaborate portrayal of it is in a monologue called 'The Case', a strange mixture of psychology and myth, whose hero is sent by his mother, who is associated with nature and afraid of death, on a quest to find his 'other half', the Father. The poem traces a progressive alienation from nature and identification with the Father, at the end of which the hero blinds himself and aspires 'to live unseeing, not watching, without judging, called "Father"'.[5]

In the same volume Redgrove published another monologue called 'The Heir'. This figure says,

> as I am a living man, Mother, I bear you no
> kind of a grudge,
> Not to you, nor to the good kind cider or beer
> Killing me and having me, for you agreed to die, and
> bear me no grudge
> For being alive and dying, and dying much as you
> did...[6]

Both speakers appear to be radically dependent on their mothers for their orientation towards nature and death; but this one seems also to be dependent on alcohol for emulating his mother's 'agreement':

> you did as you agreed
> Which was to give me life, and I agree to that too
> For the beer agrees with me as I said, and I
> undertake
> To go on agreeing so long as there's passage in my
> throat.

This is evidently the character whom Redgrove will later call 'Grand Buveur'. We meet him again in a poem called 'Full Measures':

> On the boat made out of trees I drink my beer
> And hold it up to pledge the river; it matches,
>
> It is mainly water, and stays a while in me
> Rejoicing and transmitting visions
>
> Of where it's been, some of which I see.[7]

The man is also mainly water, and by directly transmitting 'visions / Of where it's been'—unifying the water that is him with the water that is the world—the beer helps him, or so he thinks, to overcome the dualism that, in Redgrove, is always particularly associated with masculine consciousness. Similarly, for the Heir, drinking beer is 'a mixture of dreaming and feeding'. In *The Wise Wound*, you will recall, a woman's being is said to be 'more deeply actual and rooted in this physical world' than a man's. Also, in that book, the relief of menstrual distress is closely bound up with the analysis and understanding of dreams, which not merely relieves pain but releases creativity. When menstruation is accepted, 'the imaginative and interpretive energies are released in body language and symbolic form'.[8] These energies are spoken of as 'mental children', in contrast to the biological children of ovulation. This should be borne in mind to counter an impression, which might otherwise be formed, that in Redgrove's work the feminine is simply identified with nature and the body.

For Redgrove these are religious matters: the sequel to *The Wise Wound* is called *The Black Goddess*. But, in their alcoholic aspect, they are also comic, and in his Buveur poems he treads a humorous line between believing and pretending that his boozers are engaged in a serious pursuit of divine vision and oneness with the world. In 'Pheromones' for example he imagines that, like a dog, he has the power to distinguish the smell of a tennis champion from his trace in the pub gents:

> I enter and am girded with personalities,
> Long ghost snaying from the bowls
>
> And gutters; my own genius mingles with that
> Of the champion and the forty-seven assorted
> Boozers I can distinguish here in silent music,
>
> In odorous tapestries. In this Gents
> We are creating a mingled
> Essence of Gent whose powers
>
> To the attuned nose
> Are magnificent indeed
> And shall affect the umpires
>
> Who shall agree with what their noses
> Tell them strides viewless from the urinal
> Where the gentlemen sacrifice into stone bowls
>
> In silent trance.[9]

This passage exemplifies, with great success, a rhetoric that is peculiarly Redgrove's, in which grandiloquence and bathos alternate so rapidly that one ceases to be sure which is which, matching the alternation of the poet's various personae of shaman, boozer, comedian and middle-class

English eccentric: from the bizarre but undeniably poetic 'Long ghost snailing from the bowls / And gutters' via the down-to-earth 'forty-seven assorted / Boozers' to the apparently straight-faced Augustan elegance of 'odorous tapestries'.

There is a hint in the religious language of 'Pheromones' of a device that Redgrove uses extensively in his two main boozing sequences, 'Grand Buveur' and 'Buveur's Farewell' where, consciously or otherwise, he adapts the medieval topos, used by Chaucer in the *Pardoner's Tale*, and Langland in the Gluttony section of *Piers Plowman*, of the pub as the devil's church. 'Master Piss-on-Himself', for example, makes a sustained burlesque parallel between its eponymous drinker and God:

> His votives are the grassy shrines of tiles
> In continuous baptism and imageless union
> With the dew. He causes the lashing tempest.
> He rounded the fat drops of the unctuous shower.[10]

And this passage from 'Buveur's Farewell' has something of the savage humour of Chaucer's inn-scene:

> Buveur
> A gallon-an-hour man,
> He is a river below the waist
> Sliding towards the sea
> He has drunk up his legs
> Staggering from this church
> Its stained glass
> The quaffable brown light of God
> Of the Real (meaning Royal) Ale Hall;
>
> The depth and sheer well
> Of opening time not deep enough
> Not if it were all the beer in the world—
> Why, he could leak it![11]

I think Chaucer would have enjoyed the last line and 'He has drunk up his legs'. However, Redgrove uses the topos in a way that is very different from the medieval. Although—especially in 'Buveur's Farewell', which is like the hangover to the binge of 'Grand Buveur'—he self-mockingly and savagely stresses the drinker's degradation and absurdity, the values of church and pub are not neatly antithetical. Redgrove is drawn at least as much to Blake's view of them as to the Pardoner's. Elsewhere in his poetry the church is a 'Killing House' and

> The rock that has indeed become a church
>
> Is crazy with its wounds,
> Having been sliced from the hill and
> Blown up from it, and fitted together
>
> On the same hill, a little higher.[12]

Even in 'Buveur's Farewell', Buveur is not a figure from a one-dimensional moral allegory:

> He is a river below the waist
> Sliding towards the sea

This begins as a metaphor of potentially beneficent flux, the melting of the sharp outline of the masculine persona, drawing on the same imagery as the portrayal of the man drinking on the boat in 'Full Measures', where the beer connects him with the water of the river, 'Rejoicing and transmitting visions'. It is also the same imagery that Redgrove uses in the interview when speculating about why men drink. The poem's comedy is not of the nature of simple mockery, but in the shift by which this imagery is transformed, or given a double meaning, by the lines that follow:

> He has drunk up his legs
> Staggering from this church

With these lines the medieval topos, and its ruthless mockery of the drunkard, enters the poem and claims the previous lines for itself: they were no more than an image of a man unable to control his legs and/or pissing himself. To accept that claim, however, is to settle for a simpler humour than the poem offers. The same is true of another 'Buveur's Farewell' poem that uses the pub/church topos:

> The liturgy is out of hand,
> The brown eyes of God shining
> From all the tables
>
> We sit round tables
> Furnished with pint-eyes,
> Brown eyes in glass sockets—
> We blind them all, one after another,
> To obtain the Sight.[13]

Taken as simple satirical mockery, this poem is very thin. But 'blindness' is a numinous concept in other texts, both prose and poetic, by Redgrove: in *The Black Goddess* he argues, in a manner not unlike Luce Irigaray, that the privileging of vision above the other senses fosters an alienated and predatory attitude to the world, and uses the term 'blindsight' to signify a range of non-visual types of awareness that this emphasis on vision suppresses. As his title suggests, 'blindsight' is associated with the feminine, and the dominance of the visual with patriarchal culture. In a poem called 'The Quiet Woman of Chancery Lane', after a well-known misogynistic pub sign, 'blindsight' is illustrated by a blind girl's awareness of the moon:

> I take
> The blind girl by her night hand.
> With her fingers raised, she traces in the air
> The slow rising of that mountain that hangs, the
> full moon,
>
> It is like the presence of a fountain, she says,
> Like the fresh aura of falling water, or like
> That full head of the thistle I stroked in the park,
> And its sound is like a fountain too, or like snow
> thistling.[14]

So when the men 'blind' the pints in order to 'obtain the Sight', they are perhaps not simply the victims of mockery.

Despite being named after a pub, 'The Quiet Woman of Chancery Lane' is not a poem about alcohol. But Redgrove makes use of the name again in a 'Grand Buveur' poem, 'Local':

> *The Quiet Woman*: the pub where men sat suckling
> In the silence; a joke against wives. She was headless
> Yet her benefits flowed; she was tongueless
> Because we would not listen to her. A joke
> Against drinkers. The Son it was
> Who listened, whom the womb magnified from His dot,
> Who entered shining with it, and returned, the Word
> Arising always from the liquid mind, again,
> There, as you see it, again there,
> The Ever-Coming One, the same
> Again, please.[15]

This passage is a good illustration of a notable characteristic of Redgrove's later poetic style: the loosening of syntax to create an open thematic field in which various thematic strands co-exist, overlap and merge. The Quiet Woman is a pub whose sign depicts a woman who is headless, the joke being that only a headless woman will be quiet. The name stresses that the pub is a place where men go to escape from their women. Yet their drinking is described as 'suckling'; already, with this word, the joke is turned on them. The word connects interestingly with the interview comment on men's drinking: that they do it to 'create sensation', something which is bestowed on women by the menstrual cycle. 'Suckling' suggests both that this compensation is infantile and that it is somehow parasitic on women. Although the Quiet Woman is headless 'her benefits flowed': obviously the beer keeps coming, but there is perhaps a sexual connotation, following on from 'suckling'. The practised reader of Redgrove will also be prepared for the possibility that the Quiet Woman is the nature goddess herself; that it is nature, as well as women, that is headless and tongueless because men will not listen, but whose benefits flow nevertheless. We then hear of a Son who does listen, who grows in the womb, and is in a series of images parallelled to Christ, but is also associated with alcohol: 'the Word / Arising always from the liquid mind'. The threads of Christianity, nature, sexuality and alcohol are deftly and scandalously interwoven in the concluding lines of this opening passage:

> There, as you see it, again there,
> The Ever-Coming One, the same
> Again, please.

I am not at all sure who this 'Son' is, but the conclusion of the poem suggests that he might be a 'mental child', offspring of a drinker whose 'suckling' is not misogynistic but respectful of women and the Goddess:

> I lust
> To sleep, and dream; out of the windows
> I watch the misty dunes that are moored
> And suddenly on a cold wind their low cloud clears
> And their sands pour with its distillates,
> The cool dunes, the immense quartz distillaries
> Like a multifarious waterworks condense the dew,
> Foaming suddenly with dew-brooks and freshets,
>
> A giant fractionation. How can
> Such beauties be tongueless! Listen,
> The great dew condenses in the Quiet Woman's belly,
> The unborn child, the secret sharer of the bed,
> The inward drinker of the Quiet Mother,
> The child who when he is crowned will light the
> whole city.

This passage pivots around a rhetorical play on ideas of listening and speaking. When the drinker/poet instructs the reader to listen, he appears to be directing us to actual, if barely perceptible, sounds in nature, of the dew condensing, and the image of the 'unborn child' as 'The inward drinker of the Quiet Mother' appears to signify the dew. However, the exclamation, 'How can / Such beauties be tongueless!' follows a remarkable passage which has given tongue to this particular natural phenomenon. The stylistic reach of this passage is of a notably linguistically conscious character, epitomized by the alliteratively yoked 'freshets', from the lexical range that the *Oxford English Dictionary* labels '*obs*. exc. *poet.*', and 'fractionation', a technical term meaning separation by distillation. This is why the Son of the poem's opening, 'who listened', is a mental child, and why Buveur, however disgraced elsewhere, insofar as he is the author of the poem and father of the mental child, can be said to have 'suckled' the Quiet Woman to creative effect, unlike the drinkers who did not listen to her.

I will conclude by quoting and briefly commenting on one more poem that illustrates my theme: that in Redgrove's poetry the masculine consciousness is characterized by a sense of lack, which the poetic subject attempts, at some cost to his ego and dignity, to fill by various means including alcohol, but always with reference to a fullness that is given a feminine character. Here are the opening lines of 'Grand Buveur X':

> To endeavour by drinking to condense
> As far as possible the all-pervading
> Mother-body of water, to become
>
> One of her whole and rounded bald glisters.
> As the web drinks the dew
> And displays its coruscations
>
> So the body brims
> With burning internalised
> Self-interest, like light in drops.[16]

There are in this poem a number of motifs that occur frequently in Redgrove's work, often with some signification of wholeness. These associations in the imagery of water are obvious, with the notable slant that the 'all-pervading' body of water is feminine, and the male speaker attempts to become one of many 'whole and rounded bald glisters' by drinking.

The shifting and unstable body of water also signifies indeterminacy against which, Shuttle and Redgrove claim in *The Wise Wound*, the masculine consciousness protects itself with '*eternal* events, an *unchanging* god, a science made of *invariable* experimental results'.[17] With a doubleness of aspect typical of these poems, the acceptance of indeterminacy is also the fall into intoxication:

> The mind becoming water skims
> With transient patterns like the waterflies.

Another recurring motif in Redgrove's poetry is the spider's web, seen as a mandala which, following Jung, signifies the self. The fly captivated by the web and devoured by the spider which digests and extrudes it as the substance of the web is a symbolic drama of psychological transformation. The web is often, as here, hung with drops of dew, an image that Redgrove identifies with the Buddhist symbol of the net of pearls, each reflecting all the others, and signifying that the whole universe is present in every portion of it. In the following lines he also, not uncharacteristically, introduces an erotic element.

> I stroke her web, says the fly,
>
> Which is pearled with icons,
> I stroke her glittering moisture,
> I stroke her silk,
>
> I am captivated
> Says the falling-down
> Glass-reversing brittle acrobat

> Of the lipped trapezes that tilt
> On slow ropes that have elbows.

(The concluding lines show that Redgrove can write like Craig Raine when he wants to.)

One of his novels, *The Beekeepers*,[18] begins with two alcoholic poets drying out after one of them has a memorably narrated attack of DTs. Characteristically, the green beetles are described in loving detail and interpreted, not just as symptoms of poisoning, but as messengers. Nevertheless, commenting on the novel in an interview, he said that drunkenness is 'an avoidable substitute for symbolic experience'.[19] Alcohol and addiction are not central to his work, as they are to some of the writers discussed at this conference. Redgrove's ideal masculine persona derives his symbolic experience from dreaming, meditation, 'active imagination' and sexuality. But the frequency with which Buveur appears in the poetry—as well as supplying some of his best poems— signifies that, for the poet whose mission is to 'rouse the feminine energies in men',[20] it is masculinity that is the sign of lack.

NOTES

1. P. Fried, 'Scientist of the Strange: An Interview with Peter Redgrove', *Manhattan Review* 3.1 (Summer 1983), p. 20.

2. P. Shuttle and P. Redgrove, *The Wise Wound: Menstruation and Everywoman* (London: Paladin, 1986), p. 25.

3. 'Magic', in *The Mudlark Poems and Grand Buveur* (London: Rivelin Grapheme, 1986), p. 51.

4. 'The Haunted Armchair', in *Dr Faust's Sea-Spiral Spirit and Other Poems* (London: Routledge, 1972), p. 33.

5. 'The Case', in *The Force and Other Poems* (London: Routledge, 1966), p. 84.

6. 'The Heir', in *The Force and Other Poems*, pp. 27-28.

7. 'Full Measures', in *The Apple-Broadcast and Other New Poems* (London: Routledge, 1981), p. 46.

8. Shuttle and Redgrove, *The Wise Wound*, p. 75.

9. 'Pheromones', in *The Apple-Broadcast and Other New Poems*, pp. 81-82.

10. 'Master Piss-on-Himself', in *the Mudlark Poems and Grand Buveur*, p. 34.

11. 'Buveur's Farewell IX'. Extracts from the sequence, including this one, are published in *TLS*, 22 Dec. 1988; the entire sequence is published in Redgrove's *Under the Reservoir* (London: Secker & Warburg, 1992).

12. 'Rock, Egg, Church, Trumpet', in *The Apple-Broadcast and Other New Poems*, p. 29.

13. 'Buveur's Farewell XII'.

14. 'The Quiet Woman of Chancery Lane', in *The Man Named East and Other New Poems* (London: Routledge, 1985), p. 11.

15. 'Local', in *The Mudlark Poems and Grand Buveur*, p. 52.

16. 'Grand Buveur X', in *The Mudlark Poems and Grand Buveur*, p. 45.

17. Shuttle and Redgrove, *The Wise Wound*, p. 25.

18. P. Redgrove, *The Beekeepers* (London: Routledge, 1980).

19. C. Ashcroft, 'Lazarus and the Visionary Truth: An Interview with Peter Redgrove', *Arrows* (University of Sheffield Student Magazine, 1984), p. 51.

20. Letter to Neil Roberts, 19 December 1977.

HOW HOLLYWOOD TAKES THE WAITING OUT OF WANTING

Erica Sheen

I

It has been a commonplace of film study that Hollywood cinema developed its mode of narration from fictional realism; but the historical relationship between the two has been a complex ideological dialectic, not just simple semiotic appropriation. In cinema, the linear teleology of realist narrative has been adapted to provide the surface structure of a meaning that works in a quite different, even opposite way—towards repetition rather than resolution. The most important term in that last sentence is 'work': functioning as they do 'in the last instance' as resources for the reproduction of labour, the basic elements of Hollywood narrative ensure that the economic interests of cinema have priority over and within the structure of filmic signification. The progressive momentum of realist narrative, with its associated ideology of education and enlightenment, is precisely what the 'dream house' has had to deconstruct in order to assert and consolidate its positioning of the individual subject within the economic structures that maintain cinema itself.

What Hollywood has come up with in its place is a remarkably successful synthesis of narrative and institutional imperatives; a narrative with a simple quest structure, but a quest structured on regressive values; a circular rather than a linear mode of story-telling, the point of which is to get back to where it started from—even if just exactly where that was was not obvious at the time. Hollywood narrative reinterprets the realist narrative, with its characteristic concern with identity as the result of a progressive, discursive process of socialization, according to a psychoanalytical narrative, in which identity is embedded in an internalized social mythology accessed by processes of subliminal identification. In this way the individual's relationship to its culture is figured in patterns of dependence that are produced and endorsed by an apparatus that directs all its considerable resources towards a form of exchange that might as profitably be approached through the psychoanalytical description of addiction as through the economic concept of commodity circulation.

It seems to me of fundamental importance to the discussion here that we should be prepared to contextualize a concept like addiction within a description of such patterns of dependence. Every one of us—even those of us who do not take drugs or drink heavily, and are prepared to say that other people should not—use and are used by representational systems that serve primarily to advance their own material interests largely at the expense of those of their 'consumer'. An analysis of this kind helps to balance attempts to isolate the issue of addiction through the discourse of individualism either as a failure of moral choice or as an inverted form of heroism. This is *not* to say that questions of choice are unimportant or that choices cannot be made. But if they are to have any force in this discussion, it is essential to accept the structural paradox within which they exist: the position from which such choices can be made only exists by virtue of the material and ideological privilege derived from a system that works constantly towards the production of forms of dependency.

II

Between 1985 and 1990 there developed a kind of Hollywood film which made explicit the circular form and psychoanalytical investments of this deconstructive realism. By virtue of what might be considered the 'central member' of this category, I will call it the 'Back to the Future' narrative. It quickly became distinctive as a group type. Phenomena like this raise problems of description: in this case it would be counterproductive to use the term that might spring most easily to mind, 'genre', since that term, with its structuralist legacy, tends to assert decontextualized frames of reference more relevant to the concept of film than to the institution of cinema. It would thus conceal precisely the kind of issues with which I am concerned here. The term 'cycle', which has been used to focus the meaning of forms of repetition that derive from the relationship between filmic signification and the economic practices of cinema, is more appropriate. In fact it is an important aspect of the way a cycle like this works that its narrative material subsumes contrasting, even incompatible, generic material, thus maximizing its potential to dominate a market, and reinforcing the breadth of its ideological 'relevance'. (Another way of putting this would be to say that a cycle like this works by containing the diversifying momentum of film narrative production within and in the interests of the metanarrative of cinema.) The cycle in question includes executive producer Steven Spielberg's three *Back to the Future* films (directed by Robert Zemeckis in 1985, 1989 and 1990; hereafter referred to as *BTTF*) which are a cycle in their own right; Francis Ford Coppola's *Peggy Sue Got Married* (1986), and Penny Marshall's *Big* (1988). It also arguably includes the two *Terminator* films (directed by James Cameron in 1984 and 1991) which suggests something of the role the cycle has played in focusing Hollywood's most powerful resources during a period of significant economic revival. For they demonstrate most explicitly circular relationships not only within their own narratives but also between narratives and marketing strategies, such as the staggered release of videos and video games. One could, I think, go so far as to suggest that they epitomize the extent to which a circular relationship between filmic and advertising narratives has come to constitute the terms for economic survival of contemporary entertainment cinema. It is on *BTTF* and *Big* that I shall be concentrating in this discussion. As a group these films move across generic discourses ranging from sf adventure and Westerns to musical romance and comedy. They are thus similarly inclusive in the kind of audience they create, despite certain obvious basic distinctions. The *BTTF* films are ostensibly aimed at children; *Big* and *Peggy Sue Got Married* are 'adult' films, involving the explicit representation of sexual intercourse. It is of course important that any form of cinematic narrative should in practice 'transcend' the functional distinctions of age range by which the system of censorship seeks to contain its meanings. The *Terminator* films are perhaps the best example of this—in some respects both the most 'adult' *and* the most child-orientated of all the films I have mentioned. In general terms, the pervasive overlap between adult and child viewing habits is precisely the way cinema reinforces the 'universalization' of its attractions. In relation to this specific group, the circular narrative's mission to transgress—and then regress—the boundary between childhood and adulthood makes any explicit distinction between the representation or suppression of sexuality a formality. If anything there is *more* sex in *BTTF* than in *Big* (which of course makes it easier to decide whether your parents ought to be allowed to see it).

In the three *BTTF* films, as well as *Peggy Sue Got Married*, the link between 'cyclic' production and circularity of plot structure is associated with another circularity: the 'retro' momentum of the 'nostalgic' text. Nostalgia is a historically symbolized version of the act of regressive remembering which accompanies the psychoanalytical quest, creating a 'desire' that disguises highly manipulated acts of cultural reprocessing as a form of involuntary memory. As such it typically directs itself towards the retrieval of our childhood and adolescence (which is why nostalgia tends to get constructed across roughly thirty-year intervals). The self-evident reason for this is that the recreation of the personal 'prehistory' of childhood has a quite extraordinary selling power (it being a well-attested fact that many people have children in order to have an excuse to buy toys and children's clothing, a phenomenon that will bear upon my later discussion of *Big*). Cars, of course, are perhaps the single most significant symbolic vehicle for this kind of psychic space/time travel. At the start of *BTTF I*, Marty McFly—a by Californian standards deprived adolescent burdened with embarrassing parents and tasteless home—sees a trailer going past with a shiny black four-wheel drive car on it. Faced with planning a trip to the mountains with his girlfriend without this essential personal accessory, he can only gaze in desire and say succinctly, 'some day, Jennifer, some day... ' That very day Doc Brown's souped-up De Lorean takes him back to the 1950s where his intervention in his parents' courtship teaches his then adolescent father to become the kind of man he himself obviously already is so that his mother will fall in love with her husband rather than her son—and thus of course be able to give birth to him. The result? When he gets 'back to the future' Marty finds himself in a smart house with dynamic, exciting parents—and the 4 × 4 in the garage waiting for him. The film has taken the waiting out of wanting— and it does so in exactly the same way as the credit card, by setting up the kind of subjectivity it is seeking to create as the agency by which it is created. Its audience was predictably receptive to this kind of transaction. Apparently *BTTF II* produced a flood of enquiries about how to get hold of the flying skateboard that Marty uses in 'the future'. Writer/producer Bob Gale claimed to be receiving 'at least three enquiries a day from kids wanting to buy them. Someone even said he saw a magazine telling him where to get one but he had mistakenly thrown it out.'[1] To describe the extraordinary situation recorded in that last sentence as an inverted realization of 'the negation of negation' would of course be a massive methodological hyperbole; but it would draw attention to an element of parody in the way this kind of time-scheme misrepresents a dialectical analysis of history.

It is of course interesting that buying and selling are represented as interventions that can be negotiated across time without any real sense of a threat to what Doc Brown refers to as the space/time continuum; arguably this is because the function of consumer purchasing is precisely to elide the difference between the psychological and the social meanings of age difference. Significantly, the sf concept of the 'space/time continuum' has characteristically been used—particularly in literary sf— to focus the danger posed by time travel to the social order of things. Apparently in keeping with this, all of these films display a superficially 'moral' interest in the creation of 'paradoxes'—the cataclysmic disruption of the future by an intervention from the past. But it is an interest which strategically camouflages the fact that this is exactly what they themselves are doing—the covert intervention of the film itself in the nostalgic past that it purports to realize in order to appropriate the selling power of the *psychic* space/time continuum. One of the most revealing things about *BTTF I*—one might say one of the most '80s' things about it—is that it makes a point of setting up and then abandoning this moral posture, feeding that abandonment back into its own structure of desire. When Marty tries to warn the young Doc Brown that he will be shot by terrorists in the 80s, Doc prevents him: 'No man should know too much about his own destiny', he says, tearing up the letter that Marty has written to be read in 30 years' time. But of course he saves the fragments and reads them at the appropriate moment, explaining to Marty, 'well, I thought... what the hell'. Doc's 'adult' response to the priority of history gives way to the child's freedom within and from it: the self-regenerating narrative shamelessly externalizes the momentum of its own drives.

III

The narrative of Penny Marshall's *Big* is similarly shameless about its own devices. In this film, age inversion is not time travel but a 'magical' transformation that takes place *within* the hero, so the effect is one of implicit rather than historically materialized nostalgia. But notice what that means in the historical terms that it apparently denies. It means nostalgia for being a child *now* (rather than for when you actually were one). How that realizes itself in real terms is itself implicit in the film's representation of the child Joshua Baskin getting a lucrative job as an adult in a toy company designing state-of-the-art toys and spending his weekends in pleasurably expensive toy stores. Nostalgia for childhood *now* means buying in to childhood as an adult; once again 'universalized' desire turns out to have a quite specific economic subtext. And the relationship between buying in and watching a film that *authorizes* that buying in is itself marked by the film. A turning point in its narrative is indicated when the hero Josh (Tom Hanks) takes the place behind the camera that has up to this point been trained on him, and stands watching children at play—as we have been watching him. The less pleasurable implications of this voyeuristic specular economy are something to which I shall return later.

One of the most important ways that *Big* negotiates its interest in the 'timelessness' of childhood is in its identification between the film and the video screen—an effect which is becoming fundamental to the way the functions of film and television are starting to overlap, particularly in the naturalization of buying and selling as the definitive transactions of family life. This increasingly pervasive identification requires critical attention because it has serious implications for the way film organizes the 'gaze' of its audience as well as its own potential interraction with that gaze—that is to say, organizes its audience's spectatorship *as* a 'gaze'. A preoccupation with the form of attention appropriate to the video and the video game reflects the progressive glamourization by Hollywood cinema of the adolescent. As the *BTTF* films also suggests, this is a glamourization that has an essentially male bias. Childhood itself is presented as in some way *essentially* masculine—an activity which is somehow truer, more real, than the grown-up world, but to which women have no real access: even as children women seem inevitably trapped in the painful linearity of maturation. A significant point in the story of *Big* comes when Josh, having found his way back to childhood, suggests to Susan, the woman with whom he has been involved as a man, that she might like to come 'back' with him. She refuses: 'I've been there before; it's hard enough the first time—know what I mean?...no, you don't know what I mean. Oh, come on, I'll drive you home'. But in the terms of the film, Josh's ignorance is actually what there is to know, and the state to which its narrative leads us. *Big* reverses the idea of childhood as a period of stasis waiting for the go-ahead of adult life. It represents adulthood as itself a state of suspended animation and makes comic capital out of the tiresome repetitions of grown-up life. Through Josh, Susan begins to recognize how tiresome these repetitions are, and sees the possibility in her relationship with him of something more meaningful than mere success. Chatting him up at the office party, she remarks that everyone is 'having the same old conversations...like a party that was cloned in 1983'. There is in fact no point in this film at which adulthood is seen as an achievement or a progression—although Susan initially misrecognizes it as such. Rejecting the boyfriend who asks 'what's so special about Baskin?', she replies, 'he's an adult'—but there is no real contradiction between this and her essentially appreciative response at the end of the film to the revelation that he is actually only 14 years old: 'Well, that explains it'. Despite the romantic revelation (to women) of the meaninglessness of conventional success, Josh's childishness makes him very successful indeed. In fact, for masculinity in general, the circularity of game-playing becomes productive at every level of narrative meaning. The first image that presents itself to the audience is that of a video game at a crucial stage in its development: cinema screen and VDU, spectator and player are thus merged. Josh's voice becomes the spectator's voice as he reads out the words the spectator is reading, and takes control of the decision the game is soliciting:

'You are standing in the cavern of the evil wizard. All around you are the carcasses of slain ice dwarfs.' Melt wizard. 'What do you want to melt him with?' What do you think I want to melt him with?

But at this point he is interrupted by his parents, the time allotted for a response slips away, and he loses.

Your hesitation has cost you dearly. The wizard, sensing your apprehension, unleashes a fatal bolt from the ice sceptre. With luck you will thaw in several million years.

This is the first of a series of failures which Josh sees as imposed on him by his juvenile status, but he is released by another wizard, the 'Zoltar' machine which he 'plays' at the funfair and which grants his wish to be 'big'. Predictably, as far as size is concerned, the first thing he checks out is his penis—although of course we do not see it. As he looks down into his pyjama trousers the signifier of signifiers is, appropriately, off the bottom of the frame, outside the image. (This is actually an extremely telling detail, since the absent phallus is, clearly, our link—'copula'—to the metaphorical structure of the whole narrative, materializing itself metonymically in the word 'big' which functions as an invocation both inside the text as the password to Josh's magical transformation, and outside it as its title, its link to the metanarrative of cinema.)

This early sequence parodies a conventional plot structure where innocence progresses to experience, just as the kind of 'success' involved in 'playing' these wizards correctly, within the correct time, parodies and inverts the adult notion of knowledge associated with that. As the opening gambit suggests, an emphasis on luck and fortuitousness constructs a time scheme that takes its nature from electronic rather than human agency. When Josh and Billy (his best friend) try to track down the Zoltar machine, they are told that the information they seek could take two months, although they might 'get lucky' and receive a reply within six weeks. This is fed into the plot at a number of different levels within the system that Josh has to 'play' in order to get himself back to where he started—which is of course what you have to do with computer games. Here again adult (feminine) knowledge loses out to the boy's skill at game-playing. Susan asks him if he has lived on his own for very long, assuming that a desirable man without a partner must be getting over a broken relationship. His response—'they told me it would take six weeks'—is characteristic of the kind of deconstructive humour that sparks off the friction between the circular narrative that is producing the meaning of the film and the linear one that is constantly being denied in order to produce it. The time scheme of the film is in fact not merely circular but in essence a self-contained replay of the opening moment of the film as enacted on that VDU screen: a figurative expansion of that initial period of time—lost in hesitancy and apprehensiveness—allowed by the computer game. The point is that the confidence and pleasure that replace these negative states are thus not seen as interactional at all, even though they are set up as deriving from a relationship. They result merely from the child's ability to play his games well. (Josh's skill with computers parallels Marty's expertise with the skateboard in this respect.) And playing the game well does not make you want to stop playing—it makes you want to do it more. At the point when Josh realizes he wants to go 'back', he takes his software out and starts playing with it again. This time there is nothing to distract him and he is able to key in his reply to the crucial question in time:

> Melt wizard. 'What do you want to melt him with?' Throw thermal pod.

The self-determination that has become his as an adult has created him the time and space he needs in order to answer the question, but the knowledge that self-determination is seen as expressing chooses to replace him in the position that it has itself enabled him to leave. The child's hesitancy and apprehensiveness as a sexually awakening adolescent do lead to confidence and pleasure (when Josh makes love to Susan) and this 'growth' is expressed in the sexual implications of the contrast between the indeterminate period of suspended animation he suffers as a child waiting for the power and privileges of a grown-up ('with luck you will thaw in several million years') and the powerful sexual agency, and image, of the thermal pod. But as a climax (in both senses) its concern is an inversion of the adult paradigm, not a satisfying of desire but an arousal of it: the desire to 'go home' in order—presumably—to go through the process of getting to where he now is all over again. Joshua expresses quite specifically the priority of desire over fulfilment: 'There's a million reasons to go back, and only one reason to stay...'—the 'one' being his relationship with Susan. In Lacanian terms, this expresses insistently a privileging of the imaginary over the symbolic. As Catherine Clement has expressed it,

> On the side of the imaginary is variety, diversity, the multiplicity of objects of desire in one's life; on the side of the symbolic is unicity, determination, the structuration of time.[2]

Cinema of this kind has evidently got all its money on the side of the imaginary—the Utopia of the capitalist dialectic. Josh himself says that he is not 'ready' for the moves he made in this game to become real. When he goes 'back' to childhood, he picks it up again where he left off—talking sport with Billy, going home to mother. The film's circularity thus enables it to 'forget' experiences the point of which has been to get Josh— and the audience—back to this point. If it remembered them we would have on our hands *not* (as *Big* was described in its publicity) 'a wonderful new comedy' but a very old tragedy indeed, one that even Freud was afraid to put into narrative form; the story of some of the worst experiences of a society that cannot cope with the 'pleasures' of regression—sexual violation, child abuse. I referred earlier to this film's voyeuristic specular economy. The film masks its dangers by transferring them through spectatorship from the child on the screen to the adults in the auditorium—licensed to consume on the premises.

As far as mere plot is concerned, the authority that prevents the dream becoming a nightmare is not, as one might be tempted to think, the distribution and exhibition industries, but 'the power of love', which, it would seem, makes it possible to forget the sex and remember only desire. The song that accompanies Marty McFly's skateboarding flights of fancy *is* 'The Power of Love':

> Don't take money, don't take fame; don't need no credit card to ride this train...

When considering *Hollywood* production packages, money is exactly what it does take—in large and frequent doses. Of course, it is important that the whole thing should come across as 'free' if enough people are to spend enough money on it to pay off the credit that was needed to make it. In an article about product placement, Mark Crispin Miller deplores the increasing involvement of films with advertising:

> The rise of product placement has damaged movie narrative not only through the shattering effect of individual plugs but also—more pro-foundly—through the partial transfer of creative authority out of the hands of filmmaking professionals and into the purely quantitative universe of company executives.[3]

Crispin Miller dates the product placement wave from 1982, the point when Coca Cola bought 49 per cent of Columbia and began to place plugs in its films. Leaving aside the historical fact that in Hollywood 'creative authority' has in the last analysis *always* rested with 'company executives', this seems a rather innocent reading of the marketing of cinematic desire. What I have suggested in the earlier section of this paper is effectively that product placement is and always has been the implicit value system of Hollywood cinema per se, since the product being placed is 'Hollywood' itself. But it is interesting that explicit product placement as an image-making technique dates from around the time of the inception of the 'circular' narrative in film. Crispin Miller further deplores the way the predominance of advertising techniques in the making of films has resulted in losses from the cinematographic vocabulary—the loss in particular of a past tense. This clearly relates to the kind of narrative pre-occupations I have been discussing. As Catherine Clement suggests, there is no such thing as time in the imaginary—or so, at least, the symbolic system of Hollywood narrative would have us believe. Bob Gale discusses the decision to dispense with 'story so far' techniques in *BTTF III*:

> At the two or three previews we held, virtually no one had any problem—even those who had missed Part II, and we made sure they were 30-40 per cent of the audience...I don't think we'd do it like that if the videocassette did not exist. But everybody now has access to the other films.[4]

That is an extremely disingenuous 'if'. The question of video access is all-important, and it is not as innocently spontaneous as this makes it seem. Part II of the film was released in England in autumn 1989, and it concluded with the announcement 'to be continued'. Indeed, it ended with a few 'trailers' from Part III, as if the film had already been made. Despite the fact that the video distribution industry had already been pressing for a standardization of the 'window' from film release to video release, release of the video was strategically delayed until one week before the release of the film Part III in July 1990. The marketing of the video began on television two weeks before that release. I should also add that the release of the video of Part II included a plug for the video *game* of Part I. The same kind of spiralling is evident in the film's handling of its own most important 'plug', the drink Pepsi-Cola. In *BTTF I*, one of Marty's first acts in 'the past' is to go into a 1950s bar and ask for a 'Pepsi Free' (meaning the low-calorie version of the drink). 'You don't get anything for nothing', observes the soda jerk—in direct contradiction to the message of the whole film, as of course Marty goes on to prove with his success with the 4 × 4. The association between the charismatic drink and Marty's adolescent power is not merely contingent to the plot: we see him with a 1950s Pepsi bottle in his hand at some of the most productive moments in Marty's intervention in his parents' courtship. A series of television advertisements for Pepsi with Michael J. Fox followed quickly after the first part of this film. Clearly, it was neither just Pepsi or Michael J. Fox that was being marketed here. A case could, I think, be made for the suggestion that this increasingly common link-up between advertising and the star system contravenes the code of fair advertising practice that operates in this country—which would mean that product placement is not operating in our interests as viewers. But it clearly *is* operating in the interests of cinema; or perhaps more accurately, serving as a metonymic expression of what those interests are.

NOTES

1.   Quoted by Sheila Johnston in 'Keeping the time machine on the road', *The Independent*, Friday 13 July 1990.
2.   C. Clement, F. Gantheret and B. Merigot (eds.), *La Psychanalyse* (Paris: Larousse, 1976), p. 50 (quoted in C. Penley, *The Future of an Illusion: Film Feminism and Psychoanalysis* [London: Routledge, 1989], p. 187).
3.   M.C. Miller, 'Meddling with the movies', *The Guardian*, Thursday 7 June 1990.
4.   Johnston, 'Keeping the time machine on the road'.

MOURNING, MELANCHOLIA AND FEMININITY IN MALCOLM LOWRY'S *UNDER THE VOLCANO*

Sue Vice

Sigmund Freud's essay 'Mourning and Melancholia' has been used by analysts treating alcoholics, and it certainly seems the case that in *Under the Volcano* Geoffrey Firmin is a melancholic: he suffers from what he calls a 'sourceless sorrow', and loses no opportunity to speak about this and about the sick, ugly nature of his soul. The Consul is an alcoholic, his bottle both signifier and signified of his disorder; Yvonne is a woman. In their published incarnations these roles are strangely similar; they are more like the two halves of the severed rock than Yvonne guesses, and indeed their divorce has created two subjectivities out of the same set of symptoms. Geoffrey has thus chosen a version of himself to marry, but whereas the melancholia, the self-affirming sorrow, which afflicts him is seen as a debility, something out of the ordinary, its symptoms are simply the norm of womanhood.[1] Yvonne, like all women, is always already melancholic, and therefore always already in effect an alcoholic.

Geoffrey's presence in the text of *Volcano* is that of a collection of melancholic symptoms; Yvonne's own libidinal economy also crosschecks with these symptoms.

Yvonne as 'Beatrice'[2]

> ...*profoundly painful dejection*, which can be diagnosed by the absence of any libidinal activity and by the loss of interest in masturbation that occurs when the previously cathected organ and object are devalued.[3]

None of Yvonne's affairs nor her imputed sexual rapacity remains in the published version of *Volcano*. She and her womanly husband come together to share their inhibited sexuality in her bedroom soon after she returns home. They have an innocently unerotic relation: his 'problem' means that all he is capable of is allowing a woman to take care of him, whether it is the daughter of his early career whom he still calls for, or the mother he also wishes Yvonne were; her problem is that erotic signs

and gestures have a purely sentimental or totemic resonance. She notes
that they do not kiss on first seeing each other; it is not the thrill she
misses, but what the kiss, like the clasped hand in the bus to Tomalín and
in the Salón Ofélia, means:

> it was false, it was a lie, but for the moment it was almost as though they
> were returning home from marketing in days past. She took his arm,
> laughing, they fell into step.[4]

Every time the Consul struggles free of her embrace (pp. 202, 276) she
feels rejected anew, not because she has failed to get any pleasure from
their closeness, to help herself to him, but because she cannot help him.
The spectacle of a loved one introverted with suffering is positively
anaphrodisiac, impetus for a sympathetic or unhappy rather than a lustful
embrace, though Hugh and Laruelle apparently have no trouble continuing to desire the distraught and rejected Yvonne, because this is how
women always are. Her constant attempts at cheerfulness, masking her
unhappiness, are noticed even by Hugh:

> Passing her one would not have suspected agony. One would not have
> noticed lack of faith, nor questioned that she knew where she was going,
> nor wondered if she were walking in her sleep. How happy and pretty she
> looks, one would say. Probably she is going to meet her lover in the Bella
> Vista! (p. 191).

Her inability to understand innuendoes, which her earlier incarnation
had no trouble with,[5] is as suggestive of a kind of frigidity as the Consul's
own bitter bawdry reveals his impotence. The sophisticated self-mockery
he uses to present himself with failed sex on a plate—"'I think a pepped
petroot would be about my mark,' said the Consul, "after those onans"'
(p. 292)—is a substitute for and not a supplement to the act. Only the
ghostly longing in Yvonne's letter—"'I creep at night to bed and you are
waiting for me. What is there in life besides the person whom one adores
and the life one can build with that person?'" (p. 346)—remains as testimony to the strong and capable young Yvonne of the first version with
her ineffectual young man; but even this is more an expression of intense
loneliness couched in the only language available, than an avowal of
blind desire.

A Woman Without a Cause

> ...abrogation of interest in the outside world, which, in the case of the
> little girl, takes the form of a faltering effort to master the external world.
> The latter is perpetuated in women's 'weaker social interests'...and their
> 'few contributions to the discoveries and inventions in the history of civi-
> lization'.[6]

Yvonne's interest in astronomy and desire for a farm—"'Do you *know*
anything about farming?'" (p. 123)—are both seen in relation to her

anterior wish to save her ex-husband from the furnace of Mexico:

> But why was it, richly endowed in a capacity for living as she was, *she* had never found a faith merely in 'life' sufficient? If that were *all*! ...In unselfish love—in the stars! (p. 270).

Yvonne took up astronomy through a punning link with her nurturing role as the film star who supported the family, and interrupted her university course to marry what turned out to be a faithless and inept young man. Hugh and the Consul have their own ideas about the kind of interest in the world 'a woman like you' (p. 64) should have:

> Women of medium height, slenderly built, mostly divorced, passionate but envious of the male...American women, with that rather graceful swift way of walking, with the clean scrubbed tanned faces of children...the slim brown hands that do not rock the cradle, the slender feet—how many centuries of oppression have produced them? They do not care who is losing the Battle of the Ebro, for it is too soon for them to outsnort Job's warhorse. They see no significance in it, only fools going to death for a— (p. 191).

> 'Where are the children I might have wanted? You may suppose I might have wanted them. Drowned. To the accompaniment of the rattling of a thousand douche bags. Mind you, *you* don't pretend to love 'humanity', not a bit of it! You don't even need an illusion, though you do have some illusions unfortunately, to help you deny the only natural and good function you have. Though on second thoughts it might be better if women had no functions at all!' (pp. 314-15).

The Consul's grossly inappropriate comments on the subject, born of an apparent hatred of infertile women, and overheard by Hugh, are matched by Day's: the latter speaks of Yvonne's 'depressing past'—presumably depressing to the reader rather than to Yvonne—and notes that 'the number of abortions she has had seems to grow with each chapter—and most of this was judiciously excised'.[7] As the small Antoine Doinel in Truffaut's film *400 Coups* is nearly made ill by overhearing two women discussing childbirth, there are obviously subjects we cannot be expected to want to hear about.

The Day of the Dead and Mexico itself are an irrelevant backdrop to Yvonne; the Canadian dream is a paradise not in itself but because she hopes it will save her husband.

Yvonne as 'Love Goddess'

> ...*loss of the capacity for love*, which leads the little girl to 'turn away from her mother' and indeed from all women, herself included. Her desire for her father would in no way imply 'love': 'the wish with which the girl turns to her father is no doubt originally the wish for the penis which her mother has refused her and which she now expects from her father'...So there is nothing here but envy, jealousy, greed.[8]

In *Volcano* clumsy Freudian references in draft to Electra are dispersed, allowing for a less naive suggestion that the Consul is Yvonne's father-substitute; of her father's appointment as US consul to Iquique Yvonne thinks:

> Consul to Iquique! ...Or Quauhnahuac! How many times in the misery of the last year had Yvonne not tried to free herself of her love for Geoffrey by rationalizing it away, by analysing it away, by telling herself—Christ, after she'd waited, and written at first hopefully, with all her heart, then urgently, frantically...She looked at the Consul, whose face for a moment seemed to have assumed that brooding expression of her father's she remembered so well during those long war years in Chile (p. 260).

Here the merging of father and husband is less obtrusive than in the earlier version, and Yvonne interrupts herself before she can complete the sentence about Electra. However, its voicing of the unconscious is not silenced: Yvonne, her starlet-magazine biography announces, 'at twelve was a war-whooping tomboy, crazy about baseball, disobeying everyone but her adored Dad, who she called "The Boss-Boss"' (p. 263), tracing the familiar pattern. She sacrificed her independence for one Consul in her girlhood through an all-encompassing devotion, in preparation for another Consul: 'But when you've been a "Boomp Girl" and are well on your way to being an "Oomph Girl!" at eighteen, and when you've just lost your beloved "Boss-Boss", it's hard to settle down in a strict loveless atmosphere' (p. 264); as Kessel and Walton point out, 'the wife of an alcoholic, much more frequently than chance would account for, is the daughter of an alcoholic'.[9] Yvonne's envy and greed are not prominent, except as possible roots of her self-sacrificing meekness, although she is always anxious for the Consul to be her own and no one else's:

> and it is a ritual, she thought, a ritual between them, as there were once rituals between us, only Geoffrey has gotten a little bored with it at last... (p. 51).

The Consul as Yvonne's 'Armadillo'

> ...*inhibition of all activity:* 'Passivity now has the upper hand'...'It is our impression that more constraint has been applied to the libido when it is pressed into the service of the feminine function'...and 'the comparatively lesser strength of the sadistic contribution to her sexual instinct, which we may not doubt connect with *the stunted growth* of her penis, makes it easier in her case for the direct sexual trends to be transformed into aim-inhibited trends of an affectionate kind'.[10]

The only action which occurs in *Volcano* is the negative product of the Consul's attempts to flee any definitive steps being taken; Yvonne is power-less to do anything except follow her husband when he runs away or they become separated, and wait for the 'inappropriate moment' when he will let her and her mother rescue him. Her major contribution to this is

entirely inactive—the construction of a dreamworld which she is only
once able to communicate to the Consul, the details of which, quite clear to
her, remain unspoken:

> 'Darling...' They would arrive at their destination by train, a train that
> wandered through an evening land of fields beside water, an arm of the
> Pacific... (p. 279).

Melancholic evades melancholic:

> 'Geoffrey—', Yvonne began hurriedly, 'I don't expect you to—I mean—I
> know it's going to be—'
> But the Consul was finishing the habanero. He left a little for Hugh, how-
> ever (p. 280).

Yvonne's inability to act, to force herself on the Consul, meets his own
fear of action and love, and nothing happens. She has lost him. The one
externalized image of rebellion which is Yvonne's and which she can
only recognize by almost failing to—'Why was it, though, that right in
the centre of her brain, there should be a figure of a woman having
hysterics, jerking like a puppet and banging her fists upon the ground?'
(p. 281)—is a state that Primrose Wilderness, in unpublished form in *La
Mordida*, actually achieves: 'Sigbjørn wants drink and Primrose goes into
hysterics, yells, lying down on the floor, where's Sigbjørn gone?'.[11]

Door Left Open in the Mind

> ...*fall in self-esteem*, which, for the little girl, signals the end of the
> 'phallic phase' and the entry into the Oedipus complex. 'After the girl has
> discovered that her genitals are unsatisfactory', 'her self-love is mortified
> by the comparison with the boy's far superior equipment'. She is a
> 'mutilated creature' who, after she 'becomes aware of the wound to her
> narcissism...develops, like a scar, a sense of inferiority'. She acknowl-
> edges the fact of her castration and with it, too, the superiority of the male
> and her own inferiority.[12]

Recalling her past, Yvonne envies people who have a purpose in life, even
if that purpose was to accost herself, that 'bereaved and dispossessed
orphan, a failure, yet rich, yet beautiful' (p. 267). She is ashamed of her
movie career, having shown only Laruelle the photographs of herself as
'Yvonne the Terrible dressed in fringed leather shirts and riding-breeches
and high-heeled boots, and wearing a ten-gallon hat' (p. 266), never
having discussed it at all with Hugh, 'no, not even that day in Robinson'
(p. 263); and as for her ex-husband,

> How little he knew of this period of her life, of that terror, the terror,
> terror that still could wake her in the night from that recurrent night-
> mare of things collapsing...no, like Captain Constable himself, Geoffrey
> had been almost bored, perhaps ashamed, by all this: that she had,
> starting when she was only thirteen, supported her father for five years as

an actress in 'serials' and 'westerns'; Geoffrey might have nightmares, like her father in this too, be the only person in the world who ever had such nightmares, but that *she* should have them... (p. 262).

Her one period of acting, in both senses, is automatically dismissed:

Nor did Geoffrey know much more of the false real excitement, or the false flat bright enchantment of the studios, or the childish adult pride, as harsh as it was pathetic, and justifiable, in having, somehow, at that age, earned a living (p. 262).

***

Melancholics are often

far from evincing towards those around them the attitude of humiliation and submission that would alone befit such worthless people. On the contrary, they make the greatest nuisance of themselves and always seem as though they feel slighted and had been treated with great injustice.[13]

The Consul certainly behaves in this way: the injustices on which he broods occasionally reach utterance, and then he cannot easily be silenced. Yvonne only behaves thus in her earlier textual incarnations, and, unlike Geoffrey, whose particular history has pushed him into melancholia, it is central to Yvonne's very being:

The little boy is narcissized, ego-ized by his penis—since the penis is valued on the sexual market and is overrated culturally because it can be seen, specularized, and fetishized—but...in the ordeal of castration as 'accomplished fact', the little girl's ego suffers, helplessly, a defeat, a wound, whose effects are to be made out in the broad outlines of melancholia.[14]

With both Yvonne and the Consul object-loss—Yvonne's defining female lack and his unidentifiable infantile disappointment—is transformed into ego-loss, through the internalization of 'the shadow of the object' and the subsequent objectivization of the ego: 'The narcissistic identification with the object then becomes a substitute for the erotic cathexis'.[15] The Consul keeps trying to incorporate the object into himself by drinking it; for Yvonne, the relevant equivalent is 'the lack of sexual appetite attributed to women, often correctly, and also the "oral" use she makes of her sex'.[16] The Consul seems sensitive to his wife's behaviour when it imitates his own, or at least he has as much reason to be jealous of what she takes into herself as vice versa: 'I think the great rival for Jan's affections was the bottle, really':[17]

But the abominable impact on his whole being at this moment of the fact that that hideously elongated cucumiform bundle of blue nerves and gills below the steaming unselfconscious stomach had sought its pleasure in his wife's body brought him trembling to his feet. How loathsome, how incredibly loathsome was reality (p. 210).

A later incarnation of the Consul sails down what he thinks of as a *vagina dentata*, the Panama Canal.[18]

That the Consul and Yvonne are not more similar is partly due to the fact that a woman

> will not choose melancholia as her privileged form of withdrawal. She probably does not have a capacity for narcissism great enough...She functions as a *hole*...She borrows signifiers but cannot make her mark, or re-mark upon them. Which all surely keeps her deficient, empty, lacking, in a way that could be labeled 'psychotic': a *latent* but not actual psychosis, for want of a practical signifying system.[19]

This is the significance of the lost feminine anger of the earlier texts, symbolized by its remnant, the woman banging her fists on the ground; in *Volcano* there is no part for Yvonne to be angry in, let alone behave as the Consul does: she is silent but still he berates her. A further difference is emphasized by Juliet Mitchell and Jacqueline Rose in their edition of *Feminine Sexuality: Jacques Lacan and the Ecole Freudienne*. They liken the position of woman in the symbolic order to that of what Lacan calls the '*objet petit a*',[20] the lost object 'which underpins symbolization, cause of and "stand-in" for desire';[21] described in this way, it is clear how inter-changeable for the Consul are his '*objets*', Yvonne and bottle: 'the *objet a*, cause of desire and support of male fantasy, gets transposed onto the image of the woman as Other who then acts as its guarantee'.[22] The only way to stop desiring the lost object is by reuniting with it in death: 'if we accept that the end of desire (in both senses) is the logical consequence of satisfaction (if we are satisfied, we are in a position where we desire no more), we can see why Freud, in *Beyond the Pleasure Principle*, posits death as the ultimate object of desire—as Nirvana or the recapturing of the lost unity, the final healing of the split subject'.[23]

In Yvonne's history appear the reasons why, for the story of her alcoholic husband to proceed, she must take on the identity of the mutilated woman thus described.

NOTES

1. 'In point of fact, if all the implications of Freud's discourse were followed through, after the little girl discovers her own castration and that of her mother—her "object", the narcissistic representative of all her instincts—she would have no recourse other than melancholia' (L. Irigaray, *Speculum of the Other Woman* [Ithaca, NY: Cornell University Press, 1988], p. 66).

2. This and subsequent headings are quotations from the discussion of Yvonne in S. Beckoff's *Malcolm Lowry's Under the Volcano* (New York: Monarch Press, 1975).

3. Irigaray, *Speculum*, p. 66.

4. M. Lowry, *Under the Volcano* (Harmondsworth: Penguin, 1962), p. 68. Subsequent page references given in the text are to this edition.

5. In *Volcano* Yvonne 'doesn't see the joke' (p. 60), but in draft she finds it funny:

'Who was it had insisted that must mean brothel? She smiled, in spite of herself' (26 [24] II, 11). Manuscript references here and subsequently are from the University of British Columbia Special Collections Division catalogue, current 1986.

6.   Irigaray, *Speculum*, p. 66.

7.   D. Day, *Malcolm Lowry: A Biography* (New York: Oxford University Press, 1984), p. 266.

8.   Irigaray, *Speculum*, p. 66.

9.   N. Kessel and H. Walton, *Alcoholism* (Harmondsworth: Penguin 1965), p. 107.

10.   Irigaray, *Speculum*, p. 67.

11.   Malcolm Lowry, *La Mordida*, 13 (5) 265. See n. 5 for explanation of manuscript citation system.

12.   Irigaray, *Speculum*, p. 67

13.   S. Freud, 'Mourning and Melancholia', in *On Metapsychology* (trans. J. Strachey; Harmondsworth: Penguin, 1984), p. 257.

14.   Irigaray, *Speculum*, pp. 68-69.

15.   Freud, 'Mourning and Melancholia', p. 258.

16.   Irigaray, *Speculum*, p. 70.

17.   G. Bowker (ed.), *Malcolm Lowry Remembered* (London: Ariel Books, 1985), p. 104.

18.   'Through the Panama', in *Hear Us O Lord From Heaven Thy Dwelling Place* (Harmondsworth: Penguin, 1969).

19.   Irigaray, *Speculum*, p. 71.

20.   Elizabeth Wright describes this: 'in the case of the *objet a*...the fantasy pursued erases the beloved, who is repeatedly stifled beneath the "massive utterance" of the lover's discourse' (*Psychoanalytic Criticism* [London: Methuen, 1984], p. 127); see J. Lacan, 'Of the Gaze as *Objet Petit a*', in *The Four Fundamental Concepts of Psychoanalysis* (London: Hogarth Press, 1977).

21.   J. Mitchell and J. Rose, *Feminine Sexuality: Jacques Lacan and the Ecole Freudienne* (London: Macmillan, 1977), p. 48.

22.   Mitchell and Rose, *Feminine Sexuality*, p. 50.

23.   T. Moi, *Sexual/Textual Politics* (London: Methuen, 1985), p. 101.

PART IV

Addiction and Creativity

FINDING THE CLICK: ADDICTION AND THE CREATIVE SPIRIT IN SIX PLAYS OF TENNESSEE WILLIAMS

David Plumb

By the late 1940s *The Glass Menagerie* and *A Streetcar Named Desire* made Tennessee Williams, then in his late thirties, the richest American playwright. Success brought him other problems. He was a very shy man who often did not have the emotional resources to protect himself. A family history of alcoholism, and emotional if not physical incest, had also left him with a predisposition for addiction. Thirty-nine is the age when the creative process starts to fail many addicted artists and writers. Up to this point Tennessee Williams's writing appeared unaffected. Thereafter, addiction gradually became the metaphor and finally the mechanism for his work. Six plays of his middle and late periods provide a chronology of parallelism between Williams's creative process and the progression of his addictions.

In *Cat On A Hot Tin Roof* the former athlete Brick Pollitt, the Blanche Dubois character of the play, drinks because he wants to drink. Brick is trapped by his failure to tell the truth about his relationship with his friend Skipper, much as in *A Streetcar Named Desire* Blanche Dubois seeks refuge in the manners of Southern history to hide the truth of her present condition. 'Mendacity is the system we live in,' Brick says. 'Liquor's one way out an' death's the other.' Broken by self-dishonesty, Brick waits for, 'this click I get in my head, turning the hot light off and the cool night on'. The radio-phonograph-TV set and liquor cabinet is 'a very complete and compact little shrine to virtually all the comforts and illusions from which we hide behind'.

All action takes place off stage. The players are now in crisis. Who will inherit the estate? Will Maggie have a baby with alcoholic Brick? But it is the magnanimity of the characters that entices the audience—the larger than life Big Daddy, who has ruled the plantation, not the family's attempt to hide the secret of his cancer—that moves the play. It's the sexuality of Maggie the Cat that electrifies the audience, not the possibility of her reconciliation with Brick. This 1955 play tricks its audience and possibly the playwright. Even as the lies are exposed, there is no resolution (an enigma presented in later plays with less craft and conviction). This is the alcoholic saying, 'I'll stop tomorrow'; this is the codependent Maggie pouring out the liquor to get Brick to stop. The play distances and intellectualizes the realities of alcoholism and spiritual loss by accentuating the power of the characters. This is vintage Williams, an illusion of reality, a lyrical scat, and for its audience a voyeuristic 'real life' cocktail seen through Maggie and the ineffectual purist, Brick Pollitt, who has not hit bottom. There is no solution to crisis, no villain, only common guilt and denial. Brick can wait for his daily click, every day. At worst he can go to Rainbow Hill like the movie stars and dry out. He might even have to sleep with Maggie the Cat, easily the most provocative seductress since Electra and Helen of Troy. Even Big Mamma has a dignity when she has to confront the truth of Big Daddy's illness. She almost stops being fat.

Williams was aware that he was writing on the dark side of life so he entered psychoanalysis in 1958, believing it would help him free himself of his disturbances and enable him not to have to write about disturbed people. He decided to face his demons rather than to avoid them.

Suddenly Last Summer, a confessional atonement for Williams's sister Rose's lobotomy, was written in a period of several weeks. Again the action of the play takes place off stage. Again the playwright uses the collective mendacity of the relatives and enlists the aid of the doctor (his real life psychiatrist perhaps) to keep the family secret intact. The story is about Sebastian, the poet's sex addiction and his aunt who has helped procure sexual partners under the pretext of supporting his poetry. Mrs Venable has a stroke and cannot travel with Sebastian, his family of choice is disrupted, his addiction kicks into high gear and ultimately usurps his creativity. The story is told through Catherine, now institution-alized and at the mercy of Mrs Venable, who wants Catherine lobot-omized for suggesting that Sebastian used her to procure lovers and for telling the truth about his homosexuality and sex addiction. Mrs Venable denies this relationship with Sebastian, much as Tennessee Williams's mother Edwina denied Rose's profession of incest with her father. The garden on stage is an illusion of cannibalistic plant life, a hell on earth and the foreshadowing symbol of Sebastian's spiritual atonement. Catherine tells how the romantic poet Sebastian, seeking revenge for spiritual impoverishment, attached himself to Melville's vengeful god after seeing the flesh-eating birds devour newly hatched sea turtles on the narrow black beach, the color of caviar, in the Encantadas, convinced that the divine powers were as resentful as he felt. Sexual fixes blot Sebastian's resentment, until the poet sees no mystery in the world and loses his creative gift. The village boys he used cannibalize him, a ritual Sebastian believes is his only hope for atonement in a devouring world.

The irony of *Night of the Iguana* is its hopeful attempt to make peace with the word, when the playwright's life was about to plunge into chaos. There is concern for spiritual health, courage, warmth, serenity. This time the jungle is real. The players are not the gods of Williams's *Camino Real* who can overcome all odds and escape their fate. They are the disenfranchised, defrocked, addicted spirit seekers of the real world, who have arrived at the tiny resort in Mexico at the end of their ropes. Yet there is hope for compromise and acceptance.

Defrocked Reverend T. Lawrence Shannon knows who his spooks are and is well aware of his sex and alcohol addictions. Like the playwright, he never stops searching for sexual partners, dragging his victims through his personal jungle which rots quickly and only purifies him temporarily. He beats his young sexual partners afterwards as Christian recompense for their mutual sins, much as he was beaten as a child for masturbating. When Shannon raves in a drunken tirade about *his* senile and vengeful god and how *he* will show his congregation the truth, Hannah, the quick-sketch artist, realizing his tied-up shenanigans are a front, suggests forgiveness and acceptance:

> I think you will throw away the violent, furious sermon, you'll toss it into the chancel and talk about...nothing...just. Lead them beside the still waters because you know how badly they need the still waters Mr Shannon.

This big human play is about art and religion, the nature of the poet's vocation, and the half-fulfilled self. Hannah the Thin-Standing-Up-Female Buddha heats poppyseed tea on the spirit alcohol burner for Shannon, the defrocked, lushed-out sex addict, and Nonno, the ageing poet, and herself; a trinity who meet in the corrupt jungle. Earthly Maxine, whose husband died and left her the broken-down resort, and the servant boys who temporarily fulfill her sexual needs, snuff out the spirit burner. Night in the play, as in Djuna Barnes's novel *Nightwood*, is a metaphor for the characters' ego-driven addictive demons and it provides the environment for possible existential death. But unlike *Sweet Bird of Youth* and *Orpheus Descending*, which accede to atonement through castration and beating, *Iguana* graces Shannon a measure of spiritual hope for a life with Maxine. *Iguana* insists that the only way through the jungle is in the company of another. Maxine suggests they run the hotel together and that Shannon can provide sexual entertainment for the guests. She thus becomes the codependent who denies that Shannon's substance and process addictions are harbingers of physical and spiritual death. However, creativity is not completely doomed like the poet Sebastian of *Suddenly Last Summer*. Nonno finishes his poem before dying and completes the creative life-cycle.

How could this 51-year-old playwright take so many pills, drink, write, carouse and still write so well? Williams had enormous craft and discipline. He also had a huge support system, an entourage who coddled and encouraged him. His lover Frank Merlo arranged almost everything for 14 years. Tennessee Williams did not have to do anything but write.

In 1961 Merlo and Williams split up. Merlo returned briefly: 'Frank came back today which is a big relief, I don't seem to function very well on my own,' Williams said. But Williams and Merlo would soon break up for good. Within a year Frank Merlo died of lung cancer. Williams was devastated.

The family of origin or choice, no matter how dysfunctional, has a stabilizing effect on the addict. Its disintegration often sets off total dependency on the addiction of choice, a process Williams had written about in *Suddenly Last Summer*, where Mrs Venable has a stroke and cannot travel ith Sebastian anymore. Sebastian becomes totally addicted to young boys and can no longer write.

After Merlo's death, Williams's addiction was no longer the metaphor for escapism; it became the primary mechanism, dynamic, perceptive, personal, sentimental and uneven, in its fervent search for a creativity he felt was being eclipsed by younger playwrights.

In *In the Bar of a Tokyo Hotel* the Barman, the Eastern idol and spirit-maker, duels with Miriam, the Western inebriate 'bitch goddess'. The Barman tries to save face for Miriam, who smokes Panama Red which 'isn't necessary to her vitality', and for himself, through his 'inner sources of serenity'. Miriam buys off this Eastern conjugal spirit by manipulating his genitals and crossing over his bar to show him how to make a Western stinger, half brandy, half crème de menthe. Mark the painter, now beyond the click, cannot stop work even for a moment for fear of losing momentum. He crawls over the nailed canvas as Christ, painting layers upon layers of the creation, a circle of limits he must stay in. Intimacy between the painter and the I is described by Mark as 'Now it turned to me, or I turned to it, no division between us at all anymore!' He depends on Miriam to take care of him, to love him out of his madness, but will not give up his artist's studio over the spiritual bar for a loft of his own. Codependent Miriam feeds him drinks. The artist's/addict's universe is entombed; creativity is 'nerveless', or numbed. Williams's collapse in Tokyo in 1969 is thus foreshadowed by Mark's feelings of futility:

> The possibilities of color and light, discovered all at once, can make a man fall on the street...now I know the last things, the imperishable things, are color and light. Finished. No more about it.

Small Craft Warnings, the rewrite of *The Confessional*, was planned both as a revival of Williams's work and a revival of the playwright in 1972. Williams did not trust the play on merit and felt he had been forgotten as a playwright. In the tradition of *The Iceman Cometh*, written during Eugene O'Neill's sober years, a bar-room called Monk's Place is the setting for a series of sometimes brilliant monologues that often subjugate the play's action. Monk, the spirit-maker, is the proprietor of the customer's existence. The drama of their lives circles the drink in an endless mandala. Conflicts are poignant, lamentative delusions of self. Leona uses sex to keep a roof over her head, but insists she is independent; Violet masturbates men in the amusement arcade. All of the players appear destined toward spiritual deaths.

Tennessee Williams played the doctor in the first five performances to gain an audience. As the alcoholic unlicensed Doctor Bacchus who delivers the stillborn baby, which is wrapped in cloth and floated out to sea, Williams ad libbed and drank through his performances, offering himself in the dual role of addicted playwright and addicted actor. One is reminded of John Berryman's group therapy session in *Recovery/Delusions, Etc.* wherein alcoholic patient Alan Severence says of his poet self, 'I have *not* come to easy terms with my fame. I am *not* an okay person'. While Williams fuses the drinking playwright/actor to insure fame, Severence's alter ego, the amphitheater, struggling through recovery, disassociates his creative self: 'I ought to make the theater feel guilty about neglecting poor Alan [the poet]; but in fact I won't: screw him. Let him solve his own problem. I won't feel sorry for him. I am a busy amphitheater, glad to be one, useful to many'.

Williams said that he identified more closely with the ageing homosexual, Quentin. He almost writes a section of the yet-to-be written *First Step in the Big Book of Sex and Love Addicts Anonymous*:

> There's a coarseness, a deadening coarseness. The experiences are quick, hard, and brutal, and the pattern of them is practically unchanging. Their act of love is like the jabbing of a hypodermic needle to which they're addicted but which is more and more empty of real interest and surprise

and likens this knowing to a 'Sphinx who lies on her belly and portends universal wisdom, but in reality if she were woken up by a fantastic fish swimming over her head she'd say, "Oh well"'.

The psychological progression of late-stage addiction is crystallized in *Out Cry*. Unlike *The Glass Menagerie*, *Out Cry* has no external battle. Unlike Amanda and Laura, Clare and Felice are not players in the world. The brother and sister are actors abandoned by their company, acting out a play within a play for an audience which may not exist. They cannot even leave the stage to take care of basic needs. Like the addict's reality, the universe is circles of darkness where sexuality is obscured, without the sheer sexual energy of Maggie the Cat or Serafina, nor the primitive instinct of Stanley Kowalski or Big Daddy. Unlike the stark symbolism of Williams's early plays, where walls melted into heavens to defend the subjective naturalism of the characters, a statue of psychic despair dominates the stage. Insanity is seen as escape: confinement as security. Unlike *Opening Night*, the John Cassavetes film about a play about an ageing actress, where improvisation saves the play and the actors, *Out Cry* insists that improvisation causes chaos. The actors are fated to play themselves in a spiritual wasteland. As in the late stages of addiction, the actor perform rituals over and over trying to make sense of the graceful past, and how empty it has become. Clare says, 'The worst thing that's disappeared in our lives is being aware of what's going on in our lives'.

Despite countless rewrites by Williams, *Out Cry* never had a discernible ending. As the curtain falls, Felice and Clare stand in the fading light accepting the possibility that death is transcended.

By this time Williams had lost most of his friends and his long-time agent, Audrey Wood. Companions were often paid, or people who agreed with him. Human vultures fleeced the playwright. Failed poets and young hustlers cried outside his hotel door until he wrote them blank checks. Sebastian's cannibalistic death in *Suddenly Last Summer* had become for Tennessee Williams another partial, self-fulfilled prophecy.

Williams kept on writing. Most of his late work vacillated between his lost youth, his unending feelings of self-doubt, and his spiritual and creative decline following Frank Merlo's death. Amidst these shadows, Williams sensed the need to return to the era of his *tour de force*, the 1940s (knowledge that O'Neill discovered upon getting sober at thirty-seven, and which enabled him to write his finest plays). He wrote *Vieux Carré, Clothes for a Summer Hotel* and *Something Cloudy, Something Clear*, a deeply personal play that opened in 1981 and proved to be his best and most successful work in twenty years.

But Tennessee Williams, convinced he was a failure, lay prone to endless geographics, profound isolation and constant substance abuse. In 1983 he died of an apparently accidental drug overdose.

CHANGING HABITS:
JAMES JOYCE AND DRUNKEN CATHOLICS

Matthew Campbell

'Shortly after my mother's death,' wrote Stanislaus Joyce, 'my brother began to drink riotously. Until then he had not been a teetotaller, but he had always been abstemious, and none of his friends had been drinkers.'[1] Irish 'gossiples' become, in *Finnegans Wake*, 'buried teatoastally in their Irish stew',[2] and James Joyce's initial contempt for the drinker quickly turned to contempt for the temperate. According to Stanislaus, it was Oliver St. John Gogarty who wanted 'to make Joyce drink in order to break his spirit', but Joyce did not drink spirits. In fact, as Stanislaus has it, 'in emulation of Falstaff and the poets of the Mermaid Inn, my brother began drinking sack...but he soon declined upon Guinness' porter'.[3] For James Joyce, at this period, drinking became a part of the life of the poet, an engagement in a conversion to artist still maintaining the need of the sacrament, any sacrament, in his new role of priestly artificer.

The affectations of his conversion to sack, until Guinness became more palatable, involved other, more blasphemous conversions for Joyce the spoilt priest. Stanislaus could participate in the absurdities of his brother's position as he describes him 'careering along the road of excess at full gallop'. This is his description of his brother on the batter:

> My brother's tall, slender figure and Bohemian garb were bound to catch the eye: the flowing butterfly bow, the inevitable ash-plant, and the round wide-brimmed soft felt hat, which in that Dublin of the past was much in favour with Protestant ministers. The echoes of his drinking bouts generally reached my ears at once, and I could hear, as the latest and greatest jest, how after swilling all night he sank insensible under the table and was borne by his boon companions on their shoulders to some neighbouring park or garden to sleep on the grass there and digest his drunkenness in the open air. It seems that one of the group walked in front, intoning and carrying my brother's hat hoisted on his ash-plant after the manner of a processional cross. Some little ragamuffins who were still in the street at that late hour began to run and cut capers around the mock funeral, and, seeing the hat, shouted to one another:

—Yurah, come and look at the drunken Protestan' minister. Did ye ever see the like? He's blind to Jaysus.[4]

Stanislaus can only comment with his usual temperate sternness, and simply states that 'a poet, whether great or minor there is little basis for judging, was drowned in those carousals.' But his brother's head was not entirely under water, no matter how much it had sunk under the table, during this state. As the drunken party emerge from the maternity hospital in the 'Oxen of the Sun' episode of *Ulysses*, the incident repeats itself with its own gloss:

> Jay, look at the drunken minister coming out of the maternity hospal! *Benedicat vos omnipotens Deus, Pater et Filius.* A make, mister. The Denzille lane boys. Hell, blast ye! Scoot. Righto, Isaacs, shove em out of the bleeding limelight. Yous join uz, dear sir? No hentrusion in life. Lou heap good man. Allee samee dis bunch. *En avant mes enfants!* Fire away number one gun. Burke's! Thence they advanced five parasangs. Slattery's mounted foot where's that bleeding awfur? Parson Steve, apostates creed![5]

For James Joyce, this awfur's drinking is a part of a self-conscious apostate's creed. His is a negative conversion, the choice of vice rather than virtue, the change from one kind of habit into the vestments of another. For the parson Stephen Daedalus, involved in his apostate role as artist–priest, his priesthood is that of 'a priest of eternal imagination, transmuting the daily bread of experience into the radiant body of ever-living life'.[6] The sacrament is also that of the water into wine, or wine into the blood of Christ, inverted into the converting powers of another habit, the transmuting powers of the bottle.

Conversions are usually from the vicious or erroneous habits of a life-time into virtuous convictions. For the convert, the struggle is to cast aside the habits of childhood and education and to embrace a new system, forcing the mind to take the pledge, and follow another way. The converts who hover before James Joyce and his own conversion from Catholic to priest of eternal imagination are his temperate atheist brother, the saint of his middle name, Augustine, and the example given to a whole genera-tion of writers by Joyce's university's most famous Principal, John Henry Newman.

For a variety of converts, as they talk about their conversion, the metaphor of inebriation is strong, the sudden headiness of a way of thinking which appears to make sense. St Augustine, as he describes his state of mind before his full conversion, tells of the lesson learnt from the shame caused by his own writing, by watching a drunken beggar:

> I was preparing an oration in praise of the Emperor wherein I was to deliver many an untruth, and to be applauded for my untruth, even by those that knew I did so. Whilst my heart panted after these cares, and boiled again with the feverishness of these consuming thoughts; walking along one of the streets of Milan, I observed a poor beggar man, half drunk I believe, very jocund and pleasant upon the matter; but I looking

> mournfully at him, fell to discourse with my friends then in company
> with me, about the many sorrows occasioned by our own madness; for that
> all such endeavours of ours, (under which I then laboured, and galled by
> the spurs of desire, dragged after me the burden of my own infelicity,
> increased it by the dragging) we had mind of nothing but how to attain
> some joy without care, whither that beggar man had arrived before us,
> who should never perchance come at all thither. For that which he had
> attained unto by means of a few pence (and those begged too) the same was
> I now plotting for, by many a troublesome winding; namely, to compass
> the joy of a temporary felicity.[7]

Walking in the light of conviction and grace, of an everlasting happiness,
which is the state that the convert longs for, is conveyed by Augustine in
the terms of inebriation. 'Joy without care' (*laetitiam pervenire*), a 'temporary
felicity' (*temporalis felicitatis*), is the lesson of the drunken beggar. But the
context of this incident is the preparation of an oration, a pack of lies. The
temporary happiness of the drunken beggar is still more authentic than
Augustine's unsaved self. A conversion could bring him into an
everlasting happiness, like the drunken beggar, and from there his
writing might be true.

The example of the Apostles after Pentecost might have been before
Augustine at this point. When the Apostles come out of the room in which
they have received the gift of speech, and begin preaching in Jerusalem,
the general sense of amazement at these uneducated men speaking
fluently and in foreign languages receives one particularly persuasive
explanation: 'These men are full of new wine.' Peter's defense is typically
ingenuous: 'For these are not drunk, seeing it is but the third hour of the
day' (9 am) (Acts 2.13, 15 [Douai version]). This is a defense against the
fluency that intoxication brings, a desire to speak in the light of an experience which seems remarkably like drunkenness. A conversion, though,
is a change of habit into a lifetime of such feeling. When Augustine's
conversion does finally come, it is oddly stated in terms not of a new
writing but of the cessation of his lying, as he gives up his employment as
a Professor of Rhetoric. The terms are odd, though eloquent, in their
rejection of their own eloquence:

> And I resolved in thy sight, though not tumultuously to snatch away, yet
> fairly to withdraw the service of my tongue from those marts of lip-labour:
> that young students (no students in thy Law, nor in thy peace but in lying
> dotages, and law skirmishes) should no longer buy at my mouth the
> engines for their own madness.[8]

The conversions of the late nineteenth century from Anglicanism to
Catholicism were seen in these terms, especially in the figures of those
Oxford ministers who changed their habits to those of Rome. For instance
Joyce, writing in 1935 to Harriet Shaw Weaver about John Henry
Newman, said that, 'nobody has ever written English prose that can be
compared to that of a tiresome footling little Anglican parson who after-

wards became a prince of the only true church.'[9] Newman's conversion brings a nobility both to his style and to his character, and Joyce parodies and quotes from Newman in the account of Stephen's conversion away from the church into art in *A Portrait of the Artist as a Young Man* (pp. 168-69). In the 'Oxen of the Sun' episode of *Ulysses*, Newman's style is reserved for the birth of Mrs Purefoy's boy child, a 'new man' indeed. Yet contrary to Newman's eloquent example, Gerard Manley Hopkins, professor in Newman's and Joyce's Catholic University in Dublin, was, like Augustine, most anxious about writing in the light of his new-found faith. *The Wreck of the Deutschland* was his first attempt to write the poem of his conversion. The happiness of this conversion is related in the terms of Augustine's glimpse of the temporary happiness of the drunken beggar, in terms of a sudden and overwhelming alcoholic tasting. This is from the eighth stanza:

> ...Oh,
> We lash with the best or worst
> Word last! How a lush-kept plush-capped sloe
> Will, mouthed to flesh burst,
> Gush!—flush the man, the being with it, sour or sweet,
> Brim, in a flash, full!—Hither then, last or first,
> To hero of Calvary, Christ's feet—
> Never ask if meaning it, wanting it, warned of it—men go.[10]

This lush-kept plush-capped sloe of faith is lush and overgrown in its sensuousness, but it is also kept by a lush, an alcoholic hoarding of the best wine for last. This is the intoxication of faith, and in a conversion it must last. Hopkins describes himself as 'Brim, in a flash, full!' and not full as a lord, but full with the Lord, he prostrates himself before Christ's feet.

Augustine, the Apostles, Hopkins, are all intoxicated by the new. What if this becomes habit? In Thomist ethics, the conscious practice of virtue eventually becomes a habit. The body must be mortified, but the mind should take no pride in the pursuit of spiritual perfection. The human is perfectible in habit, especially through the practice of religious routine. After the shocks of his particular re-conversion back to Catholicism the pubescent Stephen Daedalus in *A Portrait of the Artist* begins to follow a rigid spiritual programme. At the point where Stephen is asked to become a priest, the urge behind his spiritual stringency is revealed in the first statement of what is to become *A Portrait's* final artistic credo:

> In vague sacrificial or sacramental acts alone his will seemed to be drawn to go forth to encounter reality: and it was partly the absence of an appointed rite which had always constrained him to inaction whether he had allowed silence to cover his anger or pride or had suffered only an embrace he longed to give.[11]

The famous closing lines of *A Portrait of the Artist* have Stephen going forth for the millionth time to encounter the reality of experience, but these lines only echo their previous occurrence in the novel, of the artistic stated in terms of the transubstantiating powers of the Catholic priest. As an artist, he is to be a writer, and Stephen replaces the 'appointed rite' of the mass with that of words. He repeats Augustine's heresy, of dwelling on words and their sentences, in this encounter with 'reality'. He realises that it is not the colours that words suggest but the sentence itself that attracts his sacrificial and sacramental attentions. Joyce reserves the Newman 'period' for the style of this move to another conversion:

> Did he then love the rhythmic rise and fall of words better than their associations of legend and colour? Or was it that, being as weak of sight as he was shy of mind, he drew less pleasure from the reflection of the glowing sensible world through the prism of a language manycoloured and richly storied than from the contemplation of an inner world of individual emotions mirrored perfectly in a lucid supple periodic prose?[12]

This is both the absence, and the willing into a presence, of an appointed rite. The liturgy is to be the 'lucid supple periodic prose'.

This may be Stephen's creed, but is it James Joyce's? In a letter to Grant Richards, part of the extraordinary sequence of artistic apologias for *Dubliners*, Joyce characterises the style of the book as one of 'scrupulous meanness',[13] and a mean style in which reality is encountered. The reality is that of turn-of-the-century Dublin. And of that, Joyce would lecture his students in the Berlitz school in Trieste:

> Dubliners, strickly speaking, are my fellow countrymen, but I don't care to speak of our 'dear, dirty Dublin' as they do. Dubliners are the most hopeless, useless and inconsistent race of charlatans I have ever come across, on the island or the continent. This is why the English Parliament is full of the greatest windbags in the world. The Dubliner passes his time gabbing and making the rounds in bars or taverns or cathouses, without ever getting 'fed up' with the double doses of whiskey and Home Rule, and at night, when he can hold no more and is swollen up with poison like a toad, he staggers from the side-door and, guided by an instinctive desire for stability along the straight line of the houses, he goes slithering his backside against all walls and corners. He goes 'arsing along' as we say in English. There's the Dubliner for you.[14]

(' "Arsing along", as we say in English': the angry man is still careful to introduce his students to a new phrase.) This is a long way from a style of scrupulous meanness, and may also be a long way from the brother that Stanislaus Joyce describes indulging in very similar practices. The style of this is not scrupulous, or mean, it is intemperate, a drunken Irishman turning on the alleged drunkenness of the Irish.

I suppose that this speaks with the zeal of the convert, of one who has changed certain habits and is working on his 'highly polished looking glass' which will expose the foolish bad habits of his native city. Among the worst of these is that city's habit of drinking. *Dubliners* carries a number of its characters in and out of public houses and in and out of various states of drunkenness. 'Grace', for instance, has its Protestant convert physically injured while drunk, and led on retreat by a number of his friends. 'The Dead' gives a dinner party which is almost ruined by the arrival of the drunk Freddy Malins, who has already reneged on the pledge he took on New Year's Eve. But it is one central story, one which was very close to Joyce's heart, which shows the horrifying social effects of drinking in its style of scrupulous meanness. This is 'Counterparts', one of the stories which was composed in Trieste and added to the earlier version of *Dubliners*. Indeed, we know more about the composition of 'Counterparts' than we do about most works of literature. Joyce said that it was written in the Adriatic summer, and that 'many of the frigidities of *The Boarding House* and *Counterparts* were written while the sweat streamed down my face on to the handkerchief which protected my collar'.[15] Joyce's frigidity is reserved for the central character, Farrington, who is described as having a 'wine-dark complexion'. In fact this Homeric epithet is used three times in the story, leading us into the final resolution of the character in drunkenness and a horrific moment of family violence. Farrington is also described as being perpetually thirsty, even when drunk. The story concerns an act of insurrection, the humiliation of a superior. Farrington drinks out on his great moment in no less than four pubs during the course of the story, but is in turn humiliated in a test of strength, an arm wrestle. He returns home drunk, and turns on his own son:

—Who is that? said the man, peering through the darkness.

—Me, pa.

—Who are you? Charlie?

—No, pa. Tom.

—Where's your mother?

—She's out at the chapel.

—That's right...Did she think of leaving any dinner for me?

—Yes, pa. I—

—Light the lamp. What do you mean by having the place in darkness? Are the other children in bed?

The man sat down heavily on one the chairs while the little boy lit the lamp. He began to mimic his son's flat accent, saying half to himself: *At the chapel, at the chapel, if you please!* When the lamp was lit he banged his fist on the table and shouted:

—What's for my dinner?

—I'm ... going to cook it, pa, said the little boy.

The man jumped up furiously and pointed to the fire.

—On that fire! You let the fire out! By God I'll teach you to do that again!

He took a step to the door and seized the walking stick which was standing behind it.

—I'll teach you to let the fire out! he said rolling up his sleeve in order to give his arm free play.

The little boy cried, *O, pa!* and ran whimpering round the table, but the man followed him and caught him by the coat. The little boy looked about him wildly but, seeing no way of escape, fell upon his knees.

—Now, you'll let the fire out the next time! said the man, striking at him vigorously with the stick. Take that, you little whelp!

The boy uttered a squeal of pain as the stick cut his thigh. He clasped his hands together in the air and his voice shook with fright.

—O, pa! he cried. Don't beat me, pa! And I'll...I'll say a *Hail Mary* for you...I'll say a *Hail Mary* for you, pa, if you don't beat me....I'll say a *Hail Mary*....[16]

According to Stanislaus Joyce, his brother took up the habit of drinking seriously after the death of his mother. This is domestic violence, perpetrated in the absence of wife and mother, against the background of the unlistening mother of God: 'I'll say a *Hail Mary* for you, pa, if you don't beat me....'

This story repudiates both old and new faiths for Joyce, that of the Church, as seen in the figures of his mother, the absent wife and mother in the story, and the unlistening mother of Christ, and that of drink. This is certainly mean, whether or not it is scrupulous, and the man, made less of a man by his drinking, his failed feats of strength and the absence of the female, is left stick in hand over the defenceless body of his child. This literary style is frigid and mean, a conversion into a 'lucid supple periodic prose' which in its tacit representation of the violence of drink does come from one brought up in the shadow of its terror.[17] Yet converted away from chapel and Hail Marys, given the impetus of a dead mother, this is a style culled from the meanness with words which Augustine wished upon himself after his conversion, a quiet withdrawing of the tongue's service from the marts of lip-labour, where the tools of madness are no longer bought at the eloquent mouth of the drunken Irish writer. There are few words, they do not stand their round, they are converted into a horrific encounter with reality.

NOTES

1.   S. Joyce, *My Brother's Keeper* (ed. R. Ellmann; London: Faber & Faber, 1958), p. 240.

2.   J. Joyce, *Finnegans Wake* (London: Faber & Faber, 1939), p. 38.

3.   S. Joyce, *My Brother's Keeper*, p. 241.

4.   S. Joyce, *My Brother's Keeper*, pp. 243-44.

5.   J. Joyce, *Ulysses* (ed. H.W. Gabler *et al.*; London: Bodley Head, 1984), 14.1444-51. (1922 text has 'Allee samee this bunch'.)

6.   J. Joyce, *A Portrait of the Artist as a Young Man* (ed. C.G. Anderson; London: Jonathan Cape, 1968), p. 225.

7.   *The Confessions of St Augustine* 6.62 (LCL edn).

8.   Augustine, *Confessions*, 9.2.2.

9.   R. Ellmann (ed.), *Letters of James Joyce* (3 vols.; London: Faber & Faber, 1966), II, p. 36.

10. Quoted from *The Poetical Works of Gerard Manley Hopkins* (ed. N.H. Mackenzie; Oxford: Oxford University Press, 1990).

11. J. Joyce, *A Portrait of the Artist*, p. 162.

12. J. Joyce, *A Portrait of the Artist*, p. 171.

13. Ellman (ed.), *Letters of James Joyce*, II, p. 134.

14. Quoted in R. Ellmann, *James Joyce* (Oxford: Oxford University Press, 2nd edn, 1982), p. 217.

15. Ellmann, *James Joyce*, p. 208.

16. J. Joyce, 'Counterparts', in *Dubliners* (ed. R. Scholes; London: Jonathan Cape, 1967), pp. 108-109).

17. See e.g., S. Joyce, *The Complete Dublin Diary* (ed. G. Healey; London: Faber & Faber, 1971), pp. 175-87.

'OH, THOSE AWFUL PRESSURES!' FAULKNER'S 'CONTROLLED' DRINKING

Tom Dardis

I

In the summer of 1987, when the Faulkner chapter of *The Thirsty Muse* (Ticknor and Fields, 1989) was nearly finished, I phoned the late Carvel Collins in California to see if he might have anything to contribute to my study of Faulkner's alcoholism. Professor Collins had amassed a huge amount of material over a period of 35 years in connection with a biography of Faulkner, a work that remained unfinished at his death. Collins indicated that he indeed had much to tell about Faulkner's drinking, but that the subject was far too complicated to be discussed on the phone; he urged me to visit him in California as soon as possible to share his knowledge of the unique qualities of Faulkner's alcoholism that he had observed at first hand in many years of acquaintanceship with the novelist. He also told me that what he wished to share was an entirely new approach to the subject and one that had never appeared in print. His invitation was certainly tempting. Collins's gracious offer was not, however, the only reason for my visiting Hollywood that summer. I had already planned such a trip in order to discuss the particulars of Faulkner's drinking with some of the friends he had known and worked with there in the 1930s and 1940s: Meta Carpenter, 'Buzz' Bezzarides and Daniel Fuchs.

Professor Collins arrived at the hotel within an hour of my arrival in Hollywood. Our talk then ran to slightly over 13 hours without a break (save for meals): he left my room at 2.15 am. I do not exaggerate. Collins was obsessed with everything about Faulkner, and while our talk was not entirely confined to his drinking habits, we kept coming back to them. Collins's knowledge of the subject was indeed encyclopedic for, as he told me, almost everyone he had interviewed had inevitably brought up the matter. The notion of saying anything much about Faulkner without mentioning the writer's fascination with alcohol was a virtual impossibility.

I soon discovered that Professor Collins's revelations were not all that startling, nor did they differ much from what I had been told by several other people who had known the man. Collins had details about some of the less famous binges, but the main element that ran through his account, as well as those of many others that I had interviewed, was that Faulkner was unique among alcoholics. It turned out that Faulkner had always been in complete control of his drinking, even including the famous 'around the clock' binges that had caused so much pain to himself and those close to him. The control Collins spoke of also applied to Faulkner's extended binges—those that could lead him to ten-day and even two-week incarcerations in hospitals and drying-out facilities. As Collins saw it, these periods of what appeared on the surface to be an uncontrollable intake of alcohol were in fact actually 'willed' by a man who had only decided to embark on non-stop drinking in the face of unbearable situations. In short, Collins believed that Faulkner only resorted to drinking binges when the life around him became too hard to handle—'those awful pressures'.

While questioning Collins about what kind of pressures were required to bring on such a binge, I asked him why Faulkner began a longish one at the time of being awarded the Nobel Prize for Literature in 1949. Surely this was good news, news that could be handled without such severe measures? Collins informed me that it really made no difference to Faulkner whether the news was good *or* bad—anything out of the ordinary would serve to produce non-stop drinking. Collins was dangerously close to the truth here when he, as well as the various other propounders of what I shall call the 'controlled drinking' myth, made it clear that Faulkner drank on any and all occasions: it did not really matter *why*. In fact, the question 'why' is beside the point.

The 'controlled drinking' myth asserts that, since we cannot consider Faulkner as an alcoholic in any commonly accepted sense of the word, if Faulkner willed his binges he must indeed have had control over his drinking. And since we surely know that alcoholics lack this capacity, Faulkner was clearly not an alcoholic as were writers like Scott Fitzgerald and Hart Crane. I will attempt to show the origins of this myth as well as its falsity.

II

There is some superficial evidence that supports the 'reaction to pressures' idea. It can be found in the imagined resemblance between Faulkner and writers like Virginia Woolf, who fell into deep, often suicidal, depressions immediately following the completion of long and difficult works. Leonard Woolf has described his wife's situation in *Downhill All the Way*:

> But there was also...a second period of passion and excitement through
> which she almost always had to pass in the process of writing a novel. This
> came upon her almost invariably as soon as she finished writing a book
> and the moment arrived for it to be sent to the printer. It was a kind of
> passion of despair, and it was emotionally so violent and exhausting that
> each time she became ill with the symptoms threatening a breakdown.[1]

In her diary entry for 7 February 1931 Virginia Woolf memorably
described the feeling of intoxicated exaltation she experienced just after
completing *The Waves*:

> Here in the few minutes that remain, I must record, heaven be praised,
> the end of *The Waves*. I wrote the words O Death fifteen minutes ago,
> having reeled across the last ten pages with some moments of such
> intensity and intoxication that I seemed only to stumble after my own
> voice, or almost, after some sort of speaker (as when I was mad) I was
> almost afraid, remembering the voices that used to fly ahead. Anyhow, it
> is done....[2]

Virginia Woolf's depressions were so deep that they often prevented her
from sleeping. Leonard Woolf would then administer doses of chloral
hydrate to his wife in order for her to cope with the problem. Her intermittent use of the drug finds its alleged counterpart in Faulkner's drinking
behavior after he had finished a number of his major works. The essential
difference between Woolf and Faulkner is that he displayed no signs of
depression whatever at these times: drink he did, but he did that without
the impact of having completed a difficult work. The resemblance
between Woolf and Faulkner is only true insofar as both writers shared an
intense, 'post-creative' state of mind that might last for days. Virginia
Woolf did not become addicted to chloral hydrate: she used it only (and
rarely) when she could not sleep. Faulkner, on the other hand, regularly
drank himself into hospitals but without any particular push. He drank
because he was an alcoholic, not because of creative pressures.

His conduct at such times was curiously repetitive. In early 1936 he took
the just-completed manuscript of *Absalom, Absalom!* to the home of some
old friends in Louisiana where he began to drink heavily, so heavily that
he could not stop. It was at this time that he was forced to undergo his first
hospitalization for detoxification, at Wright's Sanitorium in Byhalia,
Mississippi—the place of his death 26 years later. This episode is
especially interesting because Faulkner left behind him in Louisiana the
only copy of the book on which he had toiled for nearly three years. The
situation repeated itself in 1952 when Faulkner finished his nine years'
labor on *A Fable*. On this occasion Faulkner's behavior was strikingly
similar to that of 1936. On a sudden visit to the home of his old friend Ben
Wasson in Greenville, Mississippi, Faulkner began to tell Wasson and his
guests about the meaning of his epic work—uncharacteristic behavior. He
began, however, to drink so heavily that he left Wasson's house in an
unconscious state and had to be hospitalized within a few days. He

repeated his 1936 pattern by leaving behind him in Wasson's home the only copy of *A Fable*.

If these episodes had been the only ones which resulted in extended drinking bouts, we might be able to talk about 'those awful pressures' as a cause. But the facts are otherwise. Faulkner had dozens of episodes in which the factor of recently completed work—or any discernable pressure—was absent. Despite his heightened feelings on these occasions, Faulkner's drinking behavior closely resembles that of most alcoholics, which is to say that he displayed no control over his drinking.

III

The standard formulation of the legend of Faulkner's controlled drinking can be found in the pages of Joseph Blotner's 1974 biography. In the first 700 pages of this enormous work Blotner details the Faulkner family's serious involvement with alcohol. In these pages it is made abundantly clear that all the male Faulkners drank alcoholically for at least five generations. After furnishing us with countless details that show how the novelist resembled his kinsmen, Blotner suddenly asks a question that may seem to some to be unnecessary. The question is simply, 'Why did he drink?' Despite the fact that he has demonstrated conclusively that his subject was alcoholic, Blotner proceeds to answer his question by supplying us with the reasons he believes were operative. Faulkner liked the taste of alcohol; it made him feel good. Blotner also claims that Faulkner used alcohol as a general catch-all medical remedy for illnesses: take enough of it and you will not feel a thing. He also used it, apparently, as an anesthetic for anything unpleasant. In short, as Blotner sees it, Faulkner used alcohol for a good many reasons, but, nevertheless, Blotner is curiously evasive about his subject's illness. He insists that Faulkner was capable of drinking 'moderately' for long stretches of time; he ends his introductory remarks about Faulkner's drinking with these telling lines: 'his intake would be moderate, or considerable, but controlled. *It would have to be so, for him to accomplish all the work he had done*'.[3] In other words, Faulkner simply *cannot* be like other alcoholics: the work he did is too extraordinary to have been written by an alcoholic!

There is a striking similarity here between Blotner's evasiveness about the nature of Faulkner's alcoholism and Christopher Sykes's remarks about Evelyn Waugh's drinking problem in his biography of the novelist. As I indicate in *The Thirsty Muse*, Sykes absolutely refuses to accept Waugh as an alcoholic (despite the writer's own admission that he was), because no alcoholic could have written the books that have ensured his fame.

Sykes's views on Waugh deserve quoting in full, for perhaps they best state just why so many literary biographers refuse to identify their subjects as victims of alcoholism:

> While it is true that several eminent and rightly admired authors have been addicted to excessive drinking, it is also true that no such writer has gone so far as to become an alcoholic, with the dubious and, if accepted, not very impressive exceptions in English letters of Edgar Allan Poe and Dylan Thomas. Now, if Evelyn's accounts of his drinking and frequent drunkenness were not exaggerated, then he must inevitably have become an alcoholic. Equally inevitably his mental faculties would have been influenced if not impaired *and he could never have achieved literary excellence of the kind that he did....*Evelyn's work in general, though intensely imaginative, gives an immediate impression of the concentration of intellect, of mental discipline, and his prose of precise and justified choice. *None of this could conceivably be open to a man whose powers had been limited, and whose imagination had been inflamed in the manner he so fecklessly suggested.* As evidence it should be remembered that if he undoubtedly drank excessively he never was a 'slave to alcohol'. As his companion in some of his later travels, I can testify that when cut off from drink by circumstances, the inconvenience never bothered him, and it is a fact, as all his acquaintances know, that in later years he regularly gave up strong drink throughout Lent, with difficulty it is true, but with success.[4]

It is clear that Sykes and Blotner are identical in their desire to create the impression that their subjects had their drinking under control. For example, Blotner supplies his readers with the following working analysis of this touchy subject:

> A working definition of an alcoholic is that he is one who has lost control of the drinking pattern to the extent that it interferes with his interpersonal relationships, family or socioeconomic situation, or involves him with the law.[5]

After citing scores of incidents in which Faulkner displayed his conformity to the pattern outlined above, Blotner nevertheless continues his discussion of the definition by saying that, 'If WF can be said to have suffered from alcoholism, it was a kind of periodic and volitional alcoholism'. Blotner does throw the reader a bone when he concludes with: 'As he aged, the incidence of extended drinking bouts decreased'.[6]

In his immense narrative Blotner places his extended discussion of Faulkner's drinking just prior to documenting the dozens of episodes that are to be described in considerable detail. Blotner's insistence that the bouts were planned is nothing short of remarkable considering the facts he reveals:

> The bouts were usually deliberate. Faulkner would ensure a sufficient supply of liquor. He would plan when he would start and would often plan when he would stop....

Blotner then cites a tale told by Faulkner to his then Random House editor, Robert Linscott:

> The craving would come. Most often he'd fight it off. But once in a while something would 'get me all of a turmoil inside' and liquor seemed the only escape. It was only when he was caught in a situation he couldn't cope

with that he'd give in to what he called the chemistry of craving and go overboard.[7]

Faulkner's 'I just will my binges' idea is confounded by the terrifying effects that went along with them. The dreadful third-degree burns he suffered at the Hotel Algonquin in 1937 do not appear to be part of any planned or willed endeavor. That disaster simply attests to the fact that what Faulkner then experienced was part and parcel of what might happen to him when he drank, that is to say, absolutely anything.

Both Blotner and Sykes point with pride to those times when their subjects abstained from liquor. By and large, these abstentions were quite brief. After a month or a week or even a year of being 'on the wagon' both writers quickly resumed their 'normal' drinking pattern, the pattern that might involve such horrendous events as those experienced by Waugh's character Gilbert Pinfold, who believed he was going mad. This pattern of troubling events is the fate that all alcoholics suffer: an inability to know with any degree of certainty what will happen after the first few drinks are consumed. Things may go well on several occasions in a row, but inevitably the control, if it can be called that, is soon lost and the drinker ends up in the hospital, or in jail, or in the grip of the kinds of clinical depression that necessitate prolonged stays in mental institutions, often accompanied by the administration of electro-shock therapy. There is little doubt that Gilbert Pinfold's hallucinations on board ship were the same ones experienced by his creator.

Why should Blotner and Sykes feel this defensive about their subjects, so much so that their arguments fly in the face of the anecdotal material they furnish with such abundance? The answer lies, I think, in their feeling that once Faulkner and Waugh are positively identified as alcoholics, they will be 'looked down upon' as writers, as not to be taken seriously. After all, what do drunks know? Hence their stressing the 'control' factor, this apparent ability to pull in the reins on their intake of alcohol from time to time to write the books that made their reputations.

IV

Substance addiction leaves its mark on virtually every phase of human life, perhaps all the more so in the case of writers who find—in time— these addictions deadly to their creative powers. It would be pleasant to report that recent biographers have faced up to the importance of their subjects' various addictions. Some of them have, notably Green in *Capote*, Bergreen in *James Agee*, and David Roberts in *Jean Stafford*. The last of these titles has produced a curious reaction to its revelations about the degree to which Jean Stafford became involved with alcohol. The prominent American novelist and short story writer Joyce Carol Oates launched a savage attack on the book, deploring the author's thorough documentation of Stafford's difficulties. She even invented a new word, pathography, as part of her assault:

> Though this has been an era of magisterial biographies...it has also evolved a new subspecies of the genre to which the word 'pathography' might usefully be given....[Roberts] has written a seemingly well-intentioned life of Jean Stafford that falls into pathography's technique of emphasizing *the sensational underside of its subject's life to the detriment of those more scattered and less dramatic periods of accomplishment and well being.*[8]

Oates is a programmatic version of Sykes and Blotner. She is telling us that biographers should desist from giving us specific accounts of involvement with the substance that stood at the very center of their subjects' lives for decades. The notion is absurd. Without the knowledge that Faulkner, Hemingway and Fitzgerald were alcoholic, their tortured lives would strike readers as totally incomprehensible. When we understand the writers' disease, we are in a far better position to understand their triumphs and later failures.

There are many obstacles to revealing the truth about the alcoholism of major American writers, as I well recall from my own experience with *The Thirsty Muse* some years ago. I had offered the book to a major publishing house and the idea was greeted with great enthusiasm by my young and relatively inexperienced editor. A week later she told me sadly that the house simply could not afford to make me an offer for the book. She had been told by her seniors that the Hemingway and Fitzgerald estates would take a very dim view of her company's publishing any sort of book that dealt with these two writers and their deep involvement with alcohol.

It is undoubtedly the practice of viewing alcoholics as equivalent to skid-row derelicts that has caused this extreme reluctance to face the facts about these writers. 'My' Steinbeck, 'my' Henry Green, 'my' Jean-Paul Sartre cannot really have been alcoholics! It is too ignoble! Not so common a practice is understanding the existence of the highly successful writer who spends his or her days measuring out maintenance doses of alcohol in order to keep those words flowing, doses that inevitably become larger and larger until the day comes when the words either will not flow at all or emerge in the form of parodies of what the writer could accomplish in earlier days. The final years of Jack London and Ernest Hemingway come to mind here, for both men ended up unable to produce much of anything.

It is clear that the controlled drinking myth is a sort of halfway house of biographers, allowing them partially to admit their subject's acquaintance with alcohol while refusing to go the whole way and reveal that, for example, Faulkner's addiction was in the final analysis not much different than that of most other alcoholics. Things just got worse and worse and his writing was not exempt. *A Fable* is proof of what happened to the man who once wrote *As I Lay Dying*.

NOTES

1.　L. Woolf, *Downhill All the Way* (New York: Harcourt, 1967), p. 55.
2.　V. Woolf, *A Writer's Diary* (New York: Harcourt, 1954), p. 165.
3.　J. Blotner, *Faulkner: A Biography*, I (New York: Random House, 1974), p. 717.
4.　C. Sykes, *Evelyn Waugh* (Boston, MA: Little, Brown, 1975), p. 49 (italics added).
5.　Blotner, *Faulkner*, p. 107 ('Notes' section).
6.　Blotner, *Faulkner*, p. 104 ('Notes' section).
7.　Blotner, *Faulkner*, p. 719.
8.　J.C. Oates, review of Roberts, *Jean Stafford*, *New York Times*, August 28 1988, p. 3.

ALCOHOL AND WRITING:
PATTERNS OF OBSESSION IN THE WORK
OF MARGUERITE DURAS

Renate Günther

Marguerite Duras is certainly one of the most prolific writers in contemporary France. Since the beginning of her literary career in 1944 she has published over thirty novels and 'récits', eighteen plays and several collections of articles and autobiographical texts. She has also directed numerous films for which she herself wrote the scripts.

In her autobiography *L'Amant* (1984) one sentence which echoes throughout the book crystallises the fundamental motivating force in her life: 'Je veux écrire'. Writing, then, became a necessity, if not a compulsion, for Duras over a period of nearly fifty years. Yet, since the early sixties at least, Marguerite Duras's passion for literature has been accompanied and nourished by a second, complementary passion: her addiction to alcohol.

In a series of interviews with the French writer and critic Xavière Gauthier, published under the title *Les Parleuses* (1974), Duras said that one of her major novels of the sixties, *Le Ravissement de Lol V. Stein* (1964), was written during a post-withdrawal phase and that she experienced considerable anguish throughout this period, partly as a result of alcohol deprivation. Significantly the novel which was created from this experience revolves around the theme of deprivation, as the central female character loses her lover, her memory and ultimately herself.

From 1964 onwards, Duras's work became a progressive movement towards emptiness, a movement which reveals lack and absence as the paradoxically hollow core of existence, and which highlights the illusory nature of her characters' initial quest for unity and completeness, both within themselves and in their relationships with others. If for some God fills this empty space, for Duras alcohol has taken the place of God, as she herself wrote in *L'Amant*.[1] It seems, therefore, that while her writing creates an ever-increasing vacuum, drinking compensates for this sense of the void and alleviates the fear it inspires.

The relationship between alcohol and writing is mirrored in the thematic and stylistic patterns characteristic of Duras's work itself. In her early novels, which span the period from 1944–60, alcohol figures as a recurring motif and is primarily, if not exclusively, associated with her women characters. Given Duras's central concern with the question of feminine identity and the liberation of women it may be assumed that this connection between women and alcohol in her writing is not merely arbitrary, but can be interpreted within a broader thematic framework.

Duras's first women characters experience life as a series of restrictions imposed upon them either by an oppressive family environment or a suffocating marriage, which allow little room for expansion and creativity. However, most of Duras's women transgress the social norms which condemn them to a lifetime of passivity. Their desire for freedom is expressed in their search for an intense and all-consuming passion, a quest which is frequently accompanied by their consumption of alcohol. Depending on the geographical setting of her novels, Duras's earliest heroines drink Campari in Italy, manzanilla in Spain and, of course, red wine in France. In a general sense it is true that alcohol reduces inhibitions and, therefore, facilitates the transgression of social codes of behaviour. From a more gender-specific perspective, however, it seems that in Duras's novels alcohol temporarily neutralises the impact of an entire set of emotional and behavioural constraints typically associated with femininity. In particular, alcohol breaks down the social and psychological barriers which prevent her female characters from expressing their sexuality.

The role of alcohol as an agent of female transgression is most evident in one of Duras's key texts, the 1958 novel *Moderato cantabile*. In this novel the central woman character, Anne, a provincial middle-class wife and mother, has a series of encounters with a factory worker, Chauvin, in a small-town café which is frequented exclusively by men. Anne's conversations with Chauvin, highly charged with sexual and emotional intensity, are punctuated by the seemingly countless glasses of red wine which she consumes throughout this episode. From a cultural point of view it is worth drawing attention to the taboo that exists, especially in France, against women who drink alcohol, at least in public. Red wine, in particular, is seen as a typically 'masculine' drink, and in *Moderato cantabile* the social disapproval of Anne's behaviour is condensed in the reproachful glances of the landlady who reluctantly serves the other woman at the bar. The choice of red wine, then, is symbolic not only of Anne's growing awareness and expression of her sexuality but also of her explicit infringement of one of the fundamental rules concerning femininity in her culture.

But while alcohol can be seen as part of a process of liberation, it also becomes quite clearly an instrument of destruction. Throughout Duras's work women are seen to oscillate between these two poles of experience and the dividing line between them becomes dangerously blurred at times. Thus, on the one hand, her women characters seek to free themselves from a feminine identity which threatens to destroy them. However, femininity is not merely an abstract category which could simply be discarded or exchanged for a new set of definitions. It is, as Duras's work itself clearly indicates, an integral part of women's emotional world. For many of her female characters, therefore, the process of liberation from a socially constructed 'feminine' self often comes close to self-destruction in a real physical sense. This ambiguity is implicit in *Moderato cantabile*, where Anne's efforts to shed her social identity lead to her progressive loss of self, as under the influence of increasing alcohol intoxication she becomes enmeshed in an obsessive suicidal fantasy.

Moderato cantabile inaugurates a 20-year cycle in Duras's work, during which the disintegration of personal identity and the dismantling of self-boundaries become central thematic elements, especially in her representations of love and sexual relationships. Stepping beyond the confines of 'the self' is seen as a way of overcoming the self/other divide, inherent particularly in the traditional heterosexual model of love based on an assumed polarity between 'masculinity' and 'femininity'. In her attempt to come to terms with this dichotomy, Duras is constantly torn between a vision of 'absolute love' and the sense that 'love is impossible'. In so far as the ideal of love in her work is often translated by the desire for a permanent fusion between 'self' and 'other' it must, of course, remain impossible. But having glimpsed this absolute, Duras and many of her literary figures experience all the more painfully the reality of separation in relationships and the ensuing feeling of abandonment and loss. Duras's conception of love, then, fluctuates between an ideal of closeness and a deep sense of alienation and distance between individuals.

This latter version is most poignantly evoked in the short text *La Maladie de la mort*, which was written in the summer of 1982 during a phase of intense alcohol intoxication which immediately preceded Duras's admission to a hospital with cirrhosis of the liver in an advanced stage. Her subsequent experience of alcohol withdrawal and her ultimate recovery have been described by Duras's close friend and companion, Yann Andréa, in a book whose title is composed of her initials: *M.D.*

La Maladie de la mort tells of a young man's impossible desire to love and to be loved by a woman who will always remain a stranger to him, as he is unable to break down the barriers which isolate them from each other. His fear of difference and in particular of feminine 'otherness' is diagnosed by the young woman in the text as both a symptom and a cause of 'the sickness of death' which he carries within himself. In his book Andréa commented that for Duras the emotional distress of writing this text was so powerful that alcohol provided a form of relief, a 'counterpoint to the written page'.[2] This contrapuntal relationship between alcohol and writing can be interpreted more specifically with regard to both the central theme and the style of *La Maladie de la mort*. For if the text itself embodies separation and constructs an insurmountable wall between the two protagonists, alcohol can have the opposite effect of creating an (illusory) sense of unity as physical and emotional barriers seem to dissolve, allowing for the closeness which is described as 'impossible' in much of Duras's work. At the same time alcohol blurs perceptions of difference and 'otherness', both key elements in the relationship described in *La Maladie de la mort*.

On a linguistic level, the dry, almost abstract, quality of Duras's style in this text contrasts with the underlying movement in her work towards dispersal, liquefaction and merging, all associated with alcohol. The written page, then, and the alcohol which attends its composition both counteract and complement each other.

While in Duras's early novels alcohol appeared as an explicit motif, from 1960 onwards it seems to have become suppressed and channelled instead into a typically Durassian form and style. Certain aspects of these formal patterns, for example the deferral of meaning, repetition, the recurrence of liquid metaphors and the gradual paring down of language to a state of near-silence reflect an emotional world influenced by alcohol addiction.

From the outset Duras's work reveals a process of constant deferral, initially manifested in her characters' obsession with never attaining their goal of ideal love. Thus, relationships frequently remain potential, fantasised future possibilities which would be destroyed by consummation in reality. This perpetual search for an 'elsewhere' is at first overtly associated with alcohol, as in the 1952 novel *Le Marin de Gibraltar* and, of course, *Moderato cantabile*. In later texts it is implicit in the gaps and blanks which become an increasingly characteristic feature of Duras's style. Her syntax has been gradually reduced to minimal constructions, often consisting of only a noun and a verb. This suspension of meaning in the empty spaces on the page mirrors both the de-centring of the self in Duras's later work and her portrayal of relationships. Like love, writing has to remain virtual and meaning needs to be deferred, for to stabilise it would be to immobilise and thereby to suppress the very dynamics of her creativity. It is possible, therefore, that Duras's compulsion was to maintain and to nurture, through alcohol, the very sense of lack from which she wrote.

If deferral expresses the desire for an unattainable absolute in the future, a second pattern of obsession in Duras, compulsive repetition, transfers a similar desire into the past. Many Durassian characters become embroiled in their own or someone else's past which they either replay in an imaginary scenario or reproduce in reality. The past events which are thus re-enacted in the present are usually associated with a traumatic experience involving loss and separation. In one sense, repetition in Duras often indicates a refusal to accept the reality of loss as such and expresses a longing to return to an imaginary state of unity between the self and the world. This desire for non-differentiation works against her characters' potential self-creation and instead it becomes self-destructive.

Obsessive repetition is, of course, not only a central feature of Duras's texts, but also constitutes an aspect of addictive behaviour. In this context the Freudian equation between the compulsion to repeat and the death drive could be applied to Duras's writing as well as to her alcoholism, since both often take the form of suicidal regression. Although not always overtly linked with alcohol, the Durassian characters' wish to revert back to an embryonic 'original' state of harmony and completeness is nevertheless reflected in their fatal attraction towards liquid elements, particularly the sea, and in some of her later texts and films culminates in suicide through drowning. However, repetition in Duras can also have a creative function, as the desire to return is converted into an artistic activity, through which her characters enact or narrate their experience of loss as part of a scenario which they themselves have invented. Repetition also underpins the intertexuality of Duras's entire literary and cinematographic production, as she constantly retells and readapts the same core story in different contexts and through different media—novels, plays and films. Paradoxically, for the reader this vast mirror structure creates the very sense of recognition which Duras seeks to undermine in individual texts. If her characters suffer from amnesia and the loss of their identity, her work as a whole constitutes its own memory and produces an aura that is unique to Duras. Her writing, through its very existence and its internal continuity, opposes the devouring effects of alcohol.

An examination of rhetorical figures in Duras shows a clear prominence of metaphors and symbols related to various forms of liquids. If alcohol itself represents a key symbol in her earlier work, in later texts other liquids play a similar metaphorical role. Thus, for example, water imagery often translates her characters' fluid limitless way of being and their rejection of any fixed identity. The formlessness of liquids is also associated with the world of the imagination and contrasted with the solid images of ice and stone, which represent the rigid order of external reality. Similarly, food, even though a rare ingredient in Duras, is seen as part of a static social order, as in *Moderato cantabile*, where it is explicitly opposed to alcohol which becomes a means of escape from society.

The process of merging and the blurring of boundaries expressed by liquid metaphors is extended further to the gradual disintegration of language as such in Duras. If language is meaningful only as part of a system of differences, Duras's texts, on the other hand, break down the signifying chain, as her syntax becomes increasingly fragmented and the logical links between words and sentences are omitted. At the same time, her work attaches a special significance to music and to silence, as they are both seen to move beyond the rigid boundaries of language.

Marguerite Duras's writing reflects a perpetual struggle to create form and meaning out of darkness and emptiness. From this void, isolated words emerge which briefly capture sensations and impressions and then dissolve back into silence. This tension between creation and destruction, between form and formlessness is a constant element in Duras's work and mirrors the long co-existence in her life of writing and alcohol.

NOTES

1. M. Duras, *L'Amant* (Paris: Minuit, 1984), p. 15.
2. Y. Andréa, *M.D.* (Paris: Minuit, 1983), p. 116.

(UN)RELIABILITY AND PAN-(IN)SIGNIFICANCE
IN *UNDER THE VOLCANO* AND *ISLAND*:
A PRELIMINARY OVERVIEW

Tom Roder

> If you understand, things are such as they are;
> If you do not understand, things are such as they are
> (Gensha, Zen Master).

> To enter into the visions of mescaline the giraffes must grow even taller
> (H. Michaux, *Miserable Miracle*).

One of the necessary organizing features of both *Under the Volcano* and *Island* is the unreliability of experience. In *Under the Volcano* this permeates Firmin's perceptions, utterances (discourse) and relationships—nothing is fixed, definite; everything is amenable to multiple interpretation, re-working, 'inflammation',[1] disruption. In *Island* the presentation of this unreliability is less sophisticated as the bulk of this 'novel' is sermonizing, lecturing, programmatic—the authorial voice insisting on presenting its case without obstruction, dominating the fluctuations and uncertainties of Farnaby and debunking the motives of the hostile faction. However, the last chapter to some small extent disrupts, confuses, the authorial voice. Here Farnaby receives the sacramental moksha-medicine which facilitates, among other things, the reviewing and re-integrating of many of the earlier incidents or memories. This essay will look at the various means used to enact this unreliability of experience in *Under the Volcano* and *Island*, try to suggest the extent to which this unreliability is determined, ameliorated or dispersed (made reliable) by the use of alcohol and hallucinogenic drugs, and suggest ways that this (un)reliability lends itself to the presentation of pan-determinism and pan-(in)significance.

The most dramatic form of the unreliability of experience, evident in both works is seen when the infinitely benevolent vision, a 'succession of revelations' (*I*, p. 308),[2] perceived with 'limitless, undifferentiated awareness' (*I*, p. 309) flashes or flicks over to being what Huxley terms the 'Essential Horror' (*I*, p. 319)—a catch-all phrase for endless suffering, destructive forces, death, annihilation. Interestingly both works give a vivid example of this switch in terms of the perception of reptile and insect-life.[3]

In *Island* this switch between 'limitless, undifferentiated awareness', 'the fact of being blissfully one with oneness' and the 'Essential Horror' is provoked and given focus by one of Tom Krishna's pet lizards:

> The light was as bright as ever; but the brightness had changed its sign. A glow of sheer evil radiated from every grey-green scale of the creature's back, from its obsidian eyes...(*I*, p. 309).

Farnaby turns away but finds that the effect isn't invested locally; this particular object of the 'Essential Horror' has alerted him to the potential horror of everything. For example the table earlier described as a

> ...breathing apocalypse...might be thought of as a picture of some mystical Cubist, some inspired Juan Gris with the soul of Traherne and a gift for painting miracles with conscious gems and the changing moods of water lily petals (*I*, p. 317)[4]

is now perceived as an 'intricate machine for doing nothing malevolently' (*I*, p. 319). In general, 'Everything still pulsed with life but with the life of an infinitely sinister bargain basement'. The horror proliferates, reaching its apogee when a 'miniaturised machine for copulation' (a praying mantis) begins to chew off her mate's head, and then herself disappears between the jaws of the lizard:

> Protruding from between the champing jaws, the edge of a violet-tinted wing still fluttered like an orchid petal in the breeze; a pair of legs waved wildly for a moment then disappeared from view (*I*, p. 321).

This is all happening in time with the final Presto of the Fourth Brandenburg: 'What a jolly little rococo death march'. The insect-horror changes to a meditation on the doomed swarm of humanity ('Onward Nazi Soldiers') and then a memory of his kindly Aunt Mary and the 'whining malignant stranger who had taken her place during those last dreadful weeks before the final transformation into garbage' (*I*, p. 323). There is no hope—faith in a Christian redemption is devalued, debunked: 'The Agony in the Bargain Basement. The Crucifixion among the Christmas tree decorations'. One is finite except in respect to suffering:

> This dark little inspissated clot that one called 'I' was capable of suffering to infinity and in spite of death, the suffering would go on for ever (*I*, p. 323).

Farnaby has come a long way to arrive at this realization; from '*Being* it':

> Its presence was his absence. William Asquith Farnaby—Ultimately and essentially there was only a luminous bliss, only a knowledgeless understanding, only union with unity in a limitless, undifferentiated awareness (*I*, p. 309).

It is difficult to come to terms with the presentation of the on/off, infinitely good/bad perception in *Island*; and this seems to be not because there is (perhaps) no resolution but because of Huxley's unwillingness to admit there might be no resolution. Farnaby and Susila are unable to dramatize this irresolution satisfactorily because there is hardly any space between them and the authorial intention. Susila's 'as usual, it's a question of making the best of both worlds' (*I*, p. 327) is not merely inadequate but unintentionally comic. The moksha-medicine which we might have expected to help resolve the tension between the cynic, Farnaby, whose motives are directed by his awareness of the 'Essential Horror', the meaninglessness of it all, and the utopian Palanese (sane, happy, with all the benefits of sexual yoga, Mutual Adoption Clubs, heightened ecological awareness, and so on) has, in fact, taken us no further than the first few pages where we get the description of Bab's 'musty' bedroom illuminated by a neon advertising hoarding:

> Gin in royal crimson—and for ten miraculous seconds the flushed face so close to his own glowed like a seraph's, transfigured as though by an inner fire of love. Then came the yet profounder transfiguration of darkness. One, two, three, four... Ah God, make it go on for ever! But punctually at the count of ten the electric clock would turn on another revelation—but of death, of the Essential Horror; for the lights, this time, were green, and for ten hideous seconds Bab's rosy alcove became a womb of mud and on the bed, Babs herself was corpse-coloured, a cadaver galvanized into posthumous epilepsy (*I*, p. 9).

The problem with presenting a utopia is only partly that the 'energizing disgust...so good for fiction, if not for the soul'[5] is lost. The real problem is more complex and given consideration by Bakhtin in 'Discourse in the Novel'. An achieved utopia is by definition something which has discovered its truth, its singular voice, 'authoritative discourse' which 'can not be represented...only transmitted'.[6] This is why Pala's enemies don't require Huxley's irony; irony is too heavy an instrument here, they are already pitifully, transparently, wrong placed against Pala's worked-out, perfected 'system'.

As opposed to Firmin's alcoholic 'detours'[7] Farnaby can only be given an exhaustive guide tour of the island's perfected or as near perfected as is humanly possible institutions, organizations, arrangements (the book's prefatory epigraph is from Aristotle; 'In framing an ideal we may assume what we wish, but should avoid impossibilities'). Huxley presents and rationalizes this admirable world throughout the book but he complicates things for himself with his concluding moksha-medicine revelation which should have explained and confirmed his utopia. This he fails to do, and significantly, Pala is invaded.

It seems reasonable to appropriate Huxley's 'limitless, undifferentiated awareness' to describe Firmin, a 'literary man'[8] in his garden 'floating in an amber glow' (*U*, p. 143), where he becomes 'conscious for the first time of an extraordinary activity which everywhere surrounded him in the garden...' There are enormous butterflies,

> whose precise stitched marking reminded one of the blouses in the market....ants with petals or scarlet blossoms, tacking hither and thither along the paths....Where was his friend the snake now? (*U*, p. 144).

He goes on to describe how Quincey's cat catches an insect in its mouth. But instead of destroying it the cat bizarrely appears to wish to co-exist happily with the insect and its protruding wings ('lovely, luminous') fan the cat's whiskers. The cat does eventually prepare to kill it but it 'suddenly and marvellously flew out as might indeed the human soul from the jaws of death'. The biologically programmed killing routine is averted and mocked; paradise is maintained. Yvonne appears, her 'arms full of bougainvillea'. It is, perhaps, no coincidence that the first syllable of her name is homonymous with 'Eve'.

Then the Consul has a blackout and finds himself in the bathroom trying to piece together fragments of the intervening period. The paradisiacal garden has evaporated and the bathroom is a version of hell where he is 'helpless', 'sweating and trembling', 'standing under the shower waiting in an agony for the shock of cold water that never came'. The insects that had previously helped to constitute a bright fascinating, benevolent and 'natural' pattern have metamorphosed into alien, isolated, mechanistic creatures:

> the insects which lay at different angles from one another on the wall, like ships out in the roadstead....A large cricket with polished fuselage, clung to the curtain, swaying it slightly and cleaning its face like a cat [a pointer to the lost Eden of the previous scene], its eyes on stalks appearing to revolve in its head....Now a scorpion was moving slowly across towards him (*U*, p. 152).

The nightmare vision is compounded and advanced when he notices flecks of blood on the wall, reminiscent of crucifixion and invasive disease:

> all at once, the thin shadows of isolated nails, the stains of murdered mosquitoes, the very scars and cracks of the wall had begun to swarm, so that, wherever he looked, another insect was born, wriggling instantly towards his heart. It was as if, and this was what was most appalling, the whole insect world had somehow moved nearer and was now closing, rushing in upon him. (*U*, p. 152).

An important feature of both texts is the meeting of, and play between, the notions of unreliable and reliable experience, which can be usefully represented as 'unreliable/reliable': in many instances experience becomes indeterminate in terms of its reliability, it being as easy to hop from one term to the other or even to balance (teeteringly) on the dividing live itself. This indeterminacy is in large part the result of what Todorov designates 'pan-determinism', which has as a natural consequence 'pan-signification'. Todorov explains that this conviction might be derived from madness (as in Nerval's *Aurelia*) or from certain drugs, and he quotes from Alan Watt's book *Joyous Cosmology*:

> For in this world nothing is wrong, nothing is even stupid. The sense of wrong is simply failure to see where something fits into a pattern, to be confused as to the hierarchical level upon which an event belongs.

Watt makes a similar case in the introduction of his book *Nature, Man, and Woman*, and also in the chapter 'The New Alchemy', a relation of LSD experiences, in *This is IT*:

> When, therefore, our selection of sense-impressions is not organized with respect to any particular purpose, all the surrounding details of the world must appear to be equally meaningful or equally meaningless. Logically these are two ways of saying the same thing, but the overwhelming feeling of my own LSD experiences is that all aspects of the world become meaningful rather than meaningless. This is not to say that they acquire meaning in the sense of signs, by virtue of pointing to something else, but all things appear to be their own point. Their simple existence, or better, their present formation, seems to be perfect, to be an end or fulfilment without any need for justification. Flowers do not bloom in order to produce seeds, nor are seeds germinated in order to bring forth flowers. Each stage of the process—seed, sprout, bud, flower, and fruit—may be regarded as the goal. A chicken is one egg's way of producing others. In our normal experience something of the same kind takes place in music and the dance, where the point of the action is each moment of its unfolding and not just the temporal end of the performance (pp. 134-35).

As Todorov says, 'pan-determinism has as a natural consequence what we may call pan-signification since relations exist on all levels, among all elements of the world, this world become highly significant'.[9] So, for example, with Firmin the old woman from Tarasco becomes part of an undifferentiated beauty in his eyes; he gazes round him

> with the bemused unfocussed brightness of a lover's, his love asked her, 'how, unless you drink as I do, can you hope to understand the beauty of an old woman from Tarasco who plays dominoes at seven o'clock in the morning?' (*U*, p. 55).

In 'Hallucinations in *Under the Volcano*' Gilmore talks about 'naturalizing the device'. He states that two ways in which experience is made acceptable are by mediating it through alcohol and by setting it in a land (Mexico) where things are already 'objectively surreal or hallucinatory':[10]

> you would find every sort of landscape at once, the Cotswolds, Windermere, New Hampshire, the meadows of the Eure-et-Loire, even the green dunes of Cheshire, even the Sahara, a planet upon which, in the twinkling of an eye you could change climates, and if you cared to think so, in the crossing of a highway, three civilizations (*U*, pp. 15-16).[11]

The landscape both mirrors and objectifies Firmin's own perceptions and procedures.[12] During his aimless pilgrimage of the cantinas he summons, reworks, re-accentuates, conflates impression, self-image, memory, place and time which results in a loss of differentiation, of significant *detail,* because everything is unfixed, unsure and (in)significant:

> It was a fact that he was losing touch with his situation...waked him, if only, so to say, from one somnambulism into another; he was drunk, he was sober, he had a hangover; all at once...it was almost as if he were yet another kind of drunkard (*U*, p. 344).

Here we see Firmin's characteristic habit of self-(de)composition. Paradoxically what can be release can also become discomfiture or terror—the continual pressure to remake, reposition, resignify, relate, recompose. The realization or feeling that everything is connected, everything is to be found in everything else, can be heaven or hell. The bringing or stacking together of image or significance can result in positive fusion, confusion or the 'narrative's temptation to a self-cancelling over-sameness'.[13] Confusion is highlighted by the manic iridescence of Firmin's significance-seeking word-play:

> that he had sprung up and must gibber 'Coriolanus is dead!' or 'muddle, muddle, muddle' or 'I think it was, Oh! Oh!' or something really senseless like 'buckets, buckets, millions of buckets in the soup!' (*U*, p. 345).

(T.S. Eliot's *The Waste Land,* for example, also relies on a manic conflation of disparate voices and utterances, particularly in the second section, 'A Game of Chess'.)

The perceptions (and his utterances which alert us to these perceptions) are involved in two fatally opposed movements. They collide, pile up to constitute a twitching unity, but at the same time preserve a prickly time/place-locked individuality. They are amenable to only one resolution, the death of the Consul, which (perhaps) will result in a closure and fixity of his/the narrative: 'and narrative desire is ultimately, inexorably, desire for the end'.[14] Even at the end of the book, though, Lowry subverts the possibility of a symmetrical fixture and closure of the chattering Consul and chattering text. He is unable to resist the neat tagging on of a further (in)significant detail—'Somebody threw a dead dog after him down the ravine' (*U*, p. 376)—a detail which again sets the text resonating, re-alerting us to do what Firmin has done throughout; make the connections, conflate the meanings. For example we might remember the 'pariah dog that had appeared familiarly at heel' (*U*, p. 70), and the cat 'poor old Oedipuss' that died the day Yvonne left had been 'thrown down the Barranca' (*U*, p. 93).

Pan-determinism, pan-signification, then, can result in a flicking, a veering, a fluctuation between investing everything or nothing with value. In both instances 'reality' as normally understood and felt is destructured, denarratorized, because when everything has equal value/no value the pattern that exists is infinitely fine/good or bad/gruesome, and in either case moving the individual markers can do nothing to change this value because all the markers *are* this value. When the need for or possibility of ascribing relative values evaporates, desire itself loses meaning. There is no need to move, direct, achieve—these things are meaningless. This is (at least partly) why Firmin is inactive (especially when compared to the bull-riding Hugh), meandering, indecisive, unresolved (even a cadaver can have speed and direction: 'A CORPSE will be transported by express!'). Firmin is less a man acting (his primary movements are from the alcoholic's traditional repertoire: shakes, tics, trembles and shivers) than acted upon by large, powerful disorientating machines and agencies; there is the jolting bus journey, the spinning 'Infernal Machine', even the prostitute Maria acts on him with violence and gusto: 'and flinging her arms round his neck, drew him down to the bed' (*U*, p. 349).

So far we have identified one powerful feature of hallucinogenic drugs, as evinced in *Island*; an 'undifferentiated awareness', which as described might lead to entirely negative or positive feelings. However, alcohol for Firmin seems to involve two features or movements: firstly the same 'undifferentiated awareness' (a timeless 'movement' of integration and sublimation), but also a linear movement, a 'progression' towards annihilation, the narrative force which organizes the moments of awareness and, ultimately, wipes them out; completes them, fixes them, kills Firmin. The tension between these two movements achieves graphic expression in this parenthesis:

> (For his salvation might not have seemed so large with menace had not the Burkes's Irish whisky chosen suddenly to tighten, if almost imperceptibly, a screw. It was the soaring of this moment, conceived of as continuous, that felt itself threatened) (*U*, p. 88).

'Undifferentiated awareness' implies acceptance and the Consul could accept Yvonne as part of the existent pattern. But Yvonne is one *thing* he must be active against in order, as Vice makes clear, to 'keep the narrative going and his own history alive'. Vice continues, quoting Brooks:

> desire is the dynamic of signification; desire necessarily becomes textual by way of a specifically narrative impulse since desire is metonymic, a forward drive in the signifying chain, an insistence of meaning towards the occulted objects of desire.[15]

Pan-determinism, pan-signification, is also a feature of some poetry influenced by hallucinogenic drugs. In Paul Muldoon's 'Gathering Mushrooms' (*Quoof*) we see three worlds equally strange, equally real, growing out of, and into, each other: his father growing mushrooms, the magic mushroom trip and, at the end of the poem, the head of a horse ventriloquizing the song of a hunger striker:

> Come back to us. However cold and raw your feet
> were always meant

> to negotiate terms with bare cement
> Beyond this concrete wall is a wall of concrete
> and barbed wire. Your only hope
> is to come back. If sing you must, let your song
> tell of treading your own dung,
> let straw and dung give spring to your step.
> If we never live to see the day we leap
> into our own domain,
> lie down with us now and wrap
> yourself in the soiled grey blanket of Irish rain
> that will one day bleach itself white
> Lie down with us and wait.

Edna Longley does not fully understand when she says, 'the poem lets this terrible duty have its say but a Republican poet is not born'.[16] The 'terrible duty' is diluted and subverted even here; we must remember that it is a metamorphosed horse that is ventriloquizing[17] and that many elements here belong not to the world of the hunger striker but to the (not unpleasant, we might imagine) world of the horse: straw and blankets; 'dung' is animal, not human, excrement; 'a spring in your step', 'leap' often a horse's movements. Muldoon refuses to show his colours, not simply because of his chameleon nature but because he finds it dishonest, crass, reductive, to imply a particular moral or make a political gesture. Morality loses all dimension, all meaning, in a pan-significant world; and politics, suggestive of super-imposed form, organization and, thereby, the possibility of significant selection, becomes not simply a ridiculous but an impossible notion. The horror is there if we wish to see it, and interpret it in this way, but there is no way Muldoon will spell it out for us.

NOTES

1.   Sue Vice, 'Fear of Perfection, Love of Death and the Bottle', in Vice (ed.), *Malcolm Lowry: Eighty Years On* (London: Macmillan, 1989), p. 105.

2.   Abbreviations used for textual references are *I* for *Island*, *U* for *Under the Volcano*.

3.   Insects seem to have a particular resonance in both literature and life, gaining attention for endless proliferation/plagues (Exodus); metamorphoses (in their own life cycle, and in literature from human in insect form, the classic example being Kafka's *Metamorphosis*), metaphysical conceit (the lovers' blood intermingling in the living walls of jet of the flea in Donne's poem about that insect), Hughes's microscopic narration of the female spider's voracious sexual and gustatory appetites in a poem about two spiders in a children's collection. Although partly offset by the busy bee, the industrious ant and the beautiful butterfly (with the lepidopterist Nabokov in hot, eloquent pursuit), the predominant emotion seems to be one of fear capitalized in a swarm of horror B-movies. The details of this fear seem to be their pre-human/sub-human nature, unpredictable movements, ectoskeletonic structure. John Updike in his memoirs *Self-Consciousness* relates his 'morbid fear' of insects and spiders, centred especially on the fantasy (encouraged by films) that they would become very large. He reassures (himself) in a footnote: 'I need not have

worried. Insect life is limited by the fact that mass is cubed when linear dimension is doubled—an elephant-sized flea would have to have legs sturdy as an elephant's and thus would cease to be flea-like'. (In *Annie Hall* Woody Allen is summoned to tackle a spider in the bathroom. He enters it in a gust of machismo but quickly beats a retreat confessing that it's as 'big as a Buick'.) Reptiles, especially snakes, have a similarly resonant lineage, from Eden's serpent to the adder of Egdon Heath in *The Return of the Native*, and D.H. Lawrence's 'Snake'.

A further possible reason for the 'popularity' of insect and reptile-life in literature (especially visionary/hallucinogenic literature) is suggested by Huxley in *Heaven and Hell* (p. 85). These creatures often have an incandescence and colourfulness like bright stones and gems, and in visionary states 'men perceive a profusion of what Ezekiel calls "stones of fire", of what Weir Mitchell describes as "transparent fruit". These things are self-luminous, exhibit a preternatural significance. The material objects which most nearly resemble these sources of visionary illumination are gem-stones.'

A final note on spiders. In an (unlocated) edition of *National Geographic* magazine there was a feature on the effect on spiders (as evinced by their web-making abilities) of the administration of various mind-transforming chemicals. Alcohol, opiates and amphetamine caused the spider to lose interest or disrupt, deform or break the web. LSD seemed to result in the spider having a heightened interest in its web-spinning activity and the web became more symmetrical.

4.   Compare with 'the chair which looked like the Last Judgement' (Huxley, *Doors of Perception*, p. 46).

5.   F. Kermode, review in *Partisan Review* (Summer 1962), collected in D. Watt (ed.), *Aldous Huxley: The Critical Heritage* (London: Macmillan, 1975), p. 454.

6.   M.M. Bakhtin, 'Discourse in the Novel', in *The Dialogic Imagination* (University of Texas Press, 1981), p. 344.

7.   Vice, 'Fear of Perfection', p. 92.

8.   Bakhtin, 'Discourse', p. 413.

9.   T. Todorov, *The Fantastic* (Cleveland, 1973), p. 112. And another natural consequence is 'pan-eroticism' (Todorov, *Fantastic*, p. 146) elaborated on by Timothy Leary in response to the following question:

> PLAYBOY: How often have you made love under the influence of LSD?
> LEARY: Every time I've taken it. In fact, that is what the LSD experience is all about. Merging, yielding, flowing, union, communion. It's all love-making. You make love with candlelight, with sound waves from a record player, with a bowl of fruit on the table, with the trees. You're in pulsating harmony with all the energy around you. (T. Leary, 'She Comes in Colours', in *The Politics of Ecstasy* [London: Paladin, 1970], pp. 106-107).

10.   T.B. Gilmore, 'Hallucinations in *Under the Volcano*', in *Equivocal Spirits* (London: University of North Carolina Press, 1987), p. 22.

11.   Cf. the landscape described at the beginning of *Concerning a Journey to the Land of the Tarahumaras* by Antonin Artaud (London: Royal College of Arts, 1975):

> The land of the Tarahumara is full of signs, shapes, and natural effigies which do not seem to be mere products of accident, as if the gods, whose presence here is everywhere felt, had wished to signify their powers through these strange signatures in which the human form is hunted down from every side (pages unnumbered).

12. Cf. stanza 6 of Andrew Marvell's 'The Garden':

> Meanwhile the mind from pleasures less,
> Withdraws into its happiness:
> *The mind, that ocean where each kind*
> *Does straight its own resemblance find,*
> Yet it creates, transcending these
> Far other worlds, and other seas,
> Annihilating all that's made
> To a green thought in a green shade (italics mine).

13. Vice, 'Fear of Perfection', p. 92.
14. Vice, 'Fear of Perfection', p. 93.
15. Vice, 'Fear of Perfection', p. 93.
16. E. Longley, *Poetry in the Wars* (Newcastle: Bloodaxe, 1986), p. 208.
17. Cf. Lowry's ventriloquizations in *Under the Volcano*. As opposed to the humans who find it so difficult to externalize the utterances which might tell the truth, and spend much time spouting banalities and evasive anecdotes (see especially the conversations between Hugh and Yvonne in Chapter 4) inanimate objects, and plant-life, can seem to sound out more genuine feelings:

> He had to raise his voice above the renewed clamour of the plant: dungeons: dungeons: dungeons: it said... (*U*, p. 118).

Note the 'it said'; so definite compared to the unvoiced implications of human discourse:

> 'But look here, hang it all, it is not altogether darkness,' the Consul *seemed to be saying...* (*U*, p. 55, my italics)

and, a paradigmatic example:

> 'Geoffrey, I'm so thirsty, why don't we stop and have a drink?'
> 'Geoffrey, let's be reckless this once and get tight together before breakfast!'
> Yvonne said neither of these things.

Does this mean that Yvonne thought them, or that Firmin thought them, or that Firmin said them, or that they are just part of some nebulous, unattached discourse that never existed anywhere but might have done? However this may be, the immediate and startling effect is one of a subversion of expectation, a (non-)utterance of the same force as this trompe l'oeil in William Carlos Williams's 'The Right Way':

> Why bother where I went?
> for I went spinning on the
>
> four wheels of my car
> along the wet road until
>
> I saw a girl with one leg
> over the rail of a balcony

It is difficult for people to sound or at least to sound what they mean. It is far easier to borrow the voice of an animal than to say the words you wish to say for yourself:

> 'You do sound astonishingly like a horse,' Yvonne said suddenly.
> 'Wherever did you learn that?'
> 'Wh-wh-wh-wh-wh-wh-wh-wh-whwwww-u,' Hugh whistled again.

When, eventually, a 'straight' question is asked (*U*, p. 118) Yvonne chokes on her beer.

THAT FIRST INFIRMITY OF NOBLE MIND:
SINCLAIR LEWIS, FAME—AND DRINK

Roger Forseth

Always do sober what you said you'd do when you were drunk. That will teach you to keep your mouth shut!

—Ernest Hemingway

All the while I knew Sinclair Lewis he was either a drunkard or a teetotaler.

—H.L. Mencken

By 1920, after fifteen years of diligent work, Sinclair Lewis was firmly established as a hack writer. He had published six novels and a quantity of short stories, had extensive experience as a journalist, and was an accepted, if minor, figure on the New York publishing scene. Then, at the age of 35, he wrote *Main Street* (1920), followed in rapid succession by *Babbitt* (1922) and *Arrowsmith* (1925). As a result this shy, awkward, homely Grub Street Regular became, almost instantly, an international sensation. Lewis's prestige continued to accelerate until he received the Nobel Prize for Literature in 1930 (the first American to do so), after which his reputation began a steady decline from which it has yet to recover.

Concurrent with Lewis's literary fame was his celebrity as a drinker.[1] The evidence demonstrates that by the time he published *Main Street* Lewis's drinking had become a serious problem; but it was not until his public 'image' as a distinguished man of letters had been firmly established that his drinking behavior began adversely to affect his reputation. And though he continued to receive accolades as America's foremost writer for many years to come, his claim as a serious literary artist began to be compromised, damaged in large part by his alcoholism.

It is tempting to make a causal connection between the acute phase of Lewis's alcoholism and his sudden fame. Indeed, his notorious *public* drinking had become a concern of his friends and a subject of common gossip. Mark Schorer, Lewis's biographer, stated that the 'origins of

[*Arrowsmith* in late 1922] float uncertainly in the alcoholic haze of Chicago'.[2] And Lewis's publishers Alfred Harcourt and Donald Brace hoped that by encouraging him to engage the medical researcher and writer Paul de Kruif as technical collaborator for *Arrowsmith* his drinking could be controlled. In his memoir, *The Sweeping Wind*, de Kruif wrote:

> Despite ruinous rum swizzles, despite the perils of planters' punches, despite dangerous Holland gin and bitters—despite this voyage in a vapor of ethyl alcohol in all these forms—Red had brought off a miracle [by finishing the draft of *Arrowsmith*] and I knew it and there was once more a singing in my heart. To have kept my promise to Alf Harcourt and Don Brace and to Gracie...to keep our genius, Red, this side of delirium tremens.[3]

And H.L. Mencken, one of Lewis's earliest critical supporters and a drinking crony, wrote (in an unpublished volume recently made public):

> All the while I knew Sinclair Lewis [beginning in 1920] he was either a drunkard or a teetotaler...I learned at a very early stage that he was consumed by an inferiority complex, and it amused me to observe his innocent delight in the praise of persons far beneath him in intelligence and ability, and his abject subservience to his wife, Grace Hegger.[4]

One will not find that quaint term 'inferiority complex' in the *Diagnostic and Statistical Manual of Mental Disorders* of the American Psychiatric Association, but it catches precisely a crucial facet of Lewis's character, his unremitting, often embarrassing quest for approval wherever and from whomever he could find it. The pathos of his often futile search for praise, as formal recognition of his new celebrity status, from the catty American literary expatriates who were definitively 'beneath him in intelligence and ability' is poignantly dramatized in contemporary accounts. Robert McAlmon, in his autobiography, ironically titled *Being Geniuses Together*, tells of an evening [in Paris in 1923] when Djuna Barnes cut him at the Gypsy and how Lewis 'looked wistful and went away'; how, on another occasion, somewhat intoxicated at the Dôme, he stood up and announced that he not only depicted character more sharply than Flaubert, but had the better style, and someone shouted, 'Sit down. You're just a best seller', and he was crushed; and how, on still another occasion at the Jockey, a 'tough little flapper' shuddered when she saw another woman greet him with a kiss, said something loudly about his ugliness—her phrase was 'withered carrot'—that he overheard, and was not impressed when he turned redder than usual, and then quickly pale and trembling, demanding of her, 'Do you know you are speaking to a man of international fame?'[5] Samuel Putnam, in *Paris Was Our Mistress*, writes:

> A bright, sunny day in Montparnasse, bright between the unfailing Parisian showers...Things have been a bit dull of late, but, fortunately, it does not take much to provide entertainment. Conspicuously seated at the Dôme is a gaunt-looking chap with a shock of reddish hair. He is obviously

expecting that he will be noticed. I say obviously, for we have seen his kind before and know the symptoms. We are in the habit of calling this type...the 'big shot from home'. Now, there is a curious telepathy, a kind of grapevine, that operates between those terraces, and within a very short while every one on all three of them is aware that the visitor is none other than Sinclair, or 'Red' Lewis. At the same time, through a seemingly tacit and simultaneous understanding, all those at the Dôme appear to be agreed that no notice whatsoever is to be taken of Mr Lewis's presence.

It is a slap direct from the Joyce and Stein brigade to the literature that is being produced in their native land...It would be hard to say how much, if any, Mr Lewis gets; but, in any event, he very soon makes his exit, and as he does so his face is about the color of his hair. There is an unuttered snort as he stamps out, and a giggle, becoming a laugh, runs around the tables and spreads down the street to the Coupole and across the way to the Select.[6]

The 'Joyce and Stein brigade', that will shortly clutch trendy Fitzgerald and Hemingway to its bosom, contemptuously rejected the premier American literary success story, a writer moreover who was only a dozen years older than the 'lost generation'. At the age of 38 and still seven years from the Nobel (which would formally entomb him for the Left Bank crowd), the author of *Babbitt* is a has-been!

Lewis could handle what he had, in 1919, called 'hobohemia'. He could not, however, return from the grave to confront the distortions of his biographer. Mark Schorer begins his massive book on Lewis: 'He was a queer boy, always an outsider, lonely'.[7] It is a simple matter to project this perception into the adult author, and Schorer does so:

Of Martin Arrowsmith, Lewis was to write, 'he found that whisky relieved him from the frenzy of work, from the terror of loneliness—then betrayed him and left him the more weary, the more lonely. He felt suddenly old...' Friendship, for Lewis, was much like drink—a gulping, indiscriminate distraction from himself that was bound to fail.[8]

But Schorer misses the paradox that for the alcoholic liquor is the medicine to cure the disease of alcoholism. It is perhaps understandable that Lewis's contemporaries were impatient with his frequent intoxication and increasingly erratic behavior, but for his biographer contemptuously to join in the sport, as Schorer does through 800 pages, is at once distraction and distortion. Even an alcoholic deserves to retain some semblance of dignity, a status somewhere between victim and clown.

It is not that Lewis, at the height of his fame, did not attempt to 'cure' himself. In what must be the grandfather of alcoholic 'geographical escapes' the novelist returned to America from Europe in 1924 and, with his brother Claude, journeyed on a fishing trip to the Canadian wilderness, supposedly to restore his sense of place in the 'real' world. Claude Lewis's journal, *Sinclair Lewis and* Mantrap: *The Saskatchewan Trip*,[9] became a major source of Lewis's *Mantrap*, by general agreement the least accomplished of his novels. Whatever Lewis's good intentions, most of which appear to be symbolized by his extensive annotations in his copy of *Walden*,[10] he did not finish the trip; according to him, because he ran short of stamina, but actually, by the detailed account in his brother's diary, because he ran out of liquor. He was later to explain that he was simply gathering material for a novel, a transparent rationalization that not even Thoreau would have proposed.

The literary result of the Saskatchewan trip, *Mantrap*, has as its protagonist a Yale-educated lawyer (suspiciously modeled after the author) who is pointedly indifferent to alcohol! A curious book, its first half is in tone and narrative style an adolescent novel, not all that surprising from the author of *Hike and the Aeroplane*. The second half is a romantic adventure novella, antiseptically told, in which the New York lawyer and the Canadian fur trapper discover that they have more in common emotionally than either has with the trapper's opportunistic wife. A hint of the novel's style may be sensed from the following paragraph:

> 'I've given him love, and I've cooked for him, I've swept for him, I've sung for him. And now he doesn't love me any longer. I know. A woman does know! He thinks I'm a fly-by-night. Oh, he's fond of me, but he doesn't like me the way he does you...And I never did sure-enough love him. He's a peach—he's so brave and straight and everything—but he's just a regular old school-teacher, that's what he is!...I guess I know near as much about Joe and me as you do, even if you do think you invented law!'[11]

In 1941 Lewis wrote, in an odd, ironical piece titled 'The Death of Arrowsmith: An Obituary of Sinclair Lewis' that,

> Mr Lewis smote—or tried to smite—sentimentality because he knew himself to be, at heart, a sentimentalist, a romanticist, to whom green hills and barricade-jumping soldiers and smiling girls and winter storms were as childishly exciting as they were to any popular female novelist.[12]

But this is not insight; it is rationalization. For Lewis had with *Mantrap* established a pattern, a pattern driven by his alcoholic affliction, of employing his writing for therapy. It had become a defense mechanism, a necessary means of physical as well as psychic survival. Therefore, literary quality was not the desideratum. He had to embark on a major project at once to keep from drinking and to justify—to *earn*—the subsequent binge. It is an ancient and familiar pattern, striking the famous and obscure alike, a pattern Lewis was to follow with devotion to his death in 1951, thirteen novels later.

Mantrap was for the most part dismissed by the reviewers and subsequently savaged by the critics, though the naturalist Joseph Wood Krutch found in it a modest virtue: 'Once more Mr Lewis has given an anger direction and outlet. To be sure the occasion is a minor one.'[13] Indeed, Lewis's friends and editors had serious misgivings about bringing it out in book form (it had been previously serialized in *Collier's Weekly*). He wrote defensively to Alfred Harcourt: 'I still don't see any reason why we shouldn't publish *Mantrap* as a book. Looking back at it I recall nothing shoddy in it, as for the critics who insist that I have no right to do anything but social documents, they can all go to hell.'[14] And I must confess I would rather re-read *Mantrap* than, say, Hemingway's *Across the River and Into the Trees*. Perhaps my taste is influenced by the fact that I have fished the country Lewis depicts in *Mantrap* and find his descriptions accurate and his sentiments about roughing it correct. Mencken once wrote that Lewis 'was by all odds the best reporter ever heard of'.[15] In any event, Lewis, at least in *Mantrap*, is unpretentiously telling a story; and unlike Hemingway he does not do it dishonestly. *Mantrap* was composed when Lewis was at the height of his powers, whereas by the time Hemingway wrote *Across the River*, he had 'gone soft'. I think the answer as to why *Mantrap* was written—or if written, why published—lies in the self-destructive, self-loathing nature of the alcoholic. In spite of external appearances, Sinclair Lewis by the mid-1920s was living a disaster: his drinking was out of control, his daily life was chaotic, and his first marriage was falling apart.

Grace Hegger Lewis wrote a fascinating *roman à clef, Half a Loaf*,[16] that documents precisely the travails of her married life with Sinclair. What one gathers from that novel, from her later memoir of Lewis, *With Love from Gracie*,[17] and from her unpublished correspondence,[18] is a picture of a woman of considerably more substance than is suggested by Mencken's remark about her husband's 'abject subservience'. For all the remarks about Lewis's physical ugliness, which we are to believe was of mythic dimensions, he was apparently remarkably attractive to women, and the beautiful Grace Hegger time and again asserts her deep, and physical, love for her husband. But as her books and letters document, her love, far from being sentimental or uncritical, as has traditionally been thought, was in fact tough. They also demonstrate, in painful and moving detail, the profound dilemma of codependence.

I have related the corrosive treatment that Lewis received at the hands of the American expatriates in 1923 in Paris. Here, in telling reversal, is his wife's version in *Half a Loaf* (with Susan and Timothy Hale representing Grace and Sinclair Lewis):

> It was part of the sightseeing that they should spend several evenings at the Dôme...In the days of 'Trilby' there was doubtless the same playing at being artists as there was in 1921, with the difference that they were not all Americans playing at being French artists. On their first visit, the Hales had sat quietly on the sidewalk...drinking their little drinks and feeling rather lonely at a party where every one called the other by his first name. At last they were noticed by a young man, equally spotty of face and lapels, who swayed over their marble-topped table and accusingly asked, 'You're Timothy Hale, aren't you?...You don't remember me, but

you turned down a novel of mine once, said I didn't know what I was talking about. Neither did you. But you've put it over, haven't you, with a commercial best-seller? Why don't you come and live on the Rive Gauche and write a good book, now that you can afford to?'

The man was drunk; should they take offense?

'Say, would you like to meet some real writers?' and before Tim could reply the young man began to beckon in half a dozen directions. 'Come on, boys and girls, "God's own Country" has condescended to call on us.'

'Tim, this is preposterous, this gratuitous insulting. Let's go at once.'

'No, sit down! It's going to be interesting, though I hope to sock my pimply friend in the jaw before we leave.'[19]

Thus, in Walter Mitty fashion, are public drunkenness and diseased complexion melodramatically reversed by the enabling wife.

But then Timothy's own drinking becomes a problem:

What drove her to speaking to him about it was the paralyzing sight of small Roger [i.e. Wells, the Lewises' son], stealing about the drawing room one late afternoon after callers had gone, and drinking the dregs out of all the dirty cocktail glasses. Obviously he liked it.[20]

A revealing scene, that combined with Timothy's now undeniable alcoholism, leads to the Hales' separation. Grace Hegger then quotes in her novel verbatim from letters Lewis wrote to her in September 1925, now among the Lewis papers in the Beinecke Library at Yale University:

You have of late become extraordinarily bullying, you give orders grimly, as though I were a drunken private and you a colonel. Your theory had been that you had to do this because I was drinking so much I was no longer dependable, but actually you were depriving me of self-government. But here in my little apartment with all the drinks I want at hand, I have been drinking incomparably less. All my life, whether in relation to my father, my university, my bosses on jobs, or to you, I have functioned better when I have been in charge, not bullied by some one else.[21]

These same letters are quoted in *With Love from Gracie,* and they must have struck her as profound, though the mechanisms of defense here are obvious enough, revealing as they do both alcoholic denial and mortification.

The pessimism and honesty that is touchingly revealed in *Half a Loaf* was denied Lewis's own father, the sour and formidable physician of Sauk Centre, Minnesota (whom his wife invariably addresses, after a decade of marriage, as 'Dr Lewis'). Grace wrote him from Paris in February 1925 with unjustified cheer:

Think of Hal's [Sinclair's] being forty years old. Can you credit it? And he looks so very young. He has probably written you what a happy *gemütlich* time he is having in Germany...Of course I miss Hal most awfully, but I am somehow contriving to have rather a gay time on my own, and getting my wardrobe in order so that I can dash off to Hal at a telegram's notice.[22]

And Sinclair, in one of his endless travelogue-cum-bookkeeping letters to his father, wrote the following July:

> Well, I've managed to make some money since settling down to
> work...The Famous Player-Paramount Company has accepted the sce-
> nario...and they are paying me ten thousand dollars for it. This is by far
> the easiest money I have ever earned...The next news is that I *may* go to
> Japan next November.

The good doctor, before sending the letter on to Sinclair's more favored
brother, Claude, added a sardonic note: 'If I could make money as quick as
that I would go to Japan or Timbucktoo myself. It is certainly marvelous
how such a bundle of nerves can fall into the money.'[23]

These documents of Lewis's and his wife's mirror a personal deterioration just as *Mantrap* reflects an artistic lapse. Lewis was to go on to
publish the next year *Elmer Gantry*, with its dedication to Mencken and its
sardonic opening sentence, 'Elmer Gantry was drunk'. It could be argued,
to be sure, that *Mantrap* was just that, a careless or unfortunate or negligible
lapse, for in addition to *Gantry*, the author of *Main Street* would proceed to
Dodsworth and the Nobel. But in fact, *Mantrap* was anything but an
anomaly, for in 1928 came the unfortunate *The Man Who Knew Coolidge*. It
now appears clear that Sinclair Lewis had a compulsion to write as furious
and indiscriminate as was his compulsion to drink, the one obliterating
his art as the other obliterated his feelings. It is not so much that the state of
drunkenness itself directly harmed his creativity; rather, the necessity to
avoid alcohol resulted in an obsession for work, regardless of the quality of
that work. One devoutly wishes he had had a second line of employment
to use for this purpose. Perhaps one may simply urge that we have two
different writers here in the same person, the one composing those works
that led to the Nobel Prize, the other desperately scribbling to stay alive.

This tragic paradox of the destructive alcoholic discovering failure in
fame is movingly captured by Thomas Wolfe in *You Can't Go Home Again*,
with Wolfe's portrait of Sinclair Lewis as Lloyd McHarg, the sot as
genius—the genius as sot. 'I was enamored of that fair Medusa, Fame'
says Wolfe's alter-ego, George Webber:

> My desire for her was a relic of the past. All the guises of Fame's loveli-
> ness—phantasmal, ghostwise, like something flitting in a wood—I had
> dreamed of since my early youth, until her image and the image of the
> loved one had a thousand times been merged together. I had always
> wanted to be loved and to be famous. Now I had known Love, but Fame was
> still elusive...
>   Then, for the first time, I saw her. I met Mr Lloyd McHarg. That curi-
> ous experience should have taught me something. And in a way I suppose
> it did. For in Lloyd McHarg I met a truly great and honest man who had
> aspired to Fame and won her, and I saw that it had been an empty victory.
> He had her more completely than I could ever hope to have her, yet it was
> apparent that, for him, Fame was not enough. He needed something
> more, and he had not found it.[24]

No indeed; for the alcoholic Sinclair Lewis, fame was never destined to be
enough.

NOTES

1.   I have elsewhere discussed Lewis's alcoholism in some detail. See R. Forseth, '"Alcoholite at the Altar": Sinclair Lewis, Drink, and the Literary Imagination', *Modern Fiction Studies* 31 (1985), pp. 581-607.

2.   M. Schorer, *Sinclair Lewis: An American Life* (New York: McGraw, 1961), p. 360.

3.   P. de Kruif, *The Sweeping Wind: A Memoir* (New York: Harcourt, 1962), p. 92.

4.   Quoted in 'Even Dead, Mencken Has More to Criticize', *The New York Times*, 11 February 1991, B2.

5.   R. McAlmon with K. Boyle, *Being Geniuses Together, 1920–1930* (Garden City, NY: Doubleday, 1968). Quoted in Schorer, *Sinclair Lewis*, pp. 383-84.

6.   S. Putnam, *Paris Was Our Mistress: Memoirs of a Lost & Found Generation* (New York: Viking, 1947), pp. 101-102.

7.   Schorer, *Sinclair Lewis*, p. 3.

8.   Schorer, *Sinclair Lewis*, p. 363.

9.   C. Lewis, *Sinclair Lewis and* Mantrap: *The Saskatchewan Trip* (ed. J.J. Koblas and D. Page; Madison, WI: Main Street Press, 1985). See also C. Lewis, *Treaty Trip: An Abridgement of Dr Claude Lewis's Journal of an Expedition Made by himself and his Brother, Sinclair Lewis, to Northwestern Saskatchewan and Manitoba in 1924* (ed. D. Greene and G. Knox; Minneapolis: University of Minnesota Press, 1959); also D.J. Greene, 'With Sinclair Lewis in Darkest Saskatchewan: The Genesis of *Mantrap*', *Saskatchewan History* 6.2 (1953), pp. 47-52.

10.   For the influence of Thoreau on Lewis, see Schorer, *Sinclair Lewis*, pp. 769, 811, *et passim*.

11.   S. Lewis, *Mantrap* (New York: Harcourt, 1926), p. 232.

12.   S. Lewis, 'The Death of Arrowsmith: An Obituary of Sinclair Lewis' (author's typescript, Beinecke Rare Book and Manuscript Library, Yale University: 2. Later printed in *Coronet*, July 1941).

13.   J. Wood Krutch, 'Babbitt Returns to Nature', *The Nation* 122 (1926), p. 672. Robert F. Fleming argues interestingly, but in my opinion unpersuasively, that *Mantrap* is a parody of the popular Western novel ('Sinclair Lewis vs. Zane Grey: *Mantrap* as Satirical Western', *MidAmerica 9* (1982), pp. 124-38.

14.   S. Lewis, *From Main Street to Stockholm: Letters of Sinclair Lewis, 1919–1930* (ed. H. Smith; New York: Harcourt, 1952), p. 188.

15.   S.A. Young, 'The Mencken–Lewis Connection', *Menckeniana: A Quarterly Review* 94 (1985), p. 16.

16.   G. Hegger Lewis, *Half a Loaf* (New York: Liveright, 1931).

17.   G. Hegger Lewis, *With Love from Gracie: Sinclair Lewis: 1912–1925* (New York: Harcourt, 1955). See also her 'I Wrote a Biography', *Virginia Quarterly Review* 34.1 (Winter 1958), pp. 18-25.

18.   Grace Hegger Lewis's correspondence is mainly in the manuscript libraries of Yale University, The University of Texas, Syracuse University (Dorothy Thompson Collection), University of California at Berkeley (Mark Schorer Collection), and Saint Cloud State University.

19.   Hegger Lewis, *Half a Loaf*, pp. 245-46.

20.   Hegger Lewis, *Half a Loaf*, pp. 308-309.

21.   Hegger Lewis, *Half a Loaf*, pp. 317-18. The quotation is a conflation of two letters, dated 5 and 11 September 1925. See Hegger Lewis, *With Love from Gracie*, pp. 327-30; Schorer, *Sinclair Lewis*, p. 427n.

22.   Grace Hegger Lewis to Dr Edwin J. Lewis, 18 February 1925. Autograph in the Sinclair Lewis Archive, Saint Cloud State University Library.

23. Sinclair Lewis to Dr Edwin J. Lewis, 22 July 1925. Autograph in the Sinclair Lewis Archive, Saint Cloud State University Library.
24. T. Wolfe, *You Can't Go Home Again* (New York: Harper, 1940) pp. 725-26.

KEROUAC, ALCOHOL AND
THE BEAT MOVEMENT

Robin Burgess

Jack Kerouac drank himself to death, said Allen Ginsberg. This much is part of the well-known story; he died in 1969 aged 49 of an abdominal haemorrhage, brought on by years of excessive drinking. Kerouac, as far as I know, never sought specialist help for his drink problem, although he recognized it as a problem from the 1940s onwards. However, from the early 1950s Kerouac made no real attempt to control his drinking, and it cost him his life.

Kerouac is largely alone among Beat writers in succumbing to alcohol. Gregory Corso, Neal Cassady and William Burroughs were all major users of illegal drugs; Kerouac, while having no taste for hallucinogenic drugs, had periods of intense opiate, amphetamine and cannabis use, but had largely reduced his drug use by the end of the 1950s, partly because of his mother's influence during the years they lived together during his decline. His main problem was alcohol. Littered in the memoirs of Beats and others are references to the very real damage Kerouac's drinking did to his health and his friendships. Carolyn Cassady remembers the desperate time in 1960 that Kerouac later wrote about in *Big Sur.*

> Next morning everyone slept late, and Jack came inside as I was making coffee. Now that he was sober, he seemed pathetically glad to see me... He asked me to come out to the patio where we could talk alone. Once more we sat on the grass in the sun; he was full of clinging nostalgia as though he somehow knew we would never get back to the simple pleasures and sweet dreams we'd anticipated ten years ago. No longer did he make staunch vows to stop drinking; he knew he was being slowly pulled down into the quagmire, and his will was too weak to resist. His tormented eyes foretold the future; his face like a character from Poe. The usual answers from my metaphysical studies blinked on and off in my mind, but I knew now they were useless, the shame and isolation he felt deep within were too powerful to uproot with overworked admonitions. All I could do was sigh and wonder at the sense of it all, saying, 'Ah, why do we settle for pleasure when we could have bliss...and you, who've known what it is...'
>
> Jack groaned a Dantesque wail, 'I know, I know. What'll I do?' We

talked of the faithlessness of men, the easy way out. 'My unbelief is a belief to be transcended,' I quoted aloud, and he said, 'Well, I know now my Buddhism doesn't help...and why Buddha forbid alcohol...but I just *can't* stop. Thinking of those critics and the rubbish I've gone through with publishers starts filling my mind, and I reach for the bottle... Why is that? Why can't I be content?'[1]

If we examine contemporaries' reminiscences of Kerouac between 1950 and 1962 we see two clear pictures of Kerouac the drinker. Some remember the dynamic, exciting aspect of his thirst for alcohol, Kerouac the 'razor blade gone mad',[2] always partying, always lively, engaging in hectic, manic binges. Others—Amiri Baraka for example, or Charters, his first biographer, have pointed out the way in which Kerouac used alcohol as a mask to hide behind, in order to avoid people—a kind of withdrawal. The memoirs of contemporaries also contain the recurrent image of Kerouac interrupting poets' readings and bullying others when drunk. Kerouac's binges, especially those of his later years, can only properly be understood by noting that, while they may have provided occasional excitements for others, for Kerouac himself they were repetitious, damaging, lonely attempts to escape personal insecurity. This is borne out by Ginsberg's memoirs, the most complete record of these years. Common to all reminiscences is a general level of bad behaviour on Kerouac's part that was tolerated by some, reviled by others; to some it was simply boring. Kerouac illustrates this tension in his own life in the following exchange from *Dharma Bums* (written, in 1958, at the peak of his fame, a period during which it seems his drinking escalated) between himself and Japhy Ryder (the poet Gary Snyder):

I got this overwhelming urge to get drunk and feel good. I bought a poor boy of ruby port and uncapped it and dragged Japhy into an alley and we drank. 'You better not drink too much,' he said, 'you know we gotta go to Berkeley after this and attend a lecture and discussion at the Buddhist Center.'

'Aw I don't wanta go no such thing, I just wanta drink in alleys.'

'But they're expecting you, I read all your poems there last year.'

'I don't care. Look at that fog flyin over the alley and look at this warm ruby red port, don't it make you feel like singing in the wind?'

'No it doesn't. You know, Ray, Cacoethes says you drink too much.'

'And him with his ulcer! Why do you think he has an ulcer? Because he drank too much himself. Do I have an ulcer? Not on your life! I drink for joy! If you don't like my drinking you can go to the lecture by yourself. I'll wait at Coughlin's cottage.'

'But you'll miss all that, just for some old wine.'

'There's wisdom in wine, goddam it!' I yelled. 'Have a shot!'

'No I won't.'

'Well then I'll drink it!' and I drained the bottle and we went back on Sixth Street where I immediately jumped back into the same store and bought another poorboy. I was feeling fine now. Japhy was sad and disappointed. 'How do you expect to become a good bhikku or even a

Bodhisattva Mahasattva always getting drunk like that?'
    When it was time to leave for the Buddhist Center lecture I said 'I'll
just sit here get drunk and wait for you.'
    'Okay,' said Japhy, looking at me darkly. 'It's your life.'
    He was gone for two hours. I felt sad and drank too much and was dizzy.
But I was determined not to pass out and stick it out and prove something to
Japhy. Suddenly, at dusk, he came running back into the cottage drunk as a
hoot owl, yelling, 'You know what happened Smith? I went to the
Buddhist lecture and they were all drinking white raw saki out of teacups
and everybody got drunk. All those crazy Japanese saints! You were right!
It doesn't make any difference! We all got drunk and discussed prajna! It
was great!' And after that Japhy and I never had an argument again.[3]

This illustrates something central to Kerouac's drinking: he could make
very good excuses, in his fiction, for the upset it caused others. We also
need to remember that Snyder was ten years younger than Kerouac and
that in his memoirs he sees him in much the way Kerouac describes
here; as someone who wasted his gifts. Kerouac would justify his
drinking in many ways: that it made him write, that it gave him
creativity, that it was his inspiration. He once said: 'I'm descending to the
lower depths to chronicle the primitive speech patterns of the proletarian
dropouts'.[4] This attempt to draw the truth from the underbelly of the
American Dream is central to Beat thinking, but in the context of
Kerouac's increasing conservatism it begins to sound more like an excuse.
Kerouac made his own legend the subject of his books, and what we read
is how he would like to have been seen, not how he really was. Hence his
drinking is not presented as the mask for his shyness or the cure for
insecurity that it in fact was; instead he wraps around it all the
mythologies and injustices he believed about himself. Kerouac wanted his
life to be a tragedy, and he used alcohol as part of the tragic image of
himself. *Big Sur* (1962) is the only book to confront the damage involved in
his drinking in anything like a real way; indeed it not only describes
delirium tremens but also reflects its hallucinatory style.[5] In all his many
books Kerouac develops only one cause for his personal tragedy: the way
publishers, and fame, treated him. In none of his books does he escape
from the tragic victim role and thus put himself in a position to change his
drinking.

    There are many literary influences on Kerouac's writing style.
Thoreau, Miller, Celine and particularly Thomas Wolfe are cited
frequently; the rhythms of jazz are often cited. It is also possible that
another drug was equally influential: amphetamine. *On The Road* (1957),
written flat out in one mammoth sitting, was composed on one long
amphetamine binge, according to Charters, Kerouac's biographer.
Certainly its patterns replicate something of the feel of amphetamine
intoxication. Charters describes Jack's attitude to amphetamine benzedrine
as follows:

> Benzedrine made him feel stronger, more self-confident than when he
> was straight...Jack felt he was blasting so high that he was experiencing
> real insights and real fears. With benzedrine he felt he was embarking
> on a journey of self-discovery, climbing up from one level to the next,
> following his insights. Benzedrine intensified his awareness and made
> him feel more clever.[6]

Descriptions of his writing style enlarge on this; they illustrate, with
language that itself has a drug-like feel to it, the parallels between his
writing and the thrill of being high on speed:

> Like, he'd discovered a whole world of composition and rhythm—the
> rhythm of long sentences paralleling, sort of, some of the great tenor sax-
> ophones. Sentences like Charlie Parker and Lester Young. It was a kind of
> swim in the great sea of prose. Jack's sentences were unstructured, in the
> sense of like there being no single purpose to them. But they were
> structured to the actual situation, which is something *really* important. [7]

> Because he concentrates so heavily upon the writing journey rather than
> upon possible destinations, his writing is overwhelmingly kinetic and his
> primary need is to locate rhythms that will sustain his rush. When the
> rhythms fail the writing bogs down, but when he hits his stride it
> becomes a question whether Kerouac is writing the words or the words are
> writing him. *The Railroad Earth*, one masterpiece of our time, careers
> through wordscapes that flash to his feet much as one imagines colorscapes
> flashing to Jackson Pollock's hand.[8]

On The Road is amphetamine writing, about speed of all sorts. Some of
Kerouac's books may indicate other drug origins—*Doctor Sax* (1959) is said
to reflect cannabis use—but amphetamine remains the drug synonymous
with the unfettered travelling lifestyle described in *On The Road*. In this
way there is a 'fit' between the culture of the early Beat movement and its
most expressive drug. Later, alcohol would slow down and corrupt that
kinetic force in Kerouac. Certainly excessive consumption reduced
Kerouac's productivity, and in the 1960s it seemed to interfere with his
judgment; critical opinion on the 1960s works is harsh. What marks these
works most is their self-indulgence, which also indicates Kerouac's
attitude to alcohol: for alcohol, unlike other drugs, he had no cut-off point.

Kerouac, like others in the Beat movement, believed that alcohol and
other drugs were necessary definitions of personal style. They expanded
consciousness, illuminated despair and ecstasy; they were used to bring
about a 'tingling high of significance to quicken the previous inner
presence'.[9] Kerouac defined the hipster as someone able to procure drugs at
any time. In this way substance abuse had a symbolic quality within the
Beat consciousness. It was both the exit from straight society and a
gateway to the street society of the hipster, the black and the thief. It was
also much more—a search for a form of 'holy madness' that the Beats
believed an artist should possess. There is a touch of surrealism here, but
also a tradition that Tytell has indicated goes back to Blake and to

Longfellow's 'divine insanity of noble minds'. In the Beats' view madness had a dangerous quality and yet also an innocence. According to Tytell they induced 'madness' with drugs, but defined that madness as a kind of natural state the real artist 'must create at the axis between sanity and madness', an axis the Beats created by pointing at the insanity of modern, soulless society.

A noble ambition perhaps, but in reality the damage to the Beats caused by alcohol and drugs was as much physical as psychic. When this happened they blamed society, as illustrated, famously, by Ginsberg:

> I saw the best minds of my generation destroyed by madness, starving, hysterical, naked, who dragged themselves through the angry streets at dawn searching for a negro fix.[10]

Critics of the Beat movement are quick to point out that this denial of responsibility for the consequences of their own drug use and drinking is one of the major weaknesses of Beat thinking. Burroughs, in works such as *Junkie* (1953), expresses an understanding of the process of opiate or hallucinogenic addiction as a biological, almost molecular process of invasion by alien persons, thus passing the responsibility for 'addiction' onto supernatural and external forces; but he is capable of recognising that the resistance to those forces is a struggle for the individual that must be faced, rather than avoided. Kerouac was unable to face this challenge. He was content rather to wallow in his sense of injustice, paranoia and fear, unable to sustain anything more than superficial relationships with other people, particularly women. This innate sense of self-destructiveness which is so present in Beat thinking is easy to excuse away.

Hence a Beat apologia for Kerouac's drinking would take the following form—the words are Ginsberg's, but the thinking is general:

> Kerouac had tried to follow the implications of his sad–comic view of things to the bottom of his own nature, and transcribe it in its own onrushing spontaneous flow, and leave it there for others, so he drank himself to death, which is another way of living, of handling the pain and foolishness that it's all a dream, a great baffling silly emptiness.[11]

Many would see this apology—and Kerouac's own apologies—as inadequate. Beat thinking on personal tragedy can be interpreted by outsiders as self-induced martyrdom, and thrives on images derived from particularly Catholic mythology; sainthood, beatitude, innocence, angels, the fall are all features of the iconography of the Beat apologia. In a practical sense they serve to release individuals from any sense of accountability for the acts they have done, and thus prevent any change towards control of their dangerous habits. It is perhaps significant that the vision that pulls Kerouac out of delirium at the end of *Big Sur* is of the cross, not Buddha; an illustration of Kerouac's desire to seek solace in a religion that accepted, and forgave, his personal failings, rather than asking him to purify them.

Much of early Beat culture moved to the new rhythm of amphetamines, the hedonism of alcohol and other drugs. Beat writers explored all the possibilities of drug experience, and wrote about them lucidly in a new and original way. We can still consider Beat culture a prototype-subculture that sowed the seeds for others. It is simplistic to characterise all excessive substance abuse as self-destructive, but certainly there is self-destructiveness in some of the amphetamine culture described by Kerouac in his most famous books, and in the lives led by Neal Cassady, Phil Kaufman and others. Amphetamines are the appropriate drugs for the reckless unattachment of male Beat life, the race to the finish line, the Rimbaudesque pursuit of self-destruction. The Beat attitude claimed the life of Cassady, illustrating that while it may look exciting on paper, this is a lifestyle that cannot be undertaken without massive cost. Kerouac's fate was different, for while he partly created it and shared its excitement, Kerouac was unable to engage with this driving masculinist culture for long. His decline was not a fast burn-out but a creative, social, political and cultural death, as alcohol failed to hide the deficiencies of his personality. In the 1940s charm and youth could hide these insecurities; by the 1960s, perpetually drunk, he could not offer the same charisma. As Ginsberg put it,

> In 62 or 63 he said, 'I'm old, ugly, red-faced, I'm beer-bellied and I'm a drunk and nobody loves me anymore: I can't get girls.' By that time he'd gotten beer-bellied, florid faced and I no longer saw him as the romantic, handsome, young glamour-beau of post-war dark, doomed, maddened Spenglerian hippiedom.[12]

NOTES

1.   C. Cassady, 'Life with Jack and Neal', in A. Knight and K. Knight (eds.), *The Beat Vision* (New York: Paragon, 1987), pp. 33-34.

2.   B. Gifford and L. Lee, *Jack's Book: An Oral Biography* (London: Hamish Hamilton, 1979).

3.   J. Kerouac, *The Dharma Bums* (London: André Deutsch, 1959), pp. 136-37.

4.   Gifford and Lee, *Jack's Book*.

5.   J. Kerouac, *Big Sur* (London: André Deutsch, 1962).

6.   A. Charters, *Kerouac: A Biography* (San Francisco: Straight Arrow, 1973).

7.   A. Ginsberg in J. Kramer (ed.), *Ginsberg in America* (New York: Random House, 1970), p. 137.

8.   W. Tallmann, 'The Writing Life', in D. Allen and R. Greeley (eds.), *New American Story* (New York: Grove, 1965), p. 15.

9.   J. Tytell, *Naked Angels: Lives, Loves and Literature of the Beat Movement* (New York: McGraw, 1976), p. 22.

10.   A. Ginsberg, *Howl and other Poems* (San Francisco: City Lights, 1956).

11.   A. Ginsberg in B. Miles, *Ginsberg: A Biography* (London: Viking, 1989), p. 427.

12.   A. Ginsberg, 'Your own heart is your guru', *IT* 148 (1973), p. 18.

CONFESSIONS OF A HEAVY-DRINKING MARXIST: ADDICTION IN THE WORK OF PATRICK HAMILTON

Brian McKenna

In his recently-published account of literary life in 1940s London, *War Like a Wasp*, Andrew Sinclair makes mention of 'the restless and seedy novels of the alcoholic genius, Patrick Hamilton'.[1] Now, talented as he was, Patrick Hamilton was surely never a 'genius'; he was, though, an alcoholic whose consumption of whisky, for example, almost beggars belief (three bottles a day in London, and one bottle a day in the country was his brother's estimate for the late 1940s).[2] Moreover, it is also true that Hamilton's alcoholism proved conducive to his near-documentary presentation of the drinking culture of southern England between the wars. As Nigel Jones, a Hamilton biographer, has put it:

> he is the bard of the bar, the poet of the pub par excellence. Considering the high profile the public house has in the lives of most British citizens, it is odd that pub literature occupies such a small niche, but if you want to get the feel of the drinking classes, and see life through the bottom of a whisky glass, then Hamilton is your man.[3]

Polemically exaggerated though this claim may be, there can be little doubt that Hamilton's various rendition of pub life are both skilful and accurate. At times this verisimilitude can seem to be vacuous; hence Peter Widdowson's criticism that in the London trilogy *Twenty Thousand Streets under the Sky*, 'The Midnight Bell' is 'no more than a punctiliously observed pub'.[4] This stricture applies less fittingly, it seems to me, to the third volume of the trilogy, *The Plains of Cement*—written after Hamilton's intellectually enriching conversion to Marxism in 1933—where London and its pub world are metaphorized to render the human alienation at the heart of the crisis of capitalism in Britain in the 1930s in a manner comparable to (say) Martin Amis's *London Fields*.

Hamilton himself seemed to have believed that his addiction to alcohol fructified his art. In a letter to his brother Bruce (also, incidentally, a novelist of the Thirties Left), Hamilton referred to the beer glass as 'the neurotic's microscope',[5] and we also have Bruce's testimony that the fact 'that Swinburne and others seemed to have done nothing very good when they stopped drinking helped him to rationalize his own unwillingness to stop'. The knowledge of this attitude, coupled with an awareness of the premature disintegration of Hamilton as a writer, would tend to nourish the romanticized mythology which has, unfortunately, begun to surround this hitherto unjustly neglected author.

The prime mover in the propagation of this myth—of Hamilton as 'down and out' in Soho and Earl's Court—is Michael Holroyd, whose introduction to the 1987 reprint of *Twenty Thousand Streets under the Sky* exaggerates the touchstone value of this writer's personal experience. Holroyd is doubly wrong to assert that it is 'the insignificant, the needy, the homeless and the ostracized'[6] who overwhelmingly populate Hamilton's novels, and that 'he didn't write about the Upper Classes, he didn't write about the Middle Classes, he wrote about the defeated classes'.[7] On the contrary, Hamilton wrote best about the social milieux of middle-class southern England, in the voice of a bourgeois Marxist, omnisciently narrating from a socially, politically, and textually privileged position. To endorse the Holroydian myth, then, would be to gloss over several significant points about Hamilton's position of address, and to make his work vulnerable to a debunking consonant with a banal literary ideology which insists on feeling for the authorial pulse of a text.

Let us take, for example, the doss-house episode from *The Midnight Bell*, wherein Bob, the book's hero, lies amid his hung-over despair in the company of the tramps of the 'great' city:

> Within the room London's defeated slept... Slept and snored, in an extraordinarily violent way, as though grasping angrily at oblivion... One groaned...Another's breath was a recurrent whistle...Nearly all snored, and the only one awake banged ferociously at his pillow... The peace of despair was here unknown: sleep revealed the truth, and the angry souls of the downtrodden complained and raged in dreams.[8]

This *Inferno*-esque piece of writing, with its finely-cadenced evocation of the hellishness of the sleeping underworld of the 'downtrodden', gains very little from being related to the fact that its author once spent a night in a doss-house in Drury Lane in August 1927 (following a long drinking session at a pub called 'The Admiral Duncan' with his wealthy Scots-Peruvian friend Charles Mackenhenie). Of the aftermath of this 'event', Hamilton wrote:

> I came out at about half-past five, so's Mummie wouldn't miss me at home. And I had Oh such a lovely walk along the river by Westminster Bridge at six o'clock. It was divine, and I'm sure that Wordsworth's Sonnet is the best in the language.[9]

This experience was clearly an upper-class lark and the fetchingly camp description of it makes the following comments by Holroyd look rather inappropriate.

By moving into a lower social sphere, Patrick Hamilton did not shed the insecurities implanted by his upbringing; his emotional vulnerability helped to make him one of the chronically dissolute and distressed who wander the dingy London streets and find refuge in its pubs and doss houses.[10]

I wish now to develop an argument which does not simply ignore the flesh-and-blood aspect of the author, Patrick Hamilton, but which does nevertheless operate primarily at the level of the discursive. The following discussion will be informed by an articulation of the discourses of intoxication and confession and will concentrate on the theme of addiction in relation to the representation of gender and sexuality in Hamilton's work. I shall conclude the paper with some considerations on Hamilton's Marxism in the context of the coupling of confession with addiction.

In his book *Confession: Sexuality, Sin, the Subject,* Jeremy Tambling makes a telling connection between Romantic confessional discourse and the tropology of intoxication. Such texts as Rousseau's *Confessions* or Wordsworth's *Prelude,* contends Tambling, ineluctably constitute the figure of the author as guilt-bearing subject, 'constructed by something that must be gone through again'.[11] Now, the prominent figures of this particular period of literary history were avowedly important to Patrick Hamilton in terms of his self-conception as a writer (for example, one of his few critical pieces, entitled 'Random Reflections', is devoted to the English Romantic poets). In this context it is the figure of Thomas de Quincey who looms largest, since *The Confessions of an English Opium-Eater* presents the practices of confession and intoxication as conducing to the fabrication of an ostensively truth-telling subjectivity which is always–already split. The self displayed in confession (to the reader/confessor) or during intoxication (to anyone who will listen) is a fictive construct whose truth-announcing pretensions are deflated in the very *act* of enunciation. For the enunciated, as rendered by the textual confessant remains tainted with the otherness of fictionality and (in this case) the opium-munching Orient. In Tambling's words, 'the *Confessions* remains a torso as far as revelations of that other self is concerned'.[12] Little wonder then that a writter as hooked on intoxication and confession as was Patrick Hamilton should have required a seemingly truth-bellowing theodicy like Stalinism to keep him going.

Another aspect of Tambling's case of relevance here is his suggestion (apropos Puritan spiritual autobiography and the 'rise of the novel') that 'the linkup of the private, bourgeois commodification, the demand to write and to confess, produces a discourse heavily imbricated with the sexualizing of all experience';[13] and so, the sexual is discursively produced as 'that which needs to be confessed'.[14] This helps illumine that impulse to confess which is often discernible in the rendition of the sexual in the work of Patrick Hamilton—who was, incidentally, deliberately named after one of Scottish Calvinism's most celebrated martyrs.[15]

In a late—and unpublished—confessional fragment, called 'Memoirs of a Heavy-Drinking Man' and inspired by Gissing's *The Private Papers of Henry Ryecroft,* Hamilton endeavours to trace the roots of his alcoholism. In doing so he homes in on a recollected childhood tendency towards a form of obsessive-compulsive disorder. He relates how he was unable as a child 'to engage in any lark or pleasure without having the door shut'.[16] This craving for security he 'carried to extremes', for not only 'had the door to have the appearance of being shut: it was necessary to ascertain that the knob had been properly turned; and even when this had been ascertained, it had to be ascertained again and again'.[17] The remembering voice then announces that, 'here were the beginnings of the malady of doubt—the desire for the insurance of insurance of insurance indefinitely'.[18] Clearly this invocation of childhood—unlike that of George Harvey Bone in *Hangover Square*—does not signify a becalming oasis of prelapsarian stability. Elsewhere, Hamilton significantly stigmatizes the clamour of children at play as 'as ugly and unhappy as that made by adults at a cocktail party'.[19] In another part of the 'Memoirs', Hamilton narrates a farrago of anecdotes against his domineering father (and would-be novelist), Bernard,[20] and describes his own ridiculous but persistent childhood image of God.[21] Hamilton seems, then, to be suggesting a symptomatic lacuna programmed into his psychological formation—a gap to be filled with alcohol, ink and the liquid cement of Stalinism.

In common with many other male writers of his social class and generation—the so-called 'Auden generation'—Hamilton was touched by the crisis of hegemony which seems to have afflicted the British ruling order between the wars. One aspect of this crisis devolved from the problematization of Victorian and Edwardian codes of bourgeois masculinity by the eruption of 'male hysteria' during and after the Great War.[22] The deep structural determinant of the crisis of upper-class masculinity can be described, in terms borrowed from Eve Sedgewick, as 'an endemic and ineradicable state of...male homosexual panic'[23] concomitant upon the homosocial bonding between men in privileged places which subtends the marginalization of women in patriarchal culture. From his brother's various accounts and his own letters, it is not clear whether the Westminster Old Boy and Savile Club member Patrick Hamilton was repressed homosexual or simply heterosexual *manqué*,[24] but his drama and prose fiction certainly bear the alcohol-laden traces of this inter-war disturbance of bourgeois masculinity.

One possible strategy in the renegotiation of a stable masculine identity available in the inter-war period was to cultivate a fascistic sense of liquor-swilling machismo. This response is exemplified in Hamilton's work by such figures as Peter, the 'ultra-masculine'[25] Mosleyite in *Hangover Square*, and Captain Bruce Cole in the radio play *To the Public Danger*. The latter piece is an admonitory tale which enacts a punishment aimed at the evils of drinking and driving—a subject close to Hamilton ever since his near-fatal accident in Earl's Court in 1932.

Captain Cole is the whisky-sodden driver of a car which seemingly becomes involved in a hit-and-run accident.[26] One of the passengers—the male half of a young working-class couple whom Cole and his blind drunk companion, Reggie, have picked up—plead, in vain, for the car to be turned back before he succeeds in escaping (and in avoiding the collective death that is visited upon his former drinking companions). Cole's voice is endued with 'the smooth, precise, off-hand, yet arrogant tones of a slightly second-rate ex-officer and public schoolboy'.[27] But whereas the ideology of 'manliness' inculcated in the Edwardian public schools typically yoked together diametrically opposed values—'success, aggression and ruthlessness, yet victory within the rules, courtesy in triumph, compassion for the defeated'[28]—Captain Cole's outlook is rather less dialectical. For example, when Fred, the importunate Cockney bicycle mechanic, starts sobbing, Cole gives him short shrift: 'Oh My God! Now we've got to wait while he has a good cry. Can't you be a man. Can't you be a gentleman. Can't you try to imitate a gentleman?'[29] As this speech slides from 'man' to 'gentleman' to 'imitate a gentleman', class, as well as gender, swims into view. Cole's biting bark owes much to Hamilton's profound familiarity with those of Cole's kind; and indeed, when whiskied up, he too could be (in Bruce Hamilton's words) a 'bully, a braggart, and a bore'.[30] Moreover, it could be argued that, in killing off Cole with the 'water of life', Hamilton was here trying to externalize confessionally a detested aspect of himself in order to exorcise it.

Models other than Cole's of the conjunction of alcohol and masculinity are, however, evident in Hamilton's work. For instance *Rope*'s Rupert Cadell, the seemingly effeminate war-wounded ex-officer who reaffirms his problematic masculine identity by brandishing an unsheathed sword-stick at the play's pseudo-Nietzschean killers, makes liberal use of alcohol as an intellectual stimulant. A decade after *Rope*, and six years after Hamilton's declared allegiance to Communism, the avuncular figure of the proletarian Inspector Rough in *Gaslight* had come to usurp the place of Cadell, the foppish socialite, as Hamilton's avenger. To *Gaslight*'s woman-in-torture, Bella Manningham, Rough says of whisky: 'it has been employed by humanity, for several ages, for the purpose of the instantaneous removal of dark fears and doubts'. This panegyrist of whisky is recycled within the ecology of Hamilton's drama to appear in *The Governess*, where he functions, in part, as father-confessor to the baby-snatching Ethel Fry.

The confessor implicated by Hamilton's prose-fiction is, by contrast, to be located outside, in the position of the reader. *The Midnight Bell* confessionalizes the author's own involvement in the late 1920s with a prostitute called Lily Connolly.[31] Bob, the sailor-turned-waiter at the centre of the book, becomes infatuated with the prostitute Jenny Maple, and squanders his eighty pounds' savings on her before, chastened, resolving to return to life on the ocean wave. Bob is endowed with Hamilton's growing addiction to the evanescent powers of alcohol. His drinking bouts and subsequent hangovers are related in quite some detail, going beyond the mere narration of excitement followed by remorse to include such things as the 'drunkard's interlude' in the small hours, 'giddy but horribly lucid',[32] and the ravenous 'false hunger'[33] of the intoxicated. This theme of intoxication is related to the effect that Jenny—and the always-deferred promise of the pleasures she represents—has on the waiter at 'The Midnight Bell'. When Jenny and her friend Prunella enter Bob's pub it is the three beers he has already consumed which, 'plotting their subtle loosenings along his brain',[34] impell him into intercourse with them. In a later episode, having finally tracked an errant Jenny down in Shaftesbury Avenue, Bob finds his 'grammar...in pieces',[35] when she is on the point of leaving him. Thus she effects the same order of linguistic disruption as does alcohol and this goes to the very heart of Bob, who is an aspiring author.

On the third fateful occasion when Jenny breaks her appointment with him, Bob finds himself 'beyond responding to the situation. He must find her, that was all'.[36] This alcoholically paralyzed state of compulsion epitomizes the 'zombiefied' condition to which Bob has been reduced. By the time of his final disappointment (on Boxing Day, when Jenny fails to appear at Victoria when due to go on holiday to Brighton with him) Bob has become an alcoholic automaton, a self-deceiver who plays out a posturing fictional role:

> Bob conceived it his duty to get wildly drunk and do mad things. He had no authentic craving to do so: he merely objectivized himself as an abused and terrible character, and surrendered to the explicit demands of drama.[37]

The ensuing account of Bob's final spree is narrated from a seemingly recollective viewpoint, and is skewed by such devices as the rendition of speech acts in a mode between direct and indirect speech ('What, he asked, did two and two make? Four, said Bob, or did when he was a kid').[38] There then follows the night in the doss-house, referred to earlier, from which Bob emerges as someone who 'sorely needed confession'[39] and purgation—by the saline of the 'mighty and motherly sea'.[40] Just as Bob has surrendered to the 'explicit demands of drama' so Hamilton has yielded to the confessional dictates of the realist novel. And not for the last time either.

In one respect, *Hangover Square* constitutes a fictionalization of Hamilton's infatuation with an Irish actress called Geraldine Fitzgerald, whom he pestered for a time in 1936.[41] *Hangover Square* relates, it will be remembered, the story of an infernal triangle of petty-bourgeois characters who drift through a drunken existence in the pubs of Earl's

Court just before the advent of the Second World War. The narrator's favoured character is George Harvey Bone, a simple-minded version of Patrick Hamilton whose small independent income allows him to enlist in the retinue of the misogynistically-portrayed Netta Longdon—an attractive, lazy, and selfish out-of-work actress whose cruelty exacerbates Bone's innate schizoid tendencies into full-blown, murderous, schizophrenia. Eventually, in one of his 'dead moods', the alcoholic schizophrenic murders Netta and her fascist lover before gassing himself in Maidenhead.

As with Bob's relation to Jenny in *The Midnight Bell*, George's addiction to Netta is presented as classically masochistic. On the occasion of the reader's first encounter with Netta, George is to be found cowering in her presence, 'afraid of her loveliness',[42] and wincing in expectation of a delicious blow from 'some new weapon in the arsenal of her beauty'.[43] This masochistic addiction is subserved by Bone's ever-present compulsion to place himself in the ambit of his dominatrix, with whom he is neurotically obsessed. Of a piece with this obsessive-compulsive disorder is George's dependence on the bottle, which he needs in order to cope with Netta but which intensifies his schizophrenia (as well as being analogous to it).

The conception of the schizoid condition which largely informs the characterization of Bone is represented by the quotation from *Black's Medical Dictionary* which serves as the novel's epigraph: 'SCHIZOPHRENIA: a cleavage of the mental functions, associated with assumption by the affected person of a second personality'.[44] Bone's condition is, however, more complex than this since there is no absolute 'Chinese wall' inside his head. Moreover, the language patterns typical of schizophrenia—as described in the following extract from a more recent psychiatric encyclopaedia—are reminiscent of some of those of George Harvey Bone:

> Thought processes may become disturbed, so that thinking becomes vague, with unusual logic and idiosyncratic use of words or association of ideas. There may be sudden breaks in the flow of speech, which may become incomprehensible.[45]

Here, by way of comparison, is a rivulet of Bone's consciousness sourced in the 'intoxication'[46] generated by the contemplation of the very name of his sexual icon:

> Netta. The tangled net of her hair—the dark net—the brunette. The net in which he was caught—netted. Nettles. The wicked poison-nettles from which had been brewed the potion which was in his blood. Stinging nettles. She stung and wounded him with words from her red mouth. Nets. Fishing nets. Mermaids' nets. Bewitchment. Syrens—the unearthly beauty of the sea. Nets. Nest. To nestle. To nestle against her. Rest, Breast. In her Net. Netta.[47]

The snakelike slithering of the little word 'net'—its contraction from 'Netta' and its expansion into 'brunette', 'netted', 'poison nettles'—marks a trail across the terrain of Bone's split-minded desire for escape and confinement ('To nestle... In her net. Netta'). This image is literalized at the climax of the novel when Bone meticulously threads together the corpses of Netta and Peter before setting off for Maidenhead. Nevertheless, Bone remains trapped in the web of this alcoholic little world whose purblindness functions as a metaphor for the appeasement of fascism.[48]

The *Roget's Thesaurus* entries which vie for epigraphical space in *Hangover Square* with *Samson Agonistes* are of significance in this context because of their word-associationist contribution to the story's sense of intoxicated entrapment. Thesaurus entries bespeak both a futile striving for verbal accuracy and an eternal slippage of meaning from one signifier to another: the drunk and the thesaurus browser have at least this in common. The thesaurus enticingly promises precision and fixity—just as Netta and her ilk promise the 'last word' in penetrative sex—and yet it also suggests the pixilating exchangeability of words. One signifier can always do the job of another, just as one sexual partner can perform the same task as another, and one drink can allay the desire for alcohol just as another can. It is also worthy of note that the thesaurus entry typically pays scant regard to the conventional hierarchies of linguistic value. Slang words can brush shoulders with the prosaic and the orotund; a (near) 'schizophrenic' lexicon indeed, as the Roget entry for 'drunk', excerpted as follows in *Hangover Square*, should make clear:

> drunk, tipsy; intoxicated; inebri-ous, ate, ated; in one's cups; in a state of intoxication &c. n; temulent, -ive; fuddled, mellow, cut, boosy, fou, fresh, merry, elevated; flush, -ed; flustered, disguised, groggy, beery; topheavy; potvaliant, glorious; potulent; over-come, -taken; whittled, screwed, tight, primed, corned, raddled, sewn up, lushy, nappy, muddled, muzzy, obfuscated, maudlin; crapulous, dead drunk.[49]

This network of 'alcoholic' signifiers (several of which are significantly sexually charged) can be construed as figural representation of the spider-woman's web in which Bone is enmeshed. His drive to escape from this web is fuelled both by a pathetic nostalgia for Edwardian lost innocence, and by the felt need to be 'a man amongst men'[50] (in drink) once more. This ambition he realizes temporarily in the maudlin male-bonding episode in Brighton's theatre-land which precedes the double killing in Earl's Court.[51] Ambling along the sea-front, swigging a half-bottle of Haig, Bone fortuitously collapses into the solaceful arms of his friend Johnnie Littlejohn, and confesses his mistaken apprehension that Netta had enmeshed him also. Under Johnnie's wing, Bone is then admitted to a homosocial party thrown by the object of Netta's frustrated desire, the theatrical agent Eddie Carstairs. However, even the latter's misogynistic advice[52] and benediction is not enough to liberate Bone, who is left to pull his alcoholic little petty-bourgeois world down on his own head.

The female equivalent of this scene of intoxicated confession and counsel in Hamilton's fiction can be exemplified by the episode in the second volume of *Twenty Thousand Streets, The Siege of Pleasure*, wherein the comparatively 'innocent' Jenny Maple is inveigled into the world of vice 'through a glass of port'.[53] Along with her slatternly friend Violet, Jenny is hustled by two rather creepy men into a pub for the first time in her life, and is suddenly presented with the embarrassing quandary of what to order:

> She thought she had better ask for a Guinness now. Guinness she knew to be 'the ladies' drink', a fair compromise with the devil, a legitimate 'pick-me-up'... Its prime and avowed object was to 'nourish', its accidental operation to intoxicate. But outside the realms of Guinness and festive occasions, Jenny had inherited from her mother...'a horror of drink'. She knew that so soon as a 'taste' was acquired, ruin followed in clearly discernible stages. The danger lay in once starting: a single drink had been known to lead to ruin.[54]

Her choice is, of course, a *faux pas*, and she is successfully enjoined to settle for the glass of port which, ironically, does lead to her 'ruin'. In league with several more drinks, Jenny's innate snobbishness, vanity, and malleability enable her new-found male confidant to persuade her that she ought to relinquish her job as a servant and become a mannequin. Her resolution to follow this advice is given thus:

> She saw it all. She had made a 'find'!... she could be a 'gold-digger' with the rest. Why not? She rather fancied the role. Was it not, in fact, the destined part of a hot little baby straight from Paris?... Was she dreaming— or had she had too much to drink? She took another sip.[55]

It is interesting to contrast this rendition of Jenny's inebriated, internal posturing with that of Bob. For while there is something rather noble about the waiter's surrender to 'the explicit demands of drama', the servant-girl's role-playing is clearly meretricious and her supposedly internal thought processes are encrusted with cliché and twisted by the parrotting of her interlocutor's sleazy flattery. The postlapsarian Jenny becomes a 'drunken little harlot'[56] who is rendered selfish and destructive by drink where Bob is made generous and vulnerable.

With the partial exception of *The Slave of Solitude*—where 'respectable middle-class girls and women'[57] like the novel's spinster heroine, Miss Roach, discover the pleasures of pub life as a means of escaping the total war—the drinking of alcohol tends, in Hamilton's fiction, to be configured with the representation of women to produce a metaphor for corruption. *The Siege of Pleasure*'s drink-initiation scene is, significantly, repeated in *The West Pier* (where it sets in train the deception of the confessional Esther Downes by the malevolent Ernest Ralph Gorse)[58] and in Hamilton's final, unfinished, novel, *The Happy Hunting Grounds*. The other side of this corruption coin is represented by the predatory, spirits-quaffing Netta Longdon—to whose satanic sisterhood belong also the seductively 'raucous'[59] Nancy in *To the Public Danger* and the closet Hitlerite Vicki Kugelmann in *The Slaves of Solitude*. It is no accident that the most positively portrayed of Hamilton's fictional women should be Ella Dawson, the barmaid at 'The Midnight Bell' who does not drink and does not have sex—remaining, thereby, doubly uncorrupted.

It is rather difficult to imagine a 'politically correct' male novelist of today getting away with the variously sexist representations of women evident in the works of Patrick Hamilton. Yet Hamilton was a Marxist, and it is with a discussion of the mélange of Marxism, addiction and confession in his life and work that I wish to conclude this paper.

Hamilton's thematization of drinking in his one explicitly Marxist novel, *Impromptu in Moribundia*, is slight. In this novel—a satirical dystopia in the tradition of Swift and Butler—the ideas and mores of the southern English petty bourgeoisie are literalized on the 'planet' of Moribundia. Drunken deportment is here presented as an example of the willing introjection of middle-class expectations by those who seemingly transgress. Having been spurned by his cicerone and lover, the first-person narrator kowtows to social convention by togging himself up in the apparel required of Moribundia's caste of lisping drunkards—'picture postcard' top hat and tails.[60] Thus Hamilton sends up the incapacity of the straight-laced and priggish middle class to face up to anything as disturbing as drunken behaviour.

Impromptu in Moribundia is a particularly lambent example of Hamilton's obsession with unmasking hypocrisy and pretence. There is evident throughout his work a thirst for authenticity in a social world dominated by quotidian play-acting and shaped by a historically specific crisis of bourgeois gender identity. In this context, the appeal of an especially muscular form of 1930s Marxism manifestly resided in its claim to be able to penetrate the mask of reality and lay bare the essence of the real in a particularly authoritative manner.

When Michael Holroyd says of Hamilton that he 'drank to be rid of himself'[61] he is, at best, half-right. Primarily, like many (*soi-disant*) revolutionaries, he drank to get rid, temporarily, of capitalism. And, as a good Marxist, he would have recognized his drinking as an imaginary resolution of a real contradiction. The American Trotskyist leader James P. Cannon is one other of a whole legion of Marxists who have periodically hit the bottle in order to 'get away from some insurmountable problem'[62] thrown up by the political struggle against a seemingly unchangeable social system. In a recent study on the social meaning of addiction, Stanton Peele points out that, 'a society—and all the subsocieties to which people belong—creates a need for an addictive experience by setting forth key values that are not realizable'.[63] There must have been many moments in Henley-on-Thames in the 1940s when the values set forth by the subsociety to which Hamilton belonged, the CPGB, seemed unrealizable.

Matters were made much worse when Kruschev's partial denunciation of Stalin reduced Hamilton to a state of 'torment and uncertainty'[64] in 1956. Unlike other bourgeois literary Leftists of the 1930s, Hamilton had rigorously assimilated classical Marxism into his intelligence and had also come, according to his brother, to 'love'[65] Stalin. Profoundly depressed and drinking heavily, he was referred by Dr John Yerbury Dent (whose 'disease' theory of alcoholism he enthusiastically accepted)[66] to the Woodside Hospital psychiatric department at Harrow-on-the-Hill[67] for ECT treatment. This worked—temporarily—and under its influence Hamilton wrote a fifty-page letter to his brother in which (among other things) he confessed his support for the Tory Government over the Suez Crisis whilst reaffirming his addiction to that most confessional discourse of the twentieth century, Stalinism.[68]

To speak of Hamilton's continued 'addiction' to Marxism-Leninism might seem a misuse of the word. But, of course, the sense of 'addiction' as 'the state of being (self-)addicted or given *to* a habit or pursuit; devotion' ante-dates the drug sense by over two and a half centuries, according to the *OED*. Moreover, Hamilton (an inveterate *OED* addict, like the hero of *The Man Upstairs*, his last play) also recognized a wide meaning for the term. In one letter we find him chastizing Bruce for workaholism and commenting that, 'there are countless other addictions besides Work and Drink...[such as] Addiction to Money-making. America had got the latter very badly—it's the national disease'.[69] And elsewhere he spoke of his addiction to chess, remarking proudly that '60% of the Masters were violent drunks! Alekhine, perhaps the greatest of all, was completely dotty as well as incessantly drunk'.[70] Addiction in the broadest sense he saw, then, as both empowering and disempowering, constructive within the moment of its own destructiveness.

Ultimately, Hamilton's strongest addiction may well have been to the necessarily unslakeable literary practice of confession itself; witness, for example, that egregious passage in the third 'Gorse' book *Unknown Assailant* in which the narrative voice descants upon the putative unremarkability of Gorse's predilection for sexual bondage.[71] And certainly when one reads Jeremy Tambling's insight that Pepys's confession to his diary that he had been perusing a pornographic book foregrounds the puritan novelistic 'understanding that guilt should not be faced as such, but be given a smooth appearance',[72] one is reminded of much in the work of Patrick Hamilton.

NOTES

1.   A. Sinclair, *War Like a Wasp* (London: Hamish Hamilton, 1989), p. 227.

2.   B. Hamilton, *The Light Went Out: A Biography of Patrick Hamilton* (London: Constable, 1972), p. 109.

3.   N. Jones, 'Through a Glass Darkly', *The Printer's Devil* (1990), p. 84.

4.   P.J. Widdowson, 'The Saloon-Bar Society; Patrick Hamilton's Fiction in the 1930s', in J. Lucas (ed.), *The 1930s: A Challenge to Orthodoxy* (Brighton: Harvester Press, 1976), p. 123.

5.   P. Hamilton, letter to B. Hamilton from Norfolk, 22 June 1934, (in an archive of letters and manuscripts belonging to Aileen Hamilton—hereafter AHA).

6.   M. Holroyd, 'Introduction', in P. Hamilton, *Twenty Thousand Streets under the Sky* (repr.; London: Hogarth Press, 1987 [1935]), pp. 4-5.

7.   M. Holroyd, speaking on 'The Late Show', BBC 2, 27 February 1989.

8.   P. Hamilton, *Twenty Thousand Streets under the Sky*. I. *The Midnight Bell*, p. 217.

9.   Hamilton, letter to B. Hamilton from Chiswick, August 1927 (AHA).

10. Holroyd, 'Introduction', p. 5.

11. J. Tambling, *Confession: Sexuality, Sin, the Subject* (Manchester: Manchester University Press, 1990), p. 118.

12. Tambling, *Confession*, p. 125.

13. Tambling, *Confession*, pp. 99-100.

14. Tambling, *Confession*, p. 101.

15. B. Hamilton, 'Patrick—A Tragedy: the Story of a Personal Relationship', (unpublished first draft of *The Light Went Out*), p. 25.

16. P. Hamilton, 'Memoirs of a Heavy-Drinking Man' (unpublished; Version 1), pp. 23-24.

17. Hamilton, 'Memoirs (1)', pp. 23-24.

18. Hamilton, 'Memoirs (1)', p. 24.

19. P. Hamilton, 'Memoirs of a Heavy-Drinking Man' (unpublished; Version 2, 1959), p. 44.

20. Hamilton, 'Memoirs (2)', pp. 29-36. These stories relate Bernard Hamilton's pretensions to an aristocratic Scottish genealogy, his habit of 'conducting' thunderstorms, and his gift to Mussolini of a copy of his appalling historical novel about Danton, *The Giant.*

21. Hamilton, 'Memoirs (2)', pp. 46-47.

22. See E. Showalter, 'Male Hysteria: W.H.R. Rivers and the Lessons of Shell Shock', in *The Female Malady: Women, Madness, and English Culture, 1830–1980* (London: Virago, 1985), pp. 167-94.

23. E.K. Sedgewick, 'The Beast in the Closet: James and the Writing of Homosexual Panic', in R.B. Yeazell (ed.), *Sex, Politics and Science in the Nineteenth Century Novel* (Baltimore, MD: University of Baltimore, 1986), p. 151.

24. For instance, in one letter to Bruce Hamilton (dated Sheringham, Norfolk, 5 August 1959), Patrick Hamilton wrote of his hero Shelley that he was 'rather oddly sexed—in rather the same way as I am. Although clearly he slept with girls, I don't think this is what he was really after. I think he liked *yearning* for them—*spooning*'.

25. P. Hamilton, *Hangover Square: A Story of Darkest Earl's Court* (Harmondsworth: Penguin, 1974 [1941]), p. 104.

26. *To the Public Danger* is an extended treatment of a similar incident in the 1933 novel *The Plains of Cement* (see Hamilton, *Twenty Thousand Streets*, pp. 293-98). That Hamilton should repeat a story so explicitly indicates the repetitiousness typical of the (embittered) alcoholic.

27. P. Hamilton, *Money with Menaces and To the Public Danger: Two Radio Plays* (London: Constable, 1939), p. 49.

28. J.A. Morgan, *Athleticism in the Victorian and Edwardian Public Schools: The Emergence and Consolidation of an Educational Ideology* (Cambridge: Cambridge University Press, 1981), p. 135.

29. Hamilton, *Money with Menaces and To the Public Danger*, p. 76.

30. B. Hamilton, 'Patrick—A Tragedy', pp. 562-63.

31. Bruce Hamilton's possibly rather jaundiced account of this affair is given as follows: 'she played hell with her ardent but still relatively innocent and impecunious lover, taking all and giving nothing, making and breaking appointments as the whim (or the exigencies of her trade) moved her, and reducing him to a condition of helpless despair rarely broken by moments of delirious happiness' (B. Hamilton, *The Light Went Out*, p. 52).

32. Hamilton, *The Midnight Bell*, p. 131.

33. *The Midnight Bell*, p. 132.

34. *The Midnight Bell*, p. 32.

35. *The Midnight Bell*, p. 73.

36   *The Midnight Bell*

37. *The Midnight Bell*, p. 211.

38. *The Midnight Bell*, p. 212.

39. *The Midnight Bell*, p. 218.

40. *The Midnight Bell*, p. 220.

41. Bruce Hamilton characterized this relationship thus: 'For a time this passion was to cause Patrick great and only too typical frenzy, with its concomitant heavy drinking; but however it began Geraldine was in the end not responsive' (B. Hamilton, *The Light Went Out*, p. 84).

42. Hamilton, *Hangover Square*, p. 36.

43. *Hangover Square*.

44. *Hangover Square*, p. 6.

45. H.J. Eysenck, W. Arnold, R. Meili, *Encyclopaedia of Psychology* (London: Search Press, 1972), p. 175.

46. Hamilton, *Hangover Square*, p. 27.

47. *Hangover Square*.

48. A connection explicitly made in the following excerpt relating the reaction of the Netta gang to the Munich agreement: 'They went raving mad, they weren't sober for a whole week after Munich—it was just in their line. They *liked* Hitler, really. They didn't hate him anyway. They liked Musso, too. And how they cheered old Umbrella! Oh yes, it was their cup of tea all right, was Munich' (*Hangover Square*, p. 31).

49. *Hangover Square*, p. 133.

50. *Hangover Square*, p. 56.

51. See *Hangover Square*, pp. 251-61.

52. '"There is only one thing that's any good with a certain type of woman, you know," went on Eddie. "Ask her for what you want, ask her whether she means to give it to you, and if she doesn't, throw her out of the window"' (*Hangover Square*, p. 260).

53. Hamilton, *Twenty Thousand Streets under the Sky*. II. *The Siege of Pleasure*, pp. 226 and 329. In the Radio Four version of *Twenty Thousand Streets under the Sky*, adapted by F. Bradnum and broadcast in three episodes from 17 November 1989 to 1 December 1989, Jenny relates her downfall confessionally to Bob on Hampstead Heath.

54. *The Siege of Pleasure*, pp. 265-65.

55. *The Siege of Pleasure*, p. 283.

244 Beyond the Pleasure Dome

56. *The Siege of Pleasure*, p. 161.

57. P. Hamilton, *The Slaves of Solitude* (Oxford: Oxford University Press, 1982 [1947]), p. 47.

58. See P. Hamilton, *The West Pier* (Harmondsworth: Penguin, 1987 [1951]), pp. 94-95.

59. Hamilton, *Money with Menaces and To the Public Danger*, p. 52.

60. P. Hamilton, *Impromptu in Moribundia* (London: Constable, 1939), pp. 201-204.

61. M. Holroyd, speaking on 'The Late Show', BBC 2, 27 February 1989.

62. S. Gordon, in L. Evans (ed.), *James P. Cannon As We Knew Him: By Thirty-three Comrades, Friends, and Relatives* (New York: Pathfinder, 1976), p. 58.

63. S. Peele, *The Meaning of Addiction: Compulsive Experience and its Interpretation* (New York: D.C. Heath, 1985), p. 129.

64. B. Hamilton, *The Light Went Out*, p. 156.

65. *The Light Went Out*, p. 156.

66. In a letter to his brother Hamilton referred to Dent's hearty book, *Anxiety and its Treatment—With Special Reference to Alcoholism* (Belfast: W.M. Mullan & Son, 2nd edn, 1947 [1941]), as 'a magnificent work. How a man, who is himself a normal drinker, could understand the emotions and habits of the abnormal one as well as he does absolutely astonishes me' (B. Hamilton, 'Patrick—A Tragedy', p. 551). Dent's approach was unremittingly chemical and decidedly anti-psychoanalytic: 'Psychologists have ceased to be concerned with the investigation of the anatomy and physiology of the brain and have irresponsibly postulated not only the soul and will, but have invented every kind of attribute for them—complexes, fixations, repressions, libidos. Let us cut out all this' (Dent, *Anxiety*, pp. 14-15). Accordingly, he recommended a course of apomorphine tablets and aversion therapy for the treatment of alcoholism. It did Hamilton little good.

67. B. Hamilton, *The Light Went Out*, pp. 160-61. (Bruce Hamilton locates this hospital at Muswell Hill; I have been guided here by the pencilled correction made in the hand of Patrick Hamilton's first wife, Lois, in the Estate's copy of the biography.)

68. The political section of this letter is given in full in B. Hamilton, 'Patrick—A Tragedy', pp. 609-12.

69. P. Hamilton, letter to B. Hamilton, Sheringham, Norfolk, 5 August 1959 (AHA).

70. P. Hamilton, letter to B. Hamilton, Hyde Park Gate Mews, 29 January 1954 (AHA).

71. P. Hamilton, *Unknown Assailant* (London: Constable, 1955), pp. 130-31.

72. Tambling, *Confession*, p. 97.

THE BLUES, SOME BOOZE AND
KEROUAC'S LYRICAL PROSE

George Wedge

People use drugs to 'feel better' or in the belief that drugs will improve function. If a drug does not produce the desired result, they stop taking it. This is the cardinal principle anyone wishing to investigate the literature of intoxication must observe. A writer who chooses to use a drug for its effect on the process of composition usually does so to deepen awareness of a work's content or to induce a mood change, an altered state related to the work's surface phrasing or style. With habitual use of an addictive drug, good feelings or improved functioning may continue for a fairly long period—as was the case, for example, with the opium addiction of George Crabbe. But there was a price for Crabbe as for De Quincey, a price carefully spelled out in Alethea Hayter's *Opium and The Romantic Imagination*:[1] the deepened awareness of a drug-altered state makes the user both hungrier for spiritual experience and more keenly aware of human limitations that inhibit it. The drugs that awaken spiritual longing inhibit spiritual fulfillment.

Although it is commonly believed that drug addiction inevitably ends in physical and mental deterioration and death, Crabbe lived a long and productive life despite using opium for over forty years. Infirmity and death come to all sooner or later, and some artists seem willing to risk these calamities sooner if the drug pays off in the desired ways. Careful study of the work of Jack Kerouac suggests that for some time the drugs he used did pay off in the desired ways, that what he wanted included the effect on his writing as well as a sense of physical and psychic well-being, and that his spiritual hunger increased even as satisfaction became increasingly remote.

Viewed from the cold distance of the clinical standards of DSM III-R, Kerouac was dependent on drugs. His early use of benzedrine put him in the hospital with thrombophlebitis but that did not alter his use; he would endure repeated painful bouts to the end. His use of drugs and alcohol created problems with his parents, his wives and the law. In his last year, he spoke negatively of most drugs—some, like LSD, he had never found useful—but he continued to drink and, at least when writing, to use benzedrine. There is as little doubt that he used drugs for purposes related to his writing as there is that he died of hemorrhages of the esophageal varicies, a common cause of death among alcoholics. By then, he had suffered physical deterioration so severe as to be clearly visible in photographs taken over the last few years of his life. He was a man driven to write, to write about 'the big questions', that is, spiritual matters, and for him, the benefits of his substance dependence were worth the risk.

Kerouac found benzedrine useful from the beginning of his writing career. He counted on it to relieve tensions that inhibited the writing process, especially in the marathon sessions that Truman Capote said were not writing at all but 'typing'.[2] And he sought mood alterations that would assist in the search of the 'style' of his circular Duluoz Legend, the sequence of twelve novels on which his reputation rests. According to Ann Charters, he was using benzedrine for these purposes as early as 1945, prior to beginning *The Town and the City*:

> The only thing that didn't stop [among things he had been doing in New York before he returned home to help during his father's illness] was the benzedrine. Confined to the apartment most of the time, Jack took bennies late at night when his parents were in bed and he had the kitchen to himself. He told them he had to write at night, that, looking after Leo, he couldn't concentrate during the day...The benzedrine made him feel stronger, more self-confident than when he was straight and he took pride in himself for being able to take such massive doses. Jack felt he was blasting so high that he was experiencing real insights and facing real fears. With benzedrine he felt he was embarking on a journey of self-discovery, climbing from one level to the next, following his insights. As he told Allen [Ginsberg], benzedrine intensified his awareness and made him feel more clever.[3]

It is my purpose here to assert that the drug used during the gestation of each novel assisted in the development of both content and style. (Such a claim is equally valid whether one considers the mood change to be effected by the drug or by Kerouac's expectation of such an effect upon mood.) Each drug made the intensity of the composing process more bearable and each, in its effect upon mood, was consonant to the purpose of the novel at hand. A benzedrine high is different from a cannabis high or an alcohol high; the resultant mood change is different in each instance and so, correspondingly, is the mood and style of writing produced. Further, since much of Kerouac's work depends upon a contrast between the recollected past of the events described in the novel and the present of the moment of composition, the effect of the drug of choice on the functions of memory during the period of conception (classical *inventio*) is also relevant. That there are means other than drug ingestion to achieve these ends—meditation, physical and mental exercises and so on—is a subject for some other study, one that should investigate possible negative effects of *any* conscious attempt to induce creativity. The creative act itself is a high, an altered state that is both compulsive and addictive even when its source is an untraceable feature of individual personality.

In broad outline, the twelve novels of the Duluoz Legend constitute a spiritual quest, an investigation of the human condition as embodied in men and women whose vitality is their principal strength, who struggle to survive with some dignity, but whose world offers only one reward, the relief of darkness and death. Strong lyrical expressions of continuing faith in the human spirit characterize the conclusion of books as disparate in energy and style as *On the Road* and *Big Sur*.

On the Road, in the famous version that consisted of a single 125 foot long paragraph, was written over a period of three weeks in 1951, the exhausting schedule alleviated by benzedrine and coffee. By the time it was published, as Charters observes, it

> wasn't any longer the book Jack had ecstatically thrown off on the teletype roll in 1951. It was rewritten and revised countless times before being excerpted in 1955 and he was to go over it again with [Malcolm] Cowley before Viking published it in 1957.[4]

During this final rewrite, Kerouac, 'seriously concerned about his drinking...practiced temperance for a month' and abstained from cannabis.[5] At the same time he continued work on 'October in the Railroad Earth.' In fact, over the five years between teletype scroll and book, he wrote six of the twelve novels, portions of two others and a number of short pieces like 'Railroad Earth' that might or might not become part of the cycle. The cycle is largely autobiographical; nobody knows what he might have produced had he completed it. We might have viewed this cycle on the paired sadness of vitality and death as works of a 'period' in a longer career. After publication of *On the Road* came the disasters attendant on fame in twentieth-century America, heavy drug/alcohol addiction and a four-year hiatus in writing. By the last two books of the cycle, *Big Sur* and *Vanity of Duluoz*, Kerouac was less 'beat' than beaten, writing and life itself reduced to conditioned reflexes.

On the Road concludes with a paean of praise for the vast peopled continent and a continuing regard for Moriarty, from whom Sal Paradise has learned all he can bear:

> So in America when the sun goes down and I sit on the old broken-down river pier watching the long, long skies over New Jersey and sense all that raw land that rolls in one unbelievable huge bulge over to the West Coast, and all that road going, all the people dreaming in the immensity of it, and in Iowa I know by now the children must be crying in the land where they let children cry, and tonight the stars'll be out and don't you know God is Pooh Bear? the evening star must be drooping and shedding her sparkler dims on the prairie, which is just before the coming of complete night that blesses the earth, darkens all rivers, cups the peaks

and folds the final shore in, and nobody, nobody knows what's going to happen to anybody besides the forlorn rags of growing old, I think of Dean Moriarty, I even think of Old Dean Moriarty the father we never found, I think of Dean Moriarty.[6]

Much attention has been given to the phrase 'the father we never found'. Straight syntax reads it as a vision of Dean when he shall wear 'the forlorn rags of growing old'. Sadness derives not from the loss of a father but the loss of youth and, by extension, of innocence, trust, belief. In the midst of the warmth and plenty of people 'dreaming in the immensity of' the land there is only the comfort of Pooh Bear as God and a bedtime story—even for Old Moriarty, his youthful energy spent seeking IT, the ever-receding moment of pure and complete existence. Sal, like his successive Kerouac personas in the other novels, is sad but not defeated. The quest will continue; some way can be found of getting to IT, to understanding and accepting the beauty and sadness of all moments of existence. Growing old, enduring with diminished energy, being folded in with the final shore, are forlorn rags indeed to cover what was exciting, electric and immediate. Sal thinks of Dean Moriarty because the sum of their experience on the road to IT is that 'nobody knows what's going to happen to anybody' other than to grow old without increase of wisdom.

Sal Paradise is, like Kerouac, an observer more than a participant in the activity surrounding him. He called himself 'the Recording Angel', the term 'loner' occurs frequently in friends' descriptions of him and the collection that contains 'Railroad Earth' is titled *The Lonesome Traveler*. His discomfort with new people, his shyness and his use of a dream diary as a source of fictions resemble traits of George Crabbe. Anyone familiar with contemporary complaints about Kerouac's work will hear an echo in Hayter's description of how Crabbe's work was affected by his addiction. Contrasting Crabbe's *The Village* with the later poem *The Borough*, Hayter says:

> He had always a keen eye for detail, but the hyperaesthesia of opium may have intensified the poring concentration with which, in his later poems, he conveyed some trivial visual experience. The sad splendour of the flowering weeds in *The Village* is seen in a human context; they devour the poor man's wretched crop of rye, and tear and scratch his ragged children. But the weeds described in *The Borough*, that marvelous patch of intricate forms, textures, sickly smells, acrid colours, are intensely seen for themselves alone.[7]

Such heightened visual imagery is characteristic of the opium-addicted writers studied by Hayter. Alcohol, benzedrine and cannabis affect other senses. In Kerouac the prime sense is sound, especially speech rhythms, sometimes so insistent they overpower a reader. Generally, as he desired, its jazz improvisational flow carries readers along despite the cramming in of 'trivial experience'.

It is common to speak of the style of *On the Road* as if it were unmodulated, a frenetic dash—a notion encouraged by the legend surrounding the original typescript. But there is modulation. Not every sentence is a long rush of words. As Kerouac performs the ending, some phrases move swiftly, others have a slow, tender cadence. Bop, with its foundations in the blues, 'cool' in contrast to 'hot' swing music, blew both fast and slow, following the mood of the musician as Kerouac followed his mood in writing. Sal's farewell to Dean is a tender blues. As observer, he can do nothing to change the course of anybody's life, because 'nobody knows what is going to happen to anybody'. Yet spiritual bonds endure, for he thinks of Moriarty, even of Moriarty old and lost, Moriarty at the age of 'the father we never found'. The literal reading deserves emphasis because the attractive other implications, certainly also there, are universal, while the quest, as in all Kerouac's books, is personal, the context universal.

The whole of 'October in the Railroad Earth' has this lyric quality, calling upon all the senses to perceive the wonder of ordinary days and lives, their glory and squalor, through the speaker—one wants to say through the speaker's eyes, but it is through the body, the sense organs—and on the speaker's breath impulse. Originally called 'Wine in the Railroad Earth',[8] it was written while Kerouac was working as a brakeman for the Southern Pacific Railroad and living alone at the Cameo Hotel near Third and Howard Streets in San Francisco.[9] It is a good example of Kerouac's spontaneous prose sketching, an 'undisturbed flow from the mind', which sees rhythm as within the thought process rather than as a product of thought.[10] Kerouac's suggestion that the dash be used to separate breath phrasings Nicosia dismisses as based on 'idiosyncrasy and not wholly practicable.'[11] The use of the dash for this purpose in *Big Sur* may distract some readers, but has the virtue of offering the reader prepared for it the same kind of guidance the conventions of music provide to one ready to follow the score while listening to the music. But *Big Sur* is late and elliptical in ways that 'October in the Railroad Earth' is not; the reader needs no score for the latter, dense as the prose may be:

> There was a little alley in San Francisco back of the Southern Pacific station to Third and Townsend in redbrick of drowsy lazy afternoons with everybody at work in offices in the air you feel the impending rush of their commuter frenzy as soon they'll be charging en masse from Market and Sansome buildings on foot and all well-dressed thru workingman Frisco of Walkup ?? truck drivers and even the poor grime-bemarked Third Street of lost bums and even Negroes so hopeless and long left East and meanings of responsibility and try that now all they do is stand there spitting in the broken glass sometimes fifty in one afternoon against one wall at Third and Howard and here's all these Millbrae and San Carlos neat-necktied producers and commuters of America and Steel civilization rushing by the San Francisco Chronicle and green Call-Bulletin not even enough time be to be disdainful, they've got to catch 130, 132, 134, 136 all the way up to 146 till the time of evening supper in homes of the railroad

earth when high in the sky the magic stars rise above the following hotshot freight trains.—It's all in California, it's all a sea, I swim out of it in afternoons of sun hot meditation, in my jeans with head on handker-chief on brakeman's lantern or (if not working) on books, I look up at blue sky of perfect lostpurity and fell the warp of wood of old America beneath me and have insane conversations with Negroes in several-story windows above and everything is pouring in, the switching moves of boxcars in that little alley which is so much like the alleys of Lowell and I hear far off in the sense of coming night that engine calling our mountains.

> But it was that beautiful cut of clouds I could always see above the little S.P. alley, puffs floating from Oakland or the Gate of Marin to the north or San Jose south the clarity of Cal to break your heart. It was the fantastic drowse and drum hum of lum mum afternoon nathin' to do, ole Frisco with end of land sadness—the people—the alley full of trucks and cars of business nearabouts and nobody knew or far from cared who I was all my life three thousand five hundred miles from birth—O opened up and at last belonged to me in Great America.[12]

That the origin of such syntax-defying leaps is the story-telling and fast talk of men drinking together—as in experimental tapes Kerouac and Cassady made—is obvious to anyone who has listened to such speech in a bar. Its origin in bop musicians riffing can be seen in the improvisations on themes that return just as they seem to have been elaborated irrevocably into something else. End of working day at the end of the land is alternately lazy and frenzied, has a fast lane and a drowsy one, reminding the speaker of youthful afternoons and other alleys, connect-ing the theme of this time and place to the 'lostpurity' of the sky and the stars that ride over all—the city, the connecting rails and the homes of the railroad earth. To the thought at the end of *On the Road* that 'nobody knows what's going to happen to anybody' is added the thought that 'nobody knew or far from cared who I was all my life'. The syntax makes a jazz riff into the consoling faith that not to know and to be unrecognized, to be observer rather than actor, is to be free in a good place.

Given that for the six years between the first full draft of *On the Road* and its publication Kerouac was working alternately on most of the later books and that revising *On the Road* was one of the projects going on when he wrote 'October in the Railroad Earth' such a suggestion of intertextuality is less far-fetched than it might seem. In his study of style, *The Five Clocks*, Martin Joos refers to the style of printed texts as 'frozen', all other styles being open.[13] Because Kerouac could work on so many unfrozen texts simultaneously, he had an unusual opportunity to discover principles germane to the whole and apply them broadcast (unusually, but not uniquely; Proust and O'Neill provide other examples). The resulting unity of content from book to book was discounted by reviewers of the later works; they knew what Kerouac *should* be up to from the heavily edited published version of *On the Road*. When later editors wished to cut or break up sentences, repunctuate or just plain punctuate, he resisted; as Nicosia has demonstrated, he revised plenty, but on his own terms. To editors, he insisted that he knew what he was doing; the prosody of the published works shows that, for better or worse, he did.

While working on 'October in the Railroad Earth' Kerouac drank cheap sweet wines. Clark says it was 'rotgut port',[14] Charters suggests that it was 'his favorite at the time, sweet tokay'.[15] (Among the few failures of Nicosia's scholarly biography is his reluctance to relate Kerouac's addiction to his writing). What sweet wine it was is of no importance, but Charters observes, correctly, that,

> It was as if Jack imagined himself in a bar drinking his sweet wine and telling a long wild tale, his friends listening and shouting and urging him to go higher. Jack would no more go back and correct his phrases on paper than he would revise himself telling a story in a bar...Wine was perfect for describing his work on the railroad, not only because it was cheap and readily available in any corner store, but because it wasn't hallucinatory like morphine or leading him back into memory trips like marijuana, both of which he'd wanted to help shape *Doctor Sax* but didn't need with 'Railroad Earth'.[16]

While it is possible to trace the development of Kerouac's style from book to book in chronological succession, as has been done by Regina Weinreich,[17] there are passages in the full-blown manner of the mature style in all the work in progress between 1951 and 1957. Differences in tone relate both to the function of the work at hand in what Kerouac increasingly saw as not a series of novels but one long autobiographic narrative and to his choice of a facilitating drug consonant to the purpose of the work. Though he thought of 'October in the Railroad Earth' as part of this sequence, it remained independent. The drug used while writing it, sweet wine, appears from the original title to have been a conscious choice, not just a limitation of finances, his job or independent living. Perhaps because he had not yet lost his tolerance for alcohol and his living circumstances were freer, the narrative texture is firmly optimistic, liltingly lyrical and occasionally downright cheerful.

The preceding year, in Mexico City, Kerouac had worked on a book he had been planning for years, *Doctor Sax*, memories of his Lowell childhood, innocent, full of prankish comic strip mystery and centered on the basic fears of the child who has encountered death. For this work, as Charters notes, he used morphine to provide hallucination, useful even in passages as mildly surreal as the following:

> Suddenly I realized his great black cat was there. It stood four feet tall from ground to spine, with big green eyes and vast slow swishing tail like eternity on a fly—the strangest cat....A vast perwiligar balloon exploded over my head, it was a blue balloon that had risen out of the blue powders in the Forge, and so suddenly everything was blue.
> 'The Blue Era,' cried Doctor Sax, dashing to his kiln—His shroud flew

after him, he stood like a Goethe witch before his furn-forge, tall
emasculated, Nietzschean, gaunt—[18]

And he used cannabis, which has well-known properties encouraging
detailed and obsessive memory trips:

> The other night I had a dream that I was sitting on the sidewalk on
> Moody Street, Pawtucketville, Lowell, Mass., with a pencil and paper in my
> hand saying to myself 'Describe the wrinkly tar of this sidewalk, also the
> iron pickets of the Textile Institute, or the doorway where Lousy and you
> and G.J.'s always sittin and dont stop to think of words when you do stop,
> just stop to think of the picture better—and let your mind off yourself in
> this work'.[19]

Kerouac had always visualized it as a memory book with an admixture of
materials from *Shadow Magazine* tales of the mysterious and macabre. He
knew the effects of both drugs from prior experiences, experiences which
had perhaps assisted in the planning. Their use during composition was
purposeful. He was staying with William Burroughs in Mexico City and
Burroughs did not want him to smoke cannabis in the apartment, so
Kerouac took his cannabis and his notebook to the hall toilet, sat on the
closed seat, toked up and wrote. There could hardly be stronger evidence
of a connection between drug use and writing in the mind of an author.

The book ends in the gigantic clash of the Great Serpent and the Great
Bird, the bird triumphs, and Doctor Sax says, with amazement, 'I'll be
damned. The Universe disposes of its own evil'. As Weinreich observes,
the whole of the book concerns the fears and nightmares, the surreal
landscape, of Kerouac's Catholic childhood. The end of this particular part
of his spiritual journey is that the narrator outgrows Doctor Sax and his
childhood and can pass 'some old French Canadian ladies praying step
by step on their knees' outside the church, and defiantly put a rose in his
hair and go home. This statement leads into the final two-word sentence:
'By God'.

Big Sur, in contrast, ends with a vision of the cross and marks a turning
point in the spiritual quest of both Kerouac's life and work, a return to the
conventional mysticism rejected in *Doctor Sax*. Given that the book is an
account of an alcoholic breakdown, full of horrors and the waking
nightmares of delirium tremens, it is hardly surprising that both the
persona and the writer sought relief in surrender. These are not the views
found in standard critical discussion of Kerouac's work, but anyone familiar with how alcoholics desperate for relief respond to their crisis will
recognize the progress both of his painfully achieved self-knowledge and
of his willingness to seek comfort in what he believed when he was
young and innocent. However painful the belief outgrown in *Doctor Sax*, it
is easy compared to the pain in *Big Sur*.

The breakdown occurred in August 1960. Kerouac had gone to
Ferlinghetti's cabin at Bixby Canyon to escape the distracting notoriety

publication of *On the Road* had brought and to have time and space for writing. He had not had 'an extended burst of writing since 1957'.[20] Having planned to sneak into San Francisco quietly, he instead followed the self-defeating course of letting friends and hangers-on know he was there, often seeking them out to escape or to drag into the wild environment surrounding the cabin. And drinking as if there were no end.

The book was written in October, 1961, the drug of choice being benzedrine, with its deceptive energy-giving potential. It is full-force spontaneous writing with less revision than the earlier books; it was in print by 1963. Weinreich observes that 'very few sentences form thoughts in this book. Instead the book is filled with dash-joined images providing a breathy, impressionistic effect, a cataloging of detail reminiscent of Whitman's "Song of Myself" and Ginsberg's "Howl"'.[21] In the period between the breakdown itself and the writing of the book, Kerouac had continued a fifth-a-day habit, except for July 1961 when he wrote the second half of *Desolation Angels,* and much of his drunken meditation was on the events of the preceding summer and fall. Thus, though the drug in use during the writing is benzedrine, the book itself has much of the texture of a drunkologue by a person who refuses fully to engage in recovery from his alcoholism and deals interminably in self-pity. Weinreich comes close to these observations, observing that 'rather than a quest for spirituality that is suggested by an optimism, exuberance and frequent references to Christianity and Buddhism, there appears to be an attempt to justify his sins'.[22] The terrifying vision resolved in the image of the cross has led only to conventional piety, without the substance of the close of the earlier books, to self-knowledge that yields fear rather than spiritual insight:

> Any drinker knows how the process works: the first day you get drunk is okay, the morning after means a big head but so you can kill that easy with a few more drinks and a meal, but if you pass up the meal and go on to another night's drunk, and wake up to keep the toot going, and continue on to the fourth day, there'll come one day when the drinks wont take effect because you're chemically overloaded and you'll have to sleep it off but cant sleep any more because it was alcohol itself that made you sleep those last five nights, so delirium sets in—Sleeplessness, sweat, trembling, a groaning feeling of weakness where your arms are numb and useless, nightmares (nightmares of death) ....well, there's more of that up later.[23]

Weinreich quotes this passage as an example of 'wisdom on drunkenness',[24] but such eloquence can be heard from quite ordinary speakers at meetings of Alcoholics Anonymous; the 'wisdom' is hard-earned, and sincere, but if there is no resolve to change things, it expresses the 'hopeless hope' of the alcoholics in O'Neill's *The Iceman Cometh.* Flashes of Kerouac's earlier lyrical power are sad reminders of what had been possible, as in the opening of the book:

The church is blowing a sad windblown 'Kathleen' in the bells in the skid row slums as I wake up all woebegone and goopy, groaning from another drinking bout and groaning most of all because I'd ruined my 'secret return' to San Francisco by getting silly drunk while hiding in the alleys with bums and then marching forth into North Beach to see everybody altho Lorenz Monsanto and I'd exchanged huge letters outlining how I would sneak in quietly, call him on the phone using a code name like Adam Yulch or Lalagy Pulvertaft (also writers) and then he would secretly drive me to his cabin in the Big Sur woods where I would be alone and undisturbed for six weeks just chopping wood, drawing water, writing, sleeping, hiking, etc., etc.

—But instead I've bounced drunk into his City Lights bookshop at the height of Saturday night business, everyone recognized me (even tho' I was wearing my disguise-like fisherman's hat and fisherman coat and pants waterproof) and t'all ends up a roaring drunk in all the famous bars the bloody 'King of the Beatniks' is back in town buying drinks for everyone.[25]

The lyricism is there, but if the rhythm of Kerouac's spontaneous writing was 'within the thought process rather than...a product of thought', his thought process has never been quite so seedy. The casual slip from present tense in 'the church is blowing' to past in 'because I'd ruined' is uncharacteristic of the usually spell-binding tale-teller. The cut up inserted in the second sentence, 'everyone recognized me...the bloody "King of the Beatniks" is back,' is self-conscious in a way not often met in Kerouac's work. That Joan Haverty, his second wife, had used the epithet against him about the time he left for San Francisco was one of many things rankling with him.

Nicosia, Weinreich and Stephenson[26] read the twelve novels as Kerouac hoped to make them be, a single vision of a single life on a spiritual quest. That he did not live to make the books be what he intended does not prevent us from offering the kind of understanding critical appraisal these writers have given. But the life ran onto the same sad and devastating rocks that wrecked the projected life saga. The drugs which had seemed to open vast possibilities for exploration had proved, as they do for genius and fool alike, to be a snare and a delusion. But it had been a ride to thank God on. It is a disservice to Kerouac's spiritual accomplishments to miss in his ambiguous last words the admission that he did not find the 'something good [that] will come out of all things yet'. He merely completed the circle where it began, wondering what besides his animal vitality makes humanity—say in the person of Neal Cassady—such a marvel.

NOTES

1.   A. Hayter, *Opium and the Romantic Imagination* (Berkeley, CA: University of California Press, 1970).

2.   G. Nicosia, *Memory Babe* (New York: Grove, 1975), p. 588.

3.   A. Charters, *Kerouac: A Biography* (San Francisco: Straight Arrow Books, 1973), p. 63.

4.   Charters, *Kerouac*, p. 207.

5.   Nicosia, *Memory Babe*, p. 441.

6.   J. Kerouac, *On the Road* (New York: Penguin, 1976), pp. 309-10.

7.   Hayter, *Opium*, p. 189.

8.   Nicosia, *Memory Babe*, p. 423.

9.   *Memory Babe*, p. 418.

10.   *Memory Babe*, p. 454.

11.   *Memory Babe*, p. 453.

12.   J. Kerouac, 'October in the Railroad Earth', in *Lonesome Traveler* (New York: Grove Press, 1970), pp. 37-38.

13.   M. Joos, *The Five Clocks* (Bloomington, IN: Indiana University Research Center in Anthropology, Folklore and Linguistics, 1962).

14.   T. Clark, *Jack Kerouac* (New York: Paragon House, 1990), p. 118.

15.   Charters, *Kerouac*, p. 171.

16.   Charters, *Kerouac*, pp. 171-72.

17.   R. Weinreich, *The Spontaneous Poetics of Jack Kerouac* (New York: Paragon Hause, 1990).

18.   J. Kerouac, *Doctor Sax* (New York: Grove, 1975), p. 212.

19.   Kerouac, *Doctor Sax*, p. 3.

20.   Clark, *Jack Kerouac*, p. 194.

21.   Weinreich, *Spontaneous Poetics*, p. 150.

22.   Weinreich, *Spontaneous Poetics*, p. 151.

23.   J. Kerouac, *Big Sur* (New York: McGraw-Hill, 1980), pp. 74-75.

24.   Weinreich, *Spontaneous Poetics*, p. 151.

25.   Kerouac, *Big Sur*, p. 3.

26.   G. Stephenson, *The Daybreak Boys: Essays on the Literature of the Beat Generation* (Carbondale, IL: Southern Illinois University Press, 1990).

ADDICTION AND THE AVANT-GARDE: HEROIN ADDICTION AND NARRATIVE IN ALEXANDER TROCCHI'S *CAIN'S BOOK*

Sue Wiseman

There is a moment near the beginning of *On the Road* when the narrator, Sal, finds himself alone in a dreary hotel room in Des Moines:

> I...wound up in a gloomy old Plains hotel by the locomotive round-house...and that was the one distinct time in my life, the strangest moment of all, when I didn't know who I was—I was far away from home, haunted and tired with travel, in a cheap hotel room I'd never seen, hearing the hiss of steam outside, and the creak of the old wood of the hotel, and footsteps upstairs, and all the sad sounds, and I looked at the cracked high ceiling and really didn't know who I was for about fifteen strange seconds. I wasn't scared; I was just somebody else, some stranger, and my whole life was a haunted life, the life of a ghost.[1]

On the Road rapidly contextualizes this as an experience of liminality, a transition in which Sal crosses the dividing line between east and west, youth and manhood. But even so, it pinpoints the potential alienation of the narrator (and the novel), implicit in *On the Road* though disclosed only in gaps in the text's eventfulness, but always underlying—and generating—that novel's frenzied hyperproductivity of story. Instead of succumbing to the sense of pointless waiting, Sal moves on. However, the estranged space he leaves is crucial to the writing of the European and American avant-garde of the mid to late 1950s. Under the twin signs of psycho-political revolution and addiction *Cain's Book*, by the Scottish writer (and polemicist, pornographer for Olympia Press, member of the Situationist International and sigmatist) Alexander Trocchi, foregrounds the experience of 'strangeness' (or alienation, self-estrangement) which constituted Sal's experience. Where *On the Road* offers the reader 'fifteen strange seconds', *Cain's Book*[2] writes itself entirely in the 'strange' space. Written within the paradox of offering addiction as a liberatory philosophy, *Cain's Book* struggles to exist at the moment where contraries cancel each other—where addiction is both implicit, even recognized, and simultaneously refused or displaced or coded as political philosophy.

Despite some concerns shared with Beat writers, the late 1950s avant-garde writers such as William Burroughs and Samuel Beckett eschew the insistent storytelling or yarning organization of Beat prose. Trocchi, who had published Beckett and who later knew Burroughs, also disassociated himself from the novel as such (in *Merlin* he wrote 'novelists, we suppose, and by definition, do [write novels], although a serious writer, we feel, may not').[3] Although he was writing narratives in the 1950s and wrote much of *Cain's Book* at that time in New York, when the major dissident aesthetic was Beat, his fiction follows Beckett and others in refusing some aspects of novelistic narrative. Closely interwoven with this anti-novelistic approach to narrative fiction was Trocchi's heroin addiction (of which he writes, albeit ambivalently, in terms of psycho-political commitment) and its temporal rhythm. Trocchi's refusal of the novel as a genre intersects with the political and philosophical context of his last years in Paris (where he edited *Merlin* and was a member of the Situationist International). Ideas derived from situationist philosophy and an ambivalent stylistic and political commitment to the power of heroin combine to place his 'book' at the interstices of experiment in addiction, prose and politics. In the light of the interweaving of situationist and literary avant-garde ideas, the question, 'how does *Cain's Book* register and use the idea of heroin addiction?' becomes both an issue of content—of what heroin 'stands for' in the text—and a question of how addiction as the repetition of textual patterns meshes with or ultimately disrupts the anti-aesthetic of *Cain's Book*. Is *Cain's Book* a deliberate experiment in the use of heroin to 'construct situations' by transforming the protagonist's and reader's mode of perception—that is, as a kind of quasi-situationist aesthetic and political experiment—or, on the contrary, does the text register and encode addiction in ways which are other than or distruptive to its politico-philosophical impetus?

The cultural and political ideas circulating during Trocchi's time in Paris provide the insurrectionist philosophical and political contexts, inter-texts and quotations for *Cain's Book* and illuminate the text's conjunction of addiction and situationist assertion. Analogies for the thinking of the European literary anti-art, anti-culture avant-garde of the late 1950s and early 1960s can be found in the movement of *lettrisme* and later in the Situationist International which elaborated some politico-cultural ideas drawn from Dada and futurism. This is particularly pertinent because Trocchi was a member of the Situationist International after 1956 and their programme significantly underwrites his longest narrative fiction. By the mid-1950s Guy Debord and Ivan Chtcheglov had separately elaborated a social and psychic critique which centred on the tyranny of the commodity. In the first issue of *International Situationist* Chtcheglov makes clear a movement away from Marx to analysis of the psychic dominance of the image, or what Jean Baudrillard was later to call the 'simulacrum'. In 1958

Chtcheglov wrote the simulacral dominance of the commodity:

> A mental disease has swept the planet: banalisation. Everyone is hypno-
> tised by production and conveniences—sewage system, elevator, bathroom,
> washing machine.
>   This state of affairs, arising out of a struggle against poverty, has over-
> shot its ultimate goal—the liberation of material cares—and become an
> obsessive image hanging over the present...[4]

This is an analysis that sees the commodity as the focus of a quasi-
universal Western addiction, a notion which is familiar to us from
contemporary postmodern critiques. The view finds a slightly different
expression in the writing of Guy Debord, probably the best-known
member of the Situationist International. In Debord's book *The Society of the
Spectacle* (translated into English in 1963) he writes: 'The entire life of
societies in which modern conditions of production reign announces
itself as an accumulation of *spectacles*. Everything that was directly lived
has moved away into a representation'; and, 'the spectacle is the moment
when the commodity has attained the *total occupation* of social life. The
relation to the commodity is not only not visible, but one no longer sees
anything but it.'[5] The situationist insight that Debord elaborated in the
1960s was that everything, including counteractivity, is absorbed back into
the society from which it wished to dissent (or as Trocchi put it, look how
quickly Dada was mummified in books). The situationists hoped to
counter this by changing people's perception. Their ideas included a
vision of a new city and above all of a new art, which would exist both as a
continuity with life and in the act of its suppression. Above all, everyday
life might be transformed by that notoriously vague thing 'the construction of situations' which would begin to expose and thereby outflank the
addictive myths and apparatuses of hegemony.

Obviously, cultural production was crucial to the situationists' programme for the transformation of consciousness. However, as Stewart
Home points out, in terms of their thinking about 'culture' some aspects of
both *lettrisme* and situationism were limited in that they continued to think
of art as a potentially existent transcendental value rather than, as Home
puts it, 'a bourgeois construct', or as the system endlessly redeployed to
endorse the value of the dominant ideology.[6] They could be criticized for
situating any potential for change in an area which bordered the
mystical. This meant that situationist ideas, drawing on Dada and certain
other potentially elitist strands, were a perfect seed-bed and structure for
the formulation of ideologies of the avant-garde, including ideas about a
new art and artistic practice—in short, for the formation of an anti-
aesthetic.

Such thinking is echoed in the writings of Jean Baudrillard and in
Jean-François Lyotard, the latter coming to it by a slightly different route
through the redeployment of the Kantian sublime. An example is found

in *The Postmodern Condition*; Lyotard describes the kind of art which would be conscious of its own postmodernity, when, for instance, he summarizes postmodern 'art' as 'that which denies itself the solace of good forms...that which searches for new presentations, not in order to enjoy them but in order to impart a stronger sense of the unpresentable'.[7] Lyotard, like the situationists, does not really question the status of 'art' and, therefore, at least in *The Postmodern Condition* he retains (under erasure, perhaps) a category for 'art' which is more than art practices; he too looks to a new aesthetic rather than to the abolition of aesthetics.

In Trocchi's case the engagement with situationist aesthetics was also meshed with an early knowledge of Beckett, which endorsed the notion of an anti-generic anti-art. The situationist pronouncements on art were allusive and obscure in their call for a new art, but relatively clear in their assertion that the old order must be abandoned and a new kind of artistic consciousness be created if the addictive banalization of life was to be halted, reversed or rearranged. One of the formulations published in *International Situationist* put it as follows:

> 'People continue to produce plays', writes Kenneth Tynan, 'which are based on the absurd idea that people still fear and respect the crown...' The phrase 'continue to produce plays' is indicative of just how tepidly literary is the angry young man's point of view. They have simply changed their opinion about a few social conventions without understanding the *change of terrain* of the whole of cultural activity, so obvious in every truly avant-garde movement of this century.[8]

Another statement with implications for a new kind of art, and implicitly a new kind of avant-garde, can be found in Debord and Wolman's 'Methods of Detournement' from 1956:

> The literary and artistic heritage of humanity should be used for partisan and propaganda purpose... In fact, it is necessary to finish with any notion of personal property in this area. The appearance of new necessities outmodes previous 'inspired' works. They become obstacles, dangerous habits. The point is not whether we like them or not. We have to go beyond them.[9]

Burroughs's writing to some extent offers a correlative in literary practice to the situationist transformation. Like Trocchi, Burroughs recognized the need to re-evaluate writing, as is suggested in a passage analysing novelistic discourse and counterposing non-narrative prose. This occurs towards the end of *Naked Lunch*, and he emphasizes the role of the writer in registering modernity using a partial sensibility; another version of art and life being in some ways interwoven, but also, again, having a potential to disrupt the sensibility of the circuit or spectacle (though a potential which, for Burroughs, must remain unrealized):

> There is only one thing a writer can write about: *what is in front of his senses at the moment of writing*... I am a recording instrument... I do not presume to

impose 'story', 'plot', 'continuity',...Insofar as I succeed in *direct* recording
of certain areas of psychic process I may have a limited function. I am not
an entertainer...[10]

The situationists' calls for a new art are paralleled by Burroughs's assertion that a writer's function has changed. Both want a new art which
succumbs to neither classicism nor an 'empty' version of experimental art.
In Burroughs's early writing this puts the burden of finding a way to read
the text onto the reader, posing rather than solving a problem of coherence
and continuity. Accordingly, the reader in search of recurrent motifs and
paths to follow finds them in the text's obssession with heroin. It is the
'thin white line' of heroin that the reader follows throughout *Naked Lunch*,
like punctuation or the closest thing the text offers to reassuring narrative
return or repetition. The centrality of heroin in the novel, and the reader's
focus on it, is reinforced by the way the text eschews linear narration and
the exploration of problems more familiar from novelistic discourse. Thus,
in *Naked Lunch* heroin addiction is crucial to the way the anti-aesthetic
operates in the text, offering the reader a structuring device 'alternative' to
the traditional ones of story, plot and continuity.

In *Cain's Book* heroin is even more emphatically at the centre of self-
consciousness. It can be explicitly related to Trocchi's engagement with
situationist ideas and appropriation of them for his particular heroin-based
anti-aesthetic. Like Burroughs's work, Trocchi's was defended by contemporaries as a text which would act as a disincentive rather than as an
incentive to take heroin. But Trocchi never denounced heroin in the way
Burroughs has repeatedly. When *Cain's Book* underwent its one trial for
obscenity (in Sheffield) John Calder as witness claimed that the book was
more likely to repel a reader from the addict's way of life than to incite the
consumption of drugs—a position required by the obscenity laws in
England.[11] The records of the trial make explicit the grounds on which
the publisher and others were prepared to defend *Cain's Book*: principally,
its alliances with the American Beats and with Beckett, its representation
of an outsider and its place in the tradition of drug classics—as a witness
John Calder read out part of the Sherlock Holmes story *The Sign of Four*.[12]
Understandably, witnesses understated the link between the novel's
politics and its use of heroin, but when questioned Calder did say that 'the
author was in revolt against society, rightly or wrongly'. Only one of the
witnesses, however, was willing to reply unequivocally that the text
presented the addict's way of life as repellant—perhaps because heroin
and addiction is so central to the dynamic whereby the text embroils the
reader.[13] Indeed, heroin plays perhaps *the* central role as the object of
desire—the narrator's, and, in terms of structure, the reader's.

In *Cain's Book* heroin carries the weight of the book's desire to disrupt
mere novelistic aesthetics in tandem with producing a new psycho-
political consciousness. It structures the text to facilitate its attempt to refuse
the difference between the literary text and the world, using the idea of

'expression' to cover both. As Trocchi puts it in *Cain's Book*:

> It wasn't that writing shouldn't be written, but that a man should annihi-
> late prescriptions of all past form in his own soul, refuse to consider what
> he wrote in terms of literature, judge it solely in terms of his living
> (p. 131).

Thus, we find in *Cain's Book* an interweaving of past and present, Glasgow childhood, London, Paris, and the New York that Trocchi moved to in the later 1950s where he did, indeed, work on the scows on the Hudson River. He was also a heroin addict. Obviously, to read *Cain's Book* as a memoir would be to miss the point of the interwoven relations of life and text, in the book's terms. Alongside Trocchi's insistence on the writer as a 'cosmonaut of inner space' was an insistence on the breakdown of barriers of genre and between fictional and 'real' worlds—pointed to by the narrator's name (Necchi, echoing Trocchi) and the narrator's project to write *Cain's Book*.

The search for heroin is the text's motif, which links the disparate aims of the prose. The reader is always reading in relation to the text's next 'fix' (or injection of energy) which, when it comes, releases the text's flood of memories, narrative. Through heroin the text is posited as functioning at the border of a literary and political programme. First, it permits the avant-garde anti-narrative text to come into existence by providing a structure of repeated 'fixing'. Secondly, this anti-aesthetic itself overlaps with a programme in which all artistic production participates in the creation of 'situations'. Heroin as narrative strategy and object of discourse links the two into a psychic politics. Ambivalently, then, in *Cain's Book* heroin is the drug to counter the spectacle and to bring about the removal of content, but it also, paradoxically, provides the fiction with a rhythm and a kind of structure. A literal addiction is posited, as potentially, countering the addictive spectacle and its banal literary commodities. The fetishistic detail with which fixing is described inaugurates the refusal of story:

> Half an hour ago I gave myself a fix.
> I stood the needle and an eye dropper in a glass of cold water and lay
> down on the bunk. I felt giddy almost at once. It's good shit, not like some
> of the stuff we've been getting lately (p. 9).

We are invited to watch the rituals of heroin consumption at close quarters, situated on the dangerous frontiers of psychic experience.

The narrative is concerned throughout with psychic experiences. Following on from the early passage just quoted is a longer one on 'the mind under heroin' which introduces us to the ways in which heroin acts as a counter-structure to everyday ways of thinking:

> Cain at his orisons, Narcissus in his mirror.
> The mind under heroin evades perception as it does ordinarily; one is
> aware of contents. But that whole way of posing the question, of dividing
> the mind from what it's aware of, is fruitless. Nor is it that the objects of

perception are intense in an eclectic way, as they are under mescalin or
lysergic acid, nor that things strike one with more intensity or in a more
enchanted or detailed way as I have sometimes experienced under marijuana; it is that the perceiving turns inward, the eyelids droop, the blood
is aware of itself, a slow phosphorescence is all the fabric of flesh and
nerve and bone; it is that the organism has a sense of being intact and
unbrittle, and, above all, unviolable (p. 10).

Thus heroin is set up as the drug for perceiving interiority, the drug
which rejects 'content' and which therefore offers a new kind of consciousness neither sharper perceptually nor hallucinogenic but inwards-
looking, and which can implicitly provide a structure for a serious book
written against the grain of novelistic writing. Evidently, heroin is present
as the drug which is complementary to the new anti-novelistic aesthetic
in which the writer is a 'cosmonaut of inner space'.

Within fifteen pages the narrator is taking another fix, and another, and
later goes out to meet friends, takes a fix, and begins a reminiscence of
childhood and a discussion of what it means to be a writer, the writer of
Cain's Book (which may, ambiguously, be the one we are reading). Thus
the narrative comes to be structured not around plot and narrative but
fixing and a sequential section of memoirs, stories, fragments about the
past of the narrator, followed by a gap and a return to the present narrative
taking place on the scows in New York where the narrator is looking for a
way to find a fix. At one point Joe Necchi, the narrator, comments: 'I
always find it difficult to get back to the narrative. It is as though I might
have chosen any one of a thousand narratives' (p. 30), but in fact there is
no central narrative to which the text 'ought' to return, rather a sequence of
memories from the past interwoven in the present, unfolded in a rhythm
structured by fixing.

The question of writing and of narrative is one to which the text returns
again and again. Once it starts a story which begins, 'It was then that I met
the murderer...' only to point out within a few paragraphs that, of course,
no such thing 'really' happened. As the narrative progresses it becomes
increasingly reflexive, informing us:

There is no story to tell.

I am unfortunately not concerned with the events which led up to this or
that. If I were my task would be simpler. Details would take their
meaning from their relation to the end and could be expanded or
contracted, chosen or rejected, in terms of how they contributed to it. In all
this, there is no it, and there is no startling event or sensational event to
which the mass of detail in which I find myself from day to day
wallowing can be related.

Here, the reflexivity of the text which is 'not concerned with the events
which lead up to this or that' but with a serious kind of writing, non-
generic, slips into a meditation of the narrator which seems to be about
life. The remark 'in all this, there is no it' is ambiguous as to whether it

refers to *Cain's Book* (possibly being written by the narrator) or to the world, and the phrase 'the mass of detail' indicates that the subject is *both* the world and the text, indistinguishably interwoven, in which there is no pattern, ultimate meaning or 'end' to be had.

The reflexive emphasis of the book emphatically and explicitly refuses novelistic structure. And the anti-novelistic impetus of the text refuses to make a distinction between the world and the text but presents both as aspects of the shapeless meaninglessness of activity—'evidence'. What does come to structure what might be a mass of detail is, inevitably, the claim of writing to be in the present, and in the present the narrator's main purpose is fixing. The presence of fixing rituals for the figures in the narrative, for the narrator and for the reader shapes the book. The cyclical search for consumption of heroin becomes a structure of waiting and expectancy (for reader as well as narrator). This, in turn, maps back on to the reflexive and self-consciously anti-aesthetic shape of the book which the narrator describes as follows:

> No beginning, no middle, no end. This is the impasse which a serious man must enter and from which only the simple-minded can retreat. Perhaps there is no harm in telling a few stories, dropping a few turds along the way, but they can only be tidbits to hook the unsuspecting with as I coax them into the endless tundra which is all there is to be explored. God knows it's a big enough confidence trick to make someone listen to you as you gabble on without pretending to explain how Bella got her bum burnt. I said to myself, well now, here's a nice barren wilderness for you to sport and gambol in, with no premises and no conclusion, with no way in and no way out, and with nary a trial for the eye to see. What more can a man want to fill his obscene horizons?

Thus the narrator places himself and reader as inhabitants of a pointless wilderness either (if simple minded) in search of diversions of narrative, or (if 'serious') accepting the inevitable meaninglessness of language which is, after all, only a staving off of the end. The psycho-political polemic permeates narrative shape and is the object of discourse.

Heroin is the drug which allows the mind to enter this 'impasse', to inhabit most properly the great empty spaces. Throughout the book it is explicitly contrasted with alcohol which (as Tom Dardis has shown) was also the drug associated with the pre-war generation of American writers and narrators. Heroin is presented as an acknowledgment, rather than an evasion, of alienation. But—problematically—while heroin is used by the book as a literal addiction to disrupt the addictivity of social organization, and stylistically to disrupt the bankrupt structures of the commodity-novel, heroin in turn attains in the text a ritualized and fetishized treatment. It becomes the ultimate reified commodity. This is true both for the narrator who searches for it and assesses its quality and dangers, and for the reader who relies on the textual structure of fixing for her kicks of narrative moments, memories and so on—both depend on it.

The text comments on the purposes of heroin serves for it, dealing partially with this web of contradiction in which the cost of countering the addiction of the commodity by using heroin to alter perception is, in some ways, a substitution of another commodity. The narrator tells us that he attempts to evoke 'not so much a line of thought as an area of experi-ence...the immediate broth; I am left with a coherence of posture(s)' (p. 230) but the way the text delimits its area of experience is increasingly defined by the interaction of the quest for heroin as a structuring principle of the narrative, in combination with the book's reflexive refusal to tell stories and its insistence rather that it is 'evidence', an 'inventory' linked to the world it expresses as part of 'the immediate broth' in which we and the narrator wallow. The book meditates on the transformative and addictive potentials of heroin in and embedded passage:

> From the bundle of papers which have withstood my periodic prunings I select a couple of sheets and read.
>
> The fix: a purposive spoon in the broth of experience.
> (Il vous faut construire les situations.)
>
> To move is not difficult. The problem is: from what posture? This question of posture, of original attitude: to get at its structure one must temporarily get outside it. Drugs provide an alternative attitude.
>
> On the virtues of heroin. Possibility waits beyond what is fixed and known; there is no language for it; *dies zeigt sich...*
>
> Heroin is habit-forming.
>
> Habit forming, rabbit-forming, Babbitt-forming.
>
> For conventional men all forms of mental derangement save drunken-ness are taboo. Being familiar, alchoholism can arouse only disgust. The alchoholic humiliates himself. The man under heroin is beyond humiliation. The junkie arouses mass hysteria (the dope fiend is the bogeyman who can be hanged in effigy and electrocuted in the flesh to calm the hysteria of the citizens).
>
> It is a significant measure of a society to scrutinize its sewage and abominations. Doctors know this, and police, and philosophers of his-tory (p. 236).

This is one significant posture among others which link heroin addic-tion and the avant-garde, or the cultural elite. Heroin can alter our under-standing of the 'broth of experience' and make it 'purposive'. The cost, as the next line points out, is that in disrupting addiction to everyday life one produces a contrary addiction, to heroin. Heroin affords insight otherwise unavailable, but the price is addiction. Ultimately, this passage (though not, perhaps, the book as a whole) attempts to resolve this contradiction by a retreat into romantic valorization of the outcast—the insightful heroin addict (unlike the alchoholic) is a significant register and monitor of the society which casts him or her out. Simultaneously, the book acknowledges that literal addiction reproduces (or reinstates) commodity-addiction and can be no solution, only a replication. While not explicitly recognizing that heroin addiction echoes this cycle of commodity-addiction, it does recognize addiction as a problem—only to displace it by making it the *solution* which injects purpose into the 'broth of experience'. Logically, the two positions (addiction versus politico-psychic transformation) cancel each other out, which is hinted at by the aphoristic and non-linear structure of this passage. Juxtaposition and reiteration—repetition—are the organizing principles which allow denial and recognition of addiction to exist, sequentially if not quite simultaneously. Taken literally, the statements cancel each other out. Moreover, they are framed by purporting to be a section of notes taken from a notebook, and their framed and aphoristic structure invites us to read them in a Nietzschean twilight, perhaps as the political philosophy of denial.

Even as *Cain's Book* integrates into itself ideas which might transform everyday life, such as 'don't work' or psychogeography, or the model for the new city, what we get is a hellishly inverted version of it. Chtcheglov's vision of everyone's transformed relation to a new, unbanalized city comes to a rather different fruition when Joe Necchi tells us: 'Under heroin one adapts naturally to a new habitat. It is possible to live in a doorway, on someone's couch, or bed, or floor, always moving, and turning up from time to time at known places' (p. 36). The literal addiction disrupts the relation to the spectacle, perhaps, but a reader of the text does not have to be very perverse to see that the counter-structure of heroin itself seems to sow the seeds of its own undermining as it collapses towards the end of the book. The commodity as the 'obsessive image hanging over the present' is reinstated in narrative desire, as heroin.

In attempting to resist an apprehension of the political in which politics is external to and other than the self, and to avoid a model of the 'novel' which fixes and stabilizes experience and identity through genre, *Cain's Book* opts for a fusion, a literary–psychic–political polemic style in which the potential for change is situated within the psyche. But the only space the text finds for writing this change is in the contradiction of opposites: between liberation from the commodity through heroin and the replication of that addiction by heroin; between the construction of situations and the incursions of heroin into any identity; between psychic and literary transformation through fixing and a repetition of structure in heroin addiction. But that is not to say that *Cain's Book* has no angle on its own self-cancelling contradictions and reinstatement of the addictive structures it attempts to disable and disrupt; at every moment even these are framed and positioned by a circular self-referentiality. As the book says, 'to move is not difficult. The problem is: from what posture?'

NOTES

1.   J. Kerouac, *On the Road* (Harmondsworth: Penguin, 1972 [1957]), p. 19.
2.   A. Trocchi, *Cain's Book* (Grove Press, 1960). Page references given in the text are to this edition.
3.   A. Trocchi, *Merlin* 2.2 (Autumn 1953), quoted by E. Morgan, 'Alexander Trocchi: A Survey', *Edinburgh Review* 70 (1985), p. 58.
4.   I. Chtcheglov, 'Formula For a New City', *International Situationist* 1(1958). Quoted by C. Gray, *Leaving the Twentieth Century* (Free Fall Publications, 1974), p. 2.
5.   G. Debord, *The Society of the Spectacle*, p. 42. Quoted by S. Home, *The Assault on Culture* (Stirling: AK Press, 1989), p. 43.
6.   Home, *Assault on Culture*, p. 15. Trocchi's *Sigma* project is an example of this; the practical aim was in part to disrupt publishing relations by 'cutting out the brokers'—portfolios were available on subscription. However it did not cut out the idea of 'art' at all.
7.   J.-F. Lyotard, *The Postmodern Condition* (Manchester: Manchester University Press, 1986), pp. 74-82. Lyotard was part of the group 'Socialisme ou Barbarie' and their ideas are linked to those of the situationists through the seminar series run by Lefebre, at which Baudrillard was also in attendence. See Home, *Assault on Culture*, p. 33.
8.   8.   'The Sound and the Fury', *International Situationist* 1 (1958). Quoted in Gray, *Leaving the Twentieth Century*, p. 8.
9.   G. Debord and J. Wolman, 'Methods of Detournement', *Les Levres Neus* 8 (May 1956).
10.   W. Burroughs, *Naked Lunch* (London: Collins, 1986 [1959]), p. 174.
11.   *The Star* (Sheffield), April 14 1964, p. 1. This trial is written up by A. Murray Scott in *Alexander Trocchi: the Making of the Monster* (Edinburgh: Polygon, 1991), pp. 1-6. Some of the local newspaper sources he must have used have been collated by Sylvia Pybus at Sheffield City Library and are as follows: *Sheffield Telegraph*, 26 February 1964, p. 5; 15 April, p. 7; 16 April, p. 7; 21 April, p. 7; 23 April p. 5; 10 December, p. 1; *The Star* (Sheffield), 25 February 1964, pp. 1, 12; 14 April, pp. 1, 14; 15 April, pp. 1, 16; 16 April, pp. 8, 11; 18 April, p. 5; 10 December, p. 1.
12.   *The Star* (Sheffield), pp. 1, 14.
13.   *The Star* (Sheffield), pp. 1, 14.

PART V

The Novel

ADDICTION AND THE 'OTHER SELF' IN THREE LATE VICTORIAN NOVELS

J. Gerard Dollar

In George Eliot's *Silas Marner* (1861) the pathetic 'fallen woman' Molly Farren trudges through a snowstorm in search of her cowardly and evasive husband, Godfrey Cass, who refuses to acknowledge her. She clutches her infant daughter in one arm while reaching with the other for the forbidden yet irresistible phial of opium concealed in her bosom. She is torn between a better self—the nurturing mother who would protect her child—and the addict's 'other self', which in this Victorian context is demonic (the narrator refers to the drug as 'the demon opium' and the 'familiar demon in her bosom'[1]). Molly's story points to two pervasive and overlapping themes in many late Victorian works: the emerging discovery that, as Stevenson's Dr Jekyll puts it, 'man is not truly one, but truly two';[2] and the fascination with—combined with a horror of—addiction.

I wish to examine the ways in which these two themes are developed and bound up with each other in three late Victorian novels: Stevenson's *Strange Case of Dr Jekyll and Mr Hyde* (1886), Hardy's *Mayor of Casterbridge* (also 1886), and Wilde's *Picture of Dorian Gray* (1891). These works all explore the 'divided self'; specifically, the split between a 'better self', which in Victorian terms is a moral, earnest and public self, and that hidden 'other self'—violent, demonic, self-gratifying yet ultimately self-destructive—to which each central character is compulsively and fatally drawn. I would argue that in each work the irresistible pull of the other self is presented in terms of an addiction, with some 'substance'—Dr Jekyll's magic potion, Michael Henchard's alcohol, Dorian Gray's opium—functioning as the key which unlocks and releases the hitherto imprisoned 'other'. Each of these self-divided central characters acts out, in one form or another, the addict's psychodrama of fascination with the 'forbidden': temptation; submission followed initially by a sense of liberation, euphoria, power, youthfulness—but then, inevitably, horror at the violence of the uncaged 'other' (Jekyll, as Mr Hyde, and Dorian Gray both commit vicious murders of innocent and defenseless people; the intoxicated Henchard sells his wife and child, which is something of a symbolic killing of them so that he can be free). In the latter acts of this psychodrama we find attempts to reform, to 'kick the habit' and return to the old self; but each character comes to see that he has lost control of his destiny, as he finds himself powerless before the 'demon within' which ends up by destroying the 'better self'.

An excellent synopsis of this 'psychodrama'—this dark journey of the enslaved and addicted character—can be found at the beginning of Conrad's *Heart of Darkness*, written at the end of this late Victorian period. The inscrutable Marlow is musing on the fate of a Roman citizen who finds himself suddenly confronted with the savagery of Britain and the mysteries of the wilderness:

> Think of a decent young citizen in a toga—coming out here in the train of some prefect…Land in a swamp, march through the woods, and in some inland post feel the savagery, the utter savagery, had closed round him—all that mysterious life of the wilderness that stirs in the forest, in the jungles, in the hearts of wild men. There's no initiation either into such mysteries. He has to live in the midst of the incomprehensible, which is also detestable. And it has a fascination, too, that goes to work upon him. The fascination of the abomination—you know, imagine the growing regrets, the longing to escape, the powerless disgust, the surrender, the hate.[3]

These lines can very effectively be applied to the addict's experience in Stevenson, Hardy and Wilde, especially concerning the suddenness of the transformation ('there's no initiation into such mysteries') and what Conrad calls the 'fascination of the abomination'—particularly the need to watch, fascinated, one's own disintegration: self-love becoming self-hatred, with a narcissistic element in the self-disgust as well. Marlow offers the remarks I have quoted as a preface to his haunting story of Mr Kurtz, who is a close cousin of Dr Jekyll; here too the attraction of the 'other'—the savage self—is addictive. We see Kurtz acting very much like an addict, late in the novella, when he compulsively drags himself out into the jungle—until stopped by Marlow—to join once more in those 'unspeakable rites' which he cannot live without.

But returning to the three novels I want to explore in terms of 'the addict's progress', a late Victorian, moralistic, tableau-by-tableau account of a tragic fall; one should probably label the first scene in this drama 'the temptation'. Dr Henry Jekyll is very much a self-tempter, creating the drug which will 'shake the very fortress of identity'[4] and transform him into Mr Hyde. He is a Faustian figure, turning to his evil concoction in pursuit of knowledge and power; but, like most addicts, he is also trying to run away from himself—from a rigid, earnest, public and perfectionist Victorian self that he obviously finds stifling. In his confessional letter at the end of the novella he claims that 'it was rather the exacting nature of my aspirations than any particular degradation in my faults that made me what I was.'[5] Jekyll enters into his experiment and subsequent addiction with his eyes open, knowing that by putting himself in the power of his drug he risks death. He is very consciously making a moral decision.

Michael Henchard's fall into intoxication at the beginning of *The Mayor of Casterbridge*, on the other hand, is a repetition of what has no doubt happened before. Here the temptation takes the form of a chance occurrence, with a good deal of Hardyan irony thrown in. One recalls that when Henchard, his wife Susan and baby daughter arrive at the Weydon-Priors fair, Susan steers her husband away from the tent where beer is sold to the presumably safer booth offering furmety; here the rather shadowy and sinister figure of Mrs Goodenough offers to lace Henchard's furmety with rum. (Henchard's 'instinct of a perverse character'[6] had quickly sensed the evil undercurrent of Mrs Goodenough's business.) Henchard's turning to drink is therefore very different from Jekyll's succumbing to temptation, although the results, as we shall see, are similar: it is the working man's need for an escape from the frustration of being unemployed, with a wife and child to support. Self-esteem and self-image are severely undercut by his failure to earn wages, leading him to escape the unhappy present and experiment with another self.

Dorian Gray's tempter in Wilde's novel is the cynical and amoral Sir Henry Wotton, who fuels Gray's narcissism. Wotton's temptation is to live only for youth, beauty and the cultivation of new sensations; what he proposes ironically takes the form of a cure—as both Jekyll and Henchard initially see their succumbing to temptation as a cure. (The term 'drug' does, after all, have the two meanings, one suggesting a cure, the other just the opposite.) 'That is one of the great secrets of life', Lord Henry says to Dorian, 'to cure the soul by means of the senses, and the sense by means of the soul'.[7] But Dorian's flirting with, and eventually succumbing to, his 'other'—an eternally youthful, beautiful, free and immoral self—must come at the price of his soul.

So what I am calling the late Victorian psychodrama of addiction does have many elements of a morality play, as well as of tragedy. The fall into the addict self is presented as something of a pact with the devil (at least with the devil within); and there are in all three of these works suggestions of some supernatural agency. Two of the three works break completely with Victorian realism; and even in Hardy's novel, the most realistic of the three, the sinister Mrs Goodenough is mysteriously gone the next day, rather like De Quincey's druggist after he first buys what he calls 'the celestial drug'.

If the first act of the drama is temptation, the second would be transformation. Dr Jekyll is, of course, physically transformed, to the accompaniment of considerable grinding of bones, nausea, and so on; he passes through this agony, which he calls a sickness, to emerge into a strange new state of power and freedom:

> There was something strange in my sensations, something indescribably new and, from its very novelty, incredibly sweet. I felt younger, lighter, happier in body; within I was conscious of a heady recklessness, a current of disordered sensual images running like a mill race in my fancy, a solution of the bonds of obligation, an unknown but not an innocent freedom of the soul. I knew myself, at the first breath of this new life, to be more wicked, tenfold more wicked, sold a slave to my original evil.[8]

So the escape from Victorian Dr Jekyll results in the unlocking of a more youthful, more powerful, yet smaller and, interestingly enough, more ape-like self (in this post-Darwinian world, Stevenson suggests some form of evolutionary regression; all three works also present a good deal of regression in a psychological sense). As Mr Hyde, Jekyll also experiences the freeing of himself from chafing social bonds, but at the cost of a new enslavement; and the loss of order and control within his mind, as disordered sensual images are released and run amok—rather like the sinister, dancing figures within the 'Haunted Palace' in Edgar Allan Poe's 'Fall of the House of Usher'. But Jekyll's fall, begun by this transformation, is not so much into madness as into sensuality, rage, violence and amoral self-gratification.

Hardy describes Michael Henchard's transformation by alcohol in terms of four distinct stages:

> At the end of the first basin [of the rum-laced furmety] the man had risen to serenity; at the second he was jovial; at the third, argumentative; at the fourth, the qualities signified by the shape of his face, the occasional clench of his mouth, and the fiery spark of his dark eye, began to tell in his conduct; he was over-bearing—even brilliantly quarrelsome.[9]

Here too we find the 'other self' as angry, uncontrolled, egocentric to the point of monomania, and all too ready to lash out at what the character thinks to be the representative of those restraints that have kept him from happiness.

The outward manifestation of Dorian Gray's inner transformation appears, of course, on the famous picture rather than on the man's face. The first signs of this change, after Dorian rejects Sybil Vane, are the marks of cruelty—a prominent characteristic of the 'other self' in all three of these works. As Dorian degenerates morally—casually and cynically attending the opera, for example, after he learns of Sybil's suicide—the portrait becomes progressively more monstrous and loathsome. Yet Dorian, like Dr Jekyll, takes perverse delight in looking at his inner hideousness reflected back at him from the portrait, which he considers to be the 'most magical of mirrors'.[10] Again, using Conrad's phrase, we see the 'fascination of the abomination'.

Whereas the unlocking of some concealed self by an addictive substance suggested to the Romantics an exhilarating and empowering
plunge into deep imaginative waters—as for example in De Quincey and
Coleridge—to the late Victorian world the empowerment is presented in
terms of releasing a pent-up anger and violence, especially a violence
directed against representatives of the moral and religious Victorian social
order. Thus Mr Hyde strikes out violently against the kindly and courte-
ous Sir Danvers Carew, a father-figure who is also a model of the Victorian
gentleman and a variation on the upright and respected Dr Jekyll.
Henchard sells his wife and daughter in the novel's first scene, but later,
when he reverts to drinking, he accosts the mild-mannered and upright
Donald Farfrae—who is a double of Henchard is so many ways (for
example becoming the Mayor of Casterbridge and the lover of Lucetta).
Dorian Gray murders his artist friend Basil Hallward, who is horrified at
Gray's immorality and begs him to begin to reform by kneeling down in
prayer. So each novel counter-balances the fallen character, who has
unleashed the monster within, with some conventional, moral figure—
the 'good' character who remains safely within the confines of society
(although he may 'peer over the brink into the abyss', as do Utterson, the
lawyer in *Jekyll and Hyde*, and Basil Hallward the painter). The addict
character projects his own self-hatred onto these morally superior figures.
In attacking the 'good angel' he is really only repeating, with a
vengeance, his initial break from society, thus digging himself further
into the hole of his own self-loathing and ultimate self-destruction.

(With late Victorian literature we are, of course, on the threshold of the
Freudian world, and it is tempting—although no doubt overly simplistic—
to read late Victorian addiction as a descent into the id, while such moral
and upright characters as Utterson, Farfrae and Hallward represent a kind
of supervising, disapproving superego.)

Part of the addict's psychodrama is the resolution to reform, to kick the
habit, and we see this doomed enterprise acted out in various ways in
these three novels. Dr Jekyll is so horrified at murdering Sir Danvers
Carew that he resolves never to become Mr Hyde again; only to find, to
his even greater horror, that he metamorphoses into Mr Hyde involuntarily. By this point we see that Jekyll's dependency on the Hyde self really
is an addiction—he has no control over his habit and becomes progressively more scheming and desperate in plotting to get the substance he
craves. When the original supply runs out and he is unable to replace it,
we see him suffer the agonies of withdrawal.

The Mayor of Casterbridge is, of course, a very different kind of addiction
story, since Henchard immediately reforms—the morning after
becoming the monster that sold his wife—and manages to swear off his
habit for years, becoming in the interim the prosperous corn factor and
the Mayor of Casterbridge. But that other, hidden self—and that
dependency on alcohol—lies dormant within him, waiting its turn to

appear and bring on destruction (rather like the unseen iceberg patiently biding its time in Hardy's famous poem about the sinking of the *Titanic*). Here the dependency on the substance is not so much physiological as psychological; Henchard exhibits a need to fall, to be publicly humiliated—as he clearly is during his drunken appearance at the visit of the royal personage—and, of course, to watch himself slide back into being the outcast Henchard of the novel's first chapter.

For Dorian Gray there is similarly no escape. Wilde emphasizes the addictive nature of Gray's behavior by the end of the novel, as, for example, when Gray compulsively seeks out the concealed, sordid life of the opium den:

> On and on plodded the hansom, going slower, it seemed to him, at each step. He thrust up the trap and called to the man to drive faster. The hideous hunger for opium began to gnaw at him. His throat burned and his delicate hands twitched nervously together. He struck at the horse madly with his stick.[11]

Dorian also struggles to break free of his habit, attempting to return to a virtuous life by giving up his love for Hetty, a beautiful and innocent village girl; but the other self, depicted on the painting, only mocks his attempted reform and Dorian quickly sees that the portrait is right, that his virtuous intentions are only a kind of posing, another kind of narcissism. Dorian can only kill the monstrous other by killing himself; as with Jekyll and Henchard, it is as the other—the pariah—that he dies.

'Each of us has heaven and hell in him'[12] Dorian Gray tells Basil Hallward after Hallward has looked upon the hideous transformation of his portrait—and no one knows this better than the addict. Whereas De Quincey can pay tribute to opium for the heaven it can lead us to, as well as acknowledging the hell into which the addict must descend, the late Victorian perspective on addiction—at least as addiction is used metaphorically by these three writers—emphasizes the addict's inevitable spiraling downward into lower and lower depths of despair and self-loathing. The initial, heady feeling of liberation achieved by Dr Jekyll, Michael Henchard and Dorian Gray leads only to another, worse enslavement; the substance which appeared to be the key to unlocking a more powerful and appealing inner self ends up as the jailer—for the 'other self' that has emerged and taken over the better self is very much a criminal. With identity so firmly rooted in the social context, as it was for the Victorians, any experimenting with another, asocial self is tantamount to striking a blow against society; hence the pattern of murdering, or attempting to murder, the virtuous and respectable man. The addiction story is therefore lodged within an ethical framework, and the addict's psychodrama clearly parallels tragedy, with the addicted character ultimately responsible for his own fall, and with the descent into the heart of darkness bringing with it a terrible self-knowledge. Perhaps the late

Victorians' outlook on the addict's terrible inner journey can best be expressed by those famous dying words of Conrad's Mr Kurtz: 'The horror, the horror'.

NOTES

1.   G. Eliot, *Silas Marner* (Harmondsworth: Penguin, 1967), p. 164.

2.   R.L. Stevenson, *The Strange Case of Dr Jekyll and Mr Hyde and Other Stories* (Harmondsworth: Penguin, 1979), p. 82.

3.   J. Conrad, *Heart of Darkness and The Secret Sharer* (New York: New American Library, 1971), p. 69.

4.   Stevenson, *Dr Jekyll and Mr Hyde*, p. 83.

5.   *Dr Jekyll and Mr Hyde*, p. 81

6.   T. Hardy, *The Mayor of Casterbridge* (Harmondsworth: Penguin, 1978), p. 75.

7.   O. Wilde, *The Picture of Dorian Gray* (New York: New American Library, 1962), p. 37.

8.   Stevenson, *Dr Jekyll and Mr Hyde*, pp. 83-84.

9.   Hardy, *Mayor of Casterbridge*, p. 74.

10.   Wilde, *Picture of Dorian Gray*, p. 119.

11.   Wilde, *Picture of Dorian Gray*, p. 197.

12.   Wilde, *Picture of Dorian Gray*, p. 169.

ALCOHOLISM AS METAPHOR
IN WILLIAM GOLDING'S *THE PAPER MEN*

Kevin McCarron

William Golding's attitude to alcohol throughout his literary career has never been celebratory. In this second novel, *The Inheritors*, alcohol is described by the Neanderthal Lok as 'honey that smells of dead things and fire'.[1] It is noticeable, too, that when the novel's major characters, Lok and Fa, are both drunk on this 'honey', Golding puns on the dual meaning of 'fall', as waterfall and as a theological concept: 'they were weeping and laughing at each other and the fall was roaring in the clearing...'.[2] In Golding's fifth novel, *The Spire*, the practical, Rationalist builder Roger Mason is driven into hopeless alcoholism by Jocelin's obsessive desire to build a spire onto the cathedral.

In *Rites of Passage*, Parson Colley is drunk when he is sodomised and when he performs fellatio on a sailor, acts which later cause him to die 'of shame'. In *Close Quarters* it is Lieutenant Deverel's habitual drunkenness which is the young Edmond Talbot's first indication that Deverel is not the gentleman he took him for, and is actually a real menace to the safety of the passengers.

But it is also within 'The Sea Trilogy' that the drunken painter Brocklebank appears, and it is this character and the uses to which his drinking is put that most clearly anticipate Wilf Barclay and his alcoholism in *The Paper Men*. The painter takes great pains to point out to Talbot that art is as much, if not considerably more, about concealing and obscuring reality as it is about revealing it. In *Rites of Passage* Talbot looks distastefully at Brocklebank: 'Another thin trickle of wine ran down the man's chin'. Brocklebank then informs Talbot that he is 'confusing art with actuality'.[3] Both the painter's alcoholism and his art avoid any connection at all with reality.

In *The Paper Men*, published in 1984, this issue is developed, and alcoholism and the question of 'reality' are central to the book. The plot of this novel is extremely straightforward. An author, Wilf Barclay, is pursued for most of the novel by an eager academic critic, Rick Tucker, who wishes to write his biography. Barclay eventually decides to write it himself, and so Tucker shoots and kills him.

The Paper Men was the most poorly received of any of Golding's novels. The *Washington Post*'s reviewer said that it was 'the weakest of the lot, so weak indeed that had it appeared before last Fall's [Nobel] committee meeting, the vote might well have been different'.[4]

This is also the way in which the novel is regarded by critics: as a rather bad-tempered grumble about academics by an author who has himself been turned into an academic 'light industry'. But Barclay's *alcoholism* has never been critically discussed at any length, and even when it is mentioned it is usually seen as a rather 'roguish' characteristic. Yet, as the psychologists Neil Kessel and Henry Walton write, 'alcoholism is an integral aspect of the alcoholic; it is difficult to separate the man from the disease because so much of his energy and his actions are bound up in the addictive drinking and its consequences'.[5] Barclay's alcoholism is of central importance to *The Paper Men* and the reader is constantly made to feel that it should not be taken at its face value, but that it invariably alludes to something else as well—that it has a metaphorical significance.

Susan Sontag writes in her book *Illness as Metaphor* that, 'illness is the night side of life, a more onerous citizenship... My subject is not physical illness itself but the uses of illness as a figure or metaphor'.[6] Although Thomas Gilmore does not refer to *The Paper Men* in his study of fictional alcoholism, *Equivocal Spirits*, he argues throughout his book that alcoholism is often used symbolically. Similarly, while writing of Malcolm Lowry's later fiction M.C. Bradbrook comments: 'alcohol is perhaps only a symbol. ("Drinking is not the problem", as the hero of *Lunar Caustic* remarked)'.[7]

But if drinking is not the problem, what is? In *The Paper Men*, the problem is, in a word, antithesis, our unshakeable belief that the world is constructed of binary opposites: light and dark, good and evil, author and critic. One of the ways this is assessed in the novel is through the ostensible conflict between the creative writer and the critic, and the principal way it is destroyed is through Barclay's alcoholism.

For instance, the morning after the encounter in his hotel room with Tucker's wife, Mary Lou, Barclay wakes up 'too early with a clear memory of the night before and the kind of parched distancing from reality which comes from considerable brandy'.[8] At this moment, and indeed throughout the novel, Golding suggests that the alcoholic Barclay, far from having some authoritative relationship with 'reality' which would justify his own sense of hierarchical superiority over the critic, is actually incapable of even apprehending this 'reality' himself.

In the course of the novel, Barclay experiences two visions: a truly horrifying one on the Sicilian island of Lipari, which is of such violence and intensity it causes him to lose consciousness; and a beatific one in Rome. These two visions, ostensibly of quite opposed characters, are finally seen by Barclay to constitute a religious totality. They show him a vision of life which is numinous, one that he perceives as truly real; and just as there is a well-known connection between alcohol and writers, there is another long-established relationship between alcohol and religion. William James writes in his *Varieties of Religious Experience*:

> The sway of alcohol over mankind is unquestionably due to its power to stimulate the mystical faculties of human nature, usually crushed to earth by the cold facts and dry criticisms of the sober hour. Sobriety diminishes, discriminates, and says no; drunkenness expands, unites, says yes.[9]

Immediately after his experience in the cathedral in Lipari, as the doctor tries to convince him he has had a stroke, Barclay says:

> I could have told him drunks like me don't have strokes, they get the horrors of one sort or another and now and then come across a real beauty, first prize, predestined and damned, the divine justice without mercy. *In Vino Veritas*, my other tag (p. 125).

In this context, the words *in vino veritas* do not seem to mean what people commonly mean when they use the phrase. The assumption that underlies its conventional meaning is psychological; it suggests that when people are drunk they lose their inhibitions and actually say what they really believe. When Barclay utters the phrase it loses this psychological implication and suggests instead that a consciousness poisoned by alcohol may actually experience some deeper reality. Significantly, however, it is only after he has sobered up that Barclay realises that the earlier experience offered only a partial glimpse of reality. This truth, or reality, is beyond the limitations of psychology and lies in the realms of the spiritual. Despite the limitations imposed on the perception of reality by alcohol, therefore, there is a suggestion in *The Paper Men* that alcohol is also capable of conveying spiritual truth and wisdom. Jack London, himself an alcoholic, articulates a similar paradox in one of his books:

> John Barleycorn is the king of liars. He is the frankest truthsayer. He is the august companion with whom one walks with the gods. He is also in league with the Noseless one. His way leads to truth naked, and to death. He gives clear vision and muddy dreams. He is the enemy of life, and the teacher of wisdom beyond life's wisdom.[10]

Alcohol in *The Paper Men*, similarly, is both 'the enemy of life and the teacher of wisdom beyond life's wisdom'.

There are, in fiction, certain types of alcoholic who seem *spiritually* orientated. In this group I would include Barclay, as well as Marmaladov in Dostoevsky's *Crime and Punishment*, Mynheer Peeperkorn in Thomas Mann's *The Magic Mountain*, Geoffrey Firmin in Malcolm Lowry's *Under the Volcano* and the protagonist of Joseph Roth's *The Legend of the Holy Drinker*. Fundamentally Platonists, such characters perceive another reality, one which is obscured and shielded by the familiar and everyday world. Their excessive use of alcohol is designed to break down that barrier, to hasten toward this *other*. All of these characters, except Barclay, fail to achieve their goal. Barclay succeeds—because two thirds of the way through the novel, he stops drinking.

After the second of his visions he never drinks again. His alcoholism, however, already indicates that he will be responsive to such revelations. As the following understanding of alcoholism, written by a recovering alcoholic, may suggest, the spiritual connotations associated with alcoholism are not only those we associate positively with Dionysus. In his book *God Is For The Alcoholic*, Jerry Dunn writes: 'There are social, psychological, and physiological reasons why a man becomes an alcoholic, but there is still one underlying cause. Alcoholism is a sickness of the soul'.[11]

Barclay is sick in precisely this way: in his soul. There is a clear sense of meaninglessness in the life he describes himself leading after his separation from his wife, Liz, a separation brought about by the prying of the critic. Entire years pass in an aimless blur of sodden travel, and it is quite clear that, as with Marmaladov in *Crime and Punishment*, for example, there is little joy in Barclay's drinking.

Just as Barclay's alcoholism has been ignored by the novel's critics, none of the criticism that has been written on *The Paper Men* assesses the possibility that the very distinction which animates the novel, the one which exists between Barclay and Tucker, between the creative and the critical, could be an artificial distinction, or at least a misleading one. But the distinction between 'creative' and 'critical' writing has been under attack by literary theorists for several decades, and never more so than during the period in which some of the most important events in *The Paper Men* take place: the late sixties.

Far from being 'the weakest of the lot', *The Paper Men* can be seen as one of Golding's most ingenious fictions, because while it seems to attack modern literary theory, it actually endorses many of its beliefs. In particular, it denies any distinction between the creative and the critical— and yet, of course, Golding is still the author, adding another level to this highly ludic text.

Perhaps the most influential of all writings on this subject is Barthes' essay 'The Death of the Author'; a title which, intriguingly, could serve as a subtitle to *The Paper Men*. Barclay introduces himself into the narrative in a manner that both emphasises his trade as an author and delays his identification by name, which conventionally precedes that of occupation: 'Author—no, well-known author—no, damn it, Wilfred Barclay...' (p. 10), and the novel concludes with this author's death.

Although the title of Golding's novel might owe a debt to T.S. Eliot's poem 'The Hollow Men', it is also possible that Golding's title is an oblique reference to these lines of Barthes' from 'The Death of the Author':

> It is not that the Author may not 'come back' in the Text, in his text, but he
> then does so as a 'guest'. If he is a novelist, he is inscribed in the novel
> like one of his characters, figured in the carpet; no longer privileged,
> paternal, aletheological, his inscription is ludic. He becomes, as it were, a
> paper-author...[12]

During the literature conference in Seville, Barclay's unquestioning
faith in the superiority of the artist to the critic, and therefore in his superiority to Tucker, is shown to him to be illusory. He begins to recognise the
truth of Barthes' observation that all texts, creative and critical, are 'tissues
of quotations, drawn from the innumerable centres of culture'. Terry
Eagleton's comment on deconstruction actually employs an image which
is splendidly appropriate for Wilf Barclay: 'literature for the deconstruc-
tionists testifies to the impossibility of language's ever doing more than
talk about its own failure, like some bar-room bore'.[13]

In the very first words of *The Paper Men* two fundamental concerns of
the novel, alcohol and language, are intertwined:

> I knew at once that it was one of those nights. The drink, such as it had
> been, was dying out of my brain and leaving a kind of sediment of irrita-
> tion, vague discomfort and even remorse. It had not been—no, indeed—a
> *bender* or *booze-up* (p. 7).

Particularly noticeable in these opening sentences are the hungover state
of the speaker, the word 'sediment' which itself evokes images of alcohol,
and the technical, linguistic relish, reminiscent of Talbot and his pleasure
in Tarpaulin in *Rites of Passage*, with which the words 'bender' and 'booze-
up' are articulated and emphasized.

Any assessment of the implications Barclay's drinking has for *The
Paper Men* must begin by noting that it is not of the sort often described as
'heavy drinking'. Barclay himself has few illusions about his drinking,
referring to himself as a drunk throughout the novel, and even clinically
defining his state on the second page: 'The point where drinking can be
defined as alcoholism is precisely where the black hole is recognised as
part of it' (p. 8).

The opening paragraph immediately emphasises the traditional
relationship that writers have had with drink. This immediate depiction
within *The Paper Men*, therefore, makes Barclay more of a composite,
'Everyman' novelist. It introduces the reader to the possibility of a double-
layered narrative, in which Barclay can be seen as both an autonomous
character functioning purely on the level of social realism, and yet also as
an allegorical, representative figure.

Barclay's struggle to account for last night's events seizes on the possibility of empirical proof, and already, with this failure to *remember* the actions
of the previous night, the novel announces the existence of a metaphorical
alternative that will remain as one of the two narrative levels throughout
The Paper Men.

Such memory losses as Barclay experiences upon awakening are not, of course, exclusively metaphorical in themselves. On the level of social realism they are extremely common among alcoholics, as Donald Newlove suggests in his book *Those Drinking Days*:

> Blackouts weren't new... Then gaps started appearing in my nights...But it was clear enough: blackouts were a commonplace (so common they had no name), a drinker's burden, and a lost hour here and there was not too harsh a price, and could be weirdly amusing.[14]

However, Kessel and Walton note a more sinister implication in their scientifically objective assessment of alcohol addiction. They write:

> *Losses of memory occur.* On recovery from a drinking session the alcoholic finds he has no memory for its later stages... The term 'blackout' is often used to describe this amnesia, particularly by alcoholics themselves, but it is misleading because there has been no unconsciousness. The abnormality is a failure to register events in the memory.[15]

The Paper Men begins with just such a failure to register the events of the preceding night, and the subsequent attempts by Barclay to evade Tucker and his projected biography can also be seen as strategies on Barclay's part to try and forget his past which, he says, once again invoking *Rites of Passage*, fills him with the shame. While Vladimir Nabokov called his autobiography *Speak, Memory*, *The Paper Men* could be called *Deny Memory*. This alcoholic loss of memory serves as a metaphor for Barclay's obsession with denying his past, and this denial creates yet another artificial antithesis within the novel: this time, between past and present.

Barclay's desire to get up and count the empty bottles, which might prove he had not drunk as much as he feared the previous night, is balanced by his fear of waking his wife, so he remains motionless. But when he hears the lid fall off the dustbin, he says: 'It was at this moment that my wavering mind was made up for me' (p. 10). The sense of passivity which is implied in the phrasing of this comment is compounded by his instinctive reaction, which is to write a letter: 'Somehow that made the whole issue clear. I was no longer a repentant drinker. I was Outraged Householder. *Sir, how much longer in the guise of...*' (p. 10).

This ostensibly slight incident prefigures much of the novel's fascination with the act of writing, which is itself connected to alcohol and the author's claim to portray reality in some form or other. *The Paper Men* suggests that what writing *really* does, no less than drinking—and the two activities here are inextricably connected—is enable the writer to escape immediately from any form of confrontation with reality at all.

Some pages after Barclay's encounter with Mary Lou in his hotel room, an oblique reference is made to the Platonic Forms. As Barclay and Tucker listen to a stream, Barclay realises that the stream had 'two voices, not one. There was the cheerful babble, a kind of frivolity as if the thing, the Form, enjoyed its bounding passage downward, through space' (p. 83).

Given the preoccupation throughout the novel with Barclay's status as author, as 'teller of lies', this reference to the Platonic Forms might refer the reader to one of the most celebrated passages in Plato's *Republic*, where he writes:

> We have now indeed sufficiently, as it appears at least, settled these things: that the imitator knows nothing worth mentioning in those things which he imitates, but that imitation is a sort of amusement, and not a serious affair; and likewise, that those who apply to tragic poetry in iambics and heroics are all imitators in the highest degree.[16]

This is, of course, the inevitable result of Plato's assertion that this world is but an imitation of the Ideal, and that consequently the artist's claim to portray 'reality' is a lie because, even at best, the author can only approximate to that which is itself distanced from the 'real'. This is an issue of considerable interest to post-modernism and is also raised, for example, in Peter Ackroyd's novel *Chatterton*, in which the following exchange occurs:

> 'I think I understand your Drift, sir. You wish me to forge the work of these men.'
> 'I did not say Forge. Is the work of Rowley a forgery?' He hesitated, collecting his Words. 'Is it not, as the Platonists tell us, an imitation in a world of Imitations?'[17]

Golding goes further than this in *The Paper Men*, for by presenting Barclay as an alcoholic who is by his own admission 'distanced from reality', that is, not even able to confront a reality which is itself an illusion, the novel suggests that art is further removed from reality than even Plato cared to consider.

But the novel's real imperatives are spiritual, and the alcoholic author who moved soddenly through the first two thirds of the novel dies in a state of complete sobriety, noting: 'I know with absolute, inward certainty that I have drunk my last drink' (p. 190). Alcohol has played little part in the novel since the joyous vision in Rome, since, once Barclay had experienced reality in *all* of its totality and power, there was no longer any need for alcohol. Barclay dies happy: 'I am happy, quietly happy' (p. 190) he says on the penultimate page; this is the only remotely happy ending in all of Golding's fiction, and clearly far from being unequivocally joyous as Barclay is then promptly murdered.

Ironically, while Barclay's decision to write his own biography proves that he is finally able to confront his past, Tucker, now frustrated at what he sees as the usurpation of *his* role, steals a gun and brings about the death of the author. Barclay's final word is cut off, forever subject to interpretation: 'How the devil did Rick L. Tucker manage to get hold of a gu' (p. 191).

The author dies happy nonetheless, and does so because of his hard-won *sobriety*. No longer lost in the bewildering confusion of over half a century's alcoholic distancing from reality, he finally experiences what he calls 'Isness', or what we might call 'reality'.

NOTES

1. W. Golding, *The Inheritors* (London: Faber & Faber, 1955), p. 195.

2. Golding, *The Inheritors*, p. 203.

3. W. Golding, *Rites of Passage* (London: Faber & Faber, 1980), p. 169.

4. *The Washington Post*, volume 109, issue 38, section R, 12th January 1986.

5. N. Kessel and H. Walton, *Alcoholism* (London: Penguin, 1965), p. 74.

6. S. Sontag, *Illness As Metaphor* (London: Penguin, 1979), p. 7.

7. M.C. Bradbrook, *Malcolm Lowry* (Cambridge: Cambridge University Press, 1974), p. 66.

8. W. Golding, *The Paper Men* (London: Faber & Faber, 1984), p. 78. All subsequent page references are to this edition.

9. W. James, *The Varieties of Religious Experience* (Glasgow: Fontana, 1977), p. 373.

10. J. London, *John Barleycorn, Or Alcoholic Memoirs* (London: Mills & Boon, 1914), p. 2.

11. J.G. Dunn, *God Is For The Alcoholic* (Chicago: Moody Press, 1967), p. 18.

12. R. Barthes, 'The Death of the Author', in *Image—Music—Text* (trans. S. Heath; New York: Hill & Waugh, 1977), p. 161.

13. T. Eagleton, *Literary Theory* (Oxford: Basil Blackwell, 1983), p. 146.

14. D. Newlove, *Those Drinking Days* (New York: Junction Books, 1981), p. 31.

15. Kessel and Walton, *Alcoholism*, p. 17.

16. Plato, *The Republic* (trans. H. Spens; London: Penguin, 1906), p. 325.

17. P. Ackroyd, *Chatterton* (London: Grove Press, 1987), p. 91.

'WORD-MAGIC': ADDICTION TO WORDS IN FOWLES'S 'POOR KOKO'

Danielle Schaub

Most conventionally, addiction is understood as a person's acute or compulsive need for a substance be it food, alcohol, cigarettes or any kind of drug. But, as long-distance runners and workaholics would have it, the endless repetition of a favoured activity can also 'produce a compulsion to act that is beyond the individual's self-control'.[1] This is what the protagonist and narrator of John Fowles's 'Poor Koko' seems to suffer from. He indeed gives a good example of an uncommon intoxication: an old conservative writer, he is addicted to words to the extent that it prevents him from 'existing'[2] in the existentialist sense. Face to face with a burglar in a lonely cottage borrowed from Hampstead friends, he fails to take the necessary steps to save his 'lifetime's ambition'[3]—the manuscript of his comprehensive study on Peacock. Indeed his sole action—or rather inaction—is to embark on a philosophical discourse à la Sartre's *Huis Clos* with the burglar. As with most addictions, he can only postpone the fatal issue, the burning of his manuscript. Eventually the reader is left with an open ending: notwithstanding his ordeal, the narrator is re-producing his definitive biography on Peacock, his dependence getting the upper hand.

Ironically, the narrator is not fully aware of his being addicted although many of his comments indirectly report his condition. Physically weak and timid, he proves incapable of forceful deeds. As his peers receive his wit extremely well from an early age onwards, he becomes highly susceptible to word addiction. He simply shuns action by becoming absorbed with words and abstract ideas. 'I have never pretended to be a man of action' (p. 146); 'I live by words' (p. 182), he confesses, as one who 'trusts and reveres language' (p. 182). Spellbound and consequently confined to literature, he values books more than anything else: 'books—writing them, reading, reviewing, helping to get them into print—have been [his] life rather than life itself' (p. 147). He has buried himself in a literary world where any real dialogue becomes unnecessary. To compensate for the loss of human interaction resulting from his immersion, he resorts to language compulsively: his narration and presumably also his writing bear the marks of affectation, grandiloquence and ostentation. He is totally incapable of sustaining true communication with his peers: he only wants to impress others with his wit. In the case of the burglar, he does not even bother trying to establish a channel: during their conversation, his short answers and silences suggest that he prefers writing to speaking. He is clearly so fascinated with words that they become 'the major focus of his...existence'.[4] To satisfy his cravings, he simply substitutes intellectual energy and verbal aggression for physical activity and human interaction or intimacy.

The narrator/focaliser can thus easily be compared to the addict who needs drugs 'because they bring welcome relief from other sensations and feelings which [he or she] finds unpleasant'.[5] For he makes use of words to postpone—or even better to nullify—his 'distasteful consciousness of...life'.[6] Instead of using words with their original communicative function, he clings to them as a shield against the intrusion of the 'abominable' (p. 147) modern world, its norms, beliefs and values. His aversion for modern approaches he discloses in the description of the construction works in his London neighbourhood:

> It was not only the din and the dust of the initial demolition and the knowledge that the wretched pseudo-skyscraper progress intended to erect on the rubble of what had been a quietly solid Italianate terrace would very soon deprive me of a treasured westward view. I came to see it as the apotheosis of all that Peacock had stood against; all that was not humane, intelligent and balanced. Resentment at this intrusion began to affect what work I did; certain draft passages merely used Peacock as an excuse for irrelevant diatribes against my own age (pp. 147-48).

Ample alliterations, consonances and onomatopoeia, together with circumlocution and personification, convey his aggravation at witnessing changes around him. The inconveniences endured—a mere side effect of the works after all—are for him the perfect ground for a hyperbolic criticism of progress. His allusion to Peacock, the stronghold of reasoned balance and reactionary views, only reinforces his rejection of change, development and evolution in society; like Peacock, he uses his magic power to substantiate his conservatism. As the last balanced sentence shows, he strings together words as a relief from his antagonistic surroundings.

Understandably uncomfortable with the whole experience of the burglary, the narrator feebly fends for himself with pompous, formal, flowery language full of negations, circumlocutions, adjectives and adverbs, as well as words of Latin origin and foreign terms or phrases. The high proportion of verbs of cognition or perception and of abstract terms emphasizes his preoccupation with the intellectual and contemplative aspects of life. When he refers to the immediate action—his discovery of the presence of an intruder and their subsequent interactions—short

sentences in simple and terse style express his tension and fear. But these
narrative passages are interspersed with reflections and recollections that
minimize the unpleasant incident. Throughout, these are full of pompous
abstract words, awkward constructions, verbs in the passive voice, negations, witty allusions and the like. His written report of his ordeal
curiously ends up resembling a philosophical treatise; with abstractions,
negations and verbose circumlocutions as extensive means of information, his discourse fails to evoke the immediacy of a crucial experience.
Take for instance the pedantic prolegomena of his account:

> Certain melodramatic situations derived from the detective story and the
> thriller have been so done to death by the cinema and the television that I
> suspect a new and nonsensical law of inverse probability has been estab-
> lished—the more frequently one of these situations is shown on the
> screen, the less chance there is of its taking place in the viewer's real
> life...I had to climb down, needless to say, and to admit that the latterday
> Pangloss in all of us who regards tragedy as a privilege of other people was
> a thoroughly wicked and anti-social creature (p. 145).

George Orwell might have taken these lengthy, wordy sentences for his
essay on 'Politics and the English Language' to illustrate the decline of the
English language. For all the narrator means is 'although I always
believed nothing would ever happen to me, I had to accept that it was not
so'. The original long string of words merely reduces the distastefulness
of the experience[7].

The narrator is so engrossed in words, and thus remote from life, that
even the structure of his narration discloses his need to alter his
consciousness. His account of his ordeal reads more like an essay than a
story; after his pretentious exposition, his text combines narrative passage
and dialogues strewn with reflective and philosophical digressions.
Rather than sustaining the flow of the narrative, the writer continually
breaks off to recall different periods of past time. He is unable to relate to
the present without referring to the past, and his recollections and earlier
indirect experiences form the basis for his present judgment and evaluation. The looseness of the account thus destroys the impact of real
experience.

As with most addicts, 'the ordinary, rational, self-aware state [is]
uncomfortable'[8] and addiction smooths things out. The protagonist's
narrative is a good measure for it since it shows a marked difference in
length between the narrated and narrative time. The actual confrontation
lasts for a relatively short time; yet the narration is lengthy. In fact, the
unpleasant effect of the events is buffered with long semi-philosophical
asides; a barrier is built between the narrator and what he calls his 'deeply
distressing experience' (p. 145). Moreover, as he philosophizes and turns
the incident into a witty account, he prevents himself from taking in the
meaning of the conversation he had with the thief. All he does amounts to
a mere attempt to convince the reader and himself that the generation gap

that separates him from the young burglar cannot be bridged.
Responsibility for it, he claims, lies squarely with the younger generation. However, his rendering or the dialogue and his comments on it
prove that he is not open to discussion. 'Guilty of deafness' (p. 183), he
refuses to listen properly so as to avoid contact with reality.

Similarly his verbose analysis of the situation compensates for his
inability to act. However, as with most addicts, 'the gratifications that [he]
acknowledges are inferior to genuinely pleasurable and satisfying
involvements'.[9] The narrator is aware of the essence of his personality, but
will only reluctantly acknowledge it. The epigraph appears first
cryptically as a motto in Old Cornish, before the confession/translation in
contemporary English—'Too long a tongue, too short a hand'—(p. 184)
appropriately defines his verbal ostentation and physical passivity.

His inaction is precisely what Sartre would define as the typical
behaviour of the merely 'being'[10] as opposed to that of the 'existing'.[11]
Existentialists see life as constantly presenting the individual with a series
of choices. Human beings truly exist only when they take control of their
lives and exercise their power of choice and free will. This is totally
beyond the narrator's reach because of his dependence. His goals in life
are defined by, indeed restricted to, literature: the teachers he values are
not people, or life itself, but books which have taught [him] to admire and
desire truth' (p. 146). However, his sole concern is 'truth in writing'
(p. 146). He observes, writes on and philosophises about life rather than
living it. A keen observer, the burglar equates him with his writing: 'that's
you on the table down there' (p. 160), he says. The image aptly conveys
the inertia in which the writer vegetates. Indeed, at 66 he has never had
any of the '"vital" experiences' (p. 146) he once enumerated with a friend
at a dinner party. His nicknames at school—'bookworm' (p. 147), 'swot'
(p. 147) and 'shrimp' (p. 151)—all reflect his passive approach to life. He is
so remote from it that he prefers 'nature in art to nature in actuality'
(p. 148). He only retreats to the country because he is unable to concentrate
in his flat owing to the construction works in the neighbourhood. In other
words, from the faked heights of his addiction, he contemplates life rather
than 'discovering reality by acting on it'.[12]

Similarly, his intoxication causes subversion of his powers to direct his
life. He characteristically exerts no control over things and cannot cope
with change. He is indeed subjected to the burglary rather than taking
actual measures to prevent its taking place. The first could have been to
leave signs of his presence in the cottage, but he fails to do so—a proof of
his non-existence. The next step could have been to make enough noise to
scare the burglar off, indeed the most effective action according to the
intruder himself. But that too is beyond his physical power: he says, 'I was
more frightened of my own terror than of its cause. What kept me frozen
was the saner knowledge that I must not act upon it' (p. 152). For him,
sanity lies in refraining from acting. He thus becomes powerless before

he even meets the intruder, owing to his own fear and overwhelming sense of futility. He can only grab his glasses, thereby substituting contemplation for action. Later he rejects any effort to escape, resist or summon help, for he is convinced that it would be pointless even to try. Not even passive non-compliance succeeds: he fails, for want of determination, to conceal that his wallet is behind the door. He can only cooperate: he is too helpless to be in control; words have taken up all his energy.

The narrator's attitudes and outlook on life, conveyed effectively by his limited point of view, also differ greatly from an existentialist approach. Existentialists reject stereotyped thinking for it allows no changes. Similarly, they disapprove of the tendency to label others because it denies them their essential individuality, uniqueness and propensity for change. To exist fully, one should constantly struggle against conformity to other people's perception of oneself. Owing to his addiction to words, the narrator has been nicknamed from his earliest age. He in turn continually generalizes about others—from the 'crassly athletic' (p. 147) and 'baffling...new world of the classless British young' (p. 156) to Hampstead liberals (p. 163)—and labels them in most deprecatory terms. At one point he accuses the younger generation of cultural narrowness, but his own comments on other people reveal his snobbery, prejudice and standard thinking. Similarly, his preconceived and derogatory idea of who and what the intruder is—'a nervous village amateur' (p. 149) or a 'long-haired village lout with fists like hams and a mind to match' (p. 150)—are typical of his rigidity. He expects an unintelligent, 'semi-literate' (p. 150) young man with 'an aggressively uneducated accent' (p. 153). He is therefore surprised and disconcerted to discover that the young man does not conform to his expectations. On the contrary, the thief is intelligent, low-voiced, mild-mannered and considerate of the narrator's needs, attempting, even when tying him up, to minimize his physical discomfort. As the thief progressively reveals his mult-dimensional nature and the different, sometimes contradictory, facets of his personality, he becomes more of an enigma to the discomfited narrator. The latter finds it increasingly difficult to cope with the challenge the intruder presents to his preconceived notions based on 'all the fictional horrors connected with the situation that [he has] ever seen or read of' (p. 158). Instead of being relieved not to be confronted with the brutal, violent, vicious criminal he had imagined, he is disgruntled: he says 'I would have preferred a devil I knew—or who at least conformed better to one's general notion of his kind' (p. 156). He therefore constantly tries to fit the thief into a group—that of his friends' son Richard, 'the classless British young' (p. 156), 'youth in revolt' (p. 164), 'would-be world changers' (p. 165), or 'right-users' (p. 182). An expression of his inability to accept and deal with the other man's essential individuality, it clearly manifests his own conformist outlook. In his constant search for analogies, the narrator does not perceive that the burglar, like every human being, is a unique individual, continually evolving and thus defying any absolute definition. A victim of his dependence on words and, by extension, labels, he cannot take others as they are without trying to fit them into a closely-defined category.

'Being' rather than 'existing' for all his cravings, he can only be a 'word-magician' (p. 183) who reveres the power of language, 'its secrets and its magics' (p. 183). But language is in fact merely a weapon, his only means of self-defence. From childhood onwards, he has compensated for his lack of physical stature and athletic prowess through his verbal wit, not unlike Sartre whose autobiography *Les Mots* reveals similar characteristics and compensations.[13] He even admits that in his writing he has indulged in malicious humour at the expense of others. His pride in his skill at 'puncturing the pretentious' (p. 147) is particularly ironic in view of his own pomposity and pretentiousness. During the burglary, he begins to recover from his initial terror as soon as he can mentally ridicule the thief and anticipate entertaining his friends with stories and anecdotes about the incident. He looks forward to making the intruder the target for 'his skill at mimicking accents...for telling anecdotes that rely on that rather cruel ability' (p. 162). The thought of making fun of the burglar's linguistic and intellectual idiosyncracies gives the narrator a sense of superiority and power.[14] However, his powers are always confined to intellectual and verbal skills only. Likewise, when he considers a course of action against the intruder, it is either safely hypothetical when physical (as for instance when, tied to a chair, he feels like attacking the thief who is burning his papers) or limited to verbal aggression and abuse. As ever, action for him is only verbal, confirming his self-definition as a man who lives by and depends on words.

The narrator's dependence on the powers of his addiction is also reflected in his choice of language and imagery when he refers to his writing. Only then does he use words and metaphors associated with energetic or violent action, power and potency, which contrast with his usual tendency to abstraction. Expressions such as 'I had duly cleared decks for the assault of the final summit' (p. 147), 'fertile concentration' (p. 151), 'kill off the final draft' (p. 151) and words such as 'vigorous' (p. 151), 'confident' (p. 151) and 'determination' (p. 151) are only applied to intellectual life and pursuit. The man clearly lives through and for his writing. He contemplates murder or physical violence only when his writing is attacked either verbally by an unfair review or physically when it is burnt. Similarly, he considers his book to be a living being, though sterile, as conveyed in the oxymoron 'alive and on the polished page' (p. 151). As he makes no reference to a wife and/or children, he can be fairly assumed to be unmarried and childless. He substitutes his writing for them: he claims that his earlier work on Peacock was 'torn from the womb' (p. 177), the book thus being his child—the only manifestation of his fertility and potency. He describes the 'bestial...act' (p. 172) of burning his papers with terms usually associated with the death and destruction of human beings: 'holocaust' (p. 172), 'savage retribution' (p. 178), 'consigned to the flames' (p. 172), 'pyre' (p. 172). He compares the smell of cremated human knowledge (p. 173) to that of 'burnt human flesh' (p. 173), finding it almost as distressing. For him, writing and intellectual pursuits replace human relationships and attachments; they provide his only outlet for energy and aggression.

In the end, in spite of the vital experience, he reverts to his past mistakes. True, he finally concedes that he was not entirely blameless for what took place but deep down his outlook has not changed. Unlike Antoine de Roquentin in *La Nausée*,[15] he has not learnt that 'a life devoted to biography is a wasted life'.[16] He has finished rewriting his comprehensive book on Peacock and refuses to see the real meaning of his ordeal. Indeed his explanation of the story's title points to the persistent concern of the older man for 'the proper attitude of son to father' (p. 184). He may well have achieved some kind of awareness—he hints at the limitations of both the man of action and the man of words in his epigraph—but it remains superficial, for the contrast is formulated in such a way that it stresses his feeling of superiority while the enigmatic message and play on words are symptomatic of his resumed cravings. Notwithstanding the revelation of his true nature, he proudly offers his lifetime's addiction to the world, his dependence on words as firmly rooted as ever.

NOTES

1.   S. Peele, *The Meaning of Addiction: Compulsive Experience and its Interpretation* (Lexington, MA: D.C. Heath, 1985), p. xi.

2.   J.-P. Sartre, *Being and Nothingness* (trans. H.E. Barnes; London: Routledge, 1969), pp. 73-102.

3.   J. Fowles, 'Poor Koko', in *The Ebony Tower* (London: Jonathan Cape, 1974), p. 146. All subsequent references are to this edition.

4.   J. Krivanek, *Addictions* (London: George Allen & Unwin, 1988), p. 11.

5.   S. Peele and A. Brodsky, *Love and Addiction* (New York: Taplinger, 1975), p. 51.

6.   Peele and Brodsky, *Love and Addiction*, p. 61.

7.   Minimization, Dennis M. Donovan remarks, is one of 'the cognitive processes that may contribute to...addiction' ('Assessment of Addictive Behaviors: Implications of an Emerging Biopsychosocial Model', in D.M. Donovan and G.A. Marlatt [eds.], *Assessment of Addictive Behaviors* [New York: Guilford Press, 1988], p. 20).

8.   N.E. Zingberg, W.M. Harding and R. Apsler, 'What is Drug Abuse?', *Journal of Drug Issues* 8 (1978), p. 19.

9.   Peele, *The Meaning of Addiction*, p. 98.

10.   Sartre, *Being and Nothingness*, pp. 73-102.

11.   Enough evidence of Fowles's concern with existentialist issues is given in his volume *The Aristos* to argue this position safely. Besides, 'Poor Koko' consists in the meeting of two radically opposed characters corresponding to the existentialist polarity of 'being' and 'existing'. The thief, it appears, corresponds to those capable of 'existing' as he takes control of his life, constantly makes choices, and struggles to

change his station and circumstances in life. Active in all the meanings of the word, he offers a sharp contrast to the passive, conformist writer.

12. P. Wolfe, *John Fowles: Magus and Moralist* (Lewisburg, PA: Bucknell University Press, 1976), p. 25.

13. J.-P. Sartre, *Les Mots* (Paris: Gallimard, 1964). The analogy between Fowles's narrator and Sartre may be carried further, since Sartre too spent years preparing a biography, not of course of Peacock but of Gustave Flaubert.

14. A parallel can be drawn between Fowles's narrator and that of Jacques Darras in the essay 'Time and Northern Man'. The latter enjoys his humorous allusions to famous literary people. The essential difference, however, is that while the former indulges in the pretentious stringing together of words, the latter takes pleasure in developing an idea before destroying it from a sense of futility and a need to 'dis-addict himself from himself'. Totally aware of his addiction, the latter—a fictionalized representation of Darras himself—seeks to distance himself from himself rather than praising himself unconditionally like Fowles's narrator.

15. J.-P. Sartre, *La Nausée* (Paris: Gallimard, 1938).

16. S. Loveday, *The Romances of John Fowles* (London: Macmillan, 1985), p. 100.

FAULKNER'S FICTION MAKES
ADDICTS OF US ALL

Marcy Lassota Bauman

The structure of William Faulkner's fiction, as well as the structure of his personal life and the structure of his writing life, all reflect the influence of alcoholism upon him. Biographers generally acknowledge that Faulkner was an alcoholic; until recently, what they have not acknowledged are the ways in which Faulkner's alcoholism defined both his writing process and the individual works themselves. In fact, before the appearance of Donald W. Goodwin's *Alcohol and the Writer*[1] and Thomas A. Dardis's *The Thirsty Muse: Alcohol and the American Writers*,[2] virtually nothing was written about the relationship between Faulkner's writing and his drinking.

Such an oversight is striking, because in Faulkner's fiction we see the effects of his childhood in an alcoholic family and his own subsequent alcoholism in many different ways. There are numerous drinking scenes. There are alcoholic characters, although none of them is ever called an alcoholic. In one instance, Faulkner provides a clear example of a family with alcoholism. The themes and problems which interest Faulkner—grief, loss of love, the obsession with the past and with time in general, the apparently random, unpredictable, uncontrollable evil in the world—all reflect beliefs which alcoholics share. Faulkner even presents his material in ways which reflect his own alcoholic persona.

I cannot here examine all of these features in detail, so I intend to concentrate on *The Sound and the Fury*.[3] I will offer a reading of that novel which shows it to be a detailed, accurate description of a family with alcoholism, although Faulkner has embedded that reading in a tapestry of guilt and denial. Then I will explain how that novel, and Faulkner's works in general, call upon his readers to confront the same issues of knowledge, meaning and identity formation which trouble all children raised in alcoholic homes. To understand Faulkner's fictions, we must assume the meaning-making strategies that children of alcoholics are forced to assume. In a sense, to understand the works of this alcoholic writer, we ourselves must become addicts, too.

It is appropriate to begin this discussion with *The Sound and the Fury* for several reasons. First, the novel marked a change in direction for Faulkner; with the writing of *The Sound and the Fury*, Faulkner found his fictional voice. That voice sounds throughout the rest of his works, and the characters in *The Sound and the Fury* foreshadow other Faulkner characters in many important ways. Secondly, Faulkner critics generally agree that *The Sound and the Fury* is a highly autobiographical work. David Minter notes that 'in writing *The Sound and the Fury* [Faulkner] took possession of the pain and muted love of his childhood—its dislocations and vacancies, its forbidden needs and desires'.[4] Judith Bryant Wittenberg states that, '*The Sound and the Fury* seems to have been written by Faulkner in a mood of anger and despair. Underlying the book is the sense that all children are betrayed in fundamental ways by their parents and left to flounder helplessly in a world where they can find no succor'.[5] She goes on to explain: 'There are...[many] autobiographical resonances in *The Sound and the Fury*, for Faulkner patterns nearly every character in the book on some figure in his own life'.[6] John Earl Bassett explains: 'The repeated presence of motherless homes, weak or perverse parents, and family conflict in Faulkner's fiction suggests...that the loss of the mother and the ineffectuality of the father had important personal implications for him. In *The Sound and the Fury* he transforms such personal anxieties into a fiction with profound cultural implications'.[7] Finally, Faulkner himself considered the novel his greatest work; although he felt that all of his work fell short of the mark, he called *The Sound and the Fury* his 'most splendid failure'.

Let me briefly summarize the 'plot' (if one can say that there *is* a plot to this novel). In *The Sound and the Fury* Faulkner tells the story of the decline of the Compson family, an old, established family living in his fictional Yoknapatawpha County. There are four children in the family: Quentin, the eldest son; Caddy, the only daughter; Jason, the second son; and Benjy, who is mentally retarded. The novel traces the events which occur in the family over a period of about thirty years. It begins with the death of the children's grandmother, and describes several gruesome events. Caddy becomes pregnant out of wedlock and must marry hastily; when her husband learns that the child is not his, he throws her out. At this time, Quentin, distraught over his sister's marriage, kills himself. Mr Compson later brings Caddy's baby home, but Mrs Compson refuses to allow Caddy to come home, and refuses to allow her to see her baby. When Mr Compson dies, Jason takes over the family and repeatedly victimizes his niece, who is then an adolescent. The novel ends with the niece Quentin stealing upwards of $3000 from Jason, and running off. The story is presented in four sections, the first three of which are narrated by Benjy, the son Quentin, and Jason, respectively, and the fourth of which is told by an omniscient narrator, but which assumes the point of view of Dilsey, the family's black servant.

The Sound and the Fury has never been seen as a text about alcoholism. Part of the reason for this lies in the way that Mr Compson's alcoholism is presented in the text. References to his drinking occur often, but they are so embedded and camouflaged that the meaning of those moments is not clear. In the Benjy section, for example, there are several references to Mr Compson's trips to the sideboard for a toddy, but the chronology and description in the Benjy section is so confused that we are not sure whether Mr Compson drinks frequently, or whether Benjy simply remembers one scene over and over. In the Quentin section, Caddy tells Quentin that if their father does not stop drinking, he will be dead within the year, but even though this statement is very explicit, Caddy's purpose in making it has nothing to do with Mr Compson's drinking. Rather, she wants to tell Quentin why she must marry—she must save her father. Jason is particularly vituperative about his father's alcoholism, blaming his father's drinking for the unhappy condition of his own life, but his anger and bitterness surface long after his father has died, long past the point when his father has any obvious effect on him. Mrs Compson, too, acknowledges her husband's drinking when she tells Dilsey, 'Why must you encourage him to drink? That's what's the matter with him now' (p. 229). Even here, though, her purpose in acknowledging the drinking is to fault Dilsey's action, not to confront her husband. In fact, everyone talks about Mr Compson's drinking, but the only purpose of the talk seems to be to blame other family members for his alcoholism.

Such talk creates for the Compsons what Stephanie Brown calls a 'family story'. Brown notes that, 'to preserve this inherent contradiction [which is that, in reality, the family is controlled by the alcoholic's drinking, yet they must deny that reality at the same time] all family members must adapt their thinking and behavior to fit the family's "story", that is, the explanations that have been constructed to allow the drinking behavior to be maintained and denied at the same time. This "story" becomes the family's point of view. It includes core beliefs which family members share and which provide a sense of unity and cohesion, often *against* an outside world perceived as hostile and unsafe'.[8]

The Compsons have a family 'story', and they also have a scapegoat. The 'major problem' identified in *The Sound and the Fury* is Caddy's sexual maturity, promiscuity and subsequent pregnancy. The family members blame Caddy in subtle and not-so-subtle ways. Mrs Compson dresses in black the day after she first sees Caddy in the porch swing with a neighborhood boy. Benjy cries the first time Caddy wears perfume. Quentin goes to his death believing that he is killing himself over her marriage and his inability to prevent it. Jason never forgives her for the fact that her husband had promised him a job in the bank—a job that he never got because the marriage failed. This pseudo-problem allows the family's denial to continue unchecked.

When we look beyond the 'family story', we see that there are times when Mr Compson's alcoholism is presented with startling clarity, although those moments are never highlighted, and Faulkner often leaves us to make the connections for ourselves. For example, as Mr Compson's condition worsens, so do the family finances. Although Quentin's going to Harvard 'has been…[his] mother's dream since…[he was] born' (p. 204), by the time he is actually old enough to go, the Compsons must sell part of their land to pay for his education. Even so, they can only afford to pay for a single year. Quentin never blames his father for the way the family's money has been squandered; rather, he feels guilty because the land that has been sold was his brother Benjy's favorite pasture, and he feels inadequate because he fears he will not be able to repay the sacrifice the family has made for him.

We also see the effects of Mr Compson's drinking in his responses to those around him as the story progresses. Although in the early pages of the book he attempts to intervene in situations (as when he silences the children so that Quentin can study, for example), and he furnishes his children with love and moral guidance, towards the end of his life he interacts with practically no one. As Jason sardonically notes, 'after a while Father wouldn't even come down town anymore but just sat there all day with the decanter. I could see the bottom of his nightshirt and his bare legs and hear the decanter clinking until finally T.P. had to pour it for him…' (p. 290). Faulkner never tells us that Mr Compson is caught in the throes of delirium tremens. And the family simply carries on around their debilitated father.

The effects of the Compson family dynamics finally tell on the children too, in ways that are predictable to anyone familiar with research on children of alcoholics: Quentin, unable to escape childhood patterns and the family's expectation that he will 'save' them from their troubles, kills himself. Caddy takes over the care of the younger children as soon as she is able. She becomes sexually promiscuous at an early age and, once she becomes pregnant, assumes blame for the decline of the family. As an adult, she allows herself to be cruelly manipulated by her brother Jason, who extorts money from her. Jason becomes a bitter adult who trusts no one, and who masks his need for love and acceptance with an obsession with material wealth.

Thus, Faulkner presents Mr Compson's drinking in many lights. In order to see the role that his alcoholism has played in the devastation of the Compson family, we must first read beyond the versions of events presented by the various narrators—none of them offers a true reading of the circumstances. They are confused and victimized by their misreadings.

The obfuscation of meaning occurs on more levels than that of plot, however. An examination of Faulkner's stylistic choices in *The Sound and the Fury* shows that he both does and does not tell the Compson's real story. By his alternate presentations and withholdings, he forces his readers to adopt reading strategies that parallel the information-gathering strategies used by children raised in alcoholic homes. Faulkner, in fact, teaches us to learn about the world—at least, his fictional world—in the ways that children of alcoholics must do.

As I mentioned before, the story is told in four sections, each of which is narrated by a different character. *The Sound and the Fury* begins with chaos: the first section comprises the retarded Benjy's internal monologue. This section is organized as a series of memories which are triggered for Benjy by the incidental appearance of objects around him, and presents distorted, fragmentary bits of events, some of which take place in the present but most of which occurred in the distant past. In fact nearly all the major events of the story are presented here—Damuddy's death, Caddy's becoming pregnant, Quentin's suicide—but the stream-of-consciousness style makes them difficult to understand and obscures their significance.

The following section is comprised of the internal monologue of the son Quentin, which occurs on the day he kills himself. This portion, too, is characterized by a great deal of remembering; Quentin's thoughts mostly revolve around the past, not the present, although unlike Benjy, Quentin is able to make some choices and take some actions, as when, for example, he 'rescues' the lost little girl. The third section is narrated by the son Jason, when Jason has grown to manhood and assumed the responsibility of caring for his mother and niece. The narration in this section is also interrupted by memories, but it, more than the preceding two, presents information chronologically. Finally, in the fourth section, Faulkner uses an omniscient narrator to tell the end of the story from the point of view of Dilsey. The result is that bits of information are presented in one context, re-presented from another point of view, expanded upon from yet a third viewpoint, and so on.

The layering of impression upon impression, with each successive layer simultaneously reinforcing and erasing what has gone before, has posed problems of interpretation that have interested critics since the novel was first published. Olga Vickery notes that *The Sound and the Fury* was the first of Faulkner's novels to make the question of form and technique an unavoidable critical issue'.[9] Later, she explains that, 'by fixing the structure while leaving the central situation ambiguous, Faulkner forces the reader to reconstruct the story and to apprehend its significance for himself [or herself]'.[10] For Robert Parker, Faulkner does more than confuse the central situation; he deliberately conceals it:

> Radical ignorance...is the distinctive problem Faulkner imposes on his readers. Indeed, Faulkner's novels are shaped as novels, as sustained narratives, by their elaborate orchestration of that ignorance. The main thing we know reading Faulkner is that we don't know the main thing, whether it is a fact...or at the last an understanding of whether facts are possible...

> Yet Faulkner keeps pointing our attention to the very main thing we
> don't know. Like [his characters]...he calls it 'something', a natural word,
> whether consciously chosen or not, for a focus of attention identifiable but
> not definable, an even homely word that nonetheless grows to tantalize by
> the bland way it keeps labeling the key thing we do not know, without
> helping us to know it.[11]

In other words, Parker believes that learning the unknown is 'the
distinctive problem' that Faulkner poses for his readers. We have seen
how this problem operates with respect to Mr Compson's alcoholism in
The Sound and the Fury. That novel is not unique; Faulkner's readers are
often left with the problem of filling in the gaps, of discovering what is not
said or explained. In that sense, Faulkner's very stylistic choice bears the
stamp of alcoholism, for children of alcoholics face a similar problem.
Kate McElligat notes that alcoholism is often called 'the secret that everyone knows' or 'the elephant in the living room'. She goes on to explain that
most children of alcoholics, 'especially up to and often during the teenage
years, do not realize that their family's problem is alcoholism'.[12] These
children, too, must fill in the gaps, must figure out what they are not being
told. They, too, are often presented with a discrepancy between what is
happening and what is *said* about what is happening. They must learn for
themselves to construct a coherent explanation from facts which often
make no sense. Such a dilemma—resolving and making a meaning, a
personality, from the 'facts' of the 'text' of a childhood in an alcoholic
home—presents itself to all children of alcoholics as they grow up. When
we read a Faulkner novel, we participate in creating meaning as children
of alcoholics do. Our first question is always 'what is happening here?'
We, too, must grope for the central, ambiguous 'something' that will make
the text clear; and like Faulkner's characters, we may never find it.

As Faulkner's characters become paralyzed in their search for the
'truth', so, too, are we readers prevented from ever finally coming to a
resolution of the oppositions in Faulkner's fictional world. As Walter
Slatoff explains, Faulkner himself refuses to make the interpretations
which would render resolution possible, by refusing to choose between
moral responsibility and irresponsibility. Writing about the novel *Go
Down, Moses*, Slatoff notes:

> In both the form and content of Faulkner's works there is often the asser-
> tion or implication that man does not need to make choices. 'You don't
> need to choose,' says McCaslin. 'The heart already knows' (*GDM*, p. 260).
> We do need to choose. There is, of course, also, in Faulkner the frequent
> implication that we do need to choose, and Ike, himself, does seem to
> make a terribly important choice by relinquishing his land. By
> suggesting, finally, that Ike both did and did not choose, Faulkner, too,
> has made a choice, the choice which he can rarely resist, and which, I
> feel, seriously limits his stature, the choice not to choose.[13]

Faulkner, in Slatoff's view, leaves much of his fiction unresolved.

This lack of resolution often makes it difficult, if not impossible, to decide what a novel of Faulkner's is about—or even what happens in it. Critics have sometimes decided that what a book is about is immaterial or irrelevant, as for instance as Slatoff when he writes of *The Sound and the Fury*: 'In short, the ending seems designed not to interpret or to integrate but to leave the various elements of the story in much the same suspension in which they were offered, and to leave the reader with a high degree of emotional and intellectual tension'.[14] Sometimes the book is not so much about 'the facts' but about the implications of those facts, as Robert Parker points out with respect to *Absalom, Absalom!*: 'we know all the important facts, but that very knowledge is Quentin's problem. For the only ineffability that remains is a moral one, the problem of what to do or believe on the basis of those facts'.[15]

The ultimate question for Faulkner's readers, then, is one of interpretation: what difference do the facts of this text make to the characters, and to me? Whose version of the story can I believe? What is the secret no one will tell? At the end of our reading, we will be left with many impressions. We may have many theories, but we will have few answers. In the process of reading we have learned, not aphorisms to be repeated, not insights to be contemplated, but patterns of response to be followed. We have learned 'how to learn' in the way that children of alcoholics do, and we have learned that such knowledge often entails confusion and pain.

NOTES

1. D.W. Goodwin, *Alcohol and the Writer* (New York: Andrews & McMeel, 1988).

2. T.A. Dardis, *The Thirsty Muse: Alcohol and the American Writer* (New York: Ticknor & Fields, 1989).

3. W. Faulkner, *The Sound and the Fury* (New York: Vintage Books, 1929). Subsequent page references are to this edition.

4. D. Minter, *William Faulkner: His Life and Work* (Baltimore: Johns Hopkins University Press, 1980), p. 104.

5. J. Bryant Wittenberg, *Faulkner: The Transfiguration of Biography* (Lincoln: University of Nebraska Press, 1979), p. 76.

6. Bryant Wittenberg, *Faulkner*, p. 77.

7. J.E. Bassett, 'Family Conflict in *The Sound and the Fury*', *Studies in American Fiction* (1981), p. 409.

8. S. Brown, *Treating Adult Children of Alcoholics: A Developmental Perspective* (New York: John Wiley & Sons, 1988), p. 34.

9. O. Vickery, 'Worlds in Counterpoint', in M. Cowan (ed.), *Twentieth-Century Interpretations of The Sound and the Fury* (Englewood Cliffs, NJ: Prentice-Hall, 1968), p. 28.

10. Vickery, 'Worlds in Counterpoint', p. 29.

11. R.D. Parker, *Faulkner and the Novelistic Imagination* (Urbana, IL: University of Chicago Press, 1985), p. 3.

12. K. McElligat, 'Identifying and Treating Children of Alcoholic Parents', *Social Work in Education* 9 (1986), p. 55.

13. W.J. Slatoff, *Quest for Failure: A Study of William Faulkner* (Ithaca, NY: Cornell University Press, 1960), p. 178.

14. Slatoff, *Quest for Failure*, p. 170.

15. Parker, *Faulkner*, p. 22.

FORBIDDEN FRUIT:
NINETEENTH-CENTURY AMERICAN FEMALE AUTHORSHIP AND THE DISCOURSES OF DRINK

Nicholas O. Warner

In their book *Drinking in America* Mark Edward Lender and James Kirby Martin tell the old story of the American Congressman who was 'asked by a constituent to explain his attitude toward whiskey. "If you mean the demon drink that poisons the mind, pollutes the body, desecrates family life and inflames sinners, then I'm against it", the Congressman said. "But if you mean the elixir of Christmas cheer, the shield against the winter chill, the taxable potion that puts needed funds into public coffers to comfort little crippled children, then I'm for it. This is my position, and I will not compromise"'.[1]

This amusing anecdote encapsulates the ambivalence that many scholars have noted in American attitudes towards intoxicants, especially alcohol (see note 1). But the story is also significant in suggesting the widely differing ways of talking about drinking, the disparate discourses of intoxication that have been prevalent in American culture. The Congressman replies not with a comment about any reality called whiskey, but with a menu of signifiers that he can manipulate with little or no regard for anything so mundane as an actual signified beverage. Within his response, in fact, we can detect implied discourses of economics, morality, medicine, social ritual or festivity, and various possible sub-discourses buried within some or all of these (for example, within the larger framework of the discourse of 'morality' there are the associations of heavy drinking with sexual immorality implied by phrases like 'pollutes the body' and 'desecrates family life').

In nineteenth-century American fiction produced by women, the dominant discourse about drinking was that embodied in the first half of the Congressman's statement. This was the discourse of the temperance movement, which once enjoyed such great power in American society.[2] American male authors, despite the pervasiveness of temperance ideology, were free to write of intoxicated experience from a variety of viewpoints, whether positive or negative, with the temperance view only one of several possible perspectives. This diversity of approaches is apparent in the complex tensions between Dionysianism and self-control in Emerson's ideas about intoxication; in Poe's explorations of altered states of consciousness and perception; in the celebrations of what we might call 'Falstaffian' drinking and male carousing in James Fenimore Cooper and William Gilmore Simms; in the use of alcohol as a source of violence, tragedy, humor and physical enjoyment in Mark Twain; and in the manipulation of nearly all of the above modes in the unpredictable, ironic, relentlessly protean prose of Herman Melville.[3]

Female authors, on the other hand, tended overwhelmingly to write from a rigidly pro-temperance perspective, in which almost any use of intoxicants was defined as addictive, and in which teetotalism and prohibitionism edged out other approaches to intoxicant use and abuse. The reasons for this pattern in American women's writing were twofold: the existence of strict socio-literary codes governing the permissible bounds of female expression, and a predisposition of women after the 1820s (when temperance grew into a major public issue) to view nearly all drinking as inimical to their own interests and welfare. Only in the late nineteenth and early twentieth centuries do we find a significant shift toward greater pluralism in women's discourses of intoxication, as evident in the work of Sarah Orne Jewett, Kate Chopin, Edith Wharton, Gertrude Atherton and Willa Cather.

In this paper I will consider briefly some examples of nineteenth-century mainstream (as opposed to strictly temperance) American women writers' approaches to drinking. I will then examine, by way of contrast, a representative short story and novel by Willa Cather, whose work foreshadowed the more complex, multilayered depiction of drinking that we have come to expect from twentieth-century women writers. But first we need to understand more fully the reasons behind the temperance-based pattern of literature produced by women in the nineteenth-century United States.

Earlier I mentioned the existence of socio-literary codes restricting topics and attitudes permissible for women authors. These codes sprouted from intertwined roots: a long-established double standard regarding male and female use of intoxicants in Western culture; the increasingly dominant cult of female domesticity and 'purity' (the American version of the 'angel in the house' syndrome familiar in Victorian England); and the special moral scrutiny given by reviewers and readers to female authors' private lives and reputations in contrast to those of their male counterparts.

The double standard for men and women drinkers throughout Western history has been amply documented by such historians of alcohol use as Marian Sandmaier, Gregory A. Austin and Mark Edward Lender, all of whom have shown that, even when male drunkenness has been condemned, female inebriety has often been singled out for particular criticism. This 'special stigma', to use Lender's phrase, grew stronger in nineteenth-century America, which witnessed a sentimentalization and rigidification of concepts of 'ladylike' behavior and appropriate female roles. For middle-class Americans the 'ideal woman' was a 'paragon of social virtue and a guardian of the home', while the 'alcoholic' embodied all that threatened the ideal woman. Thus a drunken woman became a particularly heinous, almost unthinkable phenomenon.[4]

The deeply ingrained taboos on female intemperance, and often even on female drinking of any kind, would make it unlikely for a woman author to write about intoxication other than from the pietistic perspectives of temperance. Indeed, anything other than a temperance-oriented account might be construed as somehow reflective of the morals of the author herself. This could be a particular concern for antebellum women authors, who came under much closer personal scrutiny than did men who wrote. In the words of Nina Baym, 'while reviewers almost never considered the private lives of male authors, they did discuss the lives of women'. Accordingly, women American writers struck a bargain with their society that Baym summarizes thus: 'women may write as much as they please providing they define themselves as women writing when they do so, whether by tricks of style—diffuseness, gracefulness, delicacy; by choices of subject matter—the domestic, the social, the private; or by tone—pure, lofty, moral, didactic'.[5] Such a 'bargain' would, of course, militate against any treatment of drinking that clashed with narrowly conceived notions of both womanhood and temperance.

It is important to remember that while the codes restricting female discourses of intoxication were powerful, they accounted for only part of the picture. Even in the absence of such codes, it is doubtful that many women would have written of intoxication other than they did. The Dionysian mode of writing, for example, was not only not permissible for female authors, but in all likelihood it was not congenial either. There was just too much genuine enmity between women and the bitter fruits of male drunkenness, which often resulted in women's physical, emotional and economic suffering. From the 1850s on, drinking levels were much lower than before, but women continued to play an important role in the new campaign 'not against drinking patterns or consumption rates per se but against drinking as a symbol of rampant pluralism, individualism, and potential social disorder'[6]. In addition, temperance concerns overlapped with women's rights issues, and provided many women with 'a sense of collective purpose and solidarity'.[7]

At times, temperance itself could become a veritable addiction, as indicated in this comment by a female crusader for sobriety: 'I began going [to women's temperance meetings] twice a week, but soon got so interested that I went every day, and then twice a day in the evenings. I tried to stay home to retrieve my neglected household, but when the hour for the morning prayer meeting came around, I found the attraction irresistible. The Crusade was a daily dissipation from which it seemed impossible to tear myself. In the intervals at home, I felt as I fancy the drinker does at the breaking down of a long spree'.[8]

In light of this historical situation, it is understandable that despite some flagging in the 1850s the temperance movement soon picked up momentum again, fueled in large part by women's activism. By 1869, four years after the Civil War and five years before the founding of the powerful Women's Christian Temperance Union (WCTU), the *New York Herald* could predict quite accurately that 'the next war in this country will be between women and whiskey'.[9]

As far as mainstream literature was concerned, the chief weapon in this war was a sticky compound of tears, treacle and temperance. Most women writing about intoxication followed a predictable pattern, incorporating some or all of the following motifs: alcoholism as a disease, albeit tinged with moral overtones; the danger even (or especially) of moderate drinking; the use of intoxicants as something alien or unnatural to women; alcohol as a poisonous, literally in*toxica*ting substance; drunkenness as the cause, not the result, of poverty; the disastrousness of marriage to a drinking man; weddings arranged by force or trickery, whereby an innocent young woman is chained to an abusive drunkard; and the importance of female influence on drinkers—provided, of course, that the influence be well within the boundaries signified by the catch phrase 'woman's proper sphere'. These patterns, or slight variations on them, were common in the works of popular, influential female authors like Sarah Josepha Hale, Susan Warner, E.D.E.N. Southworth, Ann Stephens, Mary Jane Holmes, Harriet Beecher Stowe and Louisa May Alcott.

None of these particular authors was a temperance writer per se, in the sense that none published mainly for the temperance press, or was associated primarily with the temperance cause. But in general these authors—and the large school of women's domestic fiction that they represented—were strongly committed to the temperance movement and all that it implied, including rationalism, industriousness, self-discipline and emphasis on the communal rather than the individualistic. This commitment was a solemn matter. Harriet Beecher Stowe, for example, expressed indignation at Charles Dickens for having a clergyman character in *The Pickwick Papers*, the Reverend Mr Tiggins, appear drunk at a temperance meeting. And, in an essay published in 1843, Stowe took Dickens to task for ignoring American drunkenness even though he attacked the American institution of slavery. Indeed, because Dickens could 'burlesque temperance speeches, temperance hotels, and temperance societies', Stowe concluded that the published author of such novels as *The Pickwick Papers, Oliver Twist, Nicholas Nickleby* and *The Old Curiosity Shop* was 'a person of no very profound habits or capacity of reflection on moral subjects'.[10] For Stowe, it was simply impossible to make light of so weighty an issue as the battle against intoxication, a single instance of which was, in the eyes of many, a fate literally worse than death. A striking but not untypical instance of this attitude is found in *Meadow Brook*, an 1857 novel by the then immensely popular Mary Jane Holmes.[11] The fictional narrator shows us the reaction to a young man's drunkenness at a family gathering: ' "Merciful Heavens! it's as I feared!" was Aunt Charlotte's exclamation, as she sank upon the lounge, moaning bitterly, and covering her face with the cushion, that she might not see the disgrace of her only son—for Herbert was *drunk!*' At this point, the narrator thinks of her own mother, who had recently mourned the death of her infant boy: 'my mother, as she looked upon the senseless inebriate resting where once had lain the beautiful, inanimate form of her youngest born, thought how far less bitter was *her* cup of sorrow than was that of the half-fainting woman, who would rather, far rather, her boy had died with the dew of babyhood upon his brow than to have seen him thus debased and fallen'.[12]

Not only extreme inebriety, like that of the hapless Herbert, but also 'moderate' drinking was often condemned or at least seen as suspect. Thus, even when a character like Southworth's Capitola, the refreshingly spunky, irreverent heroine of the novel *The Hidden Hand*, defies the conventional pieties of Victorian femininity, she remains staunchly dry. Offered a sip of wine by her crusty old guardian, Capitola firmly refuses. She will never, she says, touch a drop, because 'my life has shown me too much misery that has come of drinking wine'.[13]

Not all women, to be sure, sang in the temperance chorus. Emily Dickinson, with her richly suggestive treatment of intoxication and her evocations of a Dionysian sensibility, is the most notable example. But Dickinson was virtually unknown and unpublished (except for eight poems) in her lifetime. The often ironic and never commercially successful Elizabeth Stoddard satirized militant temperance both in her journalism and in her novel, *The Morgesons* (1862, 1889).[14] At times, even such enthusiastically pro-temperance writers as Stowe and Alcott sounded as if they just might be about to break away from narrowly pietistic codes of alcohol depiction, to probe more adventurously the various meanings of drink and drug use embedded in conventional discourse. Stowe, no doubt influenced by her experiences as mother of an alcoholic son and morphine-addicted daughter, takes some tentative steps in such a direction (through her depiction of the alcoholic Bolton) in two novels of the 1870s, *My Wife and I* and *We and Our Neighbors*. Similarly, Alcott circles uneasily around the theme of drugs in some of her more sensationalistic fiction, for example, 'A Marble Woman' (1865), 'Perilous Play' (1869) and *A Modern Mephistopheles* (written in 1866, published in 1877). But then both authors retreat into conventional, largely external accounts of stupefaction, embarrassment, or loss of rational control, rather than exploring the nature of intoxicated consciousness or the complexities of drinking experience. And it was this mode of writing that typified women's fiction of the time.

At the turn of the century, however, we begin to see women describing intoxicant use from more varied perspectives. Even where female authors presented drinking or drugs negatively, they now did so in ways that reflected the personal complexity and multiple cultural meanings of such phenomena as intoxicant use, abuse, addiction and drunkenness. Two works by Willa Cather vividly exemplify this shift away from the genteel homogeneity of earlier women's writing on intoxication.

The title of Cather's short story 'On the Divide' (1896)[15] refers to a bleak prairie reigion between the Little Blue River and the Republican River in Nebraska. The story contains features familiar to any reader of temperance fiction: drunkenness; poverty; violence; the abduction of a young woman by a drunken, rejected suitor; the enforced marriage of the same young woman to a drunkard; a feckless father incapacitated by alcohol. But the way Cather arranges these elements and the language she uses—her patterns of description, narration and dialogue—place the story on a different plane altogether from the discourses of teetotalism.

The story revolves around the rough-hewn courtship of sensual, saucy Lena by the alcoholic Norwegian immigrant Canute Canuteson. Canute's drinking is both a parallel and an alternative to the suicide that tempts so many who live on the inhospitable divide. Expanding on alcohol's significance as something more than merely a chemically addicting substance or a sign of personal vice, Cather relates Canute's drinking to the profound madness that afflicts all those on the Divide who fail to kill themselves.

> Most men bring with them to the Divide only the dregs of the lives that they have quandered in other lands and among other peoples. Canute Canuteson was as mad as any of them, but his madness did not take the form of suicide or [as Cather informs us with an ironic jab at the conventional prairie pietism of her childhood] religion but of alcohol. He had always taken liquor when he wanted it...but after his first year of solitary life he settled down to it steadily. He exhausted whisky after a while, and went to alcohol, because its effects were speedier and surer.[16]

Cather goes on to explain that Canute does have some self-control in that he never allows his drinking to interfere with his work. But if Canute's work and drinking do not mix, his drinking and his art do. He drinks while carving his strange, crude but powerfully expressive wooden figures. It is as if the alcohol and the artistic expression of Canute's inner anguish are somehow connected. Cather does not prettify Canute's drinking or treat it as some pseudo-Romantic version of artistic inspiration. However (and this makes her, as far as the depiction of drinking is concerned, closer to a Poe or a Dostoevsky than to a Stowe or an Alcott), she does recognize intoxications's profound links to submerged drives and layers of consciousness, suffering, loneliness and longing—that is, to things that lie beyond the scope of purely rational formulation or understanding.

As I have said, Cather does not prettify Canute's drinking. Nor does she dilute the brutality of his abduction of the once taunting Lena, as Canute drags her struggling to his own hovel, which he has bizarrely decorated with snake skins and with the hideous carved dancing figures. Canute then forces Lena to marry him in a ceremony performed by a terrified clergyman. But for all that, Cather neither demonizes nor dehumanizes Canute, as we see clearly at the story's conclusion. We all know, of course, how 'On the Divide' would end in the hands of, say, a Mary Jane Holmes. In the event of an unhappy ending, we would behold Lena haggard and ill, with Canute drinking himself senseless, beating wife and children in a ceaseless cycle of violence and drunken degradation. Or, were the story to end happily, we would be edified by a vision of Lena or some other angelic woman weaning Canute away from the whisky bottle through a regular program of hymns, prayer and joyous self-sacrifice. Here, however, is how Cather ends the story. Since Lena will have none of him, the morose Canute sprawls across the threshold of his tiny cabin; meanwhile, a snowstorm rages. Terrified and lonely, Lena finally calls to Canute, complains first that she is cold, then that she is lonesome. The conclusion of the tale, which swiftly follows, is worth repeating in its entirety:

> 'I will go and get your mother.' And he got up.
> 'She won't come.'
> 'I'll bring her,' said Canute grimly.
> 'No, no, I don't want her, she will scold all the time.'
> 'Well, I will bring your father.'
> She spoke again and it seemed as though her mouth was close up to the key hole. She spoke lower than he had ever heard her speak before, so low that he had to put his ear up to the lock to hear her.
> 'I don't want him either, Canute—I'd rather have you.'
> For a moment she heard no noise at all, then something like a groan. With a cry of fear she opened the door, and saw Canute stretched out in the snow at her feet, his face in his hands, sobbing on the door step.[17]

In its open-endedness, in its sense of human complexity and contradictoriness, its refusal to punish Canute in the fashion of a stereotypical drunken villain, Cather's tale distances itself from the limited perspectives of most earlier American women's writing about intoxication. Indeed, Cather slyly undercuts the values of that fiction, at least so far as drinking is concerned, in one of her later and best-known novels, *A Lost Lady*, to which I will briefly turn now. Published in 1923, during Prohibition, the novel presents drinking in ways that differ both from the official dogma of its own time and from the temperance perspectives of the 1880s and 1890s, the period in which the novel is set and in which Cather herself grew up. It is the 'lost lady' of the title, Marian Forrester, who is the chief drinker in this book—in itself an unusual circumstance for the late Victorian era in the United States, since Mrs Forrester falls into none of the categories of scandal or, at best, grotesque comedy into which most fictional women drinkers had hitherto been placed.[18] True, Mrs Forrester's youthful admirer, Neil, is shocked at her drinking, particularly when, after becoming drunk when her lover marries another woman, she passes out. Yet even here, Mrs Forrester's intoxication is presented on a continuum with her spontaneity, 'cool impudence' and fresh, unpredictable nature. Her inclination for the elegant paraphernalia of drinking also makes her culturally superior to the petty, grasping, teetotaling townspeople whom, at the novel's end, she leaves behind. Though considered by many of them, especially after her financial misfortunes, to be a 'lost lady', Marian Forrester has the last laugh, marrying a rich Englishman who takes her to live (and, presumably, to drink) in palatial comfort in South America.

What accounts for the shift represented in Cather's work? We might cite as reasons the generally increasing emancipation of women and of women's roles as writers of fiction, the sympathy with European attitudes, including Europeans' relative tolerance of drinking, evident in both Cather and Edith Wharton, and the upper-class tastes and bohemianism of Cather's milieu in the Greenwich Village of the 1920s, a milieu towards which she was already heading, as towards a magnet, from her days as a beginning author in the 1890s. In that milieu, Prohibition and all it stood for was, at best, a joke. These are doubtless some of the factors that explain Cather's departure from the narrowness of her forebears' treatments of drinking.

Whatever the reasons, Willa Cather was bold enough to pluck the forbidden fruit of a discourse on drinking often deemed unsuitable for women, even as late as the 1920s. In so doing, she anticipated the richly significant, varied depictions of intoxicant use produced by such American writers as Djuna Barnes, Dorothy Parker, Carson McCullers, Joyce Carol Oates, Anne Sexton, Joan Didion, Lorna Dee Cervantes, Leslie Silko and Erica Jong, to name but a few. Now, as we approach the year 2000, it is appropriate to remember that the freedom and diversity of discourses on intoxication evoked by these names began to be possible for American women only relatively late in literary history—on the threshold of our own rapidly disappearing century.

NOTES

1.   M.E. Lender and J.K. Martin, *Drinking in America* (New York: Macmillan, 1982), p. 169. The anecdote serves as the epigraph to Lender and Martin's discussion of American ambivalence about alcohol on pp. 169-95. On ambivalence, see also A. Myerson, 'Alcohol: A Study of Social Ambivalence', *Quarterly Journal of Studies in Alcohol* 1 (1940), pp. 13-20; R. Room, 'Ambivalence as a Sociological Explanation: The Case of Cultural Explanations of Alcohol Problems', *American Sociological Review* 41 (1976), pp. 1047-65; and H.G. Levine, 'Temperance and Women in 19th-Century United States', in O.J. Kalant (ed.), *Alcohol and Drug Problems in Women* (New York: Plenum, 1980), pp. 30-31.

2.   Modern commentators sometimes forget that 'the 19th-century temperance movement as a whole had a very sympathetic and supportive attitude toward habitual drunkards' whose addictive condition was often called a disease; see H.G. Levine, 'The Alcohol Problem in America: From Temperance to Alcoholism', *British Journal of Addiction* 79 (1984), p. 112. However, temperance quickly began to mean total abstinence in many quarters, drinking was turned into a scapegoat for America's social problems (Levine, 'The Alcohol Problem', p. 111), and there was considerable hostility to moderate drinkers, as evidenced in S.B. Woodward's *Essays on Asylums for Inebriates* (Worcester, MA, 1938), p. 5.

3.   On Emerson, see my '"God's Wine and Devil's Wine": The Idea of Intoxication in Emerson', *MOSAIC* 19 (1986), pp. 55-68. The other authors and themes mentioned form part of a book I am now writing on the theme of intoxication in nineteenth-century American literature.

4.   M. Sandmaier, *The Invisible Alcoholics: Women and Alcohol Abuse in America* (New York: McGraw-Hill, 1980); G. Austin, *Alcohol in Western Society from Antiquity to 1800* (Santa Barbara: ABC Clio, 1985); M.E. Lender, 'A Special Stigma: Women and Alcoholism in the Late 19th and Early 20th Centuries', in D. Strug (ed.), *Alcohol Interventions* (Binghamton, NY: Haworth, 1986), pp. 41-57. The phrases quoted here are from Lender, 'A Special Stigma', pp. 47-49. Although Lender concentrates on the postbellum period, other scholars have shown that the pattern of sex roles described by Lender was developing throughout the nineteenth century; see A. Douglas, *The Feminization of American Culture* (New York: Knopf, 1977), and Levine, 'Temperance and Women', p. 33.

5.   N. Baym, *Novels, Readers, and Reviewers: Responses to Fiction in Antebellum America* (Ithaca, NY: Cornell University Press, 1984), pp. 254, 257.

6.   Lender and Martin, *Drinking in America*, p. 95.

7.   P. Aaron and D.F. Musto, 'Temperance and Prohibition in America', in M. Moore and D. Gerstein (eds.), *Alcohol and Public Policy* (Washington, D.C.: National Academy Press, 1981), p. 146.

8.   Quoted in Aaron and Musto, 'Temperance and Prohibition', p. 147.

9.   Quoted in J.C. Furnas, *The Life and Times of the Late Demon Rum* (New York: Putnam's, 1965), p. 232.

10.   Quoted in T.F. Gossett, *Uncle Tom's Cabin and American Culture* (Dallas, TX: Southern Methodist University Press, 1985), pp. 57-58.

11.   M.J. Holmes, *Meadow Brook* (New York: Carleton, 1857).

12.   Holmes, *Meadow Brook*, p. 35.

13.   E.D.E.N. Southworth, *The Hidden Hand, or, Capitola the Madcap* (ed. J. Dobson; New Brunswick, NJ: Rutgers University Press, 1988 [originally published in 1859]), p. 52.

14. The unconventional and unjustly neglected Stoddard's literary merit has been vigorously championed in a recent edition of her work; see E. Stoddard, *The Morgesons and Other Writings, Published and Unpublished* (ed. L. Buell and S.A. Zagarell; Philadelphia: University of Pennsylvania Press, 1984).

15. W. Cather, 'On the Divide', in *24 Stories* (ed. S. O'Brien; New York: New American Library, 1987), pp. 35-49.

16. Cather, 'On the Divide', p. 39.

17. 'On the Divide', p. 49.

18. In this regard see S. Shaw, 'The Female Alcoholic in Victorian Fiction: George Eliot's Unpoetic Heroine', in R.B. Nathan (ed.), *Nineteenth-Century Women Writers of the English-Speaking World* (New York: Greenwood, 1986), pp. 171-79.

General Index